Books by Albert J. Lowry, Ph.D.

How to Manage Real Estate Successfully—in Your Spare Time

How You Can Become Financially Independent by Investing in
　Real Estate

How to Become Financially Successful by Owning Your Own
　Business

Courses by Albert J. Lowry, Ph.D.

Lowry Real Estate Investment Seminar

Lowry Creative Real Estate Financing Seminar

Lowry Business Opportunities—Cash Flow and Profits Seminar

How to Become
FINANCIALLY SUCCESSFUL
by Owning
YOUR OWN BUSINESS

Albert J. Lowry, Ph.D.

SIMON AND SCHUSTER
NEW YORK

Copyright © 1981 by Dean Ambrose, as Trustee of Lowry Living Trusts III
Published by Simon and Schuster
A Division of Simon & Schuster, Inc.
Simon & Schuster Building
Rockefeller Center
1230 Avenue of the Americas
New York, New York 10020

SIMON AND SCHUSTER and colophon are registered trademarks
of Simon & Schuster, Inc.
Designed by Irving Perkins Associates
Manufactured in the United States of America
10   9   8   7

Library of Congress Cataloging in Publication Data

Lowry, Albert J
How to become financially successful by owning
your own business.

Includes index.
1. Small business.   2. Self-employed.
I. Title.
HF5356.L68   658′.022   80-25681

ISBN 0-671-41261-2

In Appreciation

The author acknowledges his sincere appreciation to Charles Colman, Ronald Moser, Oliver Ray Price, Parker Paul, Kim Perkins, Keith Monroe, Sam Meyerson, and Frederic Hills for their valued contribution and assistance in research, editing and documentation of this manuscript.

Contents

13 WINNING THE PAPERWORK WAR

**14 WHAT YOU SHOULD KNOW ABOUT MONEY
MANAGEMENT**

18 SMALL IMPROVEMENTS CAN MEAN BIG SALES   283

19 RECIPE FOR A REPUTATION   299

20 BIGGER MONEY FOR BIGGER VENTURES   319

**24 HOW TO PROTECT YOUR BUSINESS FROM
YOUR BUDDIES** 367

1
Who Wants to Buy, and Why

Unhappy Real People

Handcuffed to their attaché cases, enslaved by commuter timetables or strapped into airliners in holding patterns, badgered by stockholders or the Big Boss, trying to placate wives who complain because they're seldom home, worrying about their increasingly remote children, thousands of highly paid executives in big corporations are wondering today whether they've really achieved success.

For many, the answer is clearly "no." For some, happiness will come when they quit the corporate rat race and switch to owning a small business. At any given moment, hundreds of them are quietly searching for some enterprise they can buy and run at a decent profit.

The surprising truth is that many high-level jobs in big business are crushingly dull. Executives have to perform monotonous chores, sit in repetitive meetings, attend special clinics and seminars, read ponderous reports. The mandatory three-martini lunch in some organizations doesn't really ease the pain.

Of course, there's no harm in being bored occasionally. A little boredom can make us more zestful when we turn from dull routine to a troublesome problem. But too much boredom turns the world gray for anyone.

In that mood, an executive is likely to dream crazy dreams. Almost any opportunity that promises excitement seems inviting. This is why some corporate bigwigs speculate rashly—sometimes with their firm's funds— and why others make bad blunders in buying inferior or unsuitable businesses for themselves. An ethical business broker never assumes that men who have risen to the upper tax brackets are necessarily good judges of business opportunities. They may rely on their own judgment, over-looking the obvious facts in evidence. Thus, they may be even more in need of a broker's counsel than less exalted personages.

Bumping Against Low Ceilings

It isn't only the higher-ups who are discontented in big organizations. Middle management people, and those trapped in blind alleys lower down, may have more reasons to want out. (On the other hand, thousands of them are quite happy, because they want nothing more than an ob-scure, secure job.) Anyone who is ambitious feels frustrated in a niche where he has no chance to rise. But the lower-ranking people naturally are less impetuous than those with big bankrolls. They want to know more about a business before buying it, because they're less confident of their own all-around abilities, and certainly more hesitant to make a buy-ing decision.

Brokers often hear these people say such things as "I'm fed up to the eyebrows with my job. I've got to find a way to be my own boss and do my own thing. There must be more to life than driving in to that beehive every day. I'm tired of waiting for my department head to retire or die before I get a promotion. . . . I itch to go into business for myself. But how will I choose the right business? I could lose my shirt and pants if I plunge into something that doesn't work out." And still the entrepreneur-ial drive burns brightly within.

Whatever the answer, the fact is that most corporations are heavily larded with people who dislike their jobs. Some men at the very top are concerned about this. "Business tends to grind people down," said Thomas Watson, Jr., when he was president of IBM. "The difficulty of being creative becomes greater. In his late thirties the average fellow is likely to say, 'I'll just keep my nose clean and stay in my niche.' We have more of this than we'd like at IBM."

The same worry in different words was voiced by James Black, board chairman of a giant utility, Pacific Gas & Electric. "People may come to be secure in their own jobs, and tend not to take responsibility or initiative for fear of losing their jobs." And National Gypsum's chairman Melvin Baker said, "The 'team' concept of management has tended to eliminate originality and imagination. I have seen examples of 'yes-manship' . . . where people have agreed with the brass when they know darned well that the best thing for the company would be to do something quite different."

Only the nonconformists, the oddballs, the malcontents, the misfits are

likely to leave safe berths belowdecks and plunge into business for themselves. But these are the types who often do well in their own ventures.
They have the ego and the drive that are essential. They can understand
what young Julius Caesar meant when he said, "I would rather be first in
my village than second in Rome."

Many a clever engineer or salesman quits a good-salaried job with a
large employer and goes into business for himself. He takes some specialized know-how with him, or maybe a few customers, but not much
else. The money that he risks to buy a business comes from his own
savings account, where it might be earning six-percent interest with no
risk. Sometimes there's also capital from someone who is persuaded to
join him or back him—which adds to his debt load and sharpens his
anxiety. He knows he'll be working twice as hard, for possibly half as
much money, as with his former company. But maybe he succeeds
through hard work and sacrifice. Then later he gains more wealth than he
ever could have hoped for on a payroll—and more happiness, too.

For example, Kenneth J. Albert, a specialist in new business ventures,
tells of a chemical engineer for a large plastics company. He developed a
new plastic compound that was a combination of recycled material and a
new one. The company decided to market this new compound—but
couldn't find a supplier of the recycled material. It didn't plan to buy
more than $200,000 worth of the stuff each year, and no supplier was
interested in such a "small" order. So the chemical engineer grabbed the
chance. The company gave him a purchase order for $200,000, on
the strength of which a bank lent him the capital he needed. He left the
company, bought some equipment, and rented a small building. Five
years later, his business was grossing $4 million a year. He sold it to a
conglomerate for $2 million, an impressive figure for a company with such
a small gross. Draw your own conclusion—luck or ingenuity?

Out but Not Down

There is another large group of would-be buyers of businesses: the
people who suddenly find themselves unemployed.

This can happen at any age. But the older you are, the more vulnerable
you become to the axe, especially in a big company. You can be thrown
out of work by illness, or by a wave of layoffs. Seniority isn't always
protection when a company feels a pinch—and you may have serious
trouble finding a similar job elsewhere. The "Youth Movement" is as
prevalent in big business as it is on the baseball field.

"Nearly everyone agrees," *Reader's Digest* said a few years ago, "that
in a recession it is better to ease out people through retirement than to

swell the unemployment rolls with young married workers supporting families.'' The *Digest* was talking not about retirement at 65 or 70, but about forced ''early retirement,'' which is becoming more common.

Another corporate practice not mentioned by the *Digest* is also common: thriftily dismissing employees a few years before they become eligible for company pensions. Theoretically, this has been outlawed by recent legislation against age discrimination, but in practice it's hard to stop. Management can always invent a reason to fire someone.

These facts may be shaping a new life pattern in America. From now on, the typical breadwinner may pursue two careers in succession.

In the first career, he (or she) will struggle upward in some big company, only to be blocked sooner or later and squeezed out. Then such a person will use savings (plus a pension, perhaps) to start something totally different. It may be a career as an artist, or as some other type of freelance professional—or he may even aspire to own his own small business. . . .

No Degree? No Job

In addition to all those who buy a business of their own because of discontent or misfortunes within a corporation, there are those who buy because they can't get into a corporation in the first place, or don't want to.

The Frank Merriwell era is past when a youth could quit high school, become a clerk or office boy or coal shoveler in some company, and rise to its top through sheer diligence. Nowadays the first question asked of a job applicant is ''What is your college degree?'' If the answer is ''I didn't go to college,'' the interview is over.

Because of the GI Bill of Rights and government student-loan programs and the vast expansion of free community colleges, almost anybody can get a college degree if he is willing to endure four or more years of lecture-sitting and book-reading. The degree is considered a necessary passport into the big-business world.

But there are certain types who won't sit still. They realize that they may waste years in college without learning much that can be of practical help to them. They know where they're headed, and it isn't into a corporation or a learned profession. It's into a business of their own, although they're not always sure what kind of business this should be.

Anyone eager to be his own boss sooner or later becomes disenchanted with the academic life and finds he is out of place in college. Many college people are scornful of the grubby commercial world. Professors are breeding more professors. Technical courses turn out narrow specialists.

Even the graduate business schools are geared to produce personnel for big business—because it's big business that endows these schools, and it's big business that sends recruiters to the campuses each June.

The non–college grad often tries harder because he thinks he has to. No big corporation is out bidding for him, at least not at a management level. This, in effect, sharpens his competitive spirit. He has the will to win, and the willingness to work hard. He seldom thinks any task is beneath nis dignity—or too tough to tackle.

In fact, if you check the records of America's thirty-five richest self-made men, you'll find that about half are high school dropouts and fewer than a third bothered to finish college. Clement Stone, who started his own insurance companies and is now worth almost a half-billion dollars, quit high school because he found it a hindrance to his chosen goal of making money. William Lear, jack-of-all-trades who built five different companies and piled up $100 million, didn't even enter high school. James L. Ling was a school dropout and teenage bum, but by 25 he had a prosperous small company going, and by 30 he was a millionaire owner of Ling-Temco-Vought. Conrad Hilton dropped out of college to become a small-business man in a small New Mexico town, and went on from there to buy and build hotels all over the world.

The personal histories of these and similar men and women, recounted in articles and books, prove that if you can learn to be a reasonably skillful small-business man, you can teach yourself to be a millionaire. You don't need a formal education.

In fact, formal education is probably downright detrimental to most self-starters. Maybe campus life is wrong for the kind of youngster who will amass big money on his own. His nature makes him a maverick, whereas conformists do better in the atmosphere of colleges. Maybe he hates sitting and passively absorbing dogma from adults. Maybe he's bored because his emotional makeup demands immediate, tangible rewards such as money—rewards that are earned only in the real world, not in schools. Maybe he chafes at the tightly organized academic routine; he wants to be his own boss, instead of being told where to sit, what to read, when to arrive and depart. A personality that thrives in a university (or in military life) may not, for that very reason, find it easy to prosper in a small business—and vice versa.

At any rate, ambitious young people without college degrees often start a business or, even better, buy one if they can scrape up enough capital. Furthermore, as they grow older and more successful, these same people often keep on buying more businesses.

As a buyer or seller, you'll find yourself dealing with many of these hard-driving, self-educated, self-reliant types. Of the various groups we've considered so far in this chapter, the group with neither college nor corporation training is likely to be shrewdest in sizing up business opportunities, because of their valuable education in the famous old University of Hard Knocks.

What Do They Want? Wealth?

Why do these different groups want to be self-employed?

Sometimes the answer is simple: a lot more money.

An ambitious, optimistic buyer may expect to create his very own big business from a small start. He may know the story of Norton Simon. At 16, Simon left the University of California after six weeks and bought a small orange-juice firm. In three years his little company, located in Fullerton, California, called Val Vita, was selling $43,000 worth of orange juice per year. In another two years, its annual sales hit the half-million-dollar mark. When Simon was in his early 30s, he bought Hunt Foods for $3 million.

And there is the story of a lawyer named Elmer L. Winter, who got an idea for a new business. In 1948 he gave up his small law office and put his savings into his idea, which he called Manpower, Inc. By 1965 he headed the world's largest temporary-help service, with more than four hundred offices, grossing $93 million a year.

When H. Ross Perot was 32, he was an IBM salesman. He quit and put $1,000 into a little computer-software company, Electronic Data Systems. Six years later, the company was estimated to be worth $300 million, and he still owned 85 percent of its stock.

Sherman M. Fairchild bought a little semiconductor company working out of a garage in Palo Alto. He got the financing it needed, and it mushroomed so vastly that Fairchild earned $8.4 million from it in the first of its many good years.

When Charles B. (Tex) Thornton bought Litton Industries in 1953, it was a small firm manufacturing microwave tubes. By 1965, Litton had bought fifty other companies. By 1969, it was a billion-dollar conglomerate owning 188 plants.

In 1968, Howard Ruff came out of a meeting with associates a broken man. He had $11.36 in his pocket. But through perseverence and a determined spirit, he rebuilt his business and today he has the nationally syndicated television show "Ruff House" and produces one of the best financial newsletters around, *Ruff Times*. His book *How to Prosper During the Coming Bad Years* is a guideline for survival in the near future. If you believe in yourself, there is virtually no limit to the success you can attain.

What Simon and Winter and Perot and Fairchild and Ruff and Thornton and others have done from small starts, any ambitious small enterpriser may think he can do too. Anyhow, he knows that ownership is the only route to real wealth. Because of income-tax rates, even the highest-salaried corporate chiefs are poor in comparison with people whose wealth comes from capital gains.

Never in history have the chances to become a millionaire been better. New services, new technologies, new amusements and recreations can quickly be exploited by small entrepreneurs. Our economy is so vast, so diverse, that there is plenty of room for shoestring ventures to make millions. This happens every year. Ray Kroc turned a small hamburger stand into one of America's foremost food institutions—McDonald's.

There aren't any records that tell the exact number of U.S. millionaires, but we can deduce it from income-tax and other statistics. In 1958 *Time* magazine estimated there were 40,000 millionaires. By 1966 its estimate was 100,000. In other words, during the eight-year period, 60,000 people joined the class—which is a rate of 7,500 newly minted millionaires per year. Today, this 1966 number has more than doubled.

The number of millionaires has been growing three times as fast as the gross national product. By 1970, there were so many of them—a couple of hundred thousand, most days, depending on the oscillations of the stock market—that the only really impressive tycoon was the kind with an *income* of a million a year. The country contained 642 of these.

An encouraging fact about past and present millionaires is that many of them started with little or nothing. For example, hardly any black Americans are born with a silver spoon in their mouths, but *Ebony* magazine estimated a few years ago that there were 35 black millionaires. Most of them got rich by owning small newspapers, funeral parlors, banks, or insurance companies catering to black customers. One black businessman, S. B. Fuller of Chicago, started the Fuller Products Company (cosmetics) on $25 capital. In twenty-eight years he owned nine companies, and Fuller Products alone was grossing $10 million a year.

If we try to count the people who don't make it quite so big—who merely accumulate a net worth in five or six figures, say—we are even more encouraged. The number of Americans with a net worth between $60,000 and $100,000 grew from 3.3 million in 1964 to 4.9 million in 1972. There are at least 5 million now. By 1980, this number will top 6.5 million. That's quite a flock of successful people.

Anyone who buys a hamburger stand or a drugstore or a laundry is probably aware that he's unlikely to make a million. Nevertheless, if he's an astute businessman, he knows that even a small enterprise can bring him many monetary advantages unavailable to the salaried man.

Those Lovely Tax Breaks

The tax deductions alone can be delightful. He'll have to pay taxes on whatever his business earns, but he can deduct whatever he spends in order to make taxable income. If he works at home, a part of his housing costs can probably be deducted as a business expense—including part of what he pays for home insurance, heat, light, repairs, maintenance, real estate taxes, and so on. Most homeowners can't take a deduction for depreciation, but he can on whatever fraction of his house is used exclusively for business.

If his business loses money, he can sometimes use the loss to offset a tax he owes on other income—or it can be carried forward to use against income in a future year. On the other hand, if his business grows enough so that one of his children can be hired to help, then these wages (assuming they're reasonable) will also be tax-deductible as a business expense.

If the business really thrives, an owner's life-style can become far more luxurious without much increase in taxable income. He can take many benefits and charge them off as business expenses of the company: his wife's salary as "vice president" or "secretary"; his "company car"; life insurance, expense allowance, travel, and entertainment; personal services that are charged to the company for lawyers, accountants, and brokers; personal use of company equipment, facilities, and personnel.

Most of the owner's assets will be not in cash but in company ownership, real estate, and other nonliquid assets. When he needs more cash than his company can pay in salaries and dividends, he may have to borrow on his holdings or even sell something. But only when he sells does he pay tax on the basic source of his wealth, and then it is at the lower capital-gains rate. Meanwhile, as his company grows more valuable, there is no tax on this gain.

Why Stop with One Business?

An ambitious and astute small-business man isn't content to own just one business. He buys others. They bring him additional financial benefits.

Expense accounts, for example. Internal Revenue is taking closer looks at such deductions. But it usually permits a company to own a car for use in the business, and to pay business expenses through an expense account. If you own one business, this is what you can deduct. But if you own five businesses, you may be able to multiply some of these breaks fivefold.

One small company can probably afford only one small car for the owner. One bigger company can buy one bigger car. Maybe a boat, too, or an airplane.

With three companies, perhaps you can ride around in two cars, a plane, and a boat. With four companies, probably a camper too—for entertaining customers, of course. Five companies can give you the lifestyle of a high-flying corporate bigwig who enjoys several cars, a jet aircraft, a yacht, and apartments in Manhattan and Miami and elsewhere. More businesses provide you with more legitimate expense allowances.

More important, if you own several businesses, you can take several salaries. Three expense accounts are better than one, and three salaries are better still. They stabilize and strengthen your income by distributing it over a broader base. A bad year in one business can't hurt you as much.

Building wealth is a matter of building equity. Cash burns a hole in your pocket; it is taxed as soon as you receive it, and you can't get more than 8 or 10 percent interest from banks and savings-and-loan institutions, or, generally more than 12 to 14 percent in the purchase of a second trust deed or mortgage—which itself is taxed too—by lending or banking it. Cash can't help you get ahead unless you put it to work as capital. Inflation eats away part of the value of your cash each year. Why not plow back your cash into your own companies? Just as two or three salaries and expense accounts are better than one, you can see that two or three potential capital gains are better than one.

Small Can Be Satisfying

Of course, it isn't easy to run several enterprises at once. The overwhelming mass of small business ventures remain single, small, and unadventurous. Growth is an optional extra. For owners who opt against it, life can still be beautiful.

"I can wear only so many suits, and drive only so many cars," the head of a small business may say to himself. "Why should I work harder just for the sake of doubling my sales?"

Even though an owner may simultaneously be the janitor, the bookkeeper, the treasurer, the sales manager, the production foreman, and the chief executive, this can be a satisfying way of life. It's a very comfortable feeling to know you can't be fired. The security it provides cannot be measured in dollars alone.

Small-business owners take deep pleasure in their being their own bosses—especially if they've worked under grouchy, domineering, unreasonable superiors earlier in life. As owners, they needn't ask anyone's okay to try a new idea, or to drop an old one. They needn't conform to any set pattern of work habits, hairstyles, apparel, or social life. They can take a day or week off for golf or tennis—maybe even take a cruise whenever they see fit. Such freedom is worth a lot.

And they're likely to enjoy the work itself. To people with an ounce of imagination, creating something is great fun. Creating a business involves concocting ideas, solving puzzles, experimenting, making decisions, and seeing the results. Many owners find their enterprises so fascinating that they would almost be willing to do the work for free. When their ideas and efforts turn out well, their pride of accomplishment is deep.

Then too, there is the heady excitement of betting on oneself. It's far more exciting than rolling dice. To somebody who gambles his life savings on his own business, marching up to the $5 window at the racetrack isn't much thrill. Business is by far the better gamble, too, because luck plays less of a part in the outcome. Brains and hard work don't pay off at the roulette table, but they usually do in a business venture.

Millions of Winners

The excitement and enjoyment give a small-business man some real advantages over big business enterprises. What the little man is selling is better, quite often, because he works harder at making it better. And he does this because he sincerely wants to.

We've all heard about the theoretical advantages and economies of mass production, mass buying, huge budgets for research and development. Nevertheless, the corporate colossi often come up with shoddier quality or slacker service than their tiny competitors. A small business has a decided advantage of being able to change its ways faster than a big one. It has more freedom of choice, closer contact with employees, grassroots understanding of local market conditions. It knows its customers and suppliers personally. These are some reasons why so many commercial giants have found that the only way to stay profitable is to sell franchises to small-business men who bring drive and enthusiasm to their work.

The most successful people, in business or any other pursuit, are those who truly love what they are doing. Enjoyment is a far more common quality in the makeup of small businesses than it is in huge corporations. Consequently, success is common too in small business.

Failures? Yes, there are many. But the failures must be less prevalent than the successes, because the number of small business enterprises is growing steadily. In 1900 there were fewer than 2 million businesses of any kind, large or small, in the whole United States. By 1965 there were 7 million small businesses. In 1975 there were 9 million. About 300,000 new ones were started in 1977. Today there are more than 11 million.

(How small must a business be, in U.S. Department of Commerce eyes, to be ranked as "small"? As a general rule, an enterprise is considered small if it employs fewer than 50 people, although manufacturers stay in this category until they employ more than 100. However, if a firm with only a few employees is doing big volume, it isn't classed as small. If a retail store or a service business shows annual sales of more than $250,000, it moves up into a bigger classification. So does a wholesaler with a volume of $500,000 or more.)

According to the *Harvard Business Review,* more than 85 percent of all small businesses show a profit. Even among minority groups, who tend to be impoverished and undertrained, business ownership is growing. The Small Business Administration estimates that 300,000 people from minority ethnic groups are in business. The last census showed no fewer than 163,073 businesses owned by blacks alone; their total receipts were $4½ billion.

Of course, manufacturing is the most complex kind of small business, since it gets into problems of product design, raw materials, production, and marketing on top of the other difficulties that any business faces. Therefore, you might expect small manufacturers to be a rare breed. But in 1975, according to Dun & Bradstreet, there were about 185,000 small manufacturing companies in America, each with annual sales of $100,000 to $500,000. There were uncounted others with smaller sales, but still profitable.

Buy or Create?

Suppose you want to get into business for yourself. Should you buy an existing business or start a new one?

There is no right answer for everyone. The chemical engineer mentioned earlier who developed a new plastic compound could take advantage of it only by starting a new company. The same was true of Elmer Winter and Clement Stone; they filled needs that nobody was filling. S. B. Fuller couldn't have bought any company because he had only $25 when he started his cosmetics company.

On the other hand, Hilton, Simon, Perot, Fairchild, and Thornton did better by buying small ongoing businesses than they could have done by trying to start their own. Most small owners would probably say the same: "Buy if you can. It's quicker and safer than creating."

Of course, you can always start a tiny business on a shoestring. But then you may toil a long time before you make it big enough to pay you as much as you might earn by the same effort elsewhere. And the risk of failure is much higher in starting a new enterprise than in buying one that's already on track.

Six Advantages of Buying

Let's assume that you have enough capital to either start a business or buy one—and that the kind of business you want is for sale. Here are six viable reasons why you'd probably be smart to *buy* it:

1. You may possibly get it for a bargain price. Circumstances sometimes force an owner to accept less than his business is worth in order to sell it quickly. (Health, personal, and domestic problems are examples.)

2. You bypass start-up problems, which can be unforeseen and costly. You save the time and trouble of buying equipment and supplies. Operating methods are proven. Customers are already buying from the company.

3. Guesswork is minimized. If you start a new enterprise you can't be sure about the right location for it, right-size building, right forms of advertising, right prices, and so on. An established owner already knows most of the answers.

4. The owner can give you valuable information about competition, demand, seasonal fluctuations, community attitudes, and other variables.

5. You get a time-tested list of suppliers and service people.

6. Often you inherit trained employees who will stay on and help you learn the business.

Sometimes the Best Advice Is "Don't Buy"

A good business broker will point out these advantages to anyone who asks about buying a business. However, he sometimes meets a would-be buyer who absolutely shouldn't buy anything the broker has to sell—and the broker, if he's ethical, will say so.

Maybe the kind of business the prospect wants, and should buy, just isn't available. Maybe the prospect shouldn't pay the asking price of those available, because it would stretch him too thin financially. Maybe he simply doesn't have the personal qualities that make for success in small business. In such cases, a good broker would say, "You shouldn't buy" and will explain why.

The broker ought to know how to find other prospective purchasers. Small-business men also ought to know how—in case they want to sell, or in case they need extra financing, to keep their businesses going. Sources of capital are more plentiful than most people realize.

Who's Got the Money?

Merely by circulating, meeting as many business people as possible, you may run into a well-heeled prospective buyer or backer at any time —especially if you make it widely known that you own a business which you might sell (or that you're a broker with a portfolio of businesses available for purchase). As you circulate, you'll hear of restless people in big companies who might buy the right small business in order to run it themselves. And you'll encounter an occasional dynamic self-starter, determined to get into business for himself and actively hunting for opportunities.

But in addition to these common types, there are certain other types who are systematically seeking chances to invest into small business. They are:

1. Suppliers. A big company selling a line of supplies to small companies may buy a part ownership in some of these customers. Instead of paying for the purchase in cash, the big outfit may pay in supplies. This could solve the problem of an owner who wants to sell because he's pinched financially. He can still retain control, and get the supplies that are just as vital as cash in operating his business.

Cash-rich vendors like to buy small customers both because this helps them diversify and because it assures them that the customer will keep buying from them. In other words, it locks out rival vendors.

Actually, it's good policy for a small business to sell parts of itself to high-quality suppliers, because this often enables it to pay its bills to those suppliers later than would be allowed otherwise. And they can use the supplier as a reference to increase their credit ceilings at the banks. Then too, the supplier can often give valuable competitive information to its small partner.

2. Investment groups. Sometimes wealthy doctors, lawyers, executives, and other private investors band together through syndication to buy a small business, if they don't have to manage it. When an owner can give assurance that trained managers will stay on after he sells, they consider buying.

These people are looking for ways to minimize their tax payments while building an estate. They like to form limited partnerships under Subchapter S of the tax laws, which allows investors to write off a company's losses as the investors' direct losses. In 1976, investment groups put more than $50 million into various small enterprises.

3. Venture-capital firms. *Time* magazine estimates that some 600 privately owned venture-capital firms exist solely to pump money into other people's ventures. They invest between $700 and $900 million each year in new or existing companies—usually companies that own a promising invention or formula.

These groups vary so widely in size, operations, goals, interests, philosophies, and resources that they can't be wrapped in a tidy package. Some are Oriental groups, some are Arabs, others are South Americans —yet they comb the United States for opportunities. Some of the rumored machinery to filter money across frontiers from all over the world sounds like detective fiction. The secretiveness is perfectly legal in most cases. But an owner can feel uneasy if he doesn't know who is offering to buy part or all of his company.

Most venture-capital firms are run by salaried people. These administrators are likely to be either university graduates with Master of Business Administration degrees or former owners of small enterprises. They collect fat bonuses when they make profitable investments.

4. Major corporations. A big manufacturer, or a conglomerate, will often buy a fledgling manufacturer or technical laboratory and add its products to its sales line. This broadens the big company's line at a fraction of the time and expense needed to develop products of its own. Similarly, a big retailing chain may buy a small store for its location, or just to eliminate it as a competitor.

5. Insurance companies. They have entered the venture-capital field in a big way. They prefer to buy a slice of a small company, with first option to buy more slices as the company becomes more profitable. Like the venture-capital firms, they're interested mainly in high-technology enterprises.

6. Universities. Until recently, they invested endowment funds so conservatively that they made little old ladies look like plungers. Then they began investing in common stocks, riding the ups and downs of the market. Lately, they've begun actually buying and running businesses, or sometimes investing in a small business for the sake of a share in its expected profits. One college owns such a mundane enterprise as a spaghetti factory.

7. Cash-poor buyers. Many individuals would like to buy a business, but they think they don't have enough money. Sometimes a broker can help them raise more cash through their personal friends or others willing to be silent partners. Sometimes they don't realize they can borrow on their life insurance, or their margin accounts with stockbrokers, or on other collateral. Sometimes they don't know about getting loans from the Small Business Administration or from a small-business investment corporation.

Certain owners themselves are willing to provide financing in order to sell the business. So if a prospective buyer's financial position dictates the seller's becoming a lender, the buyer should feel out the seller early in the negotiations. Quite often, for tax reasons, sellers prefer to take no more than 30 percent of the sale price in cash over the first calendar year and let the buyer pay the rest in installments over a term of years.

So much for the people who buy, or invest in, small businesses. They represent half of the buy–sell equation that the broker must bring into balance.

In the next two chapters, we'll consider the other half of this equation: the owners who want to sell, or at least may be willing to sell.

KEEP THESE BASIC POINTS IN MIND:

- *Many people in big business, at all levels, are prospective buyers of small businesses.*
- *Some people without much education buy businesses and succeed.*
- *A small business can make a smart and energetic owner very wealthy.*
- *An owner of one or more businesses gets tax advantages not available elsewhere.*
- *In most cases, it is better to buy an ongoing business than to start a new one.*
- *Not all would-be buyers should buy.*
- *At least seven different types of individuals or organizations are prospective buyers or backers of a small business.*

2

Who Wants to Sell, and Why

Sellers, Sellers Everywhere

There are more chances today to buy a small business than there have ever been before. Even if by "small" you mean a manufacturing company churning out between $100,000 and $500,000 worth of products a year, buying opportunities are plentiful. There are about 185,000 small manufacturers in this bracket (a bracket commonly chosen by business brokers when they talk to a prosperous individual prospect, because a company in this range can be run by one owner with one layer of managers below him, yet is big enough to pay handsomely if run well). On any given day, according to Dun & Bradstreet, at least a fifth of these companies—about 37,000 of them—are for sale.

Naturally, there are infinitely more businesses for sale when you look at companies in lower brackets. If you scale down to enterprises in which the owner does all the managing, with perhaps a handful of clerks or blue-collar workers, you'll find hundreds of businesses for sale in any fair-sized county, and literally thousands of small businesses for sale in metropolitan areas like Los Angeles, Detroit, Chicago, and New York.

The number mounts into thousands per county when you include everything down to the hole-in-the-wall electronics shops, hamburger stands, ma-and-pa grocery stores, and so on. At least 100,000 businesses are sold each year in California alone. So you can afford to be choosy if you're looking for one to buy.

Nationwide, about half of all new businesses survive two years under their original owners, according to the U.S. Department of Commerce.

One-third survive for four years. Only one-fifth are still owned by the founder at the end of ten years.

Many of these businesses are sold to someone else, often at a juicy profit for the founder. Many others are liquidated because the owner is rich enough to retire and shut up shop (although he would have preferred to sell if a buyer had been in sight). Dun & Bradstreet estimates that during a typical ten-year period only one-third of the new ventures started in that period were sold or liquidated because of loss. More new businesses start up each year than are closed, so the opportunities keep growing.

Seeking Sellers? Ask Around

For the purposes of this chapter, let's suppose that you want to go into business for yourself, and that you've decided you'd rather buy one than start one.

(If you own one and want to sell it, you saw in Chapter 1 how to locate possible buyers. And in Chapter 7 you'll see how to prepare your company for sale, followed by advice in Chapter 22 on negotiating the sale.)

Where will you find a going business to buy?

The best way to begin is simply to ask around. Many potential sellers never advertise their businesses for sale. Instead, they quietly pass the word to a few lawyers and accountants, or to possible buyers they may know personally, such as their suppliers and competitors. Some of the best small businesses are bought and sold almost secretly. There are reasons for this. An owner may not want his employees worrying about a possible sale. He may be afraid that his customers or creditors will think the business is in trouble. Or he may simply not want to cope with dozens of unqualified buyers who might write, phone, and knock on his door if he advertised the business for sale. There's a chance you'll get in on one of these unadvertised buys if you scatter hints that you're in the market.

Naturally, you can locate prospective sellers faster if you have a clear idea what you're looking for. Maybe you'd like to acquire a bakery. Then start by asking around among salesmen supplying the bakeries. Look at bakery trade journals. Check with bakery trade associations. Best of all, if there's a bakery you admire in your town, it won't hurt to call up the owner, introduce yourself, and say forthrightly, "I'm interested in buying a good bakery. By any chance, have you ever thought about selling? . . . Or have you any ideas where I might find a good bakery for sale in an area of the city where I wouldn't be competing with you?"

Many a prosperous owner would be willing to sell and start another business, or move to another town, or retire, if a good offer came along.

Many a purchaser gets the inside track by asking at the right time.

Roy Thomas, a Canadian with a fabulous record of buying small enterprises and making them big, was once asked how he went about the delicate business of finding out if an owner would sell. He replied bluntly, "I ask."

It's like the old story about the direct approach to ladies: most won't but some will, and the only way to find out is to ask.

Scan, Then Screen

Surprisingly, many people are so eager to become owners that they snatch at opportunities without waiting to match their own capabilities and tastes and limitations with the business they buy. They don't even investigate its income potential and the strength of its competitors. They just follow a "hot tip" or a friend's advice. These are the ones who have to sell out sooner rather than later at reduced prices. You're not one of them, or you wouldn't be reading this book.

However, you may not have any clear idea, right now, what kind of business you'd prefer. Then you should start by setting up some rough specifications—"parameters," or a "matrix," as technical people might call them. Then take a quick look at all visible opportunities which come within these loose limits. That starts you off with a large crop of possibilities. Later you can winnow them down by methods we'll examine in Chapters 4, 5, and 6.

For example, you surely know enough about yourself to realize that some types of work *might* be well suited to you, while others would be all wrong. Some businesses—such as retailing—depend on friendliness. Others—such as a testing laboratory or a mail-order service, perhaps— may not put the owner in contact with people at all. Running a restaurant would probably involve long hours and weekends. Being a wholesaler or a manufacturer's distributor might be strictly a nine-to-five operation, weekdays only. Some businesses call for technological skills; others don't. So you can quickly rule out certain types of ventures that don't suit your personal qualities and life-style. On the other hand, you'll certainly look closely at anything involving your own spare-time recreations: if you're athletically inclined, you'll find out about the sporting-goods business, and if you love photography, you'll want to look at camera shops.

Another of your specifications, obviously, will be the selling price of the business. There's no point in looking at something offered for $100,000 if your ready cash is limited to $10,000.

However, keep in mind that the asking price is almost always higher than the eventual selling price. Furthermore, not all of the price is likely to be cash on the barrelhead. The terms are usually less than 70 percent in cash and in some instances as little as 10 percent in cash, the rest to be spread over a period of years—five or more years, in many cases—with a promissory note of 8 to 12 percent interest. An installment sale minimizes the tax that the seller must pay.

Thus, an asking price of $50,000 means that you might swing the deal for $5,000 to $10,000 cash or less. By the same ratio, $3,000 to $6,000 capital might be enough to put you in charge of a business priced at $30,000 or so.

The down payment isn't the only factor to consider, of course. You'll want to make sure that the business will net at least enough to pay off the monthly installments on the note while simultaneously paying you a living income. This whole big question of estimating "How much is the business really worth?" will be considered in Chapter 4.

For now, let's assume that you're in the early stages of seeking something to buy—strictly the window-shopping, browsing stages. Having set up your first rough screen to filter out obvious bad choices, you're mentally applying it to every opportunity you see.

You should scan everywhere you can think of—like a radar beam sweeping the horizon, or like the man in Hobbes's *Leviathan:*

> Sometimes a man knows a place within [which] he is to seek; and then his thoughts run over all the parts thereof, in the same manner as one would sweep a room to find a jewel; or as a spaniel ranges the field until he finds a scent. . . . A spaniel with the brain of an educated man could not, by an effort of will, scent a partridge in a distant part of the field. But he could so quarter the field by a voluntary arrangement that the less voluntary process of smelling would be given every chance of successfully taking place.

Sweep and ye shall find. But always bear in mind that people tend to stop looking too soon. Don't jump at one of the first few opportunities as the ideal solution. Wait until you've studied it much further and are also better able to make a comparative judgment.

The Science of Quick Scanning

Let's analyze this scanning, sweeping, sniffing process.

You've begun by asking around. Now you look around. Run your eye over the classified-advertising sections of newspapers, especially the Sunday editions, under "Business Opportunities" or "Businesses for Sale." (*The Wall Street Journal* has one of the best of these sections, although it usually advertises larger businesses than those you'll find in local advertising.)

Scan some trade journals and newsletters in all branches of industry and commerce that might conceivably interest you. You'll find many in the periodicals room of any good public library.

If you haven't anything more than the foggiest notions of which lines you might be suited for, you can clear away much fog by sending for a few of the Bank of America's series of profiles on specific types of small business. They cover just about everything from auto-parts stores through cocktail lounges and garment making to plant shops and X-ray services. Each little book costs about $3, but you can get a free catalog of all publications in the series by writing to Small Business Reporter, Bank of America, P.O. Box 37000, San Francisco 94137.

The best way to find out if you want to be in a particular line of business is to talk with people who are in it. Look in the Yellow Pages and jot down the phone numbers and addresses of some companies in a field that interests you. Include some with big ads and some with one-line listings, so that you get a good cross-section of business sizes. And while you've got the book open, study the ads. Notice what they emphasize. Is it reliability, quality, fast service, or something else?

Then when you visit a particular owner or manager, you can remark, "I noticed in your Yellow Pages ad you emphasize your company's experience. Do you find that experience is the most important attraction for customers?" He'll be flattered that you remembered the ad, and he'll loosen up as he realizes that you're serious about studying his occupation.

Try to meet an owner in a quiet setting. If he has a private office, that's usually best. But many small-business men just have a desk in a corner of the shop. Meeting with them for lunch or a cup of coffee in a quiet restaurant may be a good approach. You can invite them to your home for dinner, or for informal conversation—or you may even be invited to an owner's home.

What should you say when you ask a small-business man for an appointment? Explain that you're thinking of going into his line of business, in a location that won't compete with him. Always be sure to minimize any threat you might pose. For example, if he owns a store on the east side of a big city, explain that you may want to buy one in the far south suburbs, at least twenty miles away and well beyond his market area. (However, he just might surprise you by offering to sell you his business. In that case, he'll describe it eloquently, but you'll have to discount what he says.)

Naturally, you'll be truthful. So if you're planning a shop on the east side, you should talk with owners far to the south. If you plan to buy a business in a relatively small town, you may have to call owners in towns twenty miles distant, in order to be able to say honestly that you won't compete with them.

In bigger cities, a Buyer's Guide is published listing a wide range of business opportunities. If you want to make a quick scan nationwide, send for the National Buyer's Guide, published at 5400 Wilshire Boulevard, Los Angeles 90017. It is free.

Drop in at the nearest office of the Small Business Administration. This agency can give you good suggestions for places to look. It may even know of a few little companies that would sell out if the right buyer came along.

Two Magic Questions to Ask Seller

Two very important questions for you to ask a seller are:

How much is your profit?

What's the cash flow for your business?

Both you and your accountant will need to consider the seller's answers and records carefully.

Profit

You've probably heard people say, "Profits are the name of the game." You must, of course, make profits if you are to continue in business and get a satisfactory return on your investment. After you buy, you should have periodic, frequent, and up-to-date statements that show the profit earned in order to manage your company profitably and efficiently.

You may find that the seller, as do many businessmen, keeps his books and prepares profit-and-loss statements on a cash basis, even though he is extending credit to some customers and obtaining credit from his suppliers and vendors. As a result, a sale appears on his profit-and-loss statement only when he receives payment. Similarly, an expense is recognized only when he pays a bill. This cash method of accounting does not provide useful information on the performance of a company.

Or perhaps the seller you're talking with keeps his books on an accrual basis. The profit figures he shows do not depend upon whether he has yet been paid for goods or services rendered and whether he has yet paid for goods or services he has acquired. He considers income as earned when goods are sold or a service performed. He recognizes goods or services received as expenses when they are incurred—even though payment may be made much later. Thus, his accrual-basis accounting provides a measure of the performance of the business with respect to its profitability.

Whichever way the seller has kept his books, I recommend that after you purchase a company, you handle your accounting on an accrual basis. You will need the information to

- judge the success of your overall operation;
- judge the effectiveness of your management;
- judge the efficiency of various parts of your company;
- help in your short- and long-range planning;
- help you make decisions.

Cash Flow

"If I'm making such a good profit, why am I having so much trouble paying bills and meeting the payroll?"

"This P&L statement shows that my profit was $50,000 in the last twelve months. But my balance sheet shows that my cash increased by only $4,000. Why?"

I've heard statements like these from many small-business men. The first statement is sometimes followed by an entirely unnecessary bankruptcy on the part of a businessman whose sales are growing rapidly and whose monthly P&L statement is showing an ever-bigger profit. In most cases, you can avoid trouble of this sort by having a cash-flow statement prepared for your review along with your P&L statement.

If you're a newcomer in business, you might ask how such serious trouble could happen. Usually, it is because of items that do not show up immediately (or completely) on your P&L statement. Such items can affect your cash flow to the extent that because of a lack of cash you may find yourself unable to pay bills and/or meet your payroll, even though your profit-and-loss statement shows that you are making a good profit. The most common such items which may not affect your P&L statement quickly are

- substantial increases in your inventory
- increases in accounts receivable
- reduction of credit by your vendors or suppliers
- new equipment you've purchased
- unrecognized obsolescence of inventory
- a lump-sum payment (balloon) of a debt
- your bank's refusal to "roll" (renew) your loan.

I strongly recommend that you have a cash-flow statement made to accompany your periodic balance sheet and profit-and-loss statement. In fact, at times it can be to your advantage to make a substantial *cash* sale even at no profit on the sale. With timely and vital information about the period just ended and with planning ahead, you can handle rapid growth and get the results you want. In short—cash flow and profits are both essential to your success in business.

How to Use a Broker

Some real estate agencies do some business brokerage on the side. If so, it is probably indicated in their ads in the Yellow Pages of the phone book, or on signboards outside their offices. And of course, there are a few full-time specialists in selling businesses; they usually advertise in the Yellow Pages. Better phone them before you drop in, because many tend to specialize in particular kinds of businesses. Some limit themselves to retail stores, or to restaurants. Others handle mostly manufacturers and job shops. However, some brokers do not specialize, but prefer to list and sell many different types of business. This type of broker may even serve your needs best.

In most areas, a business listing is exclusive with whichever broker has it, so if you check only one or two, you'll miss some opportunities. Get in touch with all those which seem to deal in kinds of business you might like—or, in fact, the general business opportunities broker.

Few people know how to use brokers in buying businesses. Qualified business brokers can serve a vital function. They can be your antennae out in the field, feeding you information, not only names of would-be sellers, but sources of financing, areas where business is good, possible terms for transactions.

If you use a broker, keep in mind the limitations of the situation. The broker is the seller's agent, not yours. He's an optimist by nature. He'll talk optimistically to the seller about the price he can get. And he'll talk optimistically to you about the profits you're bound to make when you own the business.

His job is to sell for top dollar. It isn't easy, because almost always he's trying to make a sale that the owner has already failed to make on his own. When owners want to sell, they usually dangle the business first in front of relatives, friends, suppliers, and occasionally competitors. Only then do they call in a broker, to whom they must pay a commission.

Buying a Business

The purchase of a business should be free of emotional influences other than enthusiasm. It should be approached in a practical, well-organized manner, not only employing your own personal research and judgment, but also with the guidance of an attorney, an accountant, and persons knowledgeable in the field of activity you choose to enter.

Certainly some of the more important factors affecting your choice will be the amount of money you have available to invest (leaving an adequate amount for backup operating capital), the total price of the business, the track record of the business, the return on investment, the terms of the amount that might have to be financed, the adequacy of the cash flow or spendable income it will provide for your required standard of living, and a thorough review of the financial statements for at least the past three years.

Now, let us presume that after a diligent search and thorough research of all available information, you have zeroed in on one specific business. Everything points to a potential "winner."

But what about the asking price? Is it realistic in the light of the assets you will be buying—and perhaps the liabilities you will be acquiring? How much "blue sky" has been added into the price? We are all very much aware that good will has a very real asset value; but how much? How was the price of the business arrived at—by an accountant's logic, by a less-than-exact formula of employing a gross multiplier, by industry standards for comparison, or by the seller's natural greedy instincts or his inability to set a fair value consistent with the present dictates of the market?

If we start with the premise that the businessman selling his business is probably the person least able to set an equitable sale price on it, then we proceed from there armed with the knowledge and also with the fact that a business rarely sells for the original asking price.

In the final analysis, your bottom-line evaluation of the business, and thus your offer to purchase, will be based on a combination of the appraised value of the assets and your considered estimate of reasonable future expectations for the business.

How now should the negotiations begin? If you are dealing through a business broker, you can call upon his skills in attempting to bring you the most favorable price and terms based on his knowledge of the business and the seller and his innate negotiating technique. If, on the other hand, you are on a one-to-one basis with the seller, you may have to play the game under different ground rules. Do you come in with a "low-ball" offer, hoping to steal the business? This method is often counterproductive, antagonizing the seller and thus clouding further negotiations as well as your credibility.

Should you make an offer that is slightly less than what you feel you would eventually go to if the seller rejects it, and expect a counteroffer from him? You thus begin a fencing match, hoping for a mutual agreement as the negotiations continue.

Or should you go in for a full-boat offer on the terms and conditions spelled out by the seller?

Good judgment would dictate that the second, or middle-ground, choice is the most productive as far as you, the buyer, are concerned, by laying a groundwork on which confidence can be established between the two parties, with a more orderly meeting of the minds as an eventuality.

Remember—this is not a baseball game, in which there are one winner and one loser; in this match of skill, the outcome should produce two winners.

Quoting from my book *How You Can Become Financially Independent by Investing in Real Estate,* published by Simon and Schuster, Chapter 8, page 116:

> Many books have been written on selling, but buying is an art that is seldom taught. Too bad, because intelligent buying takes as much brain-work, knowledge and persuasion as selling does. A skilled buyer tries to understand the seller's viewpoint as well as his own. It's no accident that progressive schools of business now teach marketing and purchasing together; the best preparation for buying may be the knowledge of the problems and tactics of sellers.

Franchises: A Different Ball Game

Among the opportunities you'll hear or read about will be a whole giant grab bag of franchises. At least 1,200 franchise companies now offer to set you up in business for a fixed price. More than 300,000 businessmen are operating under franchise, doing a total of more than $90 billion worth of business every year.

A franchise is a license to operate under the name of a big organization with many local outlets. It combines owner-management with the advantages of group merchandising. When you are a franchisee, you're an independent owner, but you operate under the rules of the franchisor—and, if you have chosen well, under his expert guidance.

You can get a good (or sometimes a bad) franchise for an investment of anywhere from $1,000 up to $200,000. A fairly small investment can make you the boss of a franchised arts-and-crafts store, campground, candy store, cleaning establishment, coin-operated service, counseling firm, employment agency, fast-food place, hearing-aid distributorship, motel, printing-and-copying service, roadside stand, temporary-help service, or tool-rental agency.

In your preliminary scanning, you definitely should look at franchise opportunities in whatever fields appeal to you. Many will be advertised in newspapers and magazines. Each Thursday's *Wall Street Journal* has several franchise-opportunity ads. For a wider survey, write to the International Franchise Association, 7315 Wisconsin Avenue, Washington, D.C. 20014. Or send $3.10 to the U.S. Superintendent of Documents (Washington 20402) for the Commerce Department's *Franchising Opportunities Handbook*. Or ask a bookseller to get you the *Directory of Franchising Organizations* published by Pilot Books, 347 Fifth Avenue, New York City 10016; it costs $2.50. These books are packed with details about hundreds of franchise offers.

You can also go to a business show, held once or twice a year in major cities, where booths are set up by franchisors to hand out literature and talk with potential franchisees. Your chamber of commerce can tell you when and where one is scheduled nearest you.

Some of the best franchise companies are so well known that they don't need to advertise. Prospective franchisees approach them constantly. If you're interested in one of these companies, just call a local franchisee and ask him for the address of the headquarters office, where you can write for information. Slightly lesser-known companies may have ads in the Yellow Pages, with toll-free numbers you can call. Your call or letter will bring you a packet of information—followed sometimes by a call or visit from a salesman.

If you're determined to start in business within the next month or two, forget any franchisors except the small-outlet companies. You can't get a sizable franchise overnight. The company will want to investigate you thoroughly, perhaps put you through a training course. Once you sign the contract, additional weeks may pass before you can open the doors. In fact, any company that encourages you to think you can get started right away is likely to be a high-pressure promoter.

Beware the Hard Sell

In the franchise company area, as in many other business areas, there are both highly ethical and unscrupulous operators. Beware of the unscrupulous. Such operators may form a franchise company and then overload their franchisees with supplies, or furnish them with inferior equipment. They make their profits at the front end—they're not much concerned whether the franchisee succeeds.

Therefore, your first screening of franchise opportunities ought to filter out any which

1. claim you can make big money fast;
2. try to rush you into making a deposit or down payment in a hurry;
3. try to sign you to commitments rigged to the franchisor's advantage;
4. make excuses for not putting the full proposal in your hands until it's time for you to sign; and
5. are newcomers in the field, without a visible track record.

Other fast-buck operators besides these franchisors are alert for chances to contact would-be entrepreneurs. Don't give a second glance to advertisements with headlines like OWN A PART-TIME BUSINESS OF YOUR OWN—HUGE PROFITS! Before he went to prison, one con man collected $6 million through classified ads offering a worthless earn-at-home proposition. Others got rich with small ads offering to put people in the business of raising minks or chinchillas.

A more elaborate bunco game goes like this, with minor variations: A help-wanted ad proposes, "LADIES, MAKE MONEY at home. Large earnings assured. We buy what you produce. Experience unnecessary. No selling. Send $1 for information." Those who send the $1 receive enticing information about an instruction booklet, available for a price, and materials and patterns, also for a price, with which ladies can make aprons. The materials and patterns cost six times what they would at a dry-goods counter. But the big trap is in the small print of an agreement which the ladies must sign. It stipulates that the advertiser may return any aprons that don't meet his standards. Of course, all aprons sent, no matter how fine the workmanship, are rejected as "not up to standard."

Beware, too, of blind ads (giving only a phone or box number instead of a name and address) offering to sell a going business at a sacrifice price. Some of these offers are on the level. But many are swindles, even if they appear on financial pages or in trade journals. They are bait to lure you onto the hook of a smooth supersalesman who'll try to rush you into buying (often with the claim that others are bidding) and who'll find ways to keep you from reading the whole contract before signing it.

If any would-be seller wants you to sign a contract, or wants you to pay him for helping you go into business, insist on seeing the full proposal in writing. Then put it aside for intensive study. The thorough analysis of all opportunities that interest you is the second—and most important—screening that you must do before putting your money into a business venture. You'll see just how to do this screening in Chapters 4, 5, and 6.

KEEP THESE BASIC POINTS IN MIND:

• *You can probably buy a business with a cash down payment of from 10–70 percent of the asking price.*

- *In seeking a business to buy, begin by asking all acquaintances who might conceivably know of one—including owners.*
- *Then look in classified-ad columns of newspapers and trade journals.*
- *Then get acquainted with owners in fields that interest you.*
- *Watch for cash flow and profit.*
- *Investigate available franchises in your fields of interest.*
- *Check with business brokers.*
- *Use caution before buying a business.*
- *Be wary of any proposition that implies you can make big money quickly.*

3
How to Find
Hidden Bargains

A Bad Business Can Be a Good Buy

If you're a fairly capable all-around businessman, you may profit more by buying a sick business than by choosing a thriving one. You can pick it up for a handful of peanuts, usually, and then nurse it into prosperity by applying commonsense management methods.

When you know the symptoms to look for, it's no great feat to find mismanaged businesses with unhappy owners who might be overjoyed to sell if someone made them an offer. Don't look for these feebly struggling enterprises in the ads or brokers' listings. Don't even expect to hear about them through the grapevine. Owners of such anemic businesses are usually so unsophisticated that the possibility of selling out doesn't occur to them. Because of their woe, they can't imagine anyone's wanting to buy the business. So it's up to you to find such owners, and open their eyes to the possibility of selling.

Oddly, the public is often quicker to realize that a business is mismanaged than is the owner; until the late stages of decay, he's just perplexed because sales are down or payments are lagging. He doesn't see his enterprise as others can see it.

Try this experiment. Ask your acquaintances around town, "Can you think of some businessman who shouldn't be in business?" You'll be surprised how many people know several who disappointed them, and can tell you why.

The distress signals they'll mention may include:

bad temper	idleness
boredom	lateness

clutter	loose money
danger	lost articles
dinginess	rudeness
dirt	sloppiness
excuses	stock deficiencies
extravagance	waste
greed	

When these criticisms point you toward a businessman in trouble, and you visit him, he won't realize that he himself is part of the problem. He's a type who seldom sees anything wrong with himself. (Almost anybody in business for himself tends to be headstrong or he wouldn't be there. When this deepens into bullheadedness, an owner is on the skids without realizing it.)

But he's usually quick to tell you his troubles. His complaints go something like this:

"You can't get good employees nowadays."

"My competitors are unscrupulous"—or "crazy."

"Taxes are ruining me."

"A lot of my customers are deadbeats. And they walk right past without ever coming in the shop."

"I'll start advertising when customers start coming."

"Training employees is a waste of time. They keep leaving."

"Sure I hire relatives. They're loyal."

"I do all the important work myself. I don't want to depend on hired help."

"I never borrow money. I don't believe in going into debt."

Such owners are prime prospects for a buyer. Seeing themselves as innocent victims of exterior circumstances, they're likely to jump at a chance to get out of the business.

But you mustn't make the mistake of buying too quickly. The owner's incompetence may not be the only reason his business is bad. Just put him on your list of prospects, and run his business through your fine screen when you're ready for serious sifting. (Again, we'll cover this sifting technique in Chapters 4, 5, and 6.)

In addition to asking acquaintances, use your own eyes and ears to spot businesses that you might salvage. Jerome Zanar, partner in an international accounting firm, writes:

People who have built up a business from scratch have much to be proud of. However, their biggest fault is that they are too proud. In a number of firms I've seen, the boss's ego stands in the way of—

- hiring competent assistants;
- handing over responsibility to a subordinate.

The entrepreneur often rationalizes this by saying that small firms can't compete with big companies for top managers, so he must make do with what's available.

Clues that the boss is fooling himself:

- length of service and loyalty become the key reasons for promotion, rather than ability or drive;
- the boss is doing everything, not just managing; he continually steps in to fix problems;
- "little" problems (manufacturing bottlenecks, late deliveries) are brushed aside or dealt with before any facts are generated or options considered.

You may spot a clue to trouble just by sizing up the age and ability of employees. If they're mediocre, yet have been with the boss a long time, you can guess that the boss may be mediocre too.

Look for organizations that are doing everything the way they did it ten years ago. An atmosphere that's against change, a let's-leave-things-alone feeling, is sometimes easy to sense when you're inside a store or office. The fixturization may be obsolete; the displays inadequate; the carpeting ripped in places or possibly musty. Such signs as these manifest an attitude of either not caring or not knowing better.

Ask local trade associations for the names of firms that could be members but aren't; such firms tend to be types that think nothing can be learned or gained in group cooperation. Add them to your list of possible sellers, either now or when they've slid further downhill.

Watch newspapers and trade journals. You'll see news that may mean a business is in trouble, such as:

a labor dispute
a lawsuit
embezzlement or other thefts
a big loss from burglary, fire or other causes
a price war
death of an owner, partner, or manager
shortage of raw material
a mechanic's lien

If a business is seasonal or depends on climate (such as being involved with farm crops, rainwear, travel, resorts, camps, or vacations), it could be distressed after a stretch of the wrong kind of weather. Just how much business is being done at a ski resort when there is no snow?

Open Your Eyes to a Closed Business

Don't pass up the chance to investigate a business whose doors have closed; you may be missing a golden opportunity. Find out the reason it closed; how long it had been established at this location; how long the last owner ran it; and finally, who the property owner is. This information can usually be obtained from a neighboring business owner who would be happy to see it rented again; nothing is worse for a business than to have empty stores adjoining.

We are talking about a store that is not operating but has equipment and fixtures in place—not just four bare walls. The equipped store generally means that the outgoing businessman is still paying rent on these premises and has monthly payments to be met on the fixtures and equipment. You can be sure then that he is a motivated seller.

He is hurting with the ongoing contracts and leases, and chances are that any reasonable proposal on your part would be as welcome as the flowers in May. You might even get in with nothing down. And there is also the possibility that you can make monthly payments to him on a graduating scale as the business prospers. He might be amenable to a lease-purchase agreement.

Check this possibility out. This is one way you might be able to get into business with little downside risk.

Retailing: Happy Hunting Ground

You'll find it easy to go bargain hunting among retail businesses, because so much of their operation is visible to the public. You can watch employees, and often you can watch the boss. You can see whether the stock-in-trade is well displayed and well advertised. Sometimes you can judge the quality of the merchandise. Above all, whenever you see a sloppy or half-empty store in a good location, you can be sure it's a candidate for turnaround under better management.

Retailing is the field where small businesses are most plentiful—and where failures are plentiful too. It attracts a steady stream of owners who really shouldn't be in it. You see, retailing looks so simple!

Rightly or wrongly, storekeeping is considered a wide-open field for the small man, and for the mom-and-pop operation. Almost half of all U.S. business firms are retail stores. Many eventually make their owners financially independent. Yet success doesn't come as easily as most owners expect. A good location and a run of good luck may keep them alive for several years, but they don't prosper unless they learn about their customers' tastes, about inventory control, about employee relations—and especially about money management.

A retailer is always up against the problems of adequate money. He must pay taxes; meet payrolls; pay his suppliers, the landlord, and the advertising media. Yet his customers may not pay him promptly. When big companies need money, they raise money by selling stock or bond certificates. Small businesses, even when they're incorporated, can't do this because there's no established market for their stock or bonds. Consequently, some go broke prematurely on their way to making it big.

A store crowded with customers may nevertheless be plagued with hidden financial problems. Sometimes you can sense these if you check its credit rating; a flurry of past-due bills may mean it's in trouble.

Watch stores that have opened recently. Most retailing failures come within the first two or three years of operation.

As a matter of fact, retailers aren't the only small operators who have their worst troubles in their first years. The Small Business Administration reports that 80 percent of all new small businesses either sell out, merge, or go broke within three years. So you can cast a speculative eye at any fairly new start-up venture. Furthermore, if you look into enterprises that have changed hands within the last three years, you'll probably find some that are ready to change again.

Undercapitalization: The Chronic Pain

"If only I'd had more money at the start, my business would have made it." That's a common lament among entrepreneurs, not only in the retailing field but in manufacturing, wholesaling, service industries, and virtually every other kind of small venture.

One business broker is quoted as saying, "People have only a sketchy idea of how much money they need to go into business. They don't realize that they'll need some other source of income to buy groceries and clothes and maintain their accustomed standard of living for the first couple of years. Businesses with less than $10,000 of invested capital have a high mortality rate."

Under the spell of rosy dreams, many new owners underestimate their expenses. They don't budget enough for rent, operating equipment, labor, taxes, insurance premiums, licensing fees, adequate stock-in-trade, replacement due to obsolescence, interest charges on money they borrow, and the ever-rising prices that come with inflation.

Businesses that are riding high can have a money crisis too. Success can kill them if they're swamped with orders they can't fill. Or one of their big customers can fail, owing them more money than they can afford to lose.

One sure way to flirt with danger is to let yourself become heavily dependent upon one or two major customers for the bulk of your sales volume. How great it looks on the books when you are doing $3 million a year gross and 90 percent of it comes from sales to Sears and K-Mart. It will be the crash of '29 all over again if one or—God forbid—both of them change suppliers. And that has happened to a great number of smaller manufacturers who had depended too heavily on large-chain-account buying. It's the old "Too many eggs in one basket" situation.

A noteworthy example of a narrow escape from collapse through too much success is the story of an unemployed mechanic in the oil fields who thought it was ridiculous for oil companies to install permanent drilling derricks at each site. He sketched an idea for a portable drilling rig, and built one with his lifetime savings of $325. It took him three months. On his first demonstration to an oil company, the company bought the demonstrator on the spot.

The mechanic had thought of asking $7,500 for it, but the manager was so enthused that the mechanic asked $10,000 instead. When the manager didn't balk, the mechanic added $3,500 for the truck (which he had borrowed, on promise to pay for it if he sold his rig). The mechanic hitchhiked home to await the $13,500 payment. However, when the check came, it was accompanied by an order for ten more rigs at $13,500 apiece. Soon another company heard about his rig, and sent an order for fifteen.

This mechanic could barely read and couldn't write. He had no experience whatever in either management or finance. He didn't know how to get backing from banks or investors. His bookkeeping system was just a drawerful of bills and IOU's. But he could think. He thought up a way to build the twenty-five rigs with only $13,500 capital.

He offered mechanics top wages if they would work in a barn (which he rented for a few dollars), accept part of their pay in groceries, wait for the rest until the rigs were sold, and agree that no interest would be paid on back wages. Times were hard. Five applicants showed up for every job he offered, so he was able to pick top-quality men.

He found grocery stores that agreed to sell him all the food his employees needed at half price, with the balance to be paid when he collected from the oil companies. He got scrap steel for 25 percent down. And so on. When he was finally paid, his one-man company was rolling in cash —and continued so until he sold out twenty years later for about $12 million. Undercapitalized; but he solved the problem through hard work, guts, and a lot of ingenuity.

Few small entrepreneurs are so bright as our mechanic friend when coping with unexpected demand. Most let their business outgrow their ability to finance it. They tie up all-important cash in things they would be better off without, or things they should have leased instead of outright purchased. They spend money that should be held ready for emergencies to pay for store improvements or new equipment. They overstock on supposedly hot items that turn cold. They grant more credit than the business can afford, and don't press hard enough for collection. Consequently, they spend most of their waking hours scrambling to find cash, instead of working to improve the business.

Remember the story about the merchant who lost money on every item but made it up on volume? And the cartoon showing a bum telling his fellow bums, "I was always the low bidder"? They're more factual than funny. Amazingly, studies of small business show that 24 percent of the owners keep no books, and about 40 percent never take inventory. They can't possibly know the true state of their business.

A successful owner finds ways of forecasting when and where his needs will grow because he knows he can't afford a liquidity squeeze, with sudden demands for more money. As his business prospers, it will need time to get additional financing. You won't find a business on the bargain counter if it has capital for expansion.

If a proprietor's books tell him which products or services are selling best, which should be dropped as money losers, how much debt and interest payments he can handle, whether a markup is covering increases in overhead and selling costs, then he's unlikely to be in trouble. If he sells the business, he'll know what it's worth.

On the other hand, if you're acquainted with an owner who doesn't seem systematic in his ways of working and planning, you can probably buy his business, even if it looks prosperous on the surface. And the price you pay him may be well below what it could be worth potentially under your guidance.

It May Be Healthier than It Looks

Occasionally, just the opposite is true. A business is offered for sale and seems to be in worse financial shape than it really is. This can happen if an owner doesn't know how to prepare it for sale. He lets it look unattractive through errors in valuing the investment and in capitalizing the profits. So he may sell for less than the true value.

For example, he may be taking a much higher salary from the business than you'll choose to take. Or his fringe benefits may be excessive: a costly company car, high travel and entertainment expenses, pension plans, life insurance. The IRS may consider a $6,000 trip to Europe a deductible expense for the chief executive of a small company, but it probably isn't essential to the company's welfare. As you look at a balance sheet, watch for these expenses which may reflect hidden profits.

Then too, remember that owners sometimes are likely to undervalue their fixed assets. Somehow land, buildings, machinery, and equipment seem sacred. If the company has been in existence many years, these assets are usually deeply depreciated on the books. They're likely to be worth far more than book value, because of inflation. (Land, although it isn't depreciable, has usually risen in value too.)

Maybe a company has a fully tooled machine shop, although competent subcontractors are available to do all its shopwork. If you buy the company, you can close down the shop, sell off its equipment for cash, sell off supplies, free up some space, and chop your payroll.

Another example: if a company hasn't earned a profit, there hasn't been any income-tax incentive to write off uncollected debts. But if you, as the new owner, make it profitable, you might conceivably be able to charge off some debts against profits. And maybe you can collect other delinquent accounts. Poorly managed companies often neglect the job of collecting bills. Salesmen fear to annoy a customer on whom they rely for business by insisting that he really should pay up. All too often, large accounts become slower and slower in making their settlements. Thirty-day accounts turn into 60- or 90-day borrows, and many of them have the unmitigated gall to take the 1- or 2-percent discounts, as they know they will be able to get away with it. The result is that the only customers who make timely payments are those who do so automatically, without the needling that many companies expect before paying any bills. Perhaps you can restore a company's health merely by tightening its collection techniques.

Is It Weak at the Top?

A small business sometimes grows big without changing its ways—which makes it a candidate for takeover or bankruptcy. Consider the true story of one good-sized plant which burned down four months after it was built. The underlying cause of the fire was the owner's inability to adjust to the realities of a bigger enterprise.

He had started as a mechanic in the back room of his father's small shop. At first he employed three men. A quarter-century later, at the time of the fire, he employed 9,000—but he was still running a small shop. At least, he thought so. He vetoed proposals to divide the company into four small plants, and insisted that one big one be built so he could personally oversee everything. His new plant contained no fire-retarding walls because he wanted to be able to see the whole assembly floor from a gallery behind his office.

When the fire started, the owner was out to lunch. There was no other executive; the owner was still his own plant manager, production boss, quality-control expert, and chief inspector. Consequently, nobody coordinated the fire-fighting efforts; nobody hauled out the most important machines, blueprints, or records when it became clear that the building couldn't be saved. So the whole business was destroyed. The company had to be liquidated.

In this particular case, the owner wouldn't have considered selling, or even taking in a partner, before the fire. But his company might soon have fallen victim to its one-man operation in less abrupt ways, giving an outsider time to spot the storm signals and negotiate a purchase when the old owner felt the pinch.

Of course, this was an extreme example. But the condition itself is fairly common. Many a man who starts a business hasn't the innate ability to grow with it, and gets into such trouble that he would gladly sell out.

A list of "ten easy ways to run a good business into the ground" was compiled by L. S. Ring for the *Price Waterhouse Review*. Summed up, these were:

> Keep poor accounting records
> Misinterpret or don't bother to understand financial data
> Invite fraud
> Keep your costs high
> Forget to sell
> Don't plan
> Ignore working capital
> Neglect training
> Omit insurance coverage
> Avoid professional help

These are topside weaknesses, hard for an outsider to spot. They mean that money is leaking away invisibly. Eventually, they cause a company to sell out, although the owner probably offers other well-rehearsed reasons, and may even claim that the business is doing fine. He may pull out electrocardiograms which the doctor has just sent him, revealing that he has a weak heart and must give up all work. If you're an astute bargain hunter, you'll be skeptical of any claim that an owner wants to sell "for personal reasons," and will look deeper for possible weakness in the business itself.

Compare Its Prices

There's one clue to internal weakness that you can often uncover quickly: prices lower than those of competitors. Many small businesses are afraid to charge enough for their products or services. They charge only what the market will bear without strong sales effort, or even less than what it will really bear.

If a sales manager is setting prices, you can bet they're too low. Underpricing makes life easy for salesmen. Salesmen rarely believe they can get a price that includes a reasonable profit—until a tough owner forces them to try. Many owners aren't tough enough for this, or don't realize they're selling at a loss.

Small-business men tend to see growth of sales as the royal road to success. It seldom is. Higher profits don't automatically come with increased volume. In fact, shrinking the number of products, improving them, and widening the profit margin are usually safer routes to profitability.

In the long run, a lower cost has to be the result of mass production or mass buying. Small suppliers can't gain anything by undercutting price except a one-way ticket into bankruptcy.

It's surprising how often customers will pay more with little complaint, despite salesmen's cries that to raise the price is suicide. If you find an enterprise that sets prices for its merchandise or services too low, you may be able to turn it into a winner simply by charging more and thus widening the profit margin without any increase in sales volume.

I am reminded of the story of the business executive who was a frequent traveler on airplanes. He said he shuddered every time he boarded a plane because the builder of that plane had been the low bidder.

Danger! Relatives at Work

About 980,000 businesses in the United States are at least partly family-owned and family-run. Many of these are successful. Nepotism can be healthy. A husband and wife often make a good team. And a son often turns out to be a crack executive, with more drive and savvy than his father, simply because he grew up in the business. He absorbed through the skin, without even trying, the equivalent of what would have taken him years of experience. He heard his father talking about company problems at breakfast and dinner and throughout countless weekends. He probably learned to love the business, and looked forward to someday taking charge. So he took pains to get a proper education for it.

But when you see a company with other relatives at work in the business, you're probably looking at a company with internal troubles. It's worth examining as a possible bargain because of mismanaged assets.

In-laws usually drag a company downhill. Here's how it happens. The two-child family is common. Quite often, one is a girl, the other a boy. The owner-father gives equal amounts of stock to both. But he can't pick his daughter's husband. Result: His daughter may marry a man with no business experience and very little business capability.

Handsome young George, having married a few thousand shares of company stock, suddenly finds himself an executive of the company. Often, he's totally untrained for the job. So he isn't much good and can offer it nothing. The business suffers.

His wife has grown up with a certain hostility toward her brother, who seems to get more of Dad's attention. So she shuts her eyes to the fact that husband George is a disaster. Instead, she throws her stockholder's weight around. She tries to help run the company through George. Since she too has only dim notions about business, and no executive training, everything begins to fall apart. Employees don't want to be part of the family power struggle, so they look for the nearest exit.

Family-owned businesses typically reserve senior management spots for family members. They often say, "We have to support Cousin Klutz, so we might as well put him to work." And they give him important work, which he bungles. Meanwhile, competent managers around him, not related to the ruling family, get discouraged. They either quit and go elsewhere, or slack off and do just enough to get by.

One business broker says, "A company where the son is the heir apparent is probably strong and expanding. But check first to find out if he's got a sister in the background. And if you hear the word 'in-law,' beware. The same goes if you find several relatives sitting around the offices; they probably have their feet on the desk or a secretary on their lap. Their business should sell cheap."

I can remember a close friend who worked for a very successful New York food manufacturer that was a partnership, with each partner owning 50 percent of the total stock. One of the partners, age 68, used to have the office manager (whom he met as a tout at Aqueduct Race Track) drive him out to the track every day. The other partner, 72, remarried and was always in Europe traveling. Most of the key administrators were employees of forty or fifty years' service, and all well past a retirement age. Business was good, and they all drew high salaries.

A slowdown in business eventually came, and belts had to be tightened.

An efficiency team was called in to take an in-depth look at their modus operandi. After a one-month study, out of a staff of 26 in the home office and a branch manager, 11 were discharged and 5 were pensioned. Only a staff of 10 remained, and the business ran as before with a salary saving of over $230,000 per year.

Waiting for Dad to Die

And then there is the despotic type of owner who won't give relatives any power or inside information. He hangs on as others try to help manage or take over his buisness, while his heirs feel overshadowed and frustrated. There's sure to be bad trouble when his business eventually moves from one generation of top management to the next.

Sons or subordinates of first-generation entrepreneurs tell of long, worrisome waiting in the wings for their time to take over the running of the company. When the time comes, it usually comes because the "old man" dies, or is too sick to work. Until then—and afterward—there are tensions and quarreling as older and younger generations try to coexist within the company. Older relatives outside may push for fatter dividends and a place in the business for their own children. Younger, often disillusioned brothers and cousins feel varying degrees of pressure to join the firm; or else, through these pressures, potentially good working relatives shun the family power struggle and quit.

Speaking of such problems, one second-generation owner said bluntly, "Fortunately for the firm, my father died one year after I joined the company." Concerning another company, a prospective buyer said, "The old man is wrecking the company so fast that we'll pick it up for nothing before the kids can build it back up."

What to Ask Yourself While Shopping

We've outlined a wide horizon around which you can look for prospective sellers of businesses. We've noted many signals you can watch for as indications that an owner might consider selling, even though he hasn't offered to.

As you look around, as you talk to owners and brokers and other people who know something about a business you're considering, you should always keep certain questions in mind:

Do you think you can run the business as well as, or better than, the present owner? A small enterprise may be worth a heap of money under the guidance of its creator, yet be worth far less when he steps out. He must be succeeded by someone with similar abilities if the business is to keep running smoothly and profitably. Maybe two or three people will be needed to do what he did alone.

Why does the owner want to sell? Maybe his health is failing. Maybe he wants to retire. Maybe family problems necessitate a move. Maybe selling will ease his tax position. These are all common, legitimate reasons why highly profitable businesses are sold. Likewise, they are common phony excuses given for trying to unload a sick business.

As we've seen, a business in trouble doesn't necessarily make it a bad buy. Is it shrinking because of the owner's weaknesses, and can it grow under your management? Is it suffering from lack of capital or expansion, and can you obtain that needed capital?

Do you have new ideas that can make the business bloom? On the other hand, do you understand precisely what its problems are?

Will you be paying for the previous owner's mistakes? Does he have disgruntled customers? Does he have a bad reputation with suppliers and other creditors?

Will you be stuck with unsalable or outdated merchandise or materials? With inadequate fixtures? With incompetent partners or managers?

Will you be buying a bad location?

Is the owner grossly underpaying himself because he is running the business inefficiently and can't pay himself a decent salary? Is he deliberately drawing a low salary to make the company's earnings look better? Or is he making the earnings look worse by drawing an exorbitant salary?

Of course, you won't see answers to most of these questions at a glance. But you'll get glimmers, and they'll help you decide whether an opportunity is worth probing more deeply. Remember, you may be looking at only the tip of the iceberg.

KEEP THESE BASIC POINTS IN MIND:

- *Often a bad business is a good buy, if you know what is wrong with it and how to correct it.*
- *An owner of a failing business seldom realizes that anyone might buy it.*
- *You must seek out such owners and ask if they'd be interested in selling.*
- *Ask acquaintances to tell you of poorly run businesses. Watch for such businesses yourself. They often are easy to spot.*
- *Trade journals and trade associations can give you clues to businesses in trouble.*
- *Even a prosperous business may be troubled by undercapitalization, or by deteriorating bosses.*

- *Sometimes a business is worth more than the asking price because of aspects the owner doesn't realize.*
- *Underpricing by a small business is often a clue to mismanagement.*
- *Relatives in a business sometimes mean internal trouble.*
- *As you look for possible sellers, ask yourself what is wrong with their business and whether you can do better than the present owner.*

4

How Much Is This Business Worth?

Let's suppose a broker—or owner—offers you a business for sale. It's a line of business you'd like to get into. So you say, "Tell me more."

If the first hour or two of conversation gives you a feeling that you might conceivably buy the business, you say, "Let's take a look at the lease." This may save you hours of wasted conversation.

Why You Check the Lease First

Many times a would-be seller is completely unaware that his lease prevents him from selling his business, or that he must get the landlord's written consent. Even if the landlord is an "old pal" of the seller, he may not be so friendly when the seller asks him to transfer the lease to an unknown new tenant. Often a good sale breaks down right here.

Also, you'll want to know whether you can get an option to renew the lease, and at what rental. Is it a flat lease, percentage lease, escalating lease, triple-net lease? (A triple-net lease is one wherein the lessee pays the taxes, insurance and repairs.) Is there a "cost of living" or tax increase locked into the terms? Is the monthly rental figure in line with the neighboring businesses, as well as of a similar type?

A lease is really a form of long-term debt, although it doesn't show up on most firms' balance sheets. For some reason, conventional accounting doesn't include the lease as a liability. But the wrong rental terms can often strangle an owner. Until you've had the opportunity to read the lease, you'll be playing blindman's buff in negotiating to buy.

Let's say that, on the surface at least, the business looks like a potential "buy," and after inspecting the premises, you have enough interest in the business to start the negotiations by making an initial offer.

The seller has a price in mind, naturally.

So now your main problem is to determine what your opening offer should be. How can you estimate what the business is worth?

Is There a Formula for a Fair Price?

In certain lines of business, a simple rule-of-thumb is used to set a "fair selling price." For example, to fix the value of a liquor store (including its license), many sellers use the factor of 3¼ to 4 times its monthly gross, plus the value of the inventory at cost—but remember, they are attempting to get the highest price. Beer taverns are often valued at 5 to 7 times the monthly gross. The rule for cocktail lounges may be 3 to 5 times monthly gross, plus the cost of the liquor license. (Note: In most instances, liquor licenses vary in price from state to state and from county to county.)

For coffee shops, it may be 3 to 4½ times monthly gross; for hamburger stands, 4 to 5 times. For grocery stores it is more difficult to establish any workable value ground rules because they vary so widely in size, type of store, and gross volume. Sellers try for a rule-of-thumb nevertheless by adding up the cost of the inventory and the cost of the liquor license (if any), then throwing in 1½ to 3½ times the monthly gross to arrive at a total asking price.

In other types of retail stores, you'll find valuations ranging anywhere from 1 to 10 times the monthly gross, depending on many factors—including the actual *type* of retail business. For instance, you cannot establish the same formula for a shoe store, for example, as that of a jewelry store. In service businesses prices are all over the lot, because clientele counts for so much, as well as the personal relationship established by the owner with his customers, and the equipment may vary widely. Some coin laundries have equipment worth thousands, while some swimming-pool-maintenance ser ices get along with a few brushes and inexpensive tools.

The reason you will find a traditional formula used in setting prices for certain businesses is that they are often sold through small brokers—most of whom are primarily real estate brokers, usually totally inexperienced in the complexities of business-opportunities sales.

In real estate, apartment buildings are commonly priced at "gross multipliers"—that is, "six times the gross rental income," or "eight and a half times the gross," or whatever. Sometimes the multiplier is the only figure given when the property is advertised for sale. Unsophisticated investors and brokers think the gross is the key consideration in the buying or selling of income property.

Astute realty investors know better, and so do experienced buyers of liquor stores and other kinds of businesses. The so-called and often-used "magic multiplier of the gross income" is a crude guide at best. The Institute of Certified Business Counselors does not recommend this method.

What's Wrong with the Magic Multiplier

For one thing, it assumes that the gross will stay as high as it is at its present level. But past performance doesn't necessarily foretell future results. In Chapter 3 we saw various hidden weaknesses that can cause a company's gross to slump at a later date. Then too, it's not uncommon for someone selling a business to lean on his friends' extraordinary patronage to make the gross look good temporarily, or to splurge on promotion that brings in sales at an actual (but hidden) loss . . . yet on the face of things shows a very healthy gross.

Gross multipliers can mark the extreme boundaries of the ball park within which the price may fall. That is, a coffee shop priced at only twice the monthly gross would be suspiciously low; either it's a distress sale situation or there's fraud lurking somewhere, or it could be the result of a stupid owner. Likewise, a coffee shop asking seven times the monthly gross wouldn't deserve even a nibble unless perchance there is some undisclosed added value, such as a highway to be built at its front door.

One more point about gross multipliers. They can be affected by the popularity of the type of business—what brokers call "buyer appeal." The higher the appeal, the higher the gross multiplier.

To see what this means, consider a beer tavern and a children's-shoes store. Maybe the shoe store's furnishings and fixtures cost twice as much as the tavern's. Maybe the store is in a better location, and is pulling a bigger gross and net. So you'd think the shoe store would sell much faster than the tavern and for a higher price.

But it doesn't, in most cases. The beer tavern has more "buyer appeal." For every prospective buyer of a children's-shoes store, there are probably fifty prospects eager to leap into the beer business. So the latter usually sells for a higher multiple than the former.

Some investors think the gross is less important than the net profit— the bottom line. They always ask first, "How much money is he making?" They want to know what the return on their investment will be.

Others argue that the net profit depends on how efficient an owner is, and how hard he works at making the business successful. There's some truth on both sides of the argument. In making your own decision about how much to pay for a business, you'll have to judge whether or not you're likely to widen the present owner's profit margin—as well as whether you can boost the gross and maybe improve the net thereby, even though your profit margin gets thinner.

What About Book Value?

When a business is bigger—with a gross in six or seven figures, say— prospective buyers use other ways of valuing it. For one thing, they want to know its "book value."

Book value is a shorthand phrase for the net worth of the business—its total assets minus its liabilities. It is what you'd get, theoretically, if you simply closed down the business, collected all the accounts receivable, paid all the debts, and sold everything the business owned.

Victor Niederhoffer, whose Wall Street investment-banking firm represents buyers or sellers in many merger transactions, says that about half of all transactions are for 1.2 to 3 times the company's book value, with the average about 2.1 times book. Small companies who never go near Wall Street are often bought and sold at similar ratios. But you can't assume that any such ratio is a sure way of pricing the particular business you're considering.

Why not? Well, to begin with, most closely held businesses utilize two sets of books—one for tax purposes and the other for their own guidance; your accountant would be well advised to analyze both sets of books.

Then too, a business may show a high net worth and still have a bleak future. Its worth may be high because for years it hoarded earnings, yet its recent earnings may be low, with no prospect of improvement.

Also, its physical assets like building, machinery, and equipment are harder to value. Its accountant may or may not have deeply depreciated them on the books; to this day there's no agreement among accountants on how to determine the useful life of aging assets. We'll consider this further in Chapter 6.

Inventories are especially tricky. Some owners continue to value everything at what it cost them, regardless of when it was purchased, including items that really are obsolete or otherwise hard to sell. While you may be able to guess at the inventory's worth by looking at it (if you're thoroughly familiar with the type of business involved), valuation of inventory brings up accounting questions that you'll probably need to refer to a CPA. We'll get to these too in the next chapter.

For now, keep in mind that the "book" value of the assets you're buying isn't nearly as important as their current "market" value. One businessman tells of hauling out and dumping twenty-three truckloads of scrap inventory in the first three weeks after buying the business. It was worthless inventory which the previous management hadn't written off the books. He had paid for it without full knowledge of its worthlessness when inventory was taken prior to the close of escrow on the business.

For all these reasons, be skeptical of book value unless you're looking at a business with mostly liquid assets that can be accurately valued— such as a bank, an investment trust, an insurance agency or advertising agency. Even then, smart buyers don't go solely by book value. But it's a useful benchmark when used together with other measurements.

How Much Can It Earn?

The value of a going concern lies in its earning power. A dead business is worth only what its assets will bring in a sale or auction. But a business with good earnings that are growing is worth the price in the opportunity it presents to the buyer.

Profitability is also a measure of the enterprise's ability to borrow. A business with high volume and low costs will find credit cheaper and more easily available than one in less robust health. Bankers will be more cordial and receptive when asked for loans. Suppliers will be eminently more willing to grant favorable terms.

So what you really need to judge, before you decide how much to offer, is how much is the net income you're likely to get from the business. Art Hamel, past-president of Certified Business Counselors, teaches his students to value a business by estimating its future earnings and the return on whatever purchase price they would pay for it. A Small Business Seminar offered by the Education Advancement Institute covers this area quite well. For a free brochure write EAI, 50 Washington Street, Reno, Nevada 89503.

You're probably familiar with the future-net-earnings approach from reading the financial press, because this method is often used in big business and the stock market. Earnings per share and what dividends are paid largely determine how much a stock sells for. You see expressions such as "It's selling for only four times current earnings," or "The price is eighteen times estimated earnings."

Using profitability as a measure of value, most companies that are sold or merged go for between 5 and 12 times their current annual earnings; most of them are in the 8-to-11 range. But these are strong companies, seen as attractive buys.

Smart buyers often use the "capitalized earnings" method of measuring the value of a business. They start by guessing the future earnings, in the light of past performance and future prospects. Then they multiply these estimated earnings by a "capitalization rate" to arrive at the price they can pay for the business. Here's how it goes:

Suppose you want a 10-percent yearly return on your money. If a business produces a fairly certain pre-tax profit of $8,000 a year (not counting the owner's salary), you should be willing to pay $80,000 for it. This is the top price that will still yield your 10-percent return. So, as the money men say, you "capitalize" the investment at ten times earnings. But let us repeat the fact that this does not take into consideration the owner-operator's salary.

Buyers choose a capitalization rate according to the riskiness of the business. For example, if the business is unusually stable and secure, it might be comparable to government savings bonds or a bank savings certificate. Say these investments yield an annual return of 5 percent, which is one-twentieth. (The safer the investment, the lower the yield is likely to be—although low yield doesn't always betoken safety.) Then a fair market for this business might be twenty times its annual earnings. (Remember—we are talking of return only on money invested, not labor.)

So if its earnings without the owner's salary have been about $5,000 year after year, the price could conceivably be $100,000. Buyers—the elderly and cautious ones—are willing to pay a higher price for safety. But the practical likelihood is that very few businesses are sold for twenty times earnings.

But in the case of some businesses, a venturesome buyer may take a risk if the potential return looks high enough. As incentive, he may want a 25-percent prospective yield on his money. If so, he'll say the business is worth only four times earnings, and he'll pay only $20,000 if the earnings are $5,000.

Years ago someone compiled a chart of earnings multiples that would be considered the "right" price for various kinds of business. It's still a useful rough guide, although in today's turbulent business climate, some solid enterprises are selling below book value and at earnings multiples smaller than those in the following table.

As you can see from the table, the worth of a business rises with its growth potential, with its capital assets, and with its evident safety as an investment. Its worth falls as the risk rises.

So if you want to use a capitalization rate in setting the price you'll offer, ask yourself questions like these:

How vulnerable is the business to economic changes, to labor troubles, or to changes in public tastes? Is it seasonal? Would it be hurt by scarcity of key materials?

Is the business stronger than its competitors? How long has it been established in its trading area? Who and where is the competition?

What would happen if a rival business opened across the street?

Business	Capitalization Rate (number of times earnings paid for the business)
(The figures shown are for Owner-operated businesses)	
Personal-service business requiring little capital, dependent mainly on owner's talents	1
Highly competitive business requiring small capital, dependent on skills of a few key people or on a very few customers	2–3
Small, competitive business where capital assets are relatively small	4–5
Larger business relatively vulnerable to fluctuations	6–7
Established business requiring managerial talent but otherwise sound	8
Business with solid position in market and good management, but limited growth potential	10
Established business with significant growth potential	11+

How heavy is its debt load? How much heavier will the debt load be if you have to add additional mortgage payments in the financing by the seller to you? Will the interest charges, or pressure from creditors, cause problems? Is the present cash-flow rate sufficient for you to maintain your desired standard of living?

Will the present management stay on with the business, at least while you're learning to run it? Or must new and unproved people be recruited? This is an especially crucial question for a small business heavily dependent on a few key employees.

Can You Forecast Earnings?

Knowledgeable brokers and investors hate the earnings-multiple method of valuing a business because (a) it rests on the assumption that earnings will continue as they are, and (b) it assumes that risks will be the same under your management as under the old management. So you're setting your purchase price on the basis of two questionable assumptions.

They insist that past earnings aren't always a good guide to future earnings, even if they represent an average of the past five years. As for risk, you'd have to commune with occult powers to estimate it, they say. There are so many outside factors which might come into play in the near future so as to throw your best judgment out of whack.

These complaints are valid to some extent. One of the few known characteristics of the future is that those who forecast it will be wrong. The only question is, how far wrong?

And past earnings undoubtedly can fool you, especially if you're not a trained accountant. In the next chapter we'll see how your CPA should help you analyze the earnings record.

How to Allow for Risks

When you set the capitalization rate, allow a safety margin for risks. Consider the trade-offs between risk and return. The rate of return for a low-risk investment, like a mortgage or a gilt-edged bond, won't exceed 9 or 10 percent. A moderate risk, like a growth stock, may bring you a return of 20 percent if it does grow. A high-risk speculation, like raw land or a new manufacturing company, can put you in the red—or can double or triple your money. Obviously, you must try never to risk more than you can afford to lose. In any case, try to buy low enough so that the reasonably certain earnings can at least recover your capital within three years—four, at the outside.

Here are a few pointers to help you assess the risks:

1. The longer the business has been in existence, the lower your risk —unless it is on the brink of bankruptcy. Most bankruptcies occur in the first five years of business.

2. A highly competitive market generally means high risk, especially if you're entering a field you don't know well, or are little prepared for it from a skills point of view.

3. High costs of labor and materials (over 75 percent) in ratio to sales can signal high risk. These direct costs are generally hardest to cut. And when they're too high, your margin for error or profit is thin.

4. A history of dwindling earnings may not mean high risk if you know what caused the shrinkage and how to reverse it. Even if you decide to go along with the decline and sell off the assets according to a well-thought-out plan, the business may still be a good investment. Most buyers will shun it, and you can probably pick it up at a bargain price. It is altogether conceivable that the greatest bargain of all is a business that is presently closed.

5. If the owner has obviously been running the business badly, the risk may not be unacceptable if you know you can turn the business around within a year or two . . . and, of course, before you run out of cash.

6. Age of accounts receivable is an index to risk. The older the accounts, the less likely you can collect them. Although it cannot be said automatically, it would appear that a business operating on a cash basis would appear to be "safest."

7. If earnings spurted last year, make sure you know why. The owner may have slashed expenditures, or stalled creditors, in hope of selling at a fancy price to the unsophisticated buyer who looks only at the bottom line.

8. Watch out for very low owner compensation. The owner may be painfully underpaying himself because he's so inefficient that he can't afford to draw a decent salary. Or he may be taking a low salary to make the company's earnings look better.

The true earning power of the enterprise, in your eyes, is the profit it can generate under your ownership—not the profit under ideal conditions, because you'll seldom experience ideal conditions.

Don't assume that you're a genius or a dynamo who can double or triple the earnings just by taking command. Of course, if you can identify and eliminate what the seller is not doing well, you can probably count on bigger earnings. Otherwise, your safest course is to compare the firm's past performance with that of similar firms of similar size.

Information on the performance of other businesses may be hard to find; but trade associations and their publications can give you good clues. Try to get an idea of the prospect's competitive position. Talk to other people in the business. Then go to your library or bookstore and get one of the books that provide ample detail on methods of valuing various types of business. One good one is *Guide to Buying or Selling a Business,* by James M. Hanson, published in 1975 by Prentice-Hall. In addition, you can ask the nearest Small Business Administration office for its charts showing the profitability of numerous kinds of business with total assets under $250,000.

How Much Salary for the Owner?

An owner who started a business on a shoestring often tends to think of it as a job—as a source of wages rather than as an investment. Thus, he may not capitalize his assets correctly. One common error of owners is considering only their compensation and neglecting to put a fair value on the potential earning power of the assets.

Be alert for this. If you see it, point it out to the would-be seller: "Your salary is fine, but your return on investment is surprisingly small. Look at all the fixtures and equipment you've bought. Look at all the money locked up in inventory. These capital assets should be earning at least as much as they would if you'd put the money in a savings account. But they're not. When you separate your salary from the net earnings of the business, you'll see that the assets are earning hardly anything.''

An owner of a small business often shoulders a huge workload. He may be not only the chief executive but also the sales manager, the production foreman, the treasurer, and the janitor all in one. But remember, you may have to hire two or three people to replace him when you take over the business.

A business should provide more than just a handsome salary for the owner if it is to have any real value to a buyer. For example, if it is merely breaking even after paying all its expenses including a $30,000 salary to the owner, and if $30,000 is a fair salary for the manager of such a business, then it's not worth much from an investment standpoint. Why should you or, for that matter, anyone pay thousands of dollars for a business that is only going to produce a salary equal to what you might earn elsewhere—without the attendant risks of investment?

Of course, if you as the owner are drawing a much bigger salary than you'd reasonably expect to pay someone for the work he does, then you can add the excess salary to the taxable profit in estimating a potential total for the company's future yearly earnings.

In theory, at least, when you buy a business you shouldn't have to work in it in order to get your investment back in no more than five years. There should be enough income to pay a manager to run the business while you play golf, if you wish, or possibly buy this as a second business.

However, presumably you're buying the business so you can work in it yourself. You want to make it grow and prosper. You want to charge off your travel, medical benefits, business promotion, and other corporate expenses (contemplating that you set up the business as a corporation). In that case, you'll run it, draw a salary comparable to what any other corporation might pay you, and—you hope—get your investment back in five years. Base your offering price on these calculations. Unless the ''after salary'' income, or income potential, is at least equal to the earning power of outside investments, you'd be foolish to sink your money into the business.

What Owners Don't Know

Many small-business owners don't really know the value of their business. So out of their ignorance in this respect, or their naiveté, they may ask an unreasonably high price for it. Or, on the other hand, they may sell at a lower price than they should reasonably expect in the market-place.

If you ask an owner about the size or character of his company's markets, he may have to admit he has no idea. What's more, he may have no idea where to find the information. For example, some makers of specialized accessories such as milling-machine attachments don't know how many milling machines there are in their own county, to say nothing of the nation. Yet this information can easily be found in trade papers and magazines.

If you find yourself negotiating with such a muddled owner, you can probably push down his asking price by showing a greater awareness of the market than he has. Like anyone else in business, you should try to buy for the lowest possible price, as long as you do nothing unethical. After a little study of the business, you should offer less than you think it is worth, and negotiate from there. If the owner feels your offer is too low, open his eyes by showing him exactly how, on the basis of your information, you placed a value on the assets.

Almost all owners set a ridiculously high value on the "good will" factor. Good will is a catchall for all intangible assets. It includes such things as favorable location, customer lists, special connections with suppliers, old established names, trained employees, reputation for quality and service—and above all, the supposed loyalty of customers.

The average owner thinks his personal popularity has been a big factor in his success. (Maybe so, but he can't guarantee that the popularity will be transferred to a new owner.)

Some owners feel themselves so beloved by the public that they may plan to start a new business in competition with the one they're selling.

Whether you think the owner is lovable or not, you'd better make sure this doesn't happen. The less competition for you, the better. So your lawyer should insist on a written promise that the seller won't compete in a similar business in your trading area. This is known as a Covenant Not to Compete. Without this, the "good will" of the enterprise hasn't even imaginary value, because the new business will drain away whatever good will the old owner commands.

Even when the owner agrees not to compete, you'd better question his valuation of good will closely—especially if he's owned the business less than a year. Why does he want to sell so soon? You may find that instead of buying "good" will, you're smearing yourself with his bad reputation with customers and suppliers. This could mean that you'll have to go to considerable expense to change the firm name and thus its image in order to disassociate it from the former owner.

Don't Buy Imaginary Good Will

Early in the negotiations, after the seller has named his price for the business, you can inquire what he thinks the assets are worth:

"How much is your lease worth? . . .

"How much are your furniture, fixtures, and equipment worth? . . .

"How much is your inventory worth? . . .

"How much is your 'Covenant Not to Compete' worth?"

Then ask him how he arrived at the value of each of these. Can he show bills or cancelled checks to substantiate their cost? Does he know what their fair market value is today, or their replacement cost? Just how does he know?

When he's answered as fully as he can, add up the figures—and you'll almost certainly be far short of his asking price.

Request him to justify the difference between the total and his asking price. Put it to him that *you* will have to justify the difference if you later try to resell the business.

Soon he'll see, as you do, that the difference in the two figures is what can be called the "good will" factor. His own figures will show him that he's asking far too much for the intangible over the tangible assets.

Valuing the Tangibles

So now you get down to brass tacks for negotiation. This owner wouldn't know what you were talking about if you tried to discuss profit margins, budgets, price–earnings multiples, capitalization rates, potential markets, or earnings.

Instead, your discussion with him will be limited to tangibles (which, of course, are vital anyway). Land and buildings. Furniture, fixtures, equipment, machines. Inventory. Accounts receivable. Debts owed. Cash in the bank. Monthly payroll. Monthly overhead. Taxes. As you delve into these, you can probably make some educated guesses about the true earning power of the business.

Any would-be seller must expect to open up all his internal records to any serious prospective buyer after a firm offer has been made. If he won't or can't, he'll have to be satisfied with offers that reflect the buyer's doubts. The seller's "skimming" technique catches up to him at this point.

Sometimes a small-business owner tries to cover up his incompetence in a thicket of sloppy, inaccurate, and unnecessary records stuffed into boxes and bins. But he'll almost certainly have records somewhere that help show the value of his assets and liabilities. At the very least, he'll have copies of his tax returns, which can give you a fairly clear view of costs, expenses, and profits. If doubt still persists in the buyer's mind, he should protect himself by providing for a one- or two-week "observation period" in his offer to purchase, before an escrow is opened.

Incidentally, most states have laws known as "bulk sales acts" to prevent defrauding creditors by any secret sale of a firm's assets. A sale in bulk differs from an ordinary sale by a simple standard: If more than half of the entire stock is sold, then it's a bulk sale, and the seller must give the buyer a sworn list of his creditors, with their addresses and the amount of money he owes to each. He must also supply the buyer with a complete list of every item included in the sale, as well as the price he originally paid for it. Obviously, these sworn documents will be very useful to you, and you should ask for them early, if you feel it is advisable under the specific circumstances.

It often turns out that some of the assets aren't fully paid for. The owner may have gotten a chattel mortgage on some of his equipment, or bought it on the installment plan. Be sure to take these into account in setting the price you'll pay for the business and the down payment. You may agree to assume the liabilities as part of the deal, or the seller may agree to pay them off; or the seller may deposit enough money in escrow to satisfy all the debts.

Having read this far in the chapter, you undoubtedly realize that you'll need to call in your accountant and your attorney at the time you make an offer for any business. (This is the first time most sellers will be willing to open their books.) Chapter 5 will show you how to use them. But their time costs you money. Don't call them in until you're seriously considering buying.

In preliminary sparring, you should be able to make some rough judgments yourself, after even a quick tour of the premises and a few hours of conversation with the owner or broker. You'll probably look at five or ten ventures before finding one you want your expert advisers to investigate more fully. Here are a few simple steps you can take (in addition to those already mentioned) before bringing in the $80-an-hour consultant.

Take a Close Look at Assets

Look over the list of assets shown on the bulk-sale document. Occasionally you can acquire assets by purchasing a company for less money than you'd need to replace its land, buildings, machinery, and whatever else it owns—in other words, for less than book value. So if you total up the book value, you'll get a rough idea of the company's minimum worth.

But the list of assets doesn't show their book value. The seller, who drew up the list, is thinking about what he paid for them. His cost has nothing to do with their present worth. Equipment that cost him $50,000 five years ago may be worth $20,000 today, or it could have appreciated to as much as $100,000. Check into its life expectancy, and inform yourself about maintenance. Some sturdy older machines need less pampering than new and more highly technical models.

If you see equipment or office furniture that is wearing out and will have to be replaced, mention this to the owner and explain that you'll have to subtract the replacement cost—new—from his asking price or from your offer.

But in your own private calculations, don't figure on buying any new replacements at retail unless absolutely necessary. You can save big amounts by shrewd shopping for secondhand furniture, equipment, and fixtures; you'll find bargains advertised in the Sunday classified sections of most city newspapers. You can also get good cut-rate buys on new office furniture at discount stores.

Machinery for almost any kind of business can be bought second- or thirdhand for a fraction of what it would cost new. Where? Well, other businesses have failed and are eager to sell their machines. Still others have grown so big that they need larger and newer machinery, so they want to sell the used equipment. Such companies will sell good machinery for one-fourth of what it would cost new.

For example, a 17½-by-22½ offset printing press in fine condition might cost you $5,500 used, while the same-size press new from the maker would set you back $22,000 or more. Maybe the older press is slower and homelier, and will need more maintenance and repair than new equipment would. But the $16,500 difference in capital investment makes up for a lot of prettiness and speed. Unless you're running the press all week long, a new model's additional speed might not be necessary at all, and "down" time for the old model when it is not being used might not hurt you.

If you're ignorant about the equipment yourself, later on, at a more convenient time, you can ask someone who knows. In the beginning, for the sake of discussion, take the owner's valuation if you must, within the following guidelines:

1. As a general rule, new furniture and fixtures depreciate 50 percent the moment they're put in place. After a few years of service, they're worth no more than about 35 percent of their original cost. Within ten years a knowledgeable owner should depreciate them down to zero value on his books, although they may have a salvage value of 10 or 15 percent.

2. Movable furniture is worth more than fixtures in the floor, walls, ground, or ceiling.

3. Obsolete or outworn fixtures may be worth only their salvage value —or may be a downright liability, if you'll have to pay to get them ripped out and hauled away.

4. An outdoor electric sign can be estimated at 15 to 25 percent of its original cost. But if it's antiquated, or will have to be remodeled because of a change of name, value it at far less.

5. Other amenities such as air conditioning, carpeting, soundproofing, or special lighting can add to the value of the business. Expect to pay something for them, probably the replacement value in their present condition.

Just walking through the property, you can find out plenty about physical equipment. View it with a skeptical eye. Ask yourself questions— maybe even ask the owner questions. How many years have these things been used? Are they efficient? Are repair parts available, or will maintenance be slow and expensive? What losses can be expected through machine "down" time?

Accounts receivable are probably carried on the books as assets. But many of them may be worthless, if nobody has been following up on delinquent accounts. Take a look through the files. Retail customers are unlikely to pay any bills more than ninety days old. Wholesale buyers may expect lengthy (and hence costly) follow-ups before paying. Yet the "sales" to these nonpaying customers are undoubtedly included in the company's gross. If the book figure for accounts receivable is higher than the equivalent of forty to fifty days of company sales—without any compensating budget allowance for doubtful accounts—you can bet the company is headed for trouble.

Look for Assets the Owner Doesn't See

Land is an asset, if the business owns some. Maybe the land was bought several years ago for $10,000, is worth $25,000 now, but is kept on the books at cost because there's no certainty that it will be sold at the higher price. If you think the land can be improved or sold, keep it in the back of your mind as a hidden asset for which you can afford to sweeten the price.

There may be other almost invisible assets. Mailing lists and credit records, for example. If these exist and seem to be in good shape, they're worth something to you. Be sure that they're included in the sale. If good ones don't exist, their lack may be a liability.

Are there any vending contracts in force for pinball games, cigarette machines, jukeboxes, or whatever? How much cash do these bring in, and how much are you committed to pay the contractors? Are there any vendors' loans still outstanding that must be assumed by the new buyer?

Are there union contracts? If so, the terms may be an asset or a liability.

How about maintenance contracts for janitorial service, air conditioning, electric signs, protection service, burglar alarms? Like leases, these are a form of long-term debt that may not show on the balance sheet. Or maybe they've been paid in advance for a period beyond the sale—which means the paid-up periods are assets for the new owner.

Is the Location an Asset?

If the business you're thinking of buying is a retailer, its location could be an important asset—or a crippling liability.

You can evaluate the location fairly well just by visiting it a number of times at different hours of the day. If the business depends on foot traffic, it ought to be in a block teeming with pedestrian shoppers. (Beware of a block where several stores are vacant. It's probably deteriorating.)

If it depends on drive-in customers, it ought to be easily accessible to autos; ingress and egress are extremely important. So is parking. Its visibility is important. So is an attractive exterior.

The surrounding area may be almost as important as the specific block. A shop at the edge of water or wasteland will draw customers from only a few directions. A prosperous and growing area is usually better for business than a low-income area or a solidly ethnic area—although there are exceptions. An owner who has good rapport with low-income ethnics around him may prosper because of genuine good will—or just because he's selling something his customers want. For example, one chain of carry-out fried-chicken restaurants noticed a mystifying variation in gross sales between stores that seemed to show the same potential. Some did a $300,000 yearly gross, while others showed sales as low as $120,000. The chain finally realized that the biggest sales came from locations in low-income neighborhoods.

So much for the basic principles you should use in sizing up a business. They've taken quite a few pages to explain. But in using them, you'll need only one or two preliminary conversations and a careful look at the books and records.

After that much investigation, you will have reached one of three conclusions:

1. The business is a lemon and you don't want it.

2. The business is probably worth more than the owner realizes, so you'd like to grab it at his asking price (or less if possible, of course).

3. The business is overpriced, but looks like a good one for you if the owner will cut his price to what it's really worth.

If you've reached conclusion either 2 or 3, it's time to ask your attorney and CPA to take a closer look. In the next chapter we'll see how they should work with you.

KEEP THESE BASIC POINTS IN MIND:

- *Before you spend much time investigating a business, always check its lease.*
- *Traditional rules-of-thumb for valuing certain types of business are useful only as crude guides.*
- *Always try to make an informed guess about the true book value of the business and the current market value of all assets.*
- *The most important measure of the firm's value is its earning power.*
- *The riskier the business, the less its value.*
- *In computing the profitability of a business, subtract a fair salary for the owner.*
- *Sometimes a business has assets that the owner doesn't see. Look for these.*
- *Pay as little as possible for intangibles like good will.*
- *In evaluating a retail business, consider whether the location is good or bad. This is an extremely important factor.*

5
What to Ask the Analysts

We've now reached the stage, we'll assume, where you've told the prospective seller of a business, "I'll ask my CPA to make an analysis of your business. Then I should be in a position to consider making you an offer."

Don't skimp on the CPA analysis. It's essential. Only a searching audit by an expert accountant can show you the picture of a small company's past and its probable future under your management.

And don't leave this analysis entirely to the accountant. You'd better look over his shoulder—partly to make sure he asks all the right questions, and partly to learn about the business by watching him dig into it, just as the medical student learns about the condition of a patient as the surgeon begins the operation.

What You Should Know About Balance Sheets

Almost every audit will start with the company's balance sheet, just as almost every textbook on accounting begins with an explanation of the "balance-sheet approach." You need to understand the balance sheet because it's a good way to catch on to the CPA's debit-and-credit jargon, and because it's really at the beginning and end of all accounting activity.

There would be little need for a balance sheet if a venture were to be liquidated at a prearranged time; that is, if income and outgo, profits and losses were added up once and for all, debts were paid, and the books closed. In fact, that was how modern accounting came into existence, as a way of dividing up owners' profits from the caravans and voyages of the fourteenth and fifteenth centuries. Financial statements as we know them didn't evolve until the corporation, which lived on while owners came and went, began to displace partnerships and sole proprietorships as the dominant type of business enterprise.

A balance sheet is needed to show the financial position of an enterprise at a given time. The balance sheet doesn't show how the enterprise reached that position (though it may provide clues), and it doesn't show where the enterprise is heading (although you can get an idea by looking at a series of the company's balance sheets at intervals).

Amounts shown on a balance sheet all have one characteristic in common. They have been measured "as of" the same date. For example, the sheet usually has a line labeled "cash" which shows how much cash the company possessed at a certain time, such as "at the close of business December 31, 1980." Everything else on that balance sheet must be stated as it stood in dollars on that same date. The sheet mustn't show the amount of cash on December 31, the value of merchandise on December 10, and the total of accounts receivable on January 5. Accountants are too meticulous for that—with good reason.

Your own "net worth" is the total of your valuable possessions or resources less your debts. In the same way, a company balance sheet adds up a company's assets—the resources controlled by the company —and subtracts the claims against them, or liabilities. Whatever is left after this subtraction is the "owner's equity," or capital.

So if a firm's balance sheet shows assets totaling $100,000 and debts of $40,000, its net worth is $60,000. Teachers of accounting are so in love with this simple calculation that they speak of "the accounting equation" —Assets minus Liabilities equals Net Worth, or A − L = NW. The equation is also correct when you arrange it so that Assets = Liabilities + Owner's Equity, which is a sort of model of the standard balance sheet, which groups assets on the left to equal the sum of liabilities and net worth on the right. The next page gives a fairly typical example of a balance sheet.

Does a Balance Sheet Really Balance?

Basically, a balance sheet is just a pair of totals (assets and liabilities) on opposite sides of the sheet. The two sides are then made equal. How? By fill-ins on the right-hand side (the liabilities side) to make them equal!

This filling-in is the net worth—also known as our old friend "book value," an elusive and flexible figure.

About all the "accounting equation" means is that the assets of any business are claimed by either (a) the creditors, such as suppliers or

ABC COMPANY, INC.
BALANCE SHEET
December 31, 1980

Assets

Current Assets

Cash on hand and in banks		$ 5,000
Notes Receivable	4,500	
Less: Notes discounted	1,500	3,000
Accounts Receivable	19,000	
Less: Reserve for bad debts	1,000	18,000
Inventories		8,000
Prepayment of Expenses		2,500
TOTAL CURRENT ASSETS		$36,500

Plant & Equipment

Land and Building	17,000	
Equipment, fixtures & furn.	12,000	
Less: Allowance for depreciation	3,500	25,500

Intangibles

Good will	1,500	
Patents, franchises, etc.	1,000	
		2,500
TOTAL ASSETS		$64,500

Liabilities

Current Liabilities

Notes Payable (to banks)	$ 5,000
Accounts Payable (trade)	14,000
Taxes Payable	4,500
Other Payables (including accruals)	1,500
TOTAL CURRENT LIABILITIES	$25,000

Fixed Liabilities

TOTAL LIABILITIES	$31,000

Net Worth

Capital Stock (preferred)	4,000	
Capital Stock (common)	25,000	
Surplus	4,500	
TOTAL NET WORTH		$33,500
TOTAL LIABILITIES AND NET WORTH		$64,500

moneylenders (''liabilities'') or (b) the owners, who have a right to whatever is left over—owner's equity, in other words.

Once symmetrized, the sheet stays in balance, because every transaction is entered into the books in two ways—as a change in assets and liabilities, and as a revenue or an expense. This is true even of transactions that don't affect income.

For example, if the company buys a typewriter, the bookkeeper reduces the cash assets by the purchase cost of the typewriter, while increasing another asset (equipment) by the same amount. Profits and net worth haven't changed, but the balance sheet has been adjusted to show the change in the mix of assets—in this case a change of cash position, which can be important when the amounts are large.

To take another example, when the company borrows from a bank, it adds to an asset (cash) on the left side of the balance sheet and adds to a liability (notes payable) on the right. This doesn't affect net worth because it isn't figured as either a sale or an expense. Sales and/or expenses affect the owner's equity or net worth.

The ordinary business doesn't refigure its balance sheet more than once a quarter, or maybe once a year. Redoing it more often wouldn't be either practical or particularly worthwhile.

Instead, each major classification on the balance sheet is set up in the same left-and-right format as the balance sheet, and these classifications are kept up to date. Items on the left side are ''debits,'' those on the right ''credits.'' You might think that credits are good and debits are bad, but accountants don't view them this way.

A debit is just a transaction that increases the left (asset) side of the sheet or decreases the right (liability and net worth) side. Anything that decreases the left or increases the right is a credit. Revenues are credits; expenses are debits. Why do debits go on the left, credits on the right? No special reason. It's just an accepted way of doing things, like driving on the right-hand side of the road.

Any item that changes the balance sheet must also change the company's profit-and-loss statement (now more commonly called the income statement, the operating statement, or simply the P&L statement), which is the other basic accounting summary. We'll get to it a few pages from now.

For the moment, you need know only that these two sheets are made up from the same sets of numbers. For instance, a sale increases a balance-sheet asset (cash or account receivable) and also appears on the income statement as revenue. Likewise, when the company gets its telephone bill, not due until next month, this is entered on the balance sheet as an increase in liability (accounts payable) and on the income statement as an expense.

This is why the system is called double-entry bookkeeping. You may be surprised to know that the earliest users of double entry, the merchants in Genoa and Venice, saw no reason why the two sets of entries should balance. Nor did they understand why double entry worked.

Until the nineteenth century, bookkeepers thought of the accounts as people—Mr. Receivables, Mr. Inventory, Mr. Cash—and kept track of their balance as a vast series of transactions between imaginary little men. Nobody realized that all these movements were part of the two self-proving accounting equations:

$$\text{Revenues} - \text{Expenses} = \text{Net Income}$$
$$\text{Assets} - \text{Liabilities} = \text{Net Worth}$$

People who used the stewards' reports seldom worried about any numbers except those which affected them directly. Banks wanted to know whether a company could repay its bank loans, which are mostly short-term debts. So the bankers studied the totals of company cash and other assets easily convertible to cash, to make sure these exceeded the short-term liabilities.

Similarly, the company's long-term creditors, who held mortgages or bonds, wanted only to be certain of getting paid if the company went bankrupt. So they looked at the liquidating value of plant, equipment, and other depreciable assets.

Tax men studied the sheets to see whether the company was hiding any taxable income. Other investigative agencies looked for signs of fraud. As for the owners themselves, they wanted figures that would keep taxes and union demands as low as possible, keep credit flowing at easiest interest rates, and at the same time look pleasing to shareholders.

These various needs could clash, of course. Creditors (or you, as a prospective buyer of the business) are bound to prefer "conservative" accounting—that is, figures which tend to understate the value of assets but never minimize the claims against them. This, creditors think, makes the company a better credit risk. Proprietors sometimes feel the same way, because conservative accounting makes earnings look smaller to tax collectors and union negotiators.

But when the proprietor wants to sell his business, he pressures his accountants to make the earnings look bigger. This can lead to imaginative accounting.

Consider the case of Minnie Pearl's Chicken Systems. It reported $13.4 million in sales in 1968, of which $9.3 million came from selling 1,200 franchises. But only 120 of these stores were actually operating at the end of the accounting period. Which meant that true revenue from operating franchise-unit sales was probably closer to $900,000. This moved the

American Institute of Certified Public Accounts to "recommend" a change in accounting rules. Franchisers are now supposed to count as current revenue only the cash actually received from franchise fees, rather than the much larger contract price, payable over a period of ten years or more.

The point is this: No balance sheet accurately measures an enterprise's net worth. As a going concern, it may understate its worth. When it is put up for sale, it may overstate.

Be Wary of Assets

The balance sheet sets a total value on the company's assets. But this total (as well as most of the items which make up the total) is hardly ever the true current value of the assets. In fact, nobody really knows the current value of any bunch of nonmonetary assets. This may come as a shock to anyone who has looked at balance sheets, but hasn't studied accounting.

All the dollars in financial statements look alike and are added easily. What outsiders seldom realize is that these dollars come in many different sizes. Their purchasing power was different.

Costs have been rising fast in recent years. So past transactions needed fewer dollars. This brings up problems (and scope for accounting artistry) in deciding how to value inventories and such long-lived assets as land, buildings, and machinery. Who can say exactly what they are worth today, or will be worth next month?

Accountants can be flexible in accounting for gains and losses, too. Question: Does a sale occur, for their purposes, when the order is placed? Or when the shipment is billed? Or when the bill is paid?

A balance sheet usually divides assets into two broad groups: (1) current assets (consisting of cash, stock-in-trade, amounts due from customers, and other possessions easily sold for cash); (2) longer-lived assets, which have been bought for use in the business—such as land, plants, and equipment. These are often called "fixed assets," even if they're easily movable.

These fixed nonmonetary assets are arbitrarily given monetary values on the balance sheet. They show up as a conglomerate fusion of dollars representing the "current value" of things that may have been bought during the past thirty years or more.

Their current value is arrived at by guesswork. Accountants may start with an item's original cost, then subtract a guesstimate of how much it has worn out or depreciated in value. Suppose the company bought a machine for $10,000, which then is its original cost. On successive balance sheets they may list that machine (probably lumped with similar assets, so nobody can pin them down too precisely) at lower and lower amounts to reflect its theoretical decline toward some future date when it will have to be replaced. This has come about because it's worn out or nonproductive or because it no longer meets the company's needs.

However, the "depreciation allowance" for this machine on the books doesn't provide for buying another machine that will do equal or better work. Nobody knows how much that will cost. The depreciation item on the books is nothing more nor less than the spreading, or allocation, or amortization, of the cost of an asset over the period of time for which it is predicted to be useful. If the owner wanted to "provide" for its replacement, he would set aside cash in a sinking fund. This has nothing to do with what accountants think of as depreciation.

Many people think that depreciation can somehow generate cash or funds. It's true that depreciation is deductible for tax purposes, with the happy result that fewer tax dollars are paid out as more depreciation is claimed. But the depreciation doesn't create cash in any way. Cash comes from the sale of merchandise and the subsequent collections from the customers, regardless of whether the company shows $1 of depreciation or $100,000.

On the other hand, adjusting the allowance for depreciation can have magical effects on the company's apparent worth, depending on how much is allowed. For example, Continental Computer Associates, a computer-leasing company, decided that its computers would last ten years. It charged one-tenth of their cost to depreciation expense in each of the ten years, using what is called straight-line depreciation. In contrast, IBM used accelerated depreciation, charging off similar computers in just four years. Accelerated depreciation shows heavier depreciation expense in the early years, lesser depreciation expense later. Therefore, on a $1-million computer, Continental would have figured first-year depreciation at $100,000, while IBM could have used a figure of $400,000. If the computer was leased at $250,000, IBM would have shown a loss, while Continental, leasing identical equipment, would have shown a before-tax profit of $150,000.

By switching from 11-year to 12- or 14-year depreciation of its aircraft, Eastern Air Lines managed to cut a loss of $1.91 a share to a loss of $1.06 a share in 1968. That same year the eight biggest steel companies all switched from accelerated depreciation to some form of straight-line depreciation. At U.S. Steel, this bookkeeping change increased net income by $55 million.

All of which means that your accountant will want to know what form of depreciation is used in the bookkeeping of the firm you're considering. And he'll be especially inquisitive if he finds that it has switched from one form to another during the past year or two; this could mean that it is juggling figures to make itself look more profitable.

Even if the firm uses very conservative accounting, your auditor may be skeptical of its balance-sheet valuation of nonmonetary assets. The land on which its buildings stand may have high potential value in the current real estate market. So what? Is the company more valuable to you because it could sell its factory site for more than it paid years ago?

As for the buildings and equipment, their market values may be meaningless even if you could determine them. Many buildings are designed for the special purposes of a company. If the company is a going concern, it isn't interested in any possible profit from selling these buildings, unless it intends to go out of business. Equipment may be permanently in place so that it too couldn't conceivably be sold. Sometimes the only buyers would be scrap dealers. Delivery equipment designed for a plate-glass manufacturer, for example, would be useless to a food manufacturer.

Of course, the owners would need to know something about current values of their fixed assets in order to buy insurance coverage. The insurance people set their premiums according to the supposed "replacement cost" of these assets.

But what do we mean by replacement? Do we mean the literal reproduction of existing buildings and machinery, using the same materials, the same hand labor, the same building methods, and so on? Or do we mean the cost of creating, with today's dollars, similar equipment that can provide the same or better service, using today's technology? And how much should we subtract for the amount of service already obtained from the present equipment? Such questions lead into vast complexities.

Nevertheless, inflation accounting is here to stay for the big corporations, despite their vehement protests. In 1977 the Securities and Exchange Commission forced more than a thousand of the nation's biggest industrial firms to calculate the current replacement cost of most fixed assets and inventories, and to reveal these figures to securities analysts. Only in this way, said the SEC, could analysts estimate the impact of inflation on a company's future ability to grow and pay dividends. In a survey of 175 companies, it was found that their average cost of replacing productive assets would be at least double—and sometimes quintuple— what they'd spent originally.

But for small business, inflation accounting seems to be just an exercise in guesswork for the benefit of insurers. No firm except a corporate giant can afford to employ appraisers each year to make "educated" estimates of the current replacement costs of its property.

A more relevant figure may be "liquidation value"—how much money the machinery and equipment and other fixed assets would bring on the secondhand market if the business were liquidated. When you and your accountant are evaluating a sizable but shaky enterprise, liquidation value at auction may be its rock-bottom price. On the other hand, "reproduction value"—if anyone can make a guess at it—should be a ceiling price on valuations reached by other methods. The plant probably has many years of useful life ahead and won't need to be reproduced; its current assets aren't really worth the sky-high cost of replacing them, although this may be their depreciable tax base after you buy the property.

Most accountants admit that it's virtually impossible to set a value in today's dollars on all the physical assets of a business. The real worth of the business depends more on its *earning* power than on its lists of assets and liabilities. This is why the term "net worth" is seldom seen on today's balance sheets. The reigning rulemaker, the American Institute of Certified Public Accounts, has recommended substituting such terms as "stockholders' equity" or "capital stock and retained earnings" to describe the difference between total assets and total liabilities.

For similar reasons, the very term "balance sheet" is dropping out of fashion; assets and liabilities aren't truly in balance. This document is now more likely to be known as a statement of financial condition, or a statement of financial position, or simply position statement.

Whatever it's called, the statement gives only a crude picture of a company's profits and the factors contributing to them. The difference between liabilities and the supposed "current value" of assets on any particular date isn't very revealing. Therefore, your analyst, if he's worth his fee, will pay more attention to the detailed breakdown of assets and liabilities, and the ratios between them.

How to Read a Financial Statement

When a trained accountant scans a balance sheet, he looks at certain ratios. First he probably makes a rough calculation of the "current ratio," sometimes called the "working-capital ratio." It is—

$$\frac{\text{Total Current Assets}}{\text{Total Current Liabilities}}$$

For obvious reasons, he likes the top figure to be much bigger than the one under it. A 2:1 ratio is considered healthy. (In our sample balance sheet, this ratio is $36,500/$25,000, or 1.46 to 1.)

These same numbers also show the accountant how much "working capital" is available. This term is used often in business, but is poorly chosen because it implies the wrong meaning. Working capital actually means the surplus of current assets over current liabilities. Notice that cash assets aren't the same as working capital.

A business might have a million dollars in the bank, yet have no working capital at all, in the view of accountants, if it owed more than a million in short-term debts. Likewise, its bank account might be empty, while it was rich in working capital, if it had sold a lot of goods on credit—because accounts receivable, like cash, are counted as current assets. In fact, accountants who know how to make themselves clear to nonaccountants usually substitute the phrase "net current assets" for "working capital."

The analyst is also interested in the liquidity ratio:

$$\frac{\text{Cash + Marketable Securities + Accounts Receivable}}{\text{Current Liabilities}}$$

If the top total is at least equal to the lower one, the firm is in a highly liquid position, and isn't likely to need any new financing soon. However, it's bad business to hoard too much cash for too long. Unused cash is unproductive. Worse, it actually shrinks in value as inflation robs it of buying power. Also, claims to cash (accounts receivable) suffer the same shrinkage as cash does. Therefore, a business ought to plan its flow of funds in such a way as to minimize any cash balances beyond what's needed for current expenses.

Maybe the firm you're analyzing doesn't understand this—which could be a reason its owner wants to get out: he may not be making much profit. If you understand the liquidity ratio, and know how to manage the cash better (perhaps by getting better credit terms, perhaps by collecting sooner from customers), you may be able to improve the business. But if you're not a good cash manager, look out. We'll come back to cash-flow problems later in this chapter.

Ratios Can Forecast Trouble

There are several ratios that measure parts of working capital. By comparing them from one balance sheet to the next, an auditor gets some insight into reasons for changes in a firm's net current assets. One is the cash-to-sales ratio.

It can be expressed either as cash divided by net sales, or as net sales divided by cash. The latter gives dollars-of-sales per dollar-of-cash. Either figure tells an accountant how much ready cash the company needs to maintain its present sales level. In computing it, he won't include surplus cash in the calculation—but he will take seasonal variations into account if he's comparing different periods.

Another ratio he looks at is called days' receivables outstanding:

$$\frac{\text{Accounts Receivable}}{\text{Net Sales}} \quad \times \ 30 \text{ (if using monthly sales) or}$$
$$\times \ 360 \text{ (if using annual sales)}$$

As the money owed the firm by customers increases, so does the firm's need for working capital. An increase also warns that customers seem to be slow in paying, which may mean that the company needs a tougher credit manager or tighter follow-up on delinquent accounts. Or maybe the owner has been granting easier terms to customers so that he can pile up a more impressive sales total for your benefit. Are you sure you'll be able to collect from those customers if you buy the company? How big is the company's allowance for doubtful accounts?

This ratio can also be applied to accounts payable. If there's an increase in the days' outstanding, the company probably is stretching out payments. Why? Will a new owner face hostile creditors? Or is the company's credit so good that it needs less working capital now? Conversely, if there's a decrease, maybe suppliers are already dictating tougher terms —or maybe an overzealous accounts-payable department is paying invoices long before they're due.

Of all ratios used in analyzing working capital, the most important is inventory turnover:

$$\frac{\text{Cost of Goods Sold}}{\text{Inventory}}$$

Inventory usually is a company's biggest single item in its pool of working capital; that is, of its net current assets. If this is the case, the company's prosperity may depend on efficient inventory control.

You compute turnover by dividing cost of goods sold for the year by the amount of inventory at year end; or better, by the average of the beginning and ending inventories; or even by the average of the totals at the end of each quarter or each month.

For example, if the company's average inventory value is $20,000, and its cost of all goods sold during the year was $240,000, then its turnover rate is 12 times per year.

Love That Turnover!

The higher the number of inventory turns per year, the greater the efficiency. Thus, an efficient firm keeps its sales volume high while tying up less money in inventory. A slowdown in turnover is a warning to examine the inventories for slow-moving or obsolete items. Or it could also mean overstocking (overbuying) by the purchasing department, in anticipation of shortages.

How about the ratio of direct costs to sales? In a sense, it dictates where you, as a new owner, should direct your efforts. If the cost of goods is high, you had better keep a tight grip on manufacturing and purchasing procedures. If the cost of goods is relatively low, you'll probably spend more of your time on administrative and selling efforts.

However, don't expect to increase sales in a hurry unless you're intimately familiar with the market. Generally, a new owner can pick up the knowledge he needs within a year or two, just from running the company.

You'll notice we've been using language like "relatively" and "increase" and "lower than." These all imply a comparison—at least a comparison between several balance sheets from the same company, but preferably comparisons with balance sheets of similar companies as well. One of the best tools available to small-business men is statistical comparison. Comparing your own operations with your competitors' will almost always spotlight ways to improve. That's why, in choosing an accountant to analyze the business you want to buy, you should pick one familiar with other firms in the same business, if you can.

If your accountant does know similar companies, a ratio he'll use in comparing them may be their depreciation ratio:

$$\frac{\text{Allowances for Depreciation}}{\text{Gross Value of Plant and Equipment}}$$

This gives him an idea of the comparative age of each company's plant and equipment. The higher the ratio, the more fully depreciated the plant.

Thus, if Orange Company's ratio is 0.75, and White Company's is 0.5, he figures that White probably has a more modern plant. Of course, he can make the comparison only if the two companies use the same depreciation method. And he's careful to exclude the value of the land, which isn't depreciable.

Here's another important ratio:

$$\frac{\text{Net Value of Plant, Property \& Equipment}}{\text{Long-term Debt}} \quad \text{(value after allowing for depreciation)}$$

A business normally uses short-term borrowing to get whatever working capital it needs, and long-term financing to pay for its physical plant. As long as this ratio exceeds 1:1—in other words, the topside number is bigger than the number beneath it; the depreciated value of the plant exceeds the long-term debt—it is considered okay. But if the ratio tilts the other way, the company is using long-term borrowing to finance current operations. This is a real danger signal.

In judging a firm's long-term financial health, you'll pay special attention to its debt/equity ratio:

$$\frac{\text{Long-Term Debt}}{\text{Owner's Equity}}$$

The higher the ratio, the more vulnerable the company is. It won't have much cash to ride out emergencies because debt service will absorb too much of its earnings and cash flow.

In some lines of business, this ratio can safely be higher than in others. For example, financial companies such as leasing operations, personal-finance lenders, and the like can be comfortable with a 3:1 debt/equity ratio. In such companies, the assets are mostly pledged to lenders, and cash flow doesn't ebb as suddenly as it can in industrial firms. In manufacturing, the ratio should be much lower.

Analysts have dozens of other pet ratios. But you shouldn't settle for predigested rules or standards. At best the ratios are clues, or confirmation of hunches. A good accountant won't take them as final verdicts.

What he's seeking primarily is a reliable set of numbers that match costs against revenues. Nonmonetary assets are merely background. Revenue is what you collect from selling something. Cost is what you pay for something. The name of the game is to buy low and sell high.

To put this another way, a paper profit caused by changes in the estimated value of assets won't buy any groceries. It must be cashed in by actual transactions in which something is literally sold for an amount greater than its cost.

Profit is an increase in the value of a business resulting from operations. One way of measuring profit is to compare a series of balance sheets (with allowance for any changes in owner's equity that comes from other causes, such as additions to invested capital, or withdrawals from capital). A more obvious way, and certainly equally important, is to measure revenues and expenses. This is done with an "income statement," or "profit-and-loss statement," such as the one shown here:

ABC BAR & RESTAURANT
Profit & Loss Statement
12 Months Ended Dec. 31, 1980

Account Name	Percent	Year to Date
Sales		
Bar, Regular	22.20	$ 67,926.67
Bar, Restaurant	7.10	21,924.83
Restaurant	70.70	216,482.59
TOTAL NET SALES	100.00	$306,334.09
Cost of Sales		
Beginning inventory		5,067.26
Purchases, Bar		22,964.31
Purchases, Restaurant		90,288.22
Less ending inventory		5,485.39
COST OF SALES	36.83	$112,834.40
Gross Profit	63.17	$193,499.69
Operating Expense		
Advertising	1.57	$ 4,800.94
Bonus expense	1.96	6,000.00
Cash Short & (over)	.00	
Credit Card Costs	.42	1,272.94
Depreciation	3.31	10,129.45
Gas, Oil, Tires	.49	1,496.25
Insurance, general	2.45	7,504.10
Interest	2.56	7,839.02
Laundry	.98	2,999.24
Legal & Accounting	.60	1,842.50
Licenses	.26	806.78
Office expense	.15	464.88
Operating Supplies	1.59	4,859.78
Repairs & Maint.—Equipment	2.19	6,713.66
Salaries & Wages	30.32	92,873.09
Salaries, Officers	5.42	16,600.00
Taxes, Payroll	2.84	8,707.27
Taxes, Real Estate	0.89	2,741.79
Utilities	2.62	8,034.65
TOTAL OPERATING EXPENSE	60.62	$185,686.34
Net Profit	2.55	$ 7,813.35

Annual Profit & Loss—Rapid Analysis—ABC Bar & Restaurant

A. *Net Profit* $ 7,813.35

    (1) Owner's Income

        Plus Salary   16,600.00

        Plus Bonus   6,000.00

    (2) Building Lease

        Plus Depreciation   10,129.45

        Plus Interest   7,839.02

    (3) Other   ————

B. *Adjusted Net Profit* $48,381.82

    Less Manager's Salary (including benefits) $14,000.00

    Less Building Lease Cost (nnn) $18,000.00

C. *Readjusted Net Profit* $16,381.82

Food Cost

A. Per Profit & Loss Statement $90,288.22 or 29.47%

    Should be:

B. Cost of *Food* $= \dfrac{\text{Purchases}}{\text{Restaurant Sales}} = \dfrac{\$90,288.22}{\$216,482.59} = 41.71\%$

Bar Cost

A. Per Profit & Loss Statement $22,964.31 or 7.50%

    Should be:

B. Cost of *Bar* $= \dfrac{\text{Purchases}}{\text{Total Bar Sales}} = \dfrac{\$22,964.31}{\$89,851.50} = 25.56\%$

The operating expenses of a restaurant are of extreme importance to an operator, to permit him to measure each individual expense item on a realistic basis. For example, the first item of advertising is 1.57 percent; that is satisfactory in relation to advertising expenditures for the average bar-restaurant. Had it been a figure such as 0.02 percent, then it would reasonably follow that more money spent on advertising would generate more volume and hence more profits. On the other hand, if the advertising expense showed up to be 2.92 percent, then it would be clear at once that too much was being spent on advertising or that the advertising was ineffective in view of the volume of business being done.

You can apply the same kind of evaluation to each of the operating expenses, if you learn comparative figures for the industry.

In addition, you can note monthly *changes* in percentage of total expenses for each item; they are danger signals if the variation is too radical from month to month.

Failure plus Success Equals One

Howard Ruff, an internationally recognized figure in financial matters, is perhaps best known for his books *Howard Ruff—from A to Z* and *How to Prosper During the Coming Bad Years,* and his newsletter, *The Ruff Times,* published by Target, Inc. He has recently launched a new venture called Sage Associates. The president of Sage is Terry Jeffers, Mr. Ruff's partner in Target, Inc.

"Failure plus Success Equals One" (F + S = 1) means that the probability of failure plus the probability of success equals one. The theory of what Ruff calls "failure avoidance" was developed by Dr. Kent Stephens. Dr. Stephens bases the theory on applications of the formula in several fields, including operations in a hospital, school, a helicopter firm, corporations, and various segments of the U.S. Government.

The results of application of their theory are amazing, and even downright startling. As one example: after a study had been made on "How to Successfully Prevent a [ballistic missile] Launch," Dr. Stephens examined "How They Could Fail to Prevent a Launch." The results of the two studies were startlingly different.

The theory has also been applied to Target, Inc., with excellent success. The idea is, of course, that if you reduce the probability of failure, then the probability of success is automatically increased—because the sum of the two probabilities must equal one.

The "Failure Avoidance" system has been computerized. It also takes into account the human element in operations.

And what does all this have to do with you in your small business? Just this: Sage Associates offers its services to small-business men. If you're having trouble—or better yet, before you get into trouble—contact Howard Ruff c/o *The Ruff Times,* P.O. Box 2000, San Ramon, California 94853.

KEEP THESE BASIC POINTS IN MIND

- *Look on the right-hand side of a balance sheet for a company's net worth or book value, sometimes called owner's equity. But remember that this is an imaginary figure, easily distorted.*
- *Current assets are in dollars and can be measured accurately, but fixed assets are given values arrived at by guesswork.*

- *Investigate how the company figures depreciation. And be suspicious if it has recently switched from one method to another.*
- *If you can find a liquidation value for this business, use it as a guideline; you know the business is worth at least that amount.*
- *In studying a financial statement, make rough calculations of certain key ratios that can help you judge the health of the business.*
- *The higher the number of inventory turns per year, the greater the company's efficiency.*

6
A Buyer's Guide to
Income Statements

The balance sheet and the income statement are two ways of looking at changes in the value of a business resulting from its operations.

The income statement (also known as the profit-and-loss statement and as the operating statement) ignores those unmeasurable "assets" which fog up the balance sheet. It focuses on "revenues"—cash, and accounts receivable that seem likely to be converted to cash soon—and on "expenses," which are the cost of goods and services used in producing revenues. Among the important expenses are wages and salaries, rent, the cost of materials, and the cost of replacing damaged or aging equipment.

Balance sheets and income statements are the financial language of business. You need to understand how they relate to each other.

One way to understand, perhaps, is to visualize them in terms of a reservoir. The balance sheet tells the reservoir's level at a specified date. The income statement summarizes the (cash) flows into and out of the reservoir during a specified period of time.

Another way of thinking about the two documents is in terms of a football game. The balance sheet is the scoreboard at the end of each quarter. The income statement shows the statistics—yards gained and lost, passes thrown, losses from fumbles, and so on.

An income statement bridges a time period between two balance sheets. Any changes in the value of a business from one period to another must be explained by the intervening income statement. This statement is usually more enlightening than the balance sheet. Let's consider what an auditor expects to find in it.

In the first place, he wants plenty of detail, with footnotes. He dislikes condensed statements that show only a few lump sums. He wants every sum broken down into items, so that he can sift through and eliminate the misleading effect of any one-time event such as loss from a theft or disaster, or gain from selling off some capital assets.

He wants to see whether any expenses have been capitalized when they should have been written off. He's wondering whether the owner inflated earnings last year by pricing some items higher than customers would willingly pay for very long, or by cleaning out a stock of goods at sacrifice prices merely for the sake of clustering the revenues. Maybe maintenance was trimmed or the ad budget sliced, which means that the new owner will have to spend more on these items to keep the business on an even keel. Are the employees underpaid and due for a substantial raise? Were expenses buncned in 1979 to make the 1980 statement look better?

It's essential to understand how the owner arrived at his figures. Once you know that, you and your accountant can judge whether you can do a better job of keeping costs down and revenues up.

Remember that the owner was probably looking for ways to minimize his taxes. He may have charged personal expenses to the business, in order to reduce his tax liability. Maybe the business really earned more than it seemed to—and more than the owner realizes—because he cut his taxable income by paying his wife a salary as "consultant" and charging a lot of travel to the business (which you may not find necessary).

On the other hand, he may have milked the business by overborrowing, overpaying himself and others, lending to pals with no expectation they'd repay (although they might privately divvy up the proceeds with him). A good auditor will check the list of expenses and their footnotes for any unusual pension expenses, deferred-compensation arrangements, bad debts, or exceptionally high salaries. If there's no balance sheet available, he'll comb the operating statement for "interest expenses" as a clue to how much debt the business owes.

Owners have been known to engage in this sort of milking by charging the upkeep of personal cars, making the business pay for family major-medical plans, and padding the insurance-expense items.

Ratios Again

Financial analysts often use the ratio of expenses to revenues in sizing up a firm's financial efficiency. This ratio is known as the "operating ratio."

If the company is incurring $95 of expenses to produce $100 of revenue, it probably isn't run very efficiently. If you or your accountant see where and how to economize, such a company may be a fine buy because you can make it far more profitable than it is as now operated.

Digging deeper, analysts compute ratios of manufacturing costs, distribution costs, administrative costs, and other expenses as compared with those of similar companies or with the company's own past history. Is the firm controlling its expenses at past rates, or losing control? Did changes in trends hurt earnings? Increase them? An auditor will be curious about deviations in either direction, because they may be clues to hidden costs and possible savings.

If you think accounting is an exact science, you'll be disillusioned when you ask your friendly accountant how much a business is losing on any particular operation. Just what is a loss? The income statement may list expenses, and may list losses—or may not—and deduct them from revenues to arrive at profits. But often it is hard to distinguish between an expense and a loss.

In essence, an expense means "something of value given up intentionally to produce revenue." But what if the company gives up money intentionally in an effort to produce revenue, and no revenue comes in? Suppose you install a new line of goods and advertise them with a great splash, but nobody buys? The company meant the advertising to be an expense, but it produced no revenue. In an extreme case like this, accountants might agree that the expenditure was a dead loss—but how do they classify gradations between the dead-loss advertising and the advertising that reaps a bonanza?

You often can't tell whether a given expenditure produced any payoff. So the accountant usually classifies it as expense, not loss. In other words, he broadens the expense category to cover outlays that were intended to produce revenues but maybe didn't. Here he uses judgment —and accounting ceases to be an exact science.

Similarly, if the company built a new store, how do you classify wages paid to workmen during periods when they didn't work because of rain? How do you classify medical costs of employee accidents? There may be many such borderline questions. When you try to trace a given cost outlay to its end result, it's hard to be sure how much is expense and how much is loss. Revenues are good, losses are bad, expenses are in between. You try to hold down expenses, but you can't prosper unless you spend.

Where's All That Cash?

Sometimes the profit-and-loss statement shows big earnings for a company while its checkbook shows a severe shortage of cash. Why? Because of the differences between cash-basis and accrual-basis accounting.

When an accountant says he uses accrual accounting, it means that he is counting debts as soon as they are incurred, and is counting sales as soon as the goods change hands, regardless of whether they're paid for in advance or on delivery or sometime later.

If an insurance premium is paid in March, and the insurance covers a three-year period, accrual accounting charges $\frac{1}{36}$ of the premium to expense each month. Cash accounting would charge off the entire premium in March.

Most of us, as individuals, use cash accounting in figuring our personal income taxes. And of course we all have to balance our checkbooks on a cash basis. But cash accounting doesn't work too well in business.

It doesn't recognize receivables and payables, or sales and purchases until cash has been given or received. So it doesn't give an owner any idea whether he's ahead or behind. Some small-business men use this system anyhow, because they don't know any better. Some smart big farmers use it too, at least on their tax forms, because it gives them more freedom to push taxable income from one year to another by such maneuvers as paying bills earlier or later.

Accrual accounting is more realistic, but it can be tricky too. For example, let's say Mr. Black wants to sell his sick business to you, and therefore wants the books to show that he made a healthy profit last year. Maybe he spent $10,000 on advertising during the Christmas season. If he uses accrual accounting, he may decide that the $10,000 was "deferred expenditure"—that is, it was spent to produce revenue during the following year. So why not apportion the cost to the year in which the sales will come? Presto! His books show that the Black Company made $10,000 more last year than it would have otherwise!

The moral: Your auditor must study a company's operations right up to the present, not merely to the end of the last "accounting period."

Anyhow, you'll probably want to use accrual accounting in whatever business you buy—because it can give earlier warning that you're outspending your income, or can reassure you that you're operating at a long-haul profit when your bank balance is low.

But accrual accounting assumes that all customers will pay their bills, which we know isn't necessarily true. And it doesn't give you much help in forecasting cash crunches or surpluses.

Which brings us to the very important subject of "cash flow."

Sooner or later, your banker will ask to see a cash-flow chart on your business. (Or he might say "funds flow," which would be more accurate.) Probably a similar request was made to the owner of the business you're considering buying. However, don't expect to be shown one, as there is probably no such chart available—or in existence.

It's really the single most important document to a businessman, whether he realizes this or not. Taken alone, it also can be a tool for swindling a prospective buyer, as we'll see shortly.

You need cash to buy materials and services; to pay wages, taxes, and interest; and to maintain your building and equipment. Cash isn't the same as "income" or "revenue" or "profits." You have to meet your payroll by drawing checks on your bank account. (Checks, unless they're rubber, are a form of cash for business purposes, of course.) Meanwhile, the goods you've manufactured may not be sold for weeks or months. And even after you sell them (and record "income" on your books), you may not get paid until weeks or months later. All the while, you have to keep paying out cash.

In short, you can't spend "income." You must plan on keeping enough cash in the bank to meet your needs. Can the business generate enough cash from the first day you take over? To find out, your CPA should do a cash-flow analysis. It won't necessarily agree with the chart drawn up by the present owner.

How to Forecast Cash Flow

In essence, a cash-flow chart shows when the money comes in and when it goes out. It's an estimate of monthly cash expenses and cash income. In the early stages of a business, an owner may keep falling one cycle behind on the cash-flow chart, needing funds to take care of the outgo long before the inflow will provide enough.

As an illustration, let's consider a chart, taking as easy an example as possible. We'll assume a new dentist is starting practice. He draws up the cash-flow projection shown on the next page at his banker's request.

As you see, this dentist plans to rent an office for $200 a month and pay $1,000 for his equipment in January. He realizes that as a new dentist he may find patients slow in coming. He doesn't figure on getting any until February, with no payments from them until March. Also, a few patients will probably have dental insurance, but he would probably receive no payments from insurance until May, because of the paperwork.

He expects business to improve steadily. Nevertheless, he figures that he'll be deeper and deeper in the red until the end of June, the cash flow should turn positive in July, and he should be making a profit by the end of November. So this forecast tells him that he'll need a line of credit from the bank of at least $3,400, which is his low point of negative balance in June.

Scanning this statement, the banker will probably ask questions:

"How do you know you'll get any patients by March? How do you know there'll be more of them each month? . . .

Cash In	J	F	M	A	M	J	J	A	S	O	N	D
1. Patients			100	200	300	400	500	750	1000	2000	2500	2500
2. Insurance					100	200	300	300	350	350	350	350
TOTAL IN	0	0	100	200	400	600	800	1050	1350	2350	2850	2850

Cash Out	J	F	M	A	M	J	J	A	S	O	N	D
1. Equipment	1000											
2. Nurse		500	500	500	500	500	500	500	500	500	500	500
3. Rent	200	200	200	200	200	200	200	200	200	200	200	200
TOTAL OUT	1200	700	700	700	700	700	700	700	700	700	700	700

Net Cash Flow

J	F	M	A	M	J	J	A	S	O	N	D
(1200)	(700)	(600)	(500)	(300)	(100)	100	350	650	1650	2150	2150

Cumulative Balance

J	F	M	A	M	J	J	A	S	O	N	D
(1200)	(1900)	(2500)	(3000)	(3300)	(3400)	(3300)	(2950)	(2300)	(650)	1500	3650

"What controls will you use to make sure patients and insurance companies pay on schedule? . . .

"Won't you also have bills for utilities, insurance, taxes, supplies, and so on? . . .

"You've shown no cash going out to support yourself. Do you have enough savings for all your personal expenses during the ten months when you admit your cash-flow balance will be negative? . . .

"As your business grows, won't you need more equipment, another nurse or assistant, a receptionist, a bookkeeper?"

Of course, an established business can forecast its cash flow more confidently than a newly started one. So the historical data from the company that you're considering purchasing will be useful to you and the auditor in estimating how much ready cash you'll need each month to keep the business going at its present rate.

If the records show that cash flow has recently been increasing faster than earnings, that's probably a good sign; it can mean less fluff in the income statement. Just be sure to make allowances for future price changes, for the costs of making any improvements you have in mind, and for those other possible surprises we've noted in this chapter and the previous one.

One already-mentioned point is worth stressing further. A fund-flow statement has little to do with earnings. The statement may show a handsome surplus of income over outgo because it ignores depreciation, doesn't provide for replacing or enlarging any physical assets, or doesn't provide for paying off debts. So you need to compare it with the income statement and the balance sheet.

An owner who wants you to think his company is profitable can cut expenses by neglecting necessary outlays for maintenance and upkeep; by delaying buying necessary replacement equipment; by not replacing employees who leave; by not replenishing stock-in-trade; by stalling creditors.

Such tricks can temporarily enable a business that is really losing gobs of money to show a beautiful cash-flow chart. Deliberate fraud can fool auditors and analysts sometimes. The Mill Factors Corporation continued to get its annual reports certified by a leading accounting firm, and continued to enjoy millions of dollars of credit from some of Wall Street's biggest banks, for several years after it had become insolvent for all practical purposes.

The Trouble with Inventories

How much is the inventory worth? In your first quick look, you probably accepted the seller's guess for the time being—even though, as sellers often do, he may have proudly declared it to be worth more than the value shown on his balance sheet.

But now it's up to your auditor to take a much closer look. There's a double importance attached to the values at which the supplies of merchandise, materials, work in process, finished goods, and the like are recorded on the books. First, the amount shown on the balance sheet as a current asset is likely to be a large share of the firm's "working capital." Analysts are intensely curious about a company's working-capital position, and they pay special attention to the proportion of current assets that are inventories.

Second—and even more important—the valuation of inventories can materially distort profits. In arriving at net income, accountants need to figure the cost of goods sold (COGS). They figure it like this:

Value of inventory at start of period	xxx
Plus cost of goods purchased (or produced)	+xxx
Total goods to be accounted for	xxx
Minus value of inventory at end of period	−xxx
Cost of Goods Sold	xxx

Obviously, the supposed "value" of your inventory will directly affect COGS. The greater the COGS, the less your net income. The less the COGS, the bigger your income. Pursuing this, we see that the greater the value of the ending inventory, the lower your COGS will be, and hence the greater your net income.

Companies on the "full cost" system of valuing inventory sometimes play a little trick known as "selling to inventory" to make profits look better. Depreciation policies and capitalization procedures, as we've seen, can also cook the books. For all these reasons, your auditor needs to know exactly how the company values inventory, and how it figures COGS.

Beyond this, he should take a hard look at what's actually in the warehouse and on the shelves. Is there any unusually big supply of some items? Is there a surprisingly high unit cost for some? Why? In a retail business, much of the stock may be white elephants because of age, size, or poor selection. Maybe your auditor isn't familiar enough with the market to make a judgment; if he can't, he'd better call in someone who can for this needed supplemental information.

If he's analyzing a machine shop or some other manufacturing enterprise, he should see whether supplies are balanced; for example, a three-month supply of one part and a five-year supply of another is obviously bad. Any amount over a one-year supply (and less in some cases) should be valued at a lower rate than the first-year supply.

Furthermore, if this is a business in which improvements and changes happen fast, a five-year supply of some parts might be almost worthless. This doesn't necessarily mean that the company is a bad buy. If it's operating in the black despite the burden of unusable inventory, you can get tax benefits by writing down or writing off any inventory that isn't worth full value. On the other hand, a five-year supply of some common parts like nuts and bolts may be foolishly undervalued by the present owner.

The analyst should also investigate sharp changes in the totals of work in process and finished goods. If there are buildups of finished goods, why? Was the owner planning to cut production? Or if raw materials are piling up without increases in work in process, does this mean there's a worrisome production problem?

To judge whether raw materials have been bought economically, he may want to check the invoices and compare them with market prices, or to have this done by someone who is familiar with the materials you'll need. This may spotlight chances for you to reduce COGS; or it may reveal that some material the owner bought at bargain prices is no longer available at those prices.

The auditor should also go through the order books and similar records.

He may come across certain liabilities that you didn't know about, such as accumulated debts and undelivered purchases.

LIFO vs. FIFO

If the business has gone to LIFO (last-in, first-out) accounting of inventories, its books will show less "inventory profit," an imaginary figure that misleads some owners and some buyers. LIFO is based on a whopping misstatement of the order in which goods flow through the business, but it makes good sense in a cockeyed way.

In any sane business, materials go through in a first-in, first-out (FIFO) procession unless they rot in storage. Of course, the flow isn't uniform. Some goods move faster than others. Some may not move at all. But the oldest goods in each category tend to be the first ones pulled from the shelves, so the inventory at any date can realistically be assumed to consist of the more recent purchases.

But if you assume this in your bookkeeping, during a time of rising prices, you may think you're getting rich when you're not.

Suppose you bought a box of bafflegabs for $100 wholesale when the retail price was $130. You don't sell the box until later when the wholesale price has risen to $120, and prudently, you've upped the retail price to $156 (30 percent over current cost). By traditional FIFO accounting, you'd record a gross margin of $56 on the sale ($156 minus $100). But $20 of that gross margin (and a corresponding part of your net income) can be traced solely to the price rises that went on while the box was on your shelf. You've made what is known as an inventory profit.

Deceived by this profit, you may not budget enough for your next purchase of bafflegabs. The LIFO advocates say you should use today's replacement cost, rather than original cost, in figuring profits. For example, if you pay $118 wholesale for another box before you sell the first one, LIFO would figure your gross margin on the first sale this way:

Sales	$156
Cost of goods sold	118
Gross margin	$ 38

Some accountants don't like LIFO. They complain, "It artificially assumes that the goods on the shelves are the oldest ones. Theoretically, they may stay there forever. LIFO should be called FINO—first in, never out. If you begin to use LIFO when you have ten tons of steel that cost $100 per ton, and if your inventory of steel never drops below ten tons in the next century, your balance sheet for every one of those years will show the same ten tons at $100. Ridiculous.''

However that may be, LIFO does tend to make you hold on to enough working capital to cover the cost of replacing depleted inventory. It has the extra advantage of enabling you to stall off payments of income tax on those imaginary inventory profits, because LIFO is legal for tax purposes.

On the other hand, FIFO swells the apparent net income—which is nice for an owner who wants to sell his business. It also increases the tax liability for the new owner. In other words, it brings seeming profit now but real taxes later.

Still, an owner isn't necessarily trying to swindle you just because he uses FIFO accounting. He may not know any better. Or he may be in a fast-moving business where he's constantly selling out items and dropping them from his line. LIFO would be needless extra trouble for him.

Tax Traps in "Good Will"

As we said in the previous chapter, one good reason for buying a business may be its fine reputation, its popularity with customers, its large and loyal clientele. This is obviously worth something to you. But the IRS says good will is an intangible asset, so whatever you pay for it can't be included as part of your tax basis.

One possible solution, if you agree that the good will is truly valuable, is to list it as the cost of the seller's "covenant not to compete." This cost is completely tax deductible, amortized over the period of the agreement (covenant).

But this solution works against the seller. His receipts for a covenant not to compete are taxable as ordinary income. But his receipts for "good will" are taxed at capital-gains rates.

If you see that good will is going to be a big item in the purchase price, you'd better have your accountant work out a compromise adjustment in the price to even out the net after-tax effects between you and the seller. And don't forget that an installment deal reduces the seller's tax burden by spreading it over several years.

If you specify what both sides want in the sales contract, IRS is likely to go along. Sales contracts normally include some form of noncompetitive covenant.

However, your lawyer and accountant must make sure that the contract also itemizes how you allocate other components of the price. Don't allocate more to depreciable property (trucks, machinery, and the like) than fair market value; that part of the transaction may require payment of sales taxes. Allocation to the covenant is probably the simplest way for you to take the maximum deduction, if the seller will go along.

There are other alternatives. Where customer service contracts are transferred, good will can apply to them on a per-contract basis. As the contracts expire, this cost can be deducted. You wait longer to get deductions, but you still are able to write off good-will cost eventually.

Another way to write it off is available when a specific site, such as a retail store, carries the good will. Your purchase contract should allocate the cost of good will to the purchase of the leasehold and its attendant improvements. Then you can amortize the cost over the life of the lease, since the asset's value falls to zero afterward.

Now you've probably come to understand some key principles of accounting, which will be important to you as long as you're in business. (And as a side benefit, you'll have clues to whether your accountant is doing a good job.)

Before you buy the business, be sure to call in your attorney as well as your accountant. The attorney will make the search for creditors' claims, such as mortgages, back taxes, and liens. If you're going to assume any of these liabilities, their amounts should be subtracted from the purchase price. Your attorney will also make sure that any franchises, licenses, patents, or leases you want are transferable.

Your attorney is the one who should draw up the sale agreement or certainly should study it carefully, to guard your interests, if the owner or business broker draws it up. This agreement should cover all essential points, and they must be completely understood by both you and the seller.

As one final precaution, try to take possession as soon as feasible after signing the contract. This minimizes any chance that the ex-owner might remove some supplies or make any substantial changes in the business or its operation. It would best serve your interests as a buyer to handle the transaction through a recognized escrow company. Risks are greatly minimized by so doing.

A Final Reminder

The name of the game is *return on investment*. ROI is the ratio between after-tax profit and the assets employed. In evaluating a business, don't get so obsessed with the former that you neglect the latter. Keep in mind the possibility that you can sharply increase ROI by reducing the assets employed—liquidating them, in other words.

Is this a risky strategy? Not if the assets were previously idle, or used inefficiently. Putting the company in a financially sound position will be your first task.

Once the company is solid, you can go after renewed growth if you choose. Or, if you fall in love with the beauties of simplicity, you may just go on making money at that level, and live happily ever after.

KEEP THESE BASIC POINTS IN MIND

- *Accrual accounting gives you a better idea of financial position than cash accounting. But look out for deferred expenses that may not produce any revenues.*
- *Make a careful forecast of the company's month-by-month needs for cash. Revenue isn't the same as cash.*
- *Be skeptical about valuation of inventories. They can distort the profit picture.*
- *Except in businesses where the product line changes fast, LIFO accounting is more realistic than FIFO. The latter increases tax liability, while inflating apparent profits.*
- *If good will is an important asset, try to list it as the cost of the seller's covenant not to compete, or work out a compromise allocation if the seller objects.*
- *In evaluating a business, be alert for assets that can be sold off. The smaller the assets tied up in a business, the bigger your return on investment.*

7

Where to Get Financial Backing

Lenders Are Skeptics

Every new idea in business has to bore through a stone wall of skepticism. The entrepreneurs who started Xerox, Polaroid, *Reader's Digest*, Ford Motor Company, and the other legendary successes were people with almost superhuman persistence. They spent years coaxing prospective backers into putting up enough money to get their venture started. In Chapter 20 we'll look at the fastest and safest ways to get through this wall into the big money. Right now let's consider small enterprises, and how they can be set on their feet fairly easily.

Some business can be launched on just a dribble of dollars—that is, enough assured income to keep you solvent until your business can support you. These are usually service businesses: typing, dressmaking, an art service or ad agency or almost anything that one or two people can run from a small office or even a room at home. Mail-order businesses are often started with as little as $400 to $1,000.

Other types of small business need only a thousand or two to get off the ground. Even a manufacturing business can be started with $600 if it's in a basement or barn, and if it needs only hand tools or one machine. A little retail store can open its doors for not much more than the cost of its inventory and lease, plus utility deposits and the like.

As you figure your start-up costs, they may look small. But don't underestimate other needs. Ongoing costs like overhead, insurance, maybe a reserve to carry customers' charge accounts, and other expenses can grow burdensome. Many businesses go broke simply through undercapitalization.

Before you leave a full-time job and start your own business, you should have enough capital—or know where you can get it—to cover your family and business expenses for at least six months and preferably a year. If you have to dip into the cash register for groceries, you're flirting with bankruptcy.

Go over your bills or check stubs for the past couple of years. Add a cushion for unexpected medical expenses and car repairs. Increase the total by the anticipated inflation rate. If your existing resources equal this amount, and you know you needn't touch those resources for your business, then your family should be safe.

But this doesn't mean your business will be safe. How much money will it need?

Plan for a Lean Year

If you intend to buy an established business, its past records give you a reasonably good guide. If you intend to start your own business, you've presumably researched the costs. This advance spadework is essential.

When you're working up your cost estimates, the Bank of America booklets on small businesses can be a big help. Also, the Small Business Administration (Washington, D.C.) publishes a helpful guide to estimating the first year's costs in various lines of business. It is Small Markets Aid No. 71, "Checklist for Going into Business." It includes a list of the numerous one-time expenses you may run into as you get started—deposit with the phone company, sales-tax deposit, legal fees, construction of an advertising sign, and other one-shot costs you may not have foreseen.

Long before you open the doors, your regular expenses will start. Even after opening, you're likely to run in the red for months. So don't count on taking home several hundred dollars a week while you're getting under way.

Almost any new enterprise needs to plow back profits (if any) during its early months. This is true even if the business booms—because a boom means you must expand or die. (If customers don't get good service, they don't come back.) As you expand you'll need more merchandise, more supplies, more equipment—maybe a bigger place of business, bigger payroll. Meanwhile you'll have less credit than later on, so your expansion may have to be financed mostly from your reserves. Are you ready for this?

Your reserve may also be needed in case of the opposite emergency, a shortage of customers. Or unexpectedly heavy costs. Some crisis like freak weather, mechanical breakdowns, a strike, an epidemic, or any of countless other bad breaks could upset your budget. Your reserve should be big enough to pay the entire overhead during three months of zero profit.

How to Make a Projection

For all these reasons, before trying to raise any money you must know what your total capitalization should be. You must predict the all-important cash flow of the business during its first three to five years. From these you can guesstimate profit-and-loss statements for those years, called pro forma statements. Bankers love pro forma statements, which can be checked later to make sure a business is on target.

A three-year projection may seem like building a castle in the air, but it can be done scientifically. You begin by estimating (conservatively) what your sales volume will be. Then you ask yourself what proportion of this volume will be day-to-day operating expenses. The proportion of expenses to sales is called the operating ratio, from which you can figure how much capital you'll need.

If this sounds complicated, it is. Don't try to make the projection yourself unless you're a trained accountant or statistician; hire a CPA to do it.

The accountant may be able to figure how many machines you'll need, or how many employees, but he may not know how much they'll cost. It will probably be up to you to get these figures, as well as the estimates of overhead, advertising, inventory, and other outlays.

How do you get them? From trade associations, from potential suppliers, from noncompetitor acquaintances in the same business. Look back at Chapters 5 and 6 for other suggestions about places to pick up data for your estimates.

All right? Now let's assume you know how much capital you'll need. Maybe you've got that much, and more, saved up or stashed away in the form of real estate or other assets you can liquidate.

Use Other People's Money

Walt Disney once said, "I must be successful; I owe seven million dollars."

Even so, you're better off to start your business without risking much of your own cash. Why? For one thing, you'll be worrying night and day if your personal resources are at stake. Worries can warp your business judgment.

For another, you'll probably have to pay a double tax on *your* money.

First you paid income tax on it when you earned it, before investing it in the business. And when you take it out as salary or dividends or capital gains or in some other form, it may be subject to tax again.

A third reason is that you get a tax deduction for whatever interest you pay to lenders who finance you.

A fourth reason has to do with long-range planning. Suppose you sell your business later. The price will depend on its actual value, not on what you put in. Buyers won't care whether you've put in a million dollars or none. But if your company has a loan outstanding from a bank (even a loan secured by your savings account or your home), the buyers often take over the debt and repay it.

We've already touched on a fifth reason: during the early months you may need more cash to keep the business alive or help it expand. If so, your own money will be more urgently needed; you probably can't ask your original lenders or investors for more funds so soon.

The best book on how to use other people's money is *High Leverage Real Estate Investments—Inside Secrets of Using OPM,* by Dr. Oliver Ray Price, (Prentice-Hall, Inc., Englewood Cliffs, New Jersey). Dr. Price describes many creative, innovative ways for using other people's money which can be applied to whatever business area you choose—real estate or not. He also discusses many possible private sources for financing and how to approach them.

The Best Way to Use Your Own Money

On the other hand, if you try to avoid putting any of your own money into your business, you'll lack credibility with investors. They're suspicious of any entrepreneur who won't risk his own money. In fact, most institutional lenders require that an entrepreneur put up at least half the starting capital from his own funds. Even so, make your investment indirectly, not directly.

That is, put up your stocks and bonds or your savings passbook or life insurance as collateral for a bank loan directly to the company. As it repays the loan, the company establishes its own creditworthiness. Meanwhile you can truthfully say that you've put up assets of your own to get your company started.

Of course, banks hate to lend to needy strangers. Before giving you a business loan, they'll want to know all about your business. In a moment we'll see how you should package your loan application.

But first let's briefly consider some other possible kinds of financing. One is what financial people call "equity financing," which means selling people a piece of the business. Instead of simply lending in exchange for your pledge to repay on stated terms, they invest in your enterprise. If the enterprise prospers, they share in its profits.

Another way to get backing is to pull in an active partner—someone who'll share the costs and the work—or maybe a "silent" partner who'll share the costs but will stay out of the way. You can run ads to attract working or silent investors with whatever background you need. Such ads appear in the Business Opportunities section of advertising pages in *The Wall Street Journal* and big-city newspapers.

There's much more to be said about the tax, profit, and personality angles of debt vs. equity financing, and of sole proprietorship vs. partnership vs. incorporation. We'll leave those for consideration in a later chapter. Whichever kind of financing you prefer, and whichever type of business structure you choose, you'll probably find that you must operate at least partially on bank credit. So let's look at the problem of wangling a bank loan.

How to Package a Loan Application

But before we look, you may find it worthwhile to skip ahead and glance through Chapters 20, 21, and 22. Those chapters are concerned primarily with ways of getting six-figure backing, or more, from banks or venture-capital firms or highly sophisticated wealthy individuals. Presumably you're not yet in a position to seek such backing. But the chapters include certain basic advice that applies even to the simpler problem of a small firm seeking a modest loan from a bank.

Now for the loan application. The first questions in the mind of almost any banker you approach will be "Why do you need a loan? What are you going to do with the money?" You must answer these questions satisfactorily before the banker will pay much attention to the rest of your application.

To a banker, good reasons for borrowing money include:

1. To buy an existing business.
2. To buy out a partner.
3. To buy inventory.
4. To buy equipment, especially if it will pay for itself.
5. To repair or improve facilities.
6. To move to a better site.
7. To expand capacity in response to growing demand.
8. To do more advertising or sales promotion.
9. To finance accounts receivable.

You'll notice that "To start a business venture" isn't on the above list. Start-up capital is hard to obtain from a bank. You haven't much chance unless you can put up plenty of collateral—or unless you're well known as a successful manager, can point to a hungry market for whatever product or service you plan to sell, and can spell out the precise details of your operation. So if you want to start a business, try to get whatever backing you need from family or friends or from prospective partners or investors, rather than from a bank. After your firm is established, you can show its facilities and financial records to a bank, and apply for a loan with a much better chance of getting one.

When you do apply for a loan, your application ought to cover the following points:

A. Purpose of loan (preferably one of the nine listed above, with enough detail to show that the added capital will make the business more profitable. Unless your profits are going to be bigger, how can you pay back your loan?

B. How much you need, with a breakdown of how the money will be allocated. Include 90 to 180 days of fixed expenses in the sum you request.

C. Term of the loan. Unless real estate is involved, a 6-year payoff is about what a bank usually expects on a business loan.

D. Security for the loan. Sometimes the balance sheet and financial statement of the business will show such strength that the bank won't ask for any additional collateral; the bankers will figure that if you don't pay they can foreclose and take over a profitable business which somebody else will buy from them. At other times, when a business looks shaky, a bank will want the head of the business to pledge his personal assets as well—or will want somebody else as cosigner.

E. Proposed method of repayment.

F. Financial data about the business. Make sure it's complete and accurate, because the bank may want to go over your books before deciding. It's a good idea to take the meat from the past three years' records and put this on one sheet for quick scanning.

G. Advance projections of the financial performance of the business for the coming three years. Banks love this, because it gives them a simple way to update your file after granting the loan and see whether you're on target. If you are, you'll find it easier to borrow more money as needed.

H. A copy of your lease agreement. We saw in Chapter 4 how important this can be.

I. A copy of your personal financial statement. Again, be conservative in stating your assets, and be sure you list all your important debts. Any significant omissions or misstatements here could be construed as criminal fraud.

Wherever you must use words instead of numbers, be concise. Use short sentences and paragraphs. Avoid adjectives, adverbs, and rosy generalities. Anything overblown or nonfactual will make a lender suspicious.

A sample loan application will help you see how to put together your own package.

Loan Application Summary

Purpose

The purpose of the loan is to move the existing business of John's Men's Shop to the new shopping center in order to capitalize on maximum growth potential. It should be noted that John's was specifically *selected* from among all area men's shops as offering the finest selection of men's apparel in addition to offering outstanding personal service.

Amount Requested

Increase in inventory	$20,000
Architectural design, labor, material to finish leased shop @ $20 a square foot	29,200
Furniture, display racks, cash register, etc.	9,800
90 days operating capital, fixed expenses plus debt service	16,000
Total loan applied for	$75,000

Term

Estimated debt service including 10% amortized over 6 years would approximate $1,350 per month. Referral to the attached 2 year Income and Expense Statement including the projection after the move indicated $7,313 to cover interest and $8,229 net profit, which will cover $1,300 of the debt service. The balance will be taken from manager's salary.

Security for Loan

Assets, as determined from 12/31/80 Balance Sheet:

Inventory	$21,209
Cash	1,129
Accounts receivable	2,575
Furniture & fixtures	2,322
	$27,235

Additional Assets to be acquired with loan proceeds:

Inventory	$20,000
Leasehold improvements	29,200
Furniture & fixtures	9,800
Operating capital	16,000
Total security from business	$102,235

Income Statement

	1979	1980	Projected (Remainder 1981)
Net sales	$35,155	$80,651	$150,000
Cost of sales	19,833	55,387**	86,400
Gross profit	$15,322	$25,264	$ 63,600

Operating Expenses

	1979	1980	Projected
Advertising	$ 3,600	$ 6,060	$ 7,200
Wages	1,930	4,826	9,600
Rent	1,298	1,650	15,426
Insurance	944	58	800
Travel & promotion	881	1,020	1,800
Legal & accounting	450	787	960
Small tools & supplies	392	732	702
Depreciation	312	464	2,339
Telephone	286	481	600
Office	192	160	200
Payroll taxes	183	188	377
Dues & subscriptions	116	188	220
Bank fees	83	678	948
Repairs & maintenance	87	510	600
Utilities	76	58	1,500
Taxes & licenses	90	709	886
Miscellaneous	239	331	300
Manager salary			3,600
Interest	1,646	2,714	7,313
TOTAL OPERATING EXPENSE	$12,805	$21,614	$55,371

Net profit (available for debt service)

	1979	1980	Projected
	$ 2,517	$ 3,650	$ 8,229

**Inventory at end of second year increased from time store purchased by $6,543.

The 1979 and 1980 Income-Expense data are actual as taken from the Balance Sheet, Income Statement, General Ledger and Financial Position Change Report as prepared both years by the accounting firm of Doing, Good and Job.

The projection is based on an item-by-item percentage increase in certain fixed costs, actual where determinable, i.e., rent, debt service, etc.

For example, we have allowed doubling the salary figure even though we are positive the present owner-manager and employees could adequately handle the projected increased volume.

Our present advertising expense is necessary because of our little-known present location, so in reality it should go down, yet we have allowed for a 20% increase. The same goes for travel & promotion, legal & accounting, tools & supplies, repairs & maintenance, etc.

KEEP THESE BASIC POINTS IN MIND

- *In approaching lenders, remember they are skeptics—be prepared.*
- *Make projections for at least three years.*
- *Evaluate carefully how much of other people's money to use vs. your own capital.*
- *Make a carefully documented loan package; leave nothing to chance.*
- *Many loans are granted to borrowers who want to move their business to a better site, as it eliminates some of the inherent risks of bad loans by lenders.*

8

So You're the Boss

So you've started a business. Or acquired one.

Inasmuch as you're reading this book, the odds are that you wear all the hats in your business. You may be the production, sales, marketing, traffic, and personnel expert rolled into one.

In such a position, many small-business managers drift with events, leaping from crisis to crisis like a runaway crossing the ice floes. Instead of planning their operations and managing the unexpected, they let their businesses run them.

You needn't do that. Plenty of small owners, with no particular training or special education, find ways to develop smoothly running enterprises. A puzzled executive of one mammoth corporation was quoted in the *Harvard Business Review:* "Every day successful businesses are started on a shoestring by people who couldn't even get jobs in our shipping room."

This chapter will describe how it's done—what the basic principles are for running a successful small business.

Let's start by exploring the toughest situation of all. We'll suppose that you've just taken over a business—inherited it from an uncle, perhaps— only to find that it's dying. Or maybe you've been boss for some years, while the economic climate gradually changed around you, and now you suddenly find that your business is on the brink of bankruptcy.

How to Revive a Sick Company

First, stop the "blood." Forget conventional profits. Instead, focus on cash flow—just cash after costs. (This book's Chapter 14, on money management, will show you many ways to clamp down on outgo and speed up incoming cash.) Postpone as many small or routine expenditures as you can—perhaps by stretching the interval between maintenance overhauls, or temporarily curtailing some advertising. Put a limit on hiring, buy judiciously, and be careful when borrowing extra capital to make the payments as easy as possible.

Then check your backlog of orders, especially if your lead time is long. How much of the business on your books is real—not overbooking by customers? A big order from a near-bankrupt customer is much worse than no order.

Next, look around to see where you can clear out dead weight.

Maybe certain employees just aren't making things happen. Face the fact that you can't afford them. Lay them off at least temporarily, explaining that you need time to decide the future course of the business. Meet with the employees still on your payroll, level with them, and encourage them to give an all-out effort.

Go through your inventory. Probably you'll find shelves loaded with slow-moving stuff, sometimes years old. Sell it off, at giveaway prices if need be. Maybe you can run a highly promotional sale. (For example, one retailer in a wealthy area found he was failing because his customers just wouldn't pay $450 for a suit. So he advertised a liquidation sale, knocking as much as $300 off the prices of famous makers' suits. Then he switched to a semidiscount operation and heavier promotion.)

Reexamine your product lines. Look at cost–price relationships. You may find that three out of thirty products are providing all the margin or that one-fifth of your customers buy four-fifths of whatever you sell. Get rid of products going nowhere. Lighten up on marginally profitable or slow-moving items; concentrate on selling those which move fast, if their profit margin is enough to keep the business alive. You might find that you are actually losing money doing business with certain of your customers. Some probably order in quantities that are not too economical to process and ship.

But don't go in with the idea that you must raise volume or prices. Often they can't be changed at the start. If so, you must focus on cutting unit costs—which may call for more expertise than you can muster.

You Can Summon Rescue Specialists

There are consulting firms that specialize in rescuing failing businesses. Some of these even provide an infusion of cash to finance corrective action, if they can see they'll get it back through a negotiated percentage of your sales or sometimes through a fraction of the ownership.

One of the biggest and best-known of these firms is Grisanti & Galef Inc., in Los Angeles. They help about 25 businesses a year, and save approximately 90 percent of them. But their monthly fee averages around $18,000—which may be too rich for your blood.

Another is April-Marcus Inc. in New York City. They specialize in retailers, and at this writing are working with 110 of them, of which about half are "already insolvent but probably salvageable," according to Marvin Blumenfeld, president.

Alan Spiegel in New York specializes in sick manufacturing companies. He'll take clients with as little as $5 million in sales. If you're smaller than that, try some of the rescue specialists in Chicago. Or else seek free advice from the Small Business Administration (see Chapter 11) or from one of the three hundred universities and colleges that provide free consulting service for small enterprises (see Chapter 1).

How the Experts Operate

How do these consultants turn losers into winners? "There's no magic in what we try to do," Blumenfeld says. "We just recognize the realities of today's economic climate. And we urge owners to follow principles we have discovered are workable today."

By "realities of today's economic climate" he mostly means that certain markets are changing, so that what used to sell is no longer profitable. Maybe there've been changes in the laws, or in public tastes, or in competition—things that don't show up on financial statements but affect them strongly. Is there still a need for the service, the product, or the outlet in that industry?

Frank A. Grisanti takes a similar approach. "We evaluate whether there's enough gross margin for the business to be viable. Assuming it has the right margin, we ask how it is dissipating the difference. Pretty soon, we're zeroing in on the problem."

If a manufacturing firm is to be turned around, Spiegel says, its production equipment must be reasonably up-to-date compared with that of its competitors. And its location must give it access to markets, raw materials, and workers, at competitive costs.

These are simple basics. You can ask the same general questions these consultants do. If your analysis shows that the market or the economic climate is fundamentally wrong for your business, you have three options open to you: sell it, shut it down, or change it into a different kind of business.

Think Small to Stay Strong

Converting or diversifying can sometimes be done almost overnight. A small wholesaler of Christmas toys added an entirely different business —the wholesaling of beach wear. This enabled him to get more productivity out of his major economic resource, which was his trained sales force.

A small manufacturer of machine-tool parts averted failure by giving up manufacturing entirely, and confining himself to being a consultant on welding problems and techniques. His manufacturing was no better than that of hundreds of other shops. But as a welding consultant he was in a class by himself.

This is another way of saying that a business must be managed by setting objectives for it. You must decide who and where its customers are, and what they really want or need. You must figure out what it can do better than competitors—how it can make the best use of its talents and resources.

One small business which made and sold lawn-care products, such as grass seed, fertilizer, and pesticides, thought it "knew" what its skills were—manufacturing and selling, obviously. But when it analyzed itself carefully, its really profitable activities turned out to be quite different: they were research on how homeowners work on their lawns, on what they expect and will pay for; and then promotion to both the dealer and consumer, and packaging the company's products so that dealers could move them without any sales effort. Up to that time, nobody in the company was responsible for any of these activities. As soon as the activities were specifically assigned to people already in management, the company began to grow and prosper. It had found its niche.

Washington Steel found its niche by deciding to sell steel just as cigarettes and newspapers are sold—to distributors. Its president, Tom Fitch, said, "At first we tried selling direct to manufacturers. All we got was small orders that no one else wanted."

So the company used a "spare tire" argument in approaching distributors who were buying their steel almost entirely from a single maker. It pointed out that no distributor should be too dependent on one source; emergencies might arise when a second source would be invaluable. It asked to be considered as a second source. This worked. After a few years WS was the primary source for many distributors, because it was flexible enough to give excellent service.

Small merchants can find niches too. They aren't in direct competition with big stores; these giants compete among themselves. Customers don't expect a small store to offer the same prices or selection of merchandise they look for in a department store or discount chain. Instead, they seek the friendly *service* a small business can provide: prompt assistance, personal attention, special ordering, familiarity with products, and flexibility on credit terms. Just being able to greet regular customers by name is a big plus for a small operation.

"One of the surprising discoveries successful venturing companies have made is that a new business doesn't have to do everything 'right' in order to survive and prosper," writes Mack Hanan, a consultant, in the *Harvard Business Review*. "It can be wrong in some areas and even remiss in a few aspects of management, as long as its manager hits the mark where it counts: concentration on the minimum number of functions that can provide the maximum leverage for getting a venture off the ground."

What mark has your manager been aiming at? Some perfectionists keep their eyes fixed on the goal of efficiency, issuing such edicts as "Keep those credit losses down," even though more generous terms might raise profits, and "Scrap allowances must be held to 5 percent," though this might easily raise production costs. Other bosses are too cautious, passing up profits through fear of taking risks—insisting, for example, on too little plant, too much cash, and so on. Or maybe you have an order-hungry sales manager who thinks mainly of satisfying all customers, and will promise delivery at any time a customer wants—regardless of how badly his rush orders may foul up his job shop.

These are fundamentals the rescue consultants look at. If your company is in trouble, someone divorced from day-to-day details (maybe you, if you're fairly new in it, or maybe an astute banker or close friend) should analyze your business and get a fresh overview of what its real objectives should be, in light of its strengths and weaknesses.

As soon as you're sure the fundamentals are right, you can tackle the details that will pull the company out of its immediate predicament.

Don't Be Afraid of Bankruptcy

The most urgent details of a business, of course, are its debts. If it can't meet the payroll and the bank is cutting off its flow of funds, you'll have to try to work out an arrangement with lenders and creditors.

Face up to this necessity immediately. Communicate with your creditors. Tell them the whole story, numbers and all. Don't bluff. Credibility at this point may be the only thing that can help you. It may buy time—and possibly more credit, if lenders think you really can revive the business.

In laying your problem on the line with creditors, you'll have to accept the risk that one or more nervous creditors may reject your plea for patience and rush to court to force you into bankruptcy. But if you can get the major creditors behind you, they'll use their leverage to get cooperation. They can be very persuasive. Remember, creditors are businessmen, and they stand to lose a customer if you go broke.

Is the Internal Revenue Service your creditor too? The IRS has been known to compromise when a corporation can't pay in full. In fact, it follows an established procedure for arranging compromises. Fill out its Form 656, accompanied by Form 433, "Statement of Financial Condition and Other Information." Be scrupulously careful in stating facts on these forms, because a misstatement could lose you any reduction in taxes, and you might go to jail instead.

But don't let IRS agents push you around unduly. Two agents entered one grocery store and said they would close down the business unless $6,000 in back taxes was paid forthwith. The owner asked for a little more time: "If we can stay open over the weekend, we'll get enough cash to pay." The agents said no. They shut the doors immediately. Then they sold the inventory to pay the tax bill. The owner sued and got back his business, including his inventory costs. The judge ruled that the IRS had acted unreasonably and in bad faith, for the express purpose of destroying the business.

If pressure from your creditors gets too bothersome, consider taking voluntary bankruptcy, more formally known as Chapter 11 of the federal bankruptcy law. It's a legal refuge that can do wonders for small companies in trouble. In the last few years the number of Chapter 11 petitions filed each year has increased substantially. Can anything that popular be all bad? It doesn't carry as much stigma as you might think, and it doesn't necessarily mean sudden death.

Basically you're asking the court to protect you from creditors while you try to work things out. This is better than trying to stay in business with too little money, and continuing to pile up debts until you're *forced* into bankruptcy—at which time the company, its creditors, and its employees are all wiped out.

Before you file for bankruptcy, you'll be smart to get in touch with attorneys for the major creditors. This should make proceedings go more smoothly, because the attorneys will be pleased at the prospect of more legal fees. (Getting the creditors' committee as a client can be a profitable piece of business, and the attorneys will start jockeying for it.)

Under Chapter 11 a business can continue to operate, and doesn't have to pay past unsecured debts until a plan for repayment is approved by creditors and the court. The moment you file under Chapter 11, all lawsuits, creditor harassment, and problems stop. You can buy supplies and merchandise. You're not a "bankrupt" in legal terms, but the "debtor in possession." Any new creditors stand first in line for getting paid. Usually they want cash on delivery, but after a few months of positive cash flow are likely to grant you credit.

Setting up a plan for reorganizing and paying down the old debts, as required under Chapter 11, is rather like trying to put together a budget to convince your wife that you can afford a new sports car. You might have to convince some highly skeptical people.

If liquidating your business at auction would produce very little cash for the old creditors, they are more likely to allow time for repayment. But if there are assets that can pay creditors most of what's owed, the creditors will try to have a trustee run the business, and you'll need a good bankruptcy lawyer to help you stave this off.

Usually, getting a plan approved by the creditors can take two months to a year, while you continue to do business at the old stand. Generally a plan can get by if it provides for paying interest only on some of the larger debts, and reducing the smaller ones by fractional repayments each month.

When the plan is approved, you're committed to carrying it out. If you pull this off, you can then be declared out of bankruptcy. Another interesting angle of Chapter 11 is that you can even borrow more money, thereby allowing the lenders preference over the old lenders, because your new debts will be pledged against assets.

Cultivate Creditors

Don't use Chapter 11 unless there's a good chance for the company to work itself back to solvency. Once you decide to use it, keep your creditors reminded that you're doing it because of them. The worst thing you can do is avoid them. Spend a little time every week letting them know what progress you're making. Convince them they'll come out better than if they force you into total bankruptcy. Properly handled, they will probably be unanimous in their approval of your methods.

Meanwhile, spend even more time cultivating your customers. When they learn you've taken bankruptcy, they'll feel skeptical, and you must overcome this. Call them up, write them, explain that it's a temporary predicament and that their source of supply is secure. Do more advertising than you used to. Don't let your competitors bad-mouth you because of this. Make everyone understand that this is a technical maneuver to save a good business.

And of course you should call a meeting of all your employees, even before you file for bankruptcy, and explain your decision. By showing confidence instead of gloom, and telling them your plans in detail, you should be able to convince them that your strategy will mean more secure jobs for them.

One last word about bankruptcy: there are alternatives to it. Instead of being forced into bankruptcy or petitioning under Chapter 11, you can try to sell the business, and you'll have a good chance of succeeding. Plenty of capitalists like to buy going businesses at bargain prices even if they are sick.

Watch for Early Trouble Signs

So much for the worst predicament of a business, and how to meet it.

Now let's move back a stage. Before a business comes to the brink of failure, there will be many signs that it is drifting into danger. Here are distant early warnings you can recognize while there's still time for rescue without the heroic measures we've just considered:

1. Hectic confusion in any department; desks heaped with overdue paperwork.
2. Low morale among executives and employees; promotions for length of service, rather than results or ability.
3. Ballooning expenses; weak profits.
4. Frequent delays for materials, parts, tooling, maintenance; lack of inspections or supervision; increasing machinery down time; mounting scrap or rework.
5. Slow billings and collections; inventories piling up; increasing customer complaints about stock-outs or late shipments.
6. "Little" problems (bottlenecks, foul-ups) brushed aside, or handled arbitrarily before facts are gathered or options considered.
7. Decline in competitive position.
8. Recurring shortages of working capital.
9. Management does little planning, doesn't know what's going on, sets price by guesswork, merely reacts to events as they happen.
10. No communication or teamwork between departments. Sales department doesn't know or care about the problems of the production department, production about changing sales trends per sales department, sales department always at odds with credit department, and so on.

Beware of Hubris and Nemesis

Often a head man is blind to such signs. ("Wait till next year, we'll have a line that will knock 'em dead.") Kenneth Eaton, head of Associated Business Consultants, a Chicago firm, says, "An entrepreneur is an optimist. Overoptimism is what does companies in. When things are going well, the average businessman assumes they'll continue to go well. When a problem arises, he assumes it will go away. By the time he wakes up, it's often too late."

An entrepreneur is likely to be not only an optimist but an egotist. He tends to think he alone knows what's good for his company. Henry Ford thought so, and nearly wrecked his huge business by continuing to run it as a one-man company.

The Greeks had a word for this: hubris. There's a Yiddish word too: chutzpah, which has been defined as "brazen disregard for the sensibilities of others." According to the Greeks, the sin of hubris (overbearing pride) was inexorably followed by nemesis (retribution). Don't let your business be a Greek tragedy, or a Yiddish joke.

Who's Your Second Banana?

If you start as a one-man business, the first employee you hire can be a great asset at first, and a liability later. You want an assistant who is compliant, loyal, and willing to work at a comparatively low salary. But in a few years, when the business has grown and more employees have been hired, the number-two spot calls for initiative and good judgment. It's sheer luck if your first employee grows along with the business. Yet you may promote him to positions beyond his ability, just because of his seniority and fidelity (The Peter Principle).

If your business is to grow and prosper, you need a right-hand man who won't be afraid to tell you bad news or argue with you. If you recognize this early enough, you can bring in someone new as number two, moving your first loyal helper sideways instead of demoting him. Usually the first employee will accept the newcomer because he too realizes that the pace is getting too fast for him. It's easiest when frank friendly discussion is possible among all concerned.

A Quick Course in Managing People

To keep your organization lean and strong, don't hire more help until your employees are all so overworked they'll be glad to see the newcomer no matter where he sits. Meanwhile, you've got to make yourself part of a team with lots of easy give-and-take.

The best managers think of themselves as playing coaches. They are first on the field in the morning, last to leave at night, in close touch with all the action. They're just the opposite of the boss who "plays his cards close to his chest," giving everyone four jobs while nobody quite knows what anyone else is supposed to be doing. A manager should be on the scene when he's needed—to supply the blessing or the go-ahead or the missing piece of a puzzle.

Once past the problems of start-up, an entrepreneur is in danger of getting so interested in building his own fortune or perfecting his product that he forgets about developing a competent management team. Maybe you think you're delegating when you say, "You're sales manager; you run it." But that isn't delegating if the sales manager isn't sure what's expected of him, or what will happen if he steps on someone's toes—including yours. He'll probably take the path of least resistance and do whatever he thinks won't bother anyone else.

If your people tell you whenever they think something is wrong, that's healthy. Grousing is not a measure of discontent. Often the most committed are the most critical. It's even healthy when your people argue openly with each other for what they believe in. But when they start arguing among themselves by memo with copies to you, call them in. A small company can't afford time-wasting civil wars by memo. This is your chance to dramatize participative management.

Resist your temptation to pass quick judgment, like King Solomon. For example, if they're disputing over whether your new packages should be green or blue or yellow, make them support their arguments with facts. Make them listen carefully to one another. Try to encourage the group in developing more information. What do others in the company think, and why? Should we talk to customers about it? To suppliers? Whatever the final decision, don't let it be because "the boss likes blue," or "the boss's wife likes green." Make it the outcome of participation by all those responsible for reaching sound judgments.

Small companies should be fun. The key people often work at all hours, become highly expert and enjoy the challenge and opportunity for creating. That's quite an advantage over the five-day, nine-to-five week in big business.

To make the most of this advantage, get to know your people: what they do well, what their strengths and weaknesses are, what they hope to get from their jobs. Create a climate in which they'll want to help the company reach its objectives. You see, you're trying to come between your people and their families. You want them to enjoy their work so much they come in on Saturdays instead of playing tennis or cleaning the garage. Even nonprofessionals now consider wages less important than the nature of the work itself.

Keep salaries and bonuses confidential. That may seem hard in a small business, but you can do it by using a payroll service that mails checks to employees' homes. This prevents anyone's sneaking a look at office records and seeing what everyone—from you down—is making. Moreover, when checks aren't given out at work, employees don't have the chance to compare. It's comparisons, not absolute amounts, that can cause resentment.

Why Employees Quit or "Slack Off"

In a small business, you cannot afford to shrug off the important factor of employee morale; you can't accept "Everybody talks about it, but nobody does anything about it."

Personnel management consultants may spend weeks in determining why a client company has a high employee turnover or a low productivity per employee. If in your business you believe you may have a morale problem among your employees, it is vitally important that you first recognize that a problem exists and, second, *acknowledge* it!

If you are determined to try to resolve your company's morale problems without the aid of a professional, then at least consider the seven most important reasons for low morale and/or high employee turnover. (Studies have revealed that there is a sex-related factor—most men quit for occupational reasons and most women quit for "personal" reasons.) The seven major reasons for quitting are:

1. The job
2. Supervision (poor supervision or a lack of supervision)
3. Fellow employees
4. Company's personnel policies
5. The community
6. Family difficulties or family pressures
7. A better job

A recent personnel survey revealed that *poor supervision* is the dominant reason why people quit. Other reasons mentioned frequently include dislike for job, improper placement in job, poor working conditions, and unequal work loads.

Whether your company is small or large, a good procedure is to have an "exit interview" with every employee who quits. Probe—ask many questions—find out the "whys"—cover the seven major possibilities listed above. And ask "open" questions—questions that encourage the person leaving to state his reasons in his own words.

How's Your Coordination?

When General Eisenhower was elected President, his predecessor, Harry Truman, said "Poor Ike. When he was a general, he gave an order and it was carried out. Now he's going to sit in that big office and give an order and not a damn thing will happen." That's how it is where controls are clumsy, as they usually are in big business organizations. But your small organization can be just as uncoordinated, unless you build in feedback (as the Army does) whereby lower officers go out personally to make sure that everybody gets the word and is acting accordingly.

A story among management scientists illustrates the importance of the question "Who has to know?" A maker of industrial equipment decided to discontinue one type of machine. But nobody told the clerk in the purchasing department who was in charge of buying the parts from which this machine was assembled. By the time anyone noticed that these parts were piling up, there were enough for five years' production of the discontinued machine—parts that had to be written off at a serious loss.

Businesses should have a stock-control system to prevent overstocking and prevent running out. You might set up a perpetual inventory system like this: Tack up an inventory card in your supply area. On it show the maximum stock that should be on hand or on order, and the minimum below which the item shouldn't be allowed to dwindle. Between these extremes the card should show a reordering point, how much to reorder each time, and the date of each order placed but not yet received. The card should carry a running total of orders received and of removals from stock, so that it shows the actual balance on hand and on order.

A couple of times a year, check the card's total against the actual count. If there's a discrepancy because employees aren't updating the card, your displeasure and more frequent checkups should get everyone trained.

But this isn't really enough. Because demand for some items in your inventory will fluctuate, you'll need guidelines for your people in sales, manufacturing, and purchasing, so that they'll know when to boost inventory levels, when to cut down. And they should communicate their changes up and down the ladder.

To make your resources go around, you need a reporting and control system. When your business is small, this isn't as complicated as it sounds. Maybe a checklist is all you need. We'll get into it in detail in Chapter 13, which deals with simplifying paperwork.

Planning for Healthy Growth

As you grow larger, you'll probably need more sophisticated planning and control—maybe a cost-accounting system, so you can tell which parts of the business are profitable and which aren't; maybe computerized control of shopwork scheduling and inventory. Where there are too many work interruptions because of poor scheduling, or where a machine breaks down because it hasn't been adequately maintained, or where information on what to do next isn't available, your people can't work productively. Some firms have boosted productivity as much as 50 percent by computerizing their work flow.

Do you see the implication of these past few pages? It's the same point mentioned specifically in the early part of this chapter: You need a rough master plan. You need to know approximately where your business should be going. Otherwise controls won't do much good. Your business will be like a ship with a good rudder and compass but no charts.

To develop a good master plan, keep asking simple questions like:

"What advantages do we have over competitors? . . . What advantages does competition have over us? . . . What can we do to counter competitors, or take advantage of our own strengths?

"What must we do now to be ready for three years from now? . . . To get results when we need them, when must we start preparations? . . . What will not get done at all if we don't commit resources to it today?"

Getting rid of yesterday is also an important part of planning. Your top people should be asking of every activity, every product, every market: "If we weren't in this today, would we go into it?" If the answer is no, they should ask "How can we get out—fast?"

Your best financial and accounting people should be part of your inner management circle. Most entrepreneurs, being creative types, dislike accounting and leave it entirely to accountants somewhere on the fringe of the business. Frequently, operations people and money people mix like oil and water. The former think the latter are interested mainly in the past, because a typical set of financial records reads like yesterday's newspaper. "Our accounting system tells us where we fell short last month, not where we're apt to fall short next month" is a common complaint. "Our accountants are like baseball scorekeepers who don't understand baseball."

The money people might just as easily reply, "You operations guys are like baseball players who don't know how to keep score."

It's true that many fully qualified accountants really are poor businessmen. So you may easily inherit an antiquated set of financial controls that keep you shooting in the dark. But this needn't be the case. Tell your treasurer, controller, and chief accountant (maybe they're all the same person) what kind of accounting system you want. If they can't design one that meets your requirements, bring in a consultant who can. Here's what your system should do:

1. It should give you reports on past financial performances that are accurate and on time.

2. These reports should show trends—probably a comparison, in parallel columns, from month to month or year to year, and a "percentage increase or decrease" column.

3. You should get scan reports about twice weekly on who and what is generating your profits and your losses.

4. You should get estimates of future performances: projections for next month, next quarter, next half-year, and next year. These pro forma predictions really are more important than past records, because they help you set priorities, spot problems, and shut the barn door before the horse is stolen.

5. You should get a readable warning-flag report, showing dangerous changes from the norm and predicting their impact unless corrective action is taken.

6. You should get a built-in security system that will allow information to flow to even the lowest-level employees who need it, without danger of confidential information getting to your competitors.

7. Your control system should adjust to changing conditions. If sales go up, certain budget appropriations should grow, with management's okay. Your floating budgets and reserves should be set up so that they neither lead nor lag behind conditions.

An accounting group is trained to handle ledgers far better than any other group in your company. Therefore you may want to consider assigning them to handle all inventory, purchasing, production, quality assurance, marketing, and administrative ledgers—and to have them give these other groups the information they need in the language that the group understands.

The art of running an upward-bound business is encyclopedic. But all you really need is the fundamentals set forth in this chapter, plus good judgment and willingness to make decisions.

Good judgment? How do you get it? Through experience. And how do you get experience? "By having bad judgment!" someone once said. At least, you get it by finding out what works.

As for making decisions—it's scary, especially when big money or the fate of the company hangs on your judgment. But in today's business climate, he who hesitates is lost. If you're afraid to take a calculated risk on a new sales campaign or capital investment, or if you drag your feet when changes in your old established ways are needed, then your business will stop growing and may even stop existing.

KEEP THESE BASIC POINTS IN MIND:

• *If your company is near bankruptcy, the first thing to do is clamp down on outgoing cash as tightly as possible, and speed up receipts.*
• *Then check the credit of your customers, and decide how much production to discontinue. Get rid of products going nowhere.*
• *Analyze your business and its market. Maybe you should sell it, shut it down, or change it to a different kind of business.*
• *Chapter 11 bankruptcy can give you protection while you turn the business around. If you use it, keep cultivating your creditors and customers.*
• *Develop an employee team that isn't afraid to argue with you, or with each other. Look for ways to make their work satisfying, so that they'll give it their best.*
• *Set up a reporting and control system that will keep everyone in your company informed about whatever they need to know and will ensure that instructions are carried out.*
• *Develop a long-range master plan for your business.*

9

How to Tell Which Business Structure Is Best for You

The birth of a business is a life-or-death crisis. Two chores must be done to ease the birth—choosing the legal name of the enterprise (which we'll consider a little later) and choosing the legal form in which to do business. Consider carefully which type of business entity to use. The wrong choice could kill you, fiscally speaking.

There are three basic ways of doing business in the United States: (1) as a sole proprietor, (2) as a partnership, (3) as a corporation. Even insiders are sometimes mistaken about whether their enterprise is really and truly a proprietorship, a partnership, or a corporation in the eyes of the law and the Internal Revenue Service.

There's no simple test for the existence of a partnership, but the major requirements are co-ownership of a business, and making a profit. Also, since no formalities are needed to create a partnership, you may be in one and not realize it. Tax men say that as a general rule, the sharing of profits, together with dividing the work of managing the business, are enough evidence to imply the existence of a partnership whether you call it that or not.

Besides the three main forms, there are various exotic and complicated forms a business can contort itself into. You can set up an association, trust, regulated investment trust, syndicate, pool, small business corporation, small business investment company, joint stock company, or some other type of joint venture. We won't delve into the intricacies of the rarer forms. That's a task for specialists in business law and taxation. Instead, let's take a close look at the three basic forms.

Why the Differences Are Crucial

There's no form that's best for all purposes. Each has strong points which don't always meet the eye. Authorities are often appalled by small-business men's ignorance about advantages and disadvantages of the various forms. Each is great for certain purposes, terrible for others.

Surprisingly, the form of a business can make a big difference in its net profits. It can affect the taxes you must pay, your ability to attract capital needed for expansion, and the extent of the damage to your personal bankroll if the business gets into trouble. It can also minimize or maximize friction among people in the organization.

Choosing the form in which to do business is every entrepreneur's privilege. But to be recognized for tax purposes, the form you choose must be a genuine business entity—that is, it must be entered into and pursued in good faith for the purpose of making a profit. This makes it legally different from an activity carried on just for personal pleasure, or for the public good. Your activity will be classed as a business if it produces a profit in any two out of five consecutive years, unless you can get an Internal Revenue Service ruling to the contrary.

Although you have a right to mold business transactions in a way to minimize taxes, the form you use won't bind the tax collectors. They are free to look into the underlying facts and to tax the arrangement according to what it really is, rather than what you say it is. They'll ask themselves (and you), "Is this really a partnerhip? Or does it more nearly resemble a corporation?"

It's the Internal Revenue code, not local or state laws, that determines the federal tax to be paid. Thus your organization may be classified as a corporation under the laws of the state where it is formed, and a piece of imitation parchment called a charter may proclaim grandly that it is indeed a corporation. But the Treasury can tax it as a noncorporation if investigators decide that it's a vehicle for dodging taxes and doesn't have a legitimate purpose.

As we look at each form of organization, we'll explore its tax angles. But there are other angles to keep in mind. If you and your associates quarrel, and some of you decide to squeeze out someone, the tactics that can be used will vary according to the legal form of the enterprise. These are explained in Chapter 24, and you may want to skip ahead to that chapter before choosing what type you'll set up.

Some businesses start as proprietorships, go through several changes, and eventually settle into the right slot for them. This trial-and-error process isn't always the best way to evolve. It can mean yards of red tape and hefty legal fees for doing, undoing, and redoing. Theoretically, every new business ought to organize in the most advantageous way from the beginning, so that it can expand without changing form. But in practice your business may not be able to start with the legal structure that you foresee will be needed a few years from now. Talk it over with a good business lawyer at the outset. You can talk with him more intelligently after you've read this chapter.

Fewer Laws, Fewer Taxes if You're a Proprietor

If you plan to run a small, quiet mom-and-pop kind of operation, a simple proprietorship is probably your best bet. It means a one-owner operation. You alone are responsible for all the debts of the business, and you reap all its profits (after taxes).

As a sole proprietor, about all you need is a letterhead and a place to work. In most localities, you can do business under your own name without registering with anyone. You don't need a lawyer—because a proprietorship is really the absence of any legal form of business organization.

Maybe there are local rules requiring a proprietor to get an occupancy permit, a sales-tax certificate, or various other documents, but you can find out about these with a call to City Hall. (However, if you go into business as a realtor, a CPA, a medical practitioner, or a member of some other regulated profession, you'll have to be licensed by the state, and must meet its standards of training and competence.)

Do you want to use a trade name, such as Logjam Enterprises or Honest John or whatever? You'll probably need to register this name, and your own name and address, at the office of the county clerk or some similar sanctum. Any made-up business name is legally described as a "fictitious" name. Fictitious names or assumed names are considered perfectly okay unless they're deceptive, or unless you happen to pick one already being used by another enterprise nearby. A duplicate name can confuse the public, so the first user can invoke the law of unfair competition to make you stop doing business under that name.

As long as there are no complaints about you, you'll be almost totally unregulated. And of course, there are no partners or stockholders to raise bothersome questions. You're all alone in the driver's seat. That's a nice feeling if you're a take-charge, do-it-now type with special skills. Many highly successful businessmen spend their lives as sole proprietors, never taking a partner, never incorporating.

When you own a business all by your lonesome, your profits are taxed only once, as a part of your personal income. In other words, you pay no income tax on the net earnings of your business as such, but only on the combined net of your earnings and losses from the business and all other sources. You'll also pay self-employment taxes, of course, and payroll taxes and the like if you have employees.

This way of doing business is likely to be highly personal. You probably know your employees quite well, and may get emotionally involved in their accomplishments and problems. You're in close contact with many of your customers and most of your suppliers, and you learn a lot from "talking shop."

But Proprietors Run More Risks

However, there's one ominous disadvantage to individual ownership. If there are losses instead of rewards, these are entirely yours too.

You are personally liable for all the enterprise's debts, all its obligations, all claims against it. Your liability isn't limited just to the amount of capital you invest in the business. Nor is your liability limited to the total assets of the business. Your home, your car, your bank account, and your other possessions may be claimed by people to whom you owe money. Conversely, if you have unpaid personal debts, your creditors can seize assets of your business to satisfy their demands. You're stuck with what lawyers call "unlimited liability."

There are other disadvantages too.

A sole proprietor hasn't much financial flexibility. Outside capital may be hard to coax in, since it depends on his personal credit rating. Business credit is likewise limited. All those closed doors may make it hard for an owner to expand his business, or to work his way out of trouble if the cash flow goes plop. For example, he might be seriously hurt if a big customer couldn't pay him.

Then too, a sole proprietorship is almost completely dependent on the owner's abilities. If he gets sick, or if troubles at home throw him into a tizzy, the business is bound to suffer. More commonly, a one-man enterprise gets hurt because Mr. One isn't an all-around good businessman. A lack of expertise in just one side of the business, like judging credit risks, can put the whole venture into the ashcan.

Lastly, if the owner dies, his proprietary interest dies. His heirs may run into legal tangles in trying to keep the business going.

For these reasons, you may want to think about joining forces with one or more partners who can share the work, the risks, and the potential profits.

Partners Can Help You

The main advantage of having a partner is that he may supply whatever you lack. This often means investing capital. You'll need money to get started and to stay afloat. A partner can supply money of his own. And a partnership may be able to get bank loans more easily than a sole owner.

The old adage that "two heads are better than one" is often true—although "too many cooks spoil the broth" can be true too. Partners must get along well personally, and should also complement one another's talents; that is, they should be clearly able to do better as a team than they could separately. Maybe one partner is the shrewd money man while another is the production expert and another calls on customers. One may drive the truck, another buy the supplies, another answer the phone.

Partners can also give each other moral support when it's needed. This might be all-important in time of trouble. For example, suppose the business calls for slathers of personal salesmanship. Salesmen sometimes run into mysterious dry spells. A lone owner might get discouraged and give up during such a spell. But a partner who's on a "hot streak" can encourage him and help overcome the slump.

Cutting Taxes via Partnerships

Any number of people can enter into a partnership (of course, there must be at least two), investing their money or their services or both in the business of which they are co-owners. Legally speaking, a partnership is basically a group of persons having a common business interest, each doing something to make the business succeed. "Partnership does not connote the idea that each and every working partner must punch a clock in the morning and work continually through the day," in the words of one court decision.

And of course, partnership doesn't necessarily mean that each partner puts in the same money—or even any money. Maybe a penniless inventor teams up with someone who'll finance him. Maybe someone is given a big chunk of the business for free, just because his name is valuable for attracting customers or raising money. Anything is possible and legal among partners, because of the free ability of adults to contract with each other, as long as no fraud is involved.

Although it must file a federal income-tax return showing its profit or loss, a partnership as such pays no tax. Its return is only an "information return," identifying each partner and showing how much income of each type (ordinary, capital-gain, and so on) should be reported by each partner on his own income-tax return. It also shows the amounts of certain kinds of deduction that a partner may take, such as contributions and additional first-year depreciation. Each partner must attach a copy of the partnership's tax return to his own personal return.

Partnerships offer some lovely tax breaks. Consider:

1. There's no double tax on income, as there is with a corporation (except a Subchapter S corporation, a nifty little device we'll anatomize in the next chapter). Hence if an equal five-person partnership makes $50,000 in one year, each partner reports $10,000 of income.

2. A partnership is a direct conduit for each type of income. This is another difference from a corporation. Corporate income, even if it's tax-exempt or preferentially treated, is all taxed as ordinary income to the stockholders when they receive dividends from corporate earnings and profits. But any type of partnership income keeps the same character for tax purposes when transferred to the partner's own individual tax return.

3. If a partnership shows a loss for the year, proportionate shares of this loss are passed through to the partners. So they can deduct it on their personal returns to offset other income. A partner's "investment" for this purpose includes not only money he put in but also his share of the partnership liabilities.

4. If the partnership's income were taxed to a sole proprietor or to a corporation, the amount might put it into a higher bracket. In other words, a business is likely to be taxed less heavily as a partnership. But remember that if a partnership agreement seems to have tax dodging as its purpose, the tax collectors can disregard the agreement.

5. Sometimes the partners can divide different kinds of partnership income in different ratios. One partner's share might be limited to municipal-bond interest, which is tax-free. Another partner's share might take the form of capital gains or of income from foreign sources. This must be spelled out in the partnership agreement, and there must be some nontax reason for it; otherwise the Treasury can disallow it. For example, one partner's responsibilities may be for securities transactions, so his worth to the business is measured by the partnership's gains in such dealings. This can entitle him to a bigger share of these gains.

6. Partnerships are immune from all those special taxes laid on corporations, such as the accumulated-earnings tax, the personal-holding-company tax, or the excess-profit tax.

7. Partners may deduct their shares of partnership business entertaining. The courts have held that a partnership's business is each partner's business, and the partner may deduct expenses if the agreement requires him to pay them.

8. A husband and wife can be business partners and get tax breaks they couldn't get otherwise. A spouse taken into the partnership (assuming that he or she is knowledgeable in its problems and can make a real contribution to running it) can get retirement benefits under the self-employment "Keogh Plan" provisions of the tax law. His or her share of the partnership's profits are considered earnings from self-employment.

9. A partnership may refuse to show its books to tax collectors, on the ground that this would be the same as testifying against itself. In a 1972 case, *U.S.* v. *Slutsky,* the District Court of New York ruled that a partnership could invoke the Fifth Amendment to avoid turning over various records which the IRS demanded in a tax investigation.

10. If you decide to transform your partnership into a corporation, there's no big tax problem. (The reverse isn't true, however. A corporation trying to convert to a partnership would face sticky tax problems.) All the partners need do is transfer their equity interests to a corporation in exchange for at least four-fifths of its stock.

Beware These Partnership Pitfalls

Now for the gloomier side of the partnership picture:

1. To be recognized as a partner for tax purposes, a person must actually be a partner—either by putting capital into the business, or by working in it, or by making some other valuable contribution such as his name and reputation.

A joint undertaking merely to share expenses (by sharing an office, perhaps) isn't a partnership in the eyes of the IRS. Nor do people necessarily become partners when they share profits. For instance, landlords with percentage leases, commissioned salesmen, and employees on profit-sharing plans aren't legally partners, because they have no liability for losses if the business loses money.

If several people are backing you financially, or contributing their efforts in the hope of profits, you'd better check the arrangement with a tax expert. Sometimes the IRS tells a group, several years after the close of their taxable year, "We've just audited your report, and we don't consider you a partnership. We know you have a partnership certificate under state law, but we say it's a device for avoiding taxes."

2. Just as a business may not always be taxed as a partnership even though the state calls it one, the principals may sometimes be liable as partners even though no partnership agreement was drawn up.

We often hear the terms "silent partner" and "secret partner." These phrases have no special legal meaning. They merely describe the relationship between the partners. If state law requires public disclosure of all partners and there's some sort of secret relationship, then the partners are obviously breaking the law. If a business goes broke and a secret partner is discovered, then he is fully as responsible for the debts of the business as the other partners.

3. A partnership's bookkeeping can get complicated, especially if several partners buy into the business at different times, pay more or less than "book value" for their interests, own different percentages, or are drawing money for personal expenses in unequal ratios. All this affects each partner's tax liability.

4. Partnership income is taxed to each partner each year, in the percentage specified by the partnership agreement, even if the income isn't actually paid out to him. Maybe a partnership decides to hold on to the income because it needs money for expansion or other purposes. This can put a partner into the painful position of owing federal income tax without having money to pay it. He may have to pull out of a highly successful enterprise.

5. A partnership is only as stable as its weakest member. Usually it dissolves if a partner dies or if one withdraws, is declared legally insane or incompetent, or goes bankrupt. If one partner wants to withdraw and the other partners won't buy him out, he'll have trouble selling his piece of the business, since the original agreement was probably made between close personal acquaintances who'll be strangers to newcomers. Few people want to go into partnership with strangers.

You can offset a partner's death by an advance agreement, in writing, that the surviving partners will buy the dead partner's interest from his estate. Many partnerships buy life insurance on the partners ("key-man life insurance") to make sure that the business has enough cash to buy out the interest.

But for federal-income-tax purposes, a partnership is considered dissolved anyhow if half of the total capital and profits is sold or exchanged within twelve months—or if partnership activities actually halt, as they might with the death or disability of a partner.

Worse, in some states the law insists that a partnership is automatically dissolved when a partner dies, even if the partnership's business activities are continuing. This means selling all the assets, paying the debts, dividing the net proceeds among the partners, and organizing a new partnership if the surviving principals want to carry on business together.

6. If partners bicker, the business is bound to suffer. Deadlocks, backstabbing, and rule by committee have destroyed some promising ventures. Because of this danger, you should include in your partnership agreement a buy/sell clause that takes effect when partners disagree on an important issue, or when a conflict of interest arises, or when one or more partners want to pull out.

Sometimes you can lessen your risks in partnership by keeping control yourself. There's no law saying partners must share alike. You can own 60 or 75 percent yourself, and your partner 40 or 25 percent. In a three-way partnership, two partners can each control 40 percent and the other gets the remainder. This is a good way to keep a prospective partner in check if he seems likely to be troublesome. As long as the major partners are in agreement, he can't make much trouble.

7. The scariest drawback is that every partner is "the agent of the other partners," in lawyers' language. This means that one partner binds all the others when he signs a contract or a check. Therefore your partnership agreement should require that large checks carry two designated signatures, and should limit the authority to contract.

The partnership itself, as well as each of the partners, may be liable for any partner's business actions. Creditors are entitled to payment before any partner may withdraw equity capital. So if the partnership can't pay a bill, a creditor can go after any partner he chooses.

If one partner is negligent or dishonest, or just makes a costly error, all the partners get hurt. They can lose their personal assets, and find themselves in trouble for something they didn't do or approve.

Scariest of all, if a partner damages somebody while working for the business—for example, getting into an automobile accident on a sales trip —all or any of the partners may be held responsible to pay the damages. They might even be criminally prosecuted for a partner's dishonesty in business. They can't obtain bonding protection against a partner's embezzlement, thefts, or other business sins.

Obviously, you need to be supercautious about going into partnership —even with a good old buddy. It's far easier to get into a partnership than to get out—just as in a marriage—and all your personal and business life can be affected.

Too often, business owners take a partner just because he can put in needed capital. And sometimes they live unhappily ever after. You should thoroughly investigate any prospective partner's character, ability, and financial status. Learn enough about his personality to be sure he'll wear well.

Any agreement is a binding contract. A partnership agreement may be spoken, written, or simply implied by the action of the parties. Friends who plunge into business together may not feel they need anything in writing, only to discover too late that they were mistaken. Misunderstandings and disagreements can arise between the best of pals. Always put your agreement in writing. Have it drawn up by an attorney. See that it carefully specifies and limits each partner's responsibilities and rights.

This agreement should describe the proposed business in detail, and state the name under which the partnership will do business. It should tell—

> what each partner's investment will be, either in money or in other valuable considerations;
> the percentage ownership of each partner, and how profits and losses will be divided;
> how much time each partner will give to the business;
> who can sign the checks;
> who can sign contracts, incur liabilities, and sell assets;
> what each partner's functions and duties and powers are;
> how the business will be managed;
> what happens if a partner wants to get out;
> how a new partner can be admitted;
> who will arbitrate if partners disagree;
> how the partnership can be dissolved;
> how the value of any partner's interest will be computed;
> what happens when a partner dies, divorces, goes bankrupt, or becomes unable to function;
> the size and nature of key-man insurance policies to be carried.

A Law That Protects Partners

Even when there's no written agreement, in most states the Uniform Partnership Act gives you certain protections. For example, all partners must consent to any act involving assignment of the company's property, or to any act that could put it out of business. If there's a dispute about a management decision, the law says each partner has one vote, no matter how much or little he has contributed to the business—unless there's a written partnership agreement stating otherwise.

The law requires that accurate records of the business be kept, and that all partners have the right to examine them. They all are entitled to participate equally in running the business, unless the agreement states differently.

Each partner owes undivided loyalty to his partners and the business. No partner may make secret profits from its assets. No partner may carry on outside transactions that amount to a secret conflict of interest. Each partner must account for all money handled by him. If he makes secret profits, he must return them to the business.

Unless there's an agreement, partners aren't entitled to salary; they are entitled only to draw on the profits. If there's a loss, the partners must return that draw to pay their share of the loss.

All these points of the Uniform Partnership Act are worth knowing in case you have any trouble between partners.

Successful small-business men are sharply divided on whether partnerships are a good idea. Frank C. Strunk, who has owned and managed six small businesses, writes, "In my judgment, the partnership is the least attractive form of business entity for the typical small business man. It involves a great deal more than just a handshake between friends."

On the other hand Elmer L. Winter, who started Manpower, Inc., and built it into the world's largest temporary-help service, writes, "Many partnerships, entered with great care, prove very successful. Partners often complement one another, each bringing his own talents to the business, to the benefit of all. In a retail store or service operation where hours are long, the owners can divide the time so that one is always on hand."

Love Those Limited Partners

So far we've been considering "general partnerships," as they're known in legal language. Now let's turn to a less common arrangement, the "limited partnership." It's quite a different proposition—although, like a general partnership, it doesn't have to pay tax on its earnings.

In a limited partnership there's at least one general partner who takes overall responsibility for running the business—as well as unlimited personal liability for the partnership's debts. And there's at least one limited partner—more often, a flock of them.

Limited partners can't participate in managing the business. That's how they protect their "limited liability" status under law. The only money that a limited partner risks is his investment in the business. So if you buy a limited partnership in an enterprise that goes broke, you lose your investment, but creditors ordinarily can't attach your bank account or other property.

Contrariwise, if the business booms, as a limited partner you get a share of its profits—usually according to a precise mathematical formula in the partnership agreement. So this is a good way to buy a piece of a business without much risk, if you're content to keep hands off its management. (You can't become a limited partner by contributing only services, although you can simultaneously be a limited partner and an employee of the partnership.)

It's Nice to Be General Partner—Except for the Liabilities

A limited partnership is also a good way for an entrepreneur to organize a business that will need more capital than he can supply. By persuading people to join a limited partnership of which he is the general partner, he can build up capital without getting into debt and without giving up any part of his control.

He has no legal obligation to refund the investments of his limited partners when the business isn't profitable, or if it fails. His only commitment is to distribute the profits, if any, according to whatever percentages are called for in the agreement.

Obviously, he's taking far less risk than if he ran the same business as a sole proprietor. Of course, he faces the same exposure to unlimited personal liability, but the capital paid in by his limited partners gives him a cushion against losses up to the total of their contributions.

Furthermore, if he comes up short, his limited partners may be willing to put in more money. It will depend on how they see the risks, and the long-term profit potential. So he'll need to be a convincing salesman.

Usually, in starting a limited partnership, a general partner puts up a sizable chunk of his own money to show how confident he is. But since he's the only one who can go broke, investors usually are willing to sign a partnership agreement promising him a larger percentage of the profits than his cash contribution would otherwise entitle him to.

Sometimes they agree that the partnership should pay him a fee for services rendered in putting together the enterprise. And sometimes they grant him a salary or continuing management fee "for the duration." But he may run into resistance when he proposes such concessions. "Wait until you prove yourself and we see some profits," his prospective partners may say.

A fairer deal for all concerned is usually to dangle a juicy carrot—in the form of a generous share of whatever profits are made, as mentioned above—before the eyes of management, to urge it onward. Another arrangement that softens up skeptical investors is to subordinate the general partner's interest in the profits to theirs.

For example, limited partners might get all profits until they had received, say, a cumulative 15 percent yearly return on their investments, after which the general partner would take half of whatever profits were left over. Or the general partner might be promised *all* profits above a 25- or 30-percent yearly return to the limited partners.

Or there can be two classes of limited partners. A safety-first class is to get all profits up to a certain point. A high-rolling class shares the surplus with the general manager. This is the sort of proposition that an entrepreneur might consider when he's trying to raise big money, and when both conservative and speculative-minded investors are interested.

Limited partnerships are popular for real estate syndications and other fairly large-scale ventures organized by a single promoter. They also work well for a young man starting his own business, if friends want to back him but don't want any involvement in running the business. However, if they succumb to an urge to start helping him or advising him, a court may rule that they are really general partners and thus fully liable for all the debts of the business. So be careful to stay "limited" if you are a limited partner.

If you're a general partner, be sure to have a lawyer help set up the partnership. The limited partners' shares are considered investment securities, and their sale to investors is tightly regulated. Most states require that when a partnership includes a limited partner, a special document called a "limited partnership certificate" must be filed with the county clerk or some state officer. This document specifies the amount of capital supplied by limited partners, and the percentage of profit they'll be entitled to. The information in the certificate must also be published in two local newspapers. Theoretically, this puts the public on notice that the limited partner's liability extends so far and no further.

At this writing, limited partnerships are illegal in Alabama, Connecticut, Kansas, Kentucky, Louisiana, Maine, Mississippi, Oregon, and Wyoming.

How to Profit by Incorporating

The most popular structure for a business enterprise in America—big or little—is the corporation. We all know it's the structure of the mammoth companies. But it also feels comfortable for many small-business men. They choose it for various reasons, as we'll see.

A corporation isn't easy to define. It is a form of business organization created by the state solely through legislation. State laws let you incorporate an existing business (partnership or sole proprietorship) or start a new business in a corporate form.

The corporation's name must include the words "Inc." or "Corp." or "Ltd." to advise people that they may be doing business with a corporation. The word "Co." or "Company" in the corporate name isn't enough in most states.

Oddly, the law considers a corporation a kind of person. The logic behind this is that any corporation holds a string of responsibilities that set it apart from its shareholders, executives, and employees. So it has to have a personality of its own.

For example, it is responsible for its own debts; its shareholders, although they collectively own the corporation, don't have to pay these debts. (Hence, if you incorporate, your personal assets are shielded from claims against your business.)

And a corporation can own its own buildings; its members have no rights in them. It can enter into contracts. It can buy, sell, and inherit property in its own name. Its property and other assets can be seized and sold to pay debts or court judgments. It must pay taxes.

These characteristics, which free its people of so many liabilities, pump life into the corporation itself. It is just as much a person, financially and legally speaking, as Mr. Jones or Mrs. Astor.

Mr. Corporation can sue or be sued. He-she-it may even commit crimes and be tried and punished for them. (Unlike a living, breathing person, however, it can't plead possible self-incrimination as a ground for withholding corporate records from tax examiners or other authorities. Furthermore, officers of a corporation are personally responsible for any law violations they commit while working on behalf of the corporation. This means that if a corporation president defrauds someone, both he and the corporation will be liable for damages.)

Corporations are formed by filing articles of incorporation at the state capitol with the secretary of state, or some other state official. The official hands the proud parents some documents called stock certificates, indicating how much they own in terms of "shares" of the corporation's total issued "stock."

Often, when a corporation first comes alive, its founder and his family and friends are the only owners. The stock in such a corporation—which is often described as a "closed corporation" or "closely held corporation"—isn't available to outsiders. The owners don't sell any shares because they want to keep exclusive control.

Here are some of the beauties of a closely held corporation:

1. Owners risk only the money they put into their corporation. It can go broke—owing millions, conceivably—but its owners can stay solvent. The debts can't be collected from them.

2. The corporation can be immortal, in a manner of speaking, as long as it pays its bills and its shareholders want it to stay in business. It needn't come to an end, like a partnership, if Mr. Big or his partner dies.

3. The corporation generally has greater borrowing power than other business structures. It can choose among a dazzling array of financial instruments to attract lenders and investors. For example, the corporate form enables it to raise capital for expansion by selling newly issued stock. As it grows, it may also be able to sell bonds and other debt securities. It may even be able to buy other businesses, using its own stock instead of cold cash.

4. Some banks and other organizations would rather do business with corporations because of their borrowing power, relative permanence, and the like.

5. A shareholder can transfer his part ownership to someone else al-

most instantly. All he has to do is sell, give, or bequeath his stock certificates.

6. Corporate federal-income-tax rates are below the top brackets for individuals. So if big income is taxed to the corporation rather than to the owners, less tax is paid.

7. In figuring the corporation's net income, all salaries paid to employees may be deducted. The actual owners of a small corporation are usually on its payroll as executives, and their salaries and other deductions can lighten the corporation's tax load marvelously.

8. A corporate executive can deduct many expenses which he probably couldn't deduct as a sole proprietor from his gross income. For instance, the costs of health insurance can be deducted as legitimate business expenses if the insurance is offered to all employees. This means that family medical costs can be treated as a business expense under a medical reimbursement plan. Likewise, out of the goodness of its corporate heart, a corporation may pay premiums on as much as $50,000 of group term life insurance for each employee without having the payments taxed to the employees as compensation. The same is true of disability payments.

9. If an executive, or any employee, lives on company premises *for the convenience of the corporation,* he needn't pay anything for it, and the value of the lodgings (as well as company-supplied food, furniture and the like) isn't taxable to him.

10. There never are personal taxes on the corporation's income if it doesn't pay dividends, and if it can show the IRS that there are good reasons for holding on to the earnings. Maybe the company wants to expand, modernize, or get out of debt instead of enriching its stockholders; these are among the acceptable reasons for a successful corporation to pay little or no dividends.

11. During tax audits, a corporation can justify travel and entertainment deductions more easily than a partnership can. Corporate expenses are less likely to be disallowed as personal or nonbusiness for lack of proof as to whose travel and entertainment really was involved. (Still, lavish-living executives sometimes do get a corporation's expenses disallowed.)

12. If the owners of a business want to sell out, without incurring heavy taxes, their chances are better if it is incorporated. There can be a nontaxable reorganization in which shareholders trade their stock for shares of the company that buys the business, and perhaps for long-term employment contracts as well.

13. If you own stock in a corporation that goes broke, you can deduct your stock loss from your ordinary income if the corporation has processed the right papers for this special tax status. See your lawyer or CPA for details.

14. A corporation can bestow on chosen employees such goodies as qualified pension and profit-sharing plans, stock-purchase plans, and other tax-favored fringe benefits.

15. Retirement programs for corporate employees get better tax treatment than the so-called Keogh plans available to self-employed proprietors and partners. For example, a provision in ERISA (the new pension law) enables a small corporation to set up pensions for its older insiders, in a relatively short time, with pension benefits considerably larger than their compensation—and with the cost fully deductible by the corporation. Insurance companies can show you how.

16. An owner of a closely held corporation can shelter half or more of his total compensation (depending on his age) in a well-designed pension plan. There are three basic types of plans: Profit-Sharing, Money Purchase, and Defined Benefit. His company can make contributions to any of these plans in tax-free dollars. He won't be taxed until the benefits are made available to him, and then he'll get favorable tax treatment through a special ten-year averaging formula. Obviously, his benefits can pile up far faster than if he simply drew the money as current compensation, and invested it. Ask a tax expert for details.

Corporations Have Troubles Too

So much for the bright side. Now let's see what the disadvantages of the corporate tax structure can be:

1. Incorporation is costly—generally from $1,000 to $3,000. And corporations are legally required to keep detailed records, which also cost money.

2. Corporate income is taxed twice. First the corporation pays tax on its income before it can distribute any as dividends. Then the shareholders pay tax on the dividends.

3. If the corporation goes into the red, the owners can't write off the loss from their personal income taxes. In fact, the loss is "wasted." It can't be used currently by anyone. It can be carried forward, but only against profits within five years.

4. If the corporation is stingy with dividends, keeping back more money than its "reasonable needs," Uncle Sam can sock it with an accumulated-earnings tax of as much as 38.5 percent.

5. The idea that incorporating allows you to incur debts without being personally liable often turns out to be mistaken, especially when the corporation is small. Many banks and businesses won't accept a corporate signature without a personal guarantee by one or more of the execu-

tives. The persons most likely to get burned by a corporation's limited liability are tradesmen eager to extend credit for the sake of making sales.

6. Courts and the IRS may take a long skeptical look into a small corporation if it seems to be prospering yet isn't paying much tax, or if its owners don't act like persons doing business in corporate form, or if creditors complain to the authorities. Investigators know that a corporation may be only a shell. If just one or two people run a business, and their corporate label seems to be a tax fraud or an injustice to the public, courts can nullify the articles of incorporation. This is called "piercing the corporate veil." If it happens, creditors can pin personal liability on the shareholders for what would otherwise be corporate debts and liabilities. This fate often befalls sole proprietors or partnerships who switch to the corporate form. They're apt to overlook the requirements of corporate procedure (board meetings, shareholder meetings, notice of meetings, election of officers, fixing of compensation, and so on). They may neglect such simple things as getting new stationery, changing the sign on the door, notifying creditors of the change. They may treat the corporate checking account as their own. The result can be horrendous. Not only can they be held liable as if they were equal partners, but they can get hit with fraud penalties, and so can their corporation.

7. An executive's salary must be "reasonable" in IRS eyes, or it may be disallowed as a business expense, even if it's small. Salaries as low as $6,000 have been ruled unreasonable if the executives couldn't prove they did anything to earn this amount. Many businessmen who pay themselves small salaries as heads of struggling corporations never dream they'll be challenged, so they keep no documentation of the work they do.

8. Shareholders may sue a director of a corporation if his incompetence or misdeeds cause the company to lose money. Any secret profit that a director reaps because of his position (maybe through inside information, or maybe through boodle handed out to a dummy enterprise he owns) must be repaid to the corporation.

9. States often tax corporations more harshly than other enterprises. Sometimes they tax the capital stock or net worth, if the bite will be deeper this way than by a tax on net profits. Sometimes they concoct other special taxes that apply to corporate employees but not to proprietors or partners.

10. Corporations must pay unemployment-insurance taxes from which proprietors and partners are free. Also, the combined employer and employee tax under FICA is heavier than the tax on self-employed persons.

11. If corporate stock is offered to the general public, then the corporation must conform to the complicated rules of the Securities and Exchange Commission (SEC), the watchdog that seeks to protect gullible

investors from flimsy stock issues. If a closely held corporation wants to issue a little stock, individual states may regulate this under what are known as Blue Sky Laws.

However, you needn't feel too discouraged by these grim possibilities.

As we'll see in the next chapter, you can avoid many of the disadvantages of incorporation if you take certain options that the Internal Revenue Code makes available.

Meanwhile, if you want full information on ways to use the corporate form to build sheltered savings, you can ask for Judith H. McQuown's book called *Inc. Yourself: Get Rich with Your Own Corporation*. It is published by Macmillan. Any bookstore can order it for you.

Don't Incorporate Too Soon

Worldly-wise entrepreneurs hold off from incorporating their new enterprise until they've carefully studied the ideal business structure for it —and until the timing is right. Incorporating too early can bring a host of headaches.

The name and address of every new corporation application goes to federal, state, city, and county inspectors. It's their signal to research you. You'll soon get acquainted with a whole parade of auditors and inspectors bedeviling you for business licenses, zoning compliance, and umpteen other requirements. There'll be checkups to see whether you're obeying all the laws and ordinances. You'll be told to fill out dozens of forms and pay immediately for a flock of licenses.

These people work only during the busiest hours of your business day. So you'll be forced to invest a lot of prime time satisfying them. Some of them won't hestitate to interrupt you during a business conference in order to get a form filled out correctly. In one new company, the president was giving a sales talk to a prospective big customer when an investigator broke in to ask the president how much money the corporation had in the bank. The president winked at him, and nodded toward the customer, trying to indicate that this was private information. The inspector declined to take the hint, and repeated his question. This time the president told the man, "I'm with a customer. I'll answer your question as soon as I'm free." The clerk didn't want to wait. He snapped, "Obviously you have something to hide or you wouldn't mind answering."

A cash-poor enterprise can find itself pinched immediately if it incorporates too soon. Incorporation information is open to the public, and credit-bureau researchers often use it, giving the information to all their subscribers. This can deprive a new business of some of its money-leveraging options. For example, suppliers might put the corporation on a COD list.

Look before you leap. Postpone incorporating, or even drawing up a partnership agreement, until you're sure that you are ready.

KEEP THESE BASIC POINTS IN MIND:

- *Your profits, your taxes, and your ability to attract capital for expansion can be helped or hurt by the business structure you choose.*
- *Proprietorship is usually best for small, simple businesses. The rewards are solely yours—but so are the risks.*
- *If you have weak spots, consider taking one or more partners whose strengths can shore up those areas. But first make sure the prospective partners are compatible and trustworthy.*
- *Be sure to have a lawyer draw up a detailed, ironclad partnership agreement.*
- *A limited partnership is a good device when founders are short of money and backers are willing to let them run the business.*
- *Incorporating is expensive—but if it is legitimate, it offers many tax advantages and can protect owners from liabilities.*

10
Tax Breaks Through Subchapter S and Section 1244

We saw in Chapter 9 that there isn't any perfect all-purpose structure for a business, but that the corporate form is usually preferable to partnership or proprietorship. Still, business owners often groan at corporation taxes. At this writing, a corporation pays to Uncle Sam 17 percent of its first $25,000 of net income plus 20 percent of the second $25,000 plus 30 percent of the third $25,000 plus 40 percent of the fourth $25,000 plus 46 percent of net income in excess of $100,000. Then Uncle slices off another portion of this same income when it goes to shareholders as dividends. Another sad fact is that corporate losses may not be tax deductible in the year incurred, either by the company or the stockholders.

But don't despair. Luckily, the Federal Government has seen fit to let many business owners escape the heavy tax burden of the corporate form while enjoying its limited liability and other advantages.

You can form a hybrid entity called a pseudo corporation or a Subchapter S corporation after the section of the Internal Revenue Code which authorizes it. (It was passed as an add-on to the Technical Changes of 1958.)

This agreeable vehicle has other names too. You may hear it called a tax-option corporation, a small-business corporation, or an "electing small-business corporation." All these phrases stand for the same institutional form—even though an enterprise clothed in it needn't necessarily be small in anything except the number of shareholders. The amount of money involved, and the number of employees, doesn't matter. A Subchapter S corporation can be worth billions of dollars—or only hundreds of dollars—in capital or earnings.

More than 200,000 companies now are organized in this form. Known as "the workhorse" for twenty years, it is considered the old reliable of tax planning, the tried-and-true solution to many problems in closely held corporations and family businesses. If you're starting a small venture but hope to expand it into an empire without changing legal form, this could be just the compromise you need.

Sub S Corporations Don't Pay Income Taxes

Subchapter S corporations are corporations that elect not to be taxed as corporations. If an enterprise qualifies with the Internal Revenue Service as a Subchapter S corporation (you'll see how in a moment), the corporation isn't subject to federal income taxes. It files only an information return, Form 1120-S, instead of the regular corporate form.

Its income is taxed as if it were the stockholders' income. They include in their individual gross incomes their proportionate shares of the enterprise's profits and losses. This is what proprietors and partners do, of course. So their Sub S organization combines some advantages of proprietorships, partnerships, and regular corporations, yet suffers few of their disadvantages.

Only for tax purposes is this corporation a partnership. In other ways it is legally a corporation. Its owners have full corporate protection against liability for debts of the company. So if your business involves some danger of personal injury to clients or customers, or if you want to limit your risk of personal assets while retaining freedom to pay or not pay dividends as you choose—or if you just prefer to avoid the complexities of partnership—a Sub S corporation may be the way to go.

This isn't to say that Sub S is best for everyone. Wealthy owners may prefer to use a full-fledged corporation as a form of tax shelter, especially if it isn't likely to net more than $25,000—in which case its earnings will be taxed only 22 percent. Many individual taxpayers are in higher brackets than even the maximum corporate rate.

In considering Sub S, the question you and your tax adviser must decide is whether you'll come out better by reporting all your business income on your personal tax return, or by splitting the business income between a corporation and yourself through salaries, interest, and other deductible payments. There's also the factor of building up retirement benefits: you can set aside more for this purpose in a regular corporation. (More about that later in the chapter.) Generally speaking, the lower the tax bracket the business owners are in, the more advantageous Sub S becomes.

These Angles Attract Rich Investors

However, the rich can sometimes reap substantial tax savings on profits from a Sub S corporation. The juiciest of these benefits become available when they buy "Section 1244 stock." Section 1244 is worth several pages by itself, so we'll defer it momentarily. First let's look at other advantages.

One is the chance for income splitting. The owners of a profitable Sub S corporation can cut their taxes by giving or selling shares to children or other lower-tax-bracket members of the family. They can be stockholders without many of the burdens and restrictions of family partnerships. Since these relatives rarely have other income, their share of the profits is taxed at low rates or goes untaxed entirely. The investor can still claim their dependent exemptions because they don't live on their Sub S income. He can also reduce his estate taxes by gifts of stock.

In a case reported by *U.S. News & World Report,* three owners had seven children among them. By giving Sub S stock to each child, they split the income of roughly $200,000 ten ways. Thirteen personal exemptions were possible, including the owners' wives. The three officers drew salaries from their corporation; the remaining profits were reported on ten separate tax returns. The brothers saved about $17,000 in tax the first year, during which they and their families pulled $200,000 out of their corporation at an average tax rate of about 29 percent.

However, if you or your backers plan to use this tax-splitting device, you can expect the IRS to take a close look. There must be a real surrender of ownership, not just a sham. If the IRS successfully challenges your claim that minor children are bona fide shareholders, you lose Sub S status.

It's best to put children's shares in a custodial account—not a trust, because only a few types of trusts are eligible. An independent outsider, rather than a parent, is usually a preferable custodian for minors' shares. But sometimes a mother is acceptable, as shown in a 1977 case which the IRS lost. The corporation's stock was owned 52 percent by the parents (who collected 52 percent of the earnings) and 48 percent by the mother as custodian for their children, who were given interest-bearing promissory notes for their share of the earnings. Mom demonstrated to the court's satisfaction that she reviewed corporate affairs to ensure that the business was run in the kids' best interest, and she reviewed their tax returns, which reflected their proportion of the corporation's income. So the court ruled that the parents couldn't be taxed on the income allocated to their children's shares. That income is now putting the children through college.

Another talking point to potential backers with big income from other sources: they can use the start-up losses a new business usually suffers as a shelter for other income. This can slash their tax bill, as they combine their high personal income with the losses in the corporation. (Without Sub S, of course, a corporation's losses can be used only to shield corporate income, and can't ever be passed through to shield stockholders' income.)

Still other angles that sometimes attract moneyed people as well as struggling entrepreneurs:

The "double tax" on the corporation's profits is eliminated.

The corporate earnings on which the investors pay tax are regarded as dividends rather than compensation, and thus don't jeopardize any Social Security benefits the investors may be drawing. Nor do they pay self-employment tax on this income, even if they work in the company.

Unlike members of a partnership, who aren't employees in the eyes of the law, working stockholders of a Sub S corporation *are* employees. Thus they are eligible for the benign tax treatment of many fringe benefits available to employees—such as having the corporation pay their medical bills tax free, for example. Money received under an "accident or health plan for employees" isn't taxable income. A business may set up different medical plans for different classes of employees, or leave some out entirely. It isn't even essential that the plan be in writing. A tax court recently upheld hefty deductions for medical payments made, without a written plan, on behalf of just two people—the couple who owned and ran a small supply house. They'd formed a Sub S corporation (although a regular corporation probably would have done just as well in regard to medical payments) and provided no fringe benefits for a dozen part-time employees.

Until 1969, another big attraction of Sub S was the right to set up qualified pension and profit-sharing plans as generous as those available to stockholder employees of large corporations. But the Tax Reform Act of that year forbade Sub S corporations to contribute more than the Keogh Plan limits to employees owning more than 5 percent of the stock. However, the Keogh levels were later boosted to 15 percent of earned income or $7,500, whichever is less. Numerous firms find these levels adequate, so the parade into Sub S has speeded up again.

If the corporation will be buying machinery or equipment, or even furnishings, the investors can use the investment tax credit on their personal returns. (The investment credit is overlooked by many businesses, even though it can save taxes for any form of business. See Chapter 15.)

If the corporation chooses to hold on to its profits as operating capital instead of paying them out to stockholders, a Sub S corporation can do this with no danger of the penalty tax on accumulations of earnings, which is a menace to other corporations that don't pay generous dividends.

However, a Sub S shareholder must report as income his prorated share of the corporation's taxable income, even if the corporation kept it locked up. As in partnerships, where partners must pay tax on their shares of the income even though they don't withdraw it, some Sub S shareholders may be hard pressed to pay taxes on income which they haven't received. But the corporation might dole out just enough of its income so that they could pay their taxes. Remember, too, that once a shareholder has paid tax on undistributed income, it will be tax-free when he ultimately receives it. In effect, he has prepaid the tax, which is a favorite device for shifting tax from next year's expected big income to this year's smaller income.

Starting a Business with Less Investment

When you start a service business, or any kind of business that doesn't require you to lay in an inventory, you can use Sub S to get back part of your initial investment in tax savings. Here's how.

Organize the business on a cash basis. Start-up expenses, as you actually pay them, will be immediately tax-deductible. The income earned but not yet received won't be counted in your computation of taxable income. This creates a tax loss because of the negative cash flow, even though the business may be handsomely in the black on an accrual basis. The shareowners can deduct their proportion of the tax loss, just as if the business were unincorporated. This has the effect of reducing their investment.

Of course, the cash flow won't stay negative, if the business is run well. After a few months (or years), receivables will be pouring in so steadily that the cash flow should cover expenses or even create a surplus. Then you can terminate the Sub S election, if you wish. You can take advantage of Sub S for as long as it benefits you—for a year, or indefinitely. You can give up Sub S status simply by filing a statement of revocation. However, once you've switched out of it, you can't go back into it until you've waited five years.

How to Qualify as a Pseudo Corporation

Usually a corporation is eligible for Subchapter S tax treatment—

if it has no more than ten–fifteen stockholders, each of whom is a natural person (not another corporation, trust, or partnership);

if it is a domestic corporation;

if it isn't a member of an affiliated corporate group;

if all its stockholders agree to the Sub S election;

if it has only one class of stock;

if no more than 20 percent of its income is from "passive" sources such as rents, leases, dividends, royalties, interest, and sale or exchange of stock or securities.

The corporation must apply for this status through the Internal Revenue Service, using Form 2553. All shareholders of record must give written consent; a minor's consent may be given by him or his guardian.

The form must be filed at the time the corporation starts doing business, if you want it to be tax free during its first year. Or, if you choose Sub S when you're in operation, the form must be filed during a two-month interval, during the month immediately before or after the beginning of the fiscal year in which you want Sub S treatment. It's usually best to start business life in this form, rather than choosing it later, in order to take full advantage of accelerated depreciation benefits. If you incorporate at the start, the corporation will be the first user of whatever new depreciable property you buy for it, and it can take a bigger tax deduction than a later user can.

Once the election is made, and approved by the IRS, it stays in effect for all following years, unless you voluntarily terminate it or the IRS revokes it. Stay tuned and we'll soon see how you might inadvertently cause the IRS to revoke it.

After a corporation has operated under Sub S for five years, it can increase the number of stockholders to fifteen. It can also increase the number of shareholders to fifteen during its first five years if the additional shareholders get their stock by inheriting it.

One tricky point in the qualifying standards: what is "passive" income? The IRS challenged one company's Sub S status because it leased cars and trucks for a fixed rental. But the company won in court by showing that it repaired the cars and trucks, installed special equipment in them, and provided credit cards to purchase gasoline (which was billed to the corporation and then rebilled to the lessees).

Pitfalls for the Careless Corporation

As one court said in a 1972 decision, "Contrary to popular notion, pseudo-corporation status is far from simple. It has many pitfalls."

At least you don't have to worry that the IRS will revoke your Sub S privileges because you took that route in order to dodge taxes. The Internal Revenue Code is studded with clauses empowering the Treasury to annul tax advantages, even if there is full compliance with the very letter of the law, where the only purpose of an arrangement is to cut taxes. But the courts have held that a Sub S corporation may properly be formed even though the sole reason for doing so is to pay less tax. According to Russell C. Harrington, former Commissioner of Internal Revenue: "Tax evasion is illegal. Tax avoidance isn't. Every taxpayer has a right to adjust his affairs so that he minimizes his tax liability."

On the other hand, you can automatically forfeit the right to be treated as a Sub S corporation because of somebody's carelessness in not complying with some detail of the law. Here are ways this can happen:

A new stockholder neglects to give written consent.
Some of the stock becomes the property of a trust or a partnership.
The number of stockholders is increased above the legal limit.
The corporation issues another class of stock.
Stockholder loans become the equivalent of a second class of stock.
The corporation merges with another.
Changes in sources of income bring in more than 20 percent from "passive" sources.

Some of these pitfalls are worth more detail. Let's look at them.

One Stockholder Can Ruin You

The most common mistake is adding a new stockholder who doesn't consent to the Sub S election in time. This can happen when a single share of stock is given to a relative or friend. If he isn't tax-smart enough to file a written consent within thirty days, all the stockholders lose the advantages of being a Sub S corporation. Someone should follow up each transfer of stock to see that the consent is filed properly and on time.

Sometimes a Sub S stockholder tries to blackmail the corporation by threatening to revoke his consent if he isn't treated just right. To prevent this, your corporation should pass a bylaw requiring that if a consenting shareholder becomes displeased with the Sub S arrangement, he must sell his stock back to the corporation.

Another bylaw can prevent loss of Sub S status by a new shareholder's inaction whether through ignorance, negligence, or hostility: the bylaw can provide that each stock certificate must carry a proviso that no one may transfer stock without first offering it to the corporation. Then, even if the corporation doesn't intend to acquire any of its own stock, it gets a chance to tell the stockholder about the requirement for written consent before he transfers any of his stock.

Someone who wills stock to a trust for the benefit of his children, as part of an estate plan, can spoil the entire Sub S arrangement for all the shareholders. Certain trusts may now hold stock in a Sub S corporation. But many people's estate plans call for trusts that may be ineligible to hold such stock.

In one case, a Sub S stockholder included his stock in his estate, which is proper. But his will provided that the estate be divided equally among seven children—which raised the number of stockholders to sixteen. Sub S status for everyone went down the drain when the will was probated.

In another case, stock for two children was put in an estate. All was well for a year or two. But the executors kept the estate in existence long after paying all debts and all bequests. So the estate, no longer having a reason for existence as such, became a trust in the eyes of the revenuers. Good-by Sub S.

Often the original stockholders, or others later, pump more capital into a small Sub S corporation. The IRS sometimes tries to make a case that these contributions represent a second class of stock, disqualifying the company from the tax advantages. Two circuit appeals courts have ruled that this isn't necessarily so. But the IRS may keep trying.

It also contends that "loans" shareholders make to companies beyond their original equity stakes aren't really loans but rather are extra equity contributions amounting to a new class of stock. Courts have held in a few cases that the IRS rule covering such situations is tougher than Congress intended—that is, nothing in the law says a new class of stock is created just because a shareholder contributes additional equity. On the other hand, some courts say there's no such thing as nonstock equity. So you'd better be careful, and get extra-good legal advice, if you or others want to lend money to your company. One helpful precaution, often suggested by savvy tax lawyers, is to have all the shareholders make loans to the corporation in the same proportion as their stockholdings. Alternatively, a shareholder could build up his stock investment by making a capital contribution to the corporation.

Sometimes shareholders receive not only stock but notes for capital they put into the business. When most of a firm's assets are offset by such debt, the IRS says the stock doesn't mean much, and the "debt" really creates another set of ownership claims. A California partnership formed a Sub S corporation to operate a driving range. The corporation issued stock to the former partners. It also gave them notes, bearing no interest, equal to the capital each had put in. The IRS tried to revoke Sub S privileges and tax it as a standard corporation. Over six dissents, the Tax Court ruled in 1970 that simple installment debt, carrying no equity rights such as voting, didn't make another class of stock "merely because it creates disproportionate right to the assets." Better have your attorney look up this precedent if you plan to give promissory notes to your stockholders.

In another case, a shareholder tried to fatten his personal tax deduction by the amount of the corporation's indebtedness he had personally guaranteed. The court ruled that corporate debt which he guaranteed was not a loss to him—but that if the company defaults, and he has to repay the loan, he may then take the deduction.

If your corporation ceases to be classified as Sub S for any reason, it can't apply for this status again within five years, unless you obtain the Internal Revenue Commissioner's hard-to-get consent. As mentioned earlier, any merger automatically ends this delightful combination of corporate and unincorporated life. After one merger, owners squabbled, and dissolved the company with a tax-free reorganization that split it into two independent corporations again. They asked the Commissioner to let them be Sub S corporations. Sorry, he said, you relinquished favorable tax treatment when a merger seemed more desirable. Both companies had to wait five years before trying again.

If the Treasury decides that your enterprise is a regular corporation, even though you've been operating in the belief that you were Sub S, all undistributed earnings during the year in question will be vulnerable to the accumulated-earnings tax—unless by chance, you can prove that there were good business reasons for keeping the earnings in the company. It's unlikely that you can produce documentary proof, since Sub S corporations don't need it.

Another Boon for Investors: Section 1244 Stock

When setting up your corporation (Sub S or not), don't overlook a handy little section of the Small Business Tax Revision Act of 1958. This section, 1244, enables a "small business corporation," as defined therein, to issue stock. It offers one of the biggest tax breaks a small business can have, and there are absolutely no drawbacks to using it if your company is eligible.

Section 1244, enacted to encourage investments in small business, gives stockholders the right to write off against ordinary income up to $50,000 on a joint return ($25,000 on a single return) of any loss due to the failure of such a company during any tax year. Moreover, if you suffer a huge loss and your other income in the year isn't enough to absorb it, you may carry the loss back three years and deduct it from those years as well.

By contrast, if no Section 1244 plan has been adopted, only $3,000 of a net capital loss can be offset against ordinary income in any one year. Worse yet, if the loss is long-term, it takes two dollars of it to offset just one dollar of ordinary income.

Section 1244 stock is common stock (voting or nonvoting) in a "small business corporation." How small is small enough? The corporation's total equity capital—including the amount to be received under the plan—must be less than one million dollars. And the total amount of stock offered under the plan, plus other contributions to capital and paid-in surplus, must not be more than a half-million.

The written plan for issuing the stock must be adopted by resolution of the corporation's board of directors. This plan must state the maximum amount to be issued and the period—no longer than two years—during which it will be issued. It must also stipulate that no shares offered under the plan will be issued for services, or for stock or other securities. That's all. Simple, isn't it?

As implied three paragraphs ago, losses on the sale, exchange, or worthlessness of this stock are treated as ordinary losses rather than capital losses sustained by an individual. Better yet, any gain in selling the stock is still capital gain. Think about what this can mean to a high-bracket investor.

Let's say he's in the top bracket, 70 percent. If he buys stock in your company, and the company goes broke, he is assured that he'll recover 70 percent of his loss through lower income taxes. If your company thrives, he can keep for himself (except for any state taxes) 80 percent of any long-term gain. Thus Uncle Sam will share his risk of loss on an 80–20 basis, but will share only 20–80 in the potential profits. Few gambles offer such attractive odds.

As for you, the majority owner-operator, if for any reason your business fails, you'll be considerably better off with Section 1244 stock. You can probably put in for tax deductions or refunds based on a net operating loss of as much as $50,000. This is much more valuable to you than the potential use of a $50,000 net-capital-loss carry-forward, which is what you get if your equity isn't translated into Section 1244 stock. At $3,000 a year, how many years will you need to recover your $50,000?

All this and Sub S too! You don't have to choose between Sub S and

Section 1244. You can take the tax benefits of both by combining your stock issue with your election of Sub S tax treatment. If you do this, any current operating losses of your corporation are immediately deductible by the owners, and will trim down the tax basis of their stock and debt. Any additional losses suffered by the owners when they sell their stock —or when the stock becomes worthless—will be tax-deductible as ordinary losses, not capital losses.

Watch the Limit on Deductible Losses

Many people think that stockholders of a Sub S corporation may deduct their proportionate share of the corporation's net operating losses, no matter how big these losses are. They often overlook a legal limit on how much loss a shareholder may deduct. This amount may not exceed the total of—

a) the adjusted tax basis of his stock in the corporation (this usually means what he paid for it) plus

b) the adjusted tax basis of any indebtedness of the corporation to him.

This means, in general, that you must have put enough money into the corporation so that you have in effect paid for the loss you are reporting. If your pro rata share of the corporation's net operating loss exceeds this, the excess isn't deductible—not that year, nor as a carry-forward or carry-back to other years, even if you later buy more stock or make more loans to the business.

Notice that operating losses are different from capital losses. Although you report your share of the corporation's long-term capital gain, you may not deduct any capital losses it incurs. They are used by the corporation as carry-over losses to offset future capital gains.

"Thin" Can Be Beautiful

There's one other option in forming a corporation that you may not know about. It's called "thin" incorporation, and it sometimes can ease a new company's tax burden. It is an altogether separate and different device from Subchapter S incorporation.

The phrase refers to a new corporation's capital structure. In forming a company, you or other investors can transfer part of your personal assets to the new corporation, partly in exchange for stock (known as equity investment) and partly as a loan (considered a debt investment). As the corporation pays interest on the loan, this becomes a tax-deductible expense for the corporation—and as the debt is repaid, capital is returned to the investors tax-free.

Thin incorporation avoids the double tax by paying interest instead of dividends to the shareholder. Sometimes it also lets the company hoard profits for the legitimate purpose of paying debts, thus avoiding a possible penalty tax on "unreasonably" accumulated earnings.

But there can be problems. The IRS is likely to charge that interest payments are disguised dividends. Whenever it doesn't see an obvious debtor–creditor relationship, it's suspicious of borrowing arrangements.

To protect yourself and the company, make sure that the corporation draws up proper notes as proof of debt. Establish the debt in your accounts, show it on the financial statements, record it in the minutes. The note should set forth an unconditional promise to pay a reasonable, fixed rate of interest at specified intervals. It should also stipulate that the payments won't depend on corporate earnings. The debt holder's right to sue to enforce payments should be specifically recognized. The debt mustn't be subordinate to other debts.

In case you're challenged anyway, try to have evidence that outside creditors would have seriously considered making the same loan the investor did.

The amount of debt should be reasonable—no more than 3½ times the equity investment in the corporation. The schedule of repayment should show that the debt can be paid off in the normal operation of the business.

As we've seen, "thin" incorporation offers financial advantages to the corporation and its chief backers. However, there are possible disadvantages too. The debts may injure the corporation's credit rating. Moreover, the corporation is shouldering commitments for payments that it may be hard-pressed to meet. If you're starting an enterprise on a shoestring, this is a risky way to incorporate.

KEEP THESE BASIC POINTS IN MIND:

- *A Sub S corporation is taxed like a partnership or proprietorship, yet gives its owners the protections of a corporation.*
- *The owners of a profitable Sub S corporation can cut their taxes by giving shares to lower-bracket members of their families.*
- *Start-up losses of a Sub S corporation can be used to shelter the owners' personal income from other sources.*
- *A Sub S corporation can accumulate earnings without danger of the penalty tax levied on other corporations.*

- *Sub S status can be automatically forfeited through inadvertence. Make sure your corporation stays in compliance with every detail of the law.*
- *Losses on Section 1244 stock can be written off against ordinary income rather than reported as capital losses. This is a big attraction to upper-bracket investors.*
- *"Thin" incorporation avoids the double tax on dividends by paying interest on a debt to its shareholders instead of dividends. But be prepared for a challenge from the IRS.*
- *Another danger of "thin" incorporation is that the necessity of making payments on the debt can strangle the company's cash flow.*
- *Obtain professional advice on the matters discussed in this chapter.*

11

Uncle Sam Can Help You

Matt Lesko was puzzled. Should he stock up on potatoes, which were selling at high prices? Or sell what he had? He looked through the U.S. Department of Agriculture directory and found the potato expert at (202)655-4000. He learned everything he wanted to know about potatoes.

A Long Island truck driver was desperate. He'd bought a luncheonette, by mortgaging his house and borrowing from friends. His new business was shrinking. He had to keep cutting payroll. Within a year, earnings had fallen by half, and didn't even provide enough to restock supplies. His wife wrote to the Small Business Administration in Washington, D.C.:

> Each month our gross becomes less, yet our bills stay the same. We've tried so many ways to improve the business, but it is hopeless.
>
> If you can give us any information on our business, please let us hear it.

Without charge, the SBA brought together the luncheonette owner and a consultant who had spent his life in the restaurant business. In six months the little enterprise was back on firm ground.

Tack Yonemoto, a carnation grower in California, was badly hurt by foreign competition. Carnations imported from Colombia stole half his market. He turned to the Economic Development Administration, a branch of the U.S. Department of Commerce. He told a Los Angeles official of EDA: "Until 1977, I had a hundred people working at peak season and fifty employees year around. Now I have thirty people year around, and fifty at peak."

EDA can give both financial and technical help to small businesses hurt by imports. It lent Yonemoto a sizable sum to help him diversify, and put

161

him in touch with a greenhouse in Pennsylvania which taught him to grow and market geraniums in addition to his carnations.

Federal Employees Will Work for You

Few small businesses know that the U.S. Government offers literally thousands of services to business, mostly free or at low cost.

It can send one or several expert consultants to work closely with you. It can give you quick information on almost any business-related problem —such as whether to diversify into a new field, how to find products to sell, what prices to charge, and how your enterprise is likely to be affected by market conditions in any part of America or the world.

It will do free research for you. It will publicize your products in foreign markets. It will help you get government contracts. It may even help you train employees, reimburse you for the training costs, and pay part of their wages.

In this chapter we will see how the Small Business Administration makes loans to entrepreneurs who can't get backing elsewhere and we'll see how it (and other agencies) provide fund transfusions to businesses that are failing through no fault of their own.

The SBA is far more than a source of capital. Although it doesn't trumpet the fact, it can be a helpful adviser even if you haven't borrowed from it and aren't hurting. It also offers what it calls "procurement assistance," which means help in selling your product or service to some of the thousands of government workplaces, and in getting manufacturing contracts or subcontracts for defense and space programs. This chapter will show many ways you can benefit by asking help from the SBA and other government people. The nice thing is that these people are free, because they're on the public payroll.

Experiment That Never Ended

Small business represents about half of the U.S. economy, in terms of output and in terms of private payrolls. It created 5.5 million new jobs in the first eight years of the 1970s. For every big business there are about fifty small ones. The healthier they are, the stronger and more competitive the U.S. economy.

Yet it's hard for some of them to stay healthy. They seldom get the services, advice, and information that are available to a big company at the touch of a button. Washington began to realize this as long ago as the 1930s, and tried to do something to rectify the disadvantage. One after another, three temporary agencies were set up to help small business financially and otherwise—the Reconstruction Finance Corporation, the Smaller War Plants Corporation, the Small Defense Plants Administration. The last of these experiments was phased out in 1953, but Congress was determined that federal help for small business shouldn't die. So it created the present Small Business Administration.

Its purpose, as set forth by Congress, was to promote "free competitive enterprise" by helping out the smallest and weakest competitors. Yet since nobody was sure what small business really needed, the SBA's enabling statute was vague. To encourage the agency's independence, the legislation made it directly responsible to the president. Policy-making was quietly left to the SBA itself, subject only to the proviso that it act "in the public interest."

Lately, on Capitol Hill, interest in the problems of small business has sharpened. Congress has saddled the SBA with an array of additional programs—and with political hacks hired as favors to the White House and Congress. A few cases of corruption have surfaced. Turnover at the top has been dizzy. Only two chiefs have lasted more than four years, and the average stay has been twenty-one months. The SBA budget ($935 million) and its staff (about 4,300) haven't grown much.

Who Is "Small" Enough?

The SBA is also beset by another sort of trouble: deciding what size company is elgible for its services. If 98 percent of American firms have fewer than 50 employees, aren't all these—and no others—eligible? Not necessarily. Standards vary all over the lot, and can be shifted on impulse.

In 1979 the administrator of the SBA, A. Vernon Weaver, who ran a small insurance company in Arkansas and had been a classmate of President Carter at the Naval Academy, told the *Harvard Business Review:*

> What's large in some types of business is small in others. What's the definition of a small automobile manufacturer? American Motors? We once said so (because their market share was less than 5 per cent) and everybody screamed at us. For manufacturers, we say the size standard should probably be the number of employees. For service businesses, it probably should be the gross receipts. We have specific size standards for hundreds of industries. But there's no answer that everybody is going to agree on.

Earlier in this book we saw how a firm with a handful of employees might be a multimillion-dollar enterprise. Likewise, a company with thousands of workers may struggle along on small sales. Therefore manufacturing firms are considered "small" if they have fewer than 250 workers in some industries, fewer than 1,500 in others. A steel rolling mill is small until it has 2,500 workers, while a household-appliance manufacturer's ceiling is 500. Construction companies grossing under $9.5 million can usually qualify as small. A wholesaler may not gross more than $9 million —or $22 million, depending on the industry. Retail and service businesses get the "small" label when their annual volume is below a top that varies from $2 million to $7.5 million in different industries.

If you're interested in qualifying for various kinds of SBA help, investigate the standards for each kind. Being rejected for one doesn't mean you're disqualified for another. A company too big to qualify for an SBA-guaranteed loan may be small enough to bid on a procurement contract reserved for small firms.

These standards are due for an overhaul anyhow, with no hint which way they'll be rewritten. If you qualify now but are near the border, you'll be smart to enroll in SBA programs immediately, in order to be protected by a so-called grandfather clause which may allow those already in a program to stay in.

Itching to Help

The SBA is the only federal agency specifically designed to help and advise the practicing or prospective small-business man. However, hundreds of middle-level bureaucrats all over Washington (and in other federal offices around the country) are fountains of knowledge in their specialties, and are dying to tell someone about it. Federal bureaucracy, the object of everyone else's scorn, is a gold mine for information seekers. If a bureaucrat doesn't know the answer to your question, he can often refer you to someone who does, and is pleased to be asked.

The U.S. Government is concerned in various ways with virtually any business or technical problem you can imagine. There's almost nothing you can't get answered with a phone call or letter to the right desk. Here are general guidelines:

Do you need an expert on any topic? Call the Library of Congress National Referral Center. It lists thousands of specialists on university staffs, in government, or working for nonprofit organizations. Lists of experts within the government only, on any topic, are available through the Federal Information Centers in about a hundred cities. Most have toll-free tie lines. Check your phone book under United States Government.

Do you need information about a domestic company or industry—such as our competitors, for example? You can get it from one of the hundred-odd industry analysts in the Bureau of Domestic Business Development, which is a division of the Department of Commerce.

Do you need a profile of a foreign company? The Commerce Department probably has it, in the World Traders' Data Report.

Are you planning to mail many similar packages of an unusual kind—maybe tree saplings, or hookahs? Take a sample package to your postmaster; he may suggest improvements. Or get advice from higher-ups in the Postal Service.

Are you looking for a business to buy? Bargains may be available through the SBA. If a business got an SBA loan and can't meet the lenient repayment terms, the SBA may foreclose and auction it off to anyone who'll take over the loan. Such a business probably was badly run. You might turn it around without much trouble, if you have a good business head, or if you merely seek some of the help available, as described in this chapter and the next. (Remember, half of being smart is knowing where you're dumb.) Get the SBA booklet entitled "Buying and Selling a Small Business."

New Markets for You

Are you looking for new territories to enter? Maybe you need to know about population patterns, or family incomes, or business sales, or types of housing. Maybe your decision hinges on how many homes have fireplaces, or which counties have the most jewelry stores. Try the Data Users' Service at the Bureau of the Census. Every five years the Census Bureau goes out and updates its facts on most small businesses. It is now working with both the Treasury and Commerce Departments to get these data computerized.

Census data can keep you in step with your customers. One garment maker, for example, found that the population in his market area had a high concentration of teen-agers. So he added new styles aimed at this group.

A small manufacturer of automobile dashboard accessories expanded after asking the Census Bureau, "Where are the high concentrations of automobiles?" and then, "Which areas have many auto-supply stores and variety stores?" since these outlets did the best job with his products.

Let's say you're a florist, yearning to open a second shop in another city. You can find out the average number of inhabitants needed to support a florist's shop, which happens to be 9,000. You can also find out how many florists' shops already exist in any city. So if a city's population is 140,000 and there are 13 florists, you know there's room for another.

But if there are 15, you'd better look for a different city, because 15 times 9,000 is 135,000—barely enough to support the florists already there. You can find communities where there are 15,000 or more residents per florist.

For step-by-step instructions in picking good areas for various kinds of business, write to the SBA for its pamphlet "Using Census Data in Small Plant Marketing."

Help in Developing New Products

Would you like to know of inventions that are available for new-product development? The U.S. Patent Office will send you lists. The SBA also puts out a monthly "Products List Circular." These publications are fertile sources of new-product ideas. Some inventions they list can be bought. Some you can use by paying a royalty to the patent owner. Many others were developed by the government's own vast research programs; these are usually available, free but nonexclusively, to anyone who wants them. Lists of these, grouped by industry, are available from the Office of Technical Services.

Maybe you need to search scientific journals for information about a material, process, or invention. The reference workers in the Science and Technology Division of the Congressional Library will do research free, or for a fee, and mail you the results. (However, it's easier for them not to bill you, because that bureaucratic monster has to go up the big Hill to put in a $100 invoice.)

If you need research in the food field, or in textiles, leather, or chemicals, the Agricultural Marketing Service of the Department of Agriculture may give you free or low-cost help. Many other kinds of technical research is done by the National Bureau of Standards, which welcomes questions.

Maybe you have an energy-saving idea. The U.S. Department of Energy may be happy to help you develop it, by giving you free technical assistance and by guaranteeing a bank loan.

Would you like to sell a product abroad? Get in touch with the Commerce Department's Bureau of International Commerce. It keeps up-to-date lists of foreign buyers, distributors, and agents, and will help you make contact with the right ones.

To start your export program, you can ask the Commerce Department to include you in its American International Traders Index. This directory lists more than 20,000 U.S. manufacturers who want to sell in foreign markets, and gives information about their wares. Buyers abroad consult it constantly.

When your new product is ready for export, tell the Commerce Department's New Product Information Service about it. The service will probably publicize it and test the interest in foreign markets. Later you can arrange with the department to have exhibitors display it at the U.S. trade centers abroad—in Milan, Stockholm, Tokyo, London, Frankfurt, and Bangkok.

Reading for Profit

We could go on, but you get the idea. Tons of up-to-date information and advice are on tap. If you'd like an overview of the pamphlets and books available, send for a free fifteen-page booklet, "Publications for Business," published by the Department of Commerce. It lists not only commerce publications but valuable literature from other departments. To get it, write to Superintendent of Documents, Government Printing Office, Washington, D.C. 20402.

About 29,000 titles are available from the Superintendent of Documents. They range over every field in which an agency of the Federal Government takes an interest. Many are thick, bound volumes. To avoid making a blind purchase, you may be able to examine some of the books at the GPO bookstore in Boston, Chicago, Kansas City, San Francisco, Los Angeles, Atlanta, Dallas, Denver, or New York. Or you may find some in public libraries. The *complete* line of GPO publications is available only at the bookstore in the GPO's Washington headquarters.

Other ways you might look at a book before buying: Call the Federal Building in your city, and ask for the branch office of the government agency concerned with the publication. Maybe someone there will let you examine a bookshelf copy. Or phone one of the previously mentioned Federal Information Centers, and see if it can suggest where you might look at a copy.

Finding Out Where to Ask

Now let's suppose you're up against a specific problem. You don't know what agency among the hundreds in Washington, what person or persons within that agency, and what publications will be useful in solving that problem. How do you find out?

First try one of the Federal Information Centers, mentioned a few pages back as places that can find you free experts in government. These centers also do much more. They're operated by the General Services Administration, and are set up "to answer any questions about government programs, activities, or agencies."

If they can't guide you, write a short letter to your congressman. He and his staff have quick access to the Library of Congress, the Government Printing Office, the committees of Congress, and the executive agencies. Every congressional office has employees doing "casework," as it's called—helping constituents get services from the bureaucracy. On the theory that this wins votes, a congressman is happy to help any resident of his district who writes a letter requesting a reasonable service.

One small-business man wanted to see what a contract between a soft-drink manufacturer and a bottler should look like. The trade association refused to supply one. So he asked his congressman, who quickly discovered that Congress had held hearings on the topic. A sample contract was in the hearing record.

Here are services that your congressman can provide:

1. Information on the status of pending legislation.

2. Copies of public laws, House and Senate bills, committee testimony, and committee reports.

3. A list of publications in a specified field, from which you can make your choices and order direct from the Government Printing Office.

4. A call to any government agency to find its latest publications about the topic you're investigating.

5. A request to the Congressional Research Service (CRS) for research material it may have available. A CRS pamphlet addressed to congressmen explains its service this way:

> While we cannot undertake research for your constituents—please, no term papers or master's theses—we do try to help with that portion of your constituent mail which can be answered with readily available material. Rather than telephoning each inquiry, many offices find it faster and more convenient to send the letters directly to us. We will return them with the proper materials for transmittal to your constituents.

Sometimes the best the congressman can do is find out what particular agency or committee should know the answer to your question. You can take it from there, by calling or writing to the Public Information Office of that agency. The PIO is paid to give information to the public, and is usually well informed and eager to help. Always ask the PIO for citations of printed material written by that agency (or others) and available through the Government Printing Office.

Although bureaucracies prefer to answer questions through their information officers, sometimes they'll put you in direct contact with an agency expert who may be the only person in all government with the specialized information you're seeking. Generally, how much help a bureaucrat is willing to give may depend on how you ask for it. He may hang up on you, or he may spend hours digging up facts and advice. If a PIO doesn't help you, you can write for an in-house telephone directory of the agency, and try calling middle-level officials direct, as Matt Lesko did in the first paragraph of this chapter.

With a really tough problem, it may take numerous calls and a bit of luck to locate the best informant. One small-business man needed facts about the golf-cart industry. None of the manufacturers would give him sales and market data. But somebody in the Treasury Department, of all places, remembered that there had been a court case against a Polish golf-cart manufacturer charged with violating U.S. trade laws by selling carts in the United States at cut rates. In the court testimony, all the major U.S. makers divulged their sales figures, and their percentage of the market, to back up their claim that the importer hurt their business. All that testimony was available in the Public Documents Room of the Customs Service.

Help in Training Your Employees

Government wants to put people to work—especially women, minorities, and the handicapped. Most of these people need a chance as beginners—in "entry-level jobs," as social workers say—but big business can't provide many such openings. Entry-level work is a small-business specialty. Knowing this, the government offers many programs to help you train beginners on the job. Maybe you can use one of the following:

The Comprehensive Employment and Training Act provides federal funds for training unemployed or underemployed workers. If you hire them, the government reimburses you for part of their wages, for the fees to instructors you bring in to train them, and for your training materials and supplies. You do the training yourself, but CETA experts will give you advice if you have problems. They're especially interested in anyone you hire from welfare rolls, but will also help you train school dropouts and other "disadvantaged" types.

Physically or mentally handicapped workers can be trained through the government's vocational-rehabilitation programs. The handicapped often make unusually reliable and dedicated employees.

The Defense Department wants business to train servicemen who are about to be released from the Armed Forces. This cooperative effort is called Project Transition. It's useful to many small firms that are interested in hiring and training veterans.

The Labor Department's Bureau of Apprenticeship and Training will help you set up an apprentice program in your business, so that youngsters can learn a trade there. Write to this bureau for information.

Get to Know the SBA—Just in Case

The Small Business Administration may have troubles near the top, due to Washington politics, but across the country in its ninety-three local offices you'll find dedicated people with long experience in counseling all kinds of small enterprise. They can tell you how other business owners solved problems like yours.

Maybe you think you have no problems. Even so, making some personal acquaintances in the SBA would be worthwhile. By knowing ahead of time what resources are available, you can tap them in time of need.

A good first step would be to phone the nearest field office and ask it to send you a list of its 250-odd free booklets and its separate list of publications sold for $1 to $3. Just scanning these lists may awaken you to unthought-of possibilities for improving your business.

Don't send for pamphlets yet, though. Drop in at the SBA office and browse through the ones you wanted. Afterward, maybe you can chat with some of the people in the office. It's a good principle to make friends before you need them. If there's one federal office that's likely to be especially useful to you, it's your local SBA office.

Rescues from Disaster

Consider the SBA's "disaster lending" and its other programs of financial aid to firms caught in a crisis through no fault of their own. Who can predict when a flood or earthquake might wreck your business? Who knows when some other external ill wind might blow red ink all over you?

There is wide agreement that what the SBA does best is disaster lending, a specialty it inherited from the Reconstruction Finance Corporation of the 1930s. After a natural disaster, SBA lending officers, accompanied by droves of volunteers, race to the scene to hand out forms and money to owners of damaged businesses. After Hurricane Agnes in 1973, the SBA made 215,000 loans for a total of $1.3 billion. The interest rate was only 1 percent, repayment could be spread over thirty years, and the dazed borrower got "forgiveness" on the first $5,000—that is, he didn't have to pay it back.

The majestically generous terms of disaster loans tend to bring mendicants from under rocks. To deter them, Congress overhauled the entire program in 1977, eliminating the forgiveness clause and setting interest rates between 1 and 6.62 percent depending on the type of loan. Still, the SBA lends as much as $3 billion per year to small-business men hit by disasters. It processed 60,000 loan applications in the New York area alone after the great snowstorms and cold waves of 1978. These are direct loans made right out of the U.S. Treasury, and aren't counted against the SBA's budget for regular business loans. Disaster loans range from $250 all the way to a quarter-million dollars, and average around $6,600.

The SBA also lends to small businesses that are uprooted by the construction of new highways or military bases, or that lose their customers because a military base closes. When the 1972 SALT agreement cut Montana's total of Air Force missile sites and thereby hurt small enterprises thereabouts, the SBA rode to the rescue with a loan program specially for them.

These SBA loans set the stage for con games. Shysters claim to know how to package SBA loan applications and speed up approval, if the applicant pays the "consultant" a few thousand dollars. After the fee is paid, the con man may tell the victim that the loan was disapproved, when it really wasn't even sent to SBA. Another swindle offers influence in buying supplies and equipment from bankrupt SBA-backed companies. William Bowling, SBA assistant inspector general, has warned: "These characters are stating or implying that they are SBA employees or SBA-approved consultants. No loan packager has any influence with SBA loan officers. . . . And the SBA doesn't sell furniture on the phone." If you want an SBA loan, or want surplus government equipment at low prices, get in touch with the SBA office personally. It will tell you how to apply.

Harassed by Uncle Sam? Ask Him for Help

In the late 1960s the SBA took on still another job—that of righting wrongs done by other government agencies and programs. It now tries to give back to small businesses what Uncle Sam takes away, in effect, through costly and burdensome regulations. It has a "chief counsel for advocacy"—a position created by Congress to give the nation's smaller enterprises an independent spokesman and defender within the federal bureaucracy.

As the first chief advocate President Carter appointed Milton D. Stewart, a former venture capitalist and lawyer, and former president of the National Small Business Association. He organized a staff of five case-workers, and said in an interview:

> Large government feels most comfortable with large businesses. The bureaucracy is innately hostile to small business. . . . If the government does big things for big business and little things for little business, nobody should be surprised that the relative growth rate of big and small

business is disproportionate, and small business and the economy are the losers.

Take the area of regulation. The lives of 20,000 chemical companies are jeopardized by Environmental Protection Administration regulations. . . . It is my job to say to Treasury that there are other priorities than the ones the tax ideologues have. And to say to people in Labor that as anxious as we are to raise working standards, we shouldn't do it by jeopardizing many small businesses, since it is going to cost us jobs in the long run.

He's had some successes. When Agriculture Department inspectors "went out of their way to make it tough" for an egg plant in the northeast, says Nick Kalcounos, chief caseworker in the SBA Advocacy office, "we called Agriculture and the inspectors were transferred to other areas."

The SBA has handed out money to some small companies to compensate for losses they suffered at the hands of the Consumer Product Safety Commission. CPSC discovered that a chemical called Tris, used by the garment industry to make children's sleepwear meet CPSC's own flammability standard, causes cancer in experimental rats. So CPSC ordered all Tris-treated garments removed from retail stores. The agency further decreed that the 110 manufacturers of these theoretically cancer-causing pajamas and nighties must pay all costs, estimated at $200 million. The manufacturers soon challenged this order in court, and part of the burden was shifted elsewhere in the distribution chain. Nevertheless, the manufacturers were still in deep trouble. Their sleepwear was now unsalable. Many faced write-offs as high as a million dollars.

Hearing of their plight, SBA invoked a 1974 law authorizing loans to small businesses that have suffered economic injury because of any action by the Federal Government. It started sending out checks. But a snag developed. Under a quirk in SBA eligibility rules, most of the makers of little girls' nighties were "too big" to qualify for loans, although they were the same size as pajama makers who did qualify. This was because any company with fewer than 500 employees was eligible if it manufactured boys' sleepwear, but a girls'-sleepwear company couldn't qualify with more than 250.

"We got a lot of pressure from manufacturers who weren't going to get any money," said William Pellington, who had spent most of his career setting SBA size standards. "That happens all the time—and when you have a crisis, it's only reasonable to make a change." The SBA did, announcing that if a pajama or nightie maker had lost more than a quarter of its revenues because of the Tris ban, the agency wouldn't recompute the company's eligibility downward. It handed out some $6.9 million.

Since 1971 the SBA has lent more than $55 million for costs laid onto small business by consumer-protection regulations, and another $48 million for compliance with the Occupational Safety and Health Act, passed in 1970.

Learning to Live with OSHA

Throughout the 1970s, few regulation agencies have hit small companies harder than the Department of Labor's Occupational Safety and Health Administration (OSHA). Dozens of foundries in seven states had to close permanently, even with SBA loans, because they couldn't afford to meet standards set by OSHA inspectors. "Our mail is telling us the inspectors are mean, arrogant, and petty," one caseworker told United Press International. "They have an attitude that 'We're going to nail you to the wall unless you comply with our rules.' "

OSHA rules fill a 330-page book. The average small employer is hardpressed merely to read and understand the regulations, let alone obey them all. SBA can probably advise you about rules in your particular line of work—especially if you happen to be in one of five industries in which small firms are numerous: roofing and sheet metal; meat and meat products; lumber and wood products; manufacturers of mobile homes, campers, and snowmobiles; and stevedoring. These industries have relatively high injury and illness rates, so OSHA is pushing hard to make them safer.

Under the law, any one of your employees, or a labor union representing them, can file a complaint that you're violating safety or health standards—just because a crew size is "unsafe," for example. You can't fire or retaliate against anyone for filing the complaint. When OSHA inspectors arrive, usually unannounced, whoever complained is entitled to accompany them on the visit. The inspectors are required by law to inspect fully, and to cite and fine you if they find any violations—but they aren't allowed to give advice about how to correct the hazard. That's your problem.

The law even forbids OSHA from making a "dry run" inspection and warning you in advance before citing and fining you. However, you can get pointers from other sources. SBA will tell you how to request a free health-hazard evaluation from the government's National Institute of Occupational Safety and Health. If you have a safety engineer on your staff, he can get training from OSHA and from National Safety Council chapters. Your workers'-compensation-insurance carrier may also be helpful, but its approval doesn't guarantee OSHA approval.

SBA says you can get even better advice, perhaps, through trade associations, other employers who've been inspected, and equipment manufacturers. Your suppliers are probably the best advisers of all. They constantly visit plants, and know the day-to-day problems. Ask a lift-truck salesman to look at your forklift procedures, a fuse salesman to examine wiring, a pneumatic-tube dealer to check your air lines. Their word isn't final, but can alert you to worrisome points.

Anyhow, OSHA is beginning to ease off, because of widespread howls from business. In 1979 it eliminated more than two thousand detailed rules. For example, its new manual simply says fire extinguishers "must be accessible," instead of spelling out how high above the floor they must be mounted.

But as OSHA calms down, consumer complaints about defective or dangerous products seem to be getting louder. For example, sellers of old machines can be haled into court for defects in the machines, if the original maker is out of business. In such a case, the last seller becomes liable for injuries caused by the machine. Consequently, some companies are junking machinery rather than take the risk of selling it.

Washington will help you keep up with what's brewing in this field too. Weekly listings of the last product-safety actions, and the problems under scrutiny, are available free from the Consumer Product Safety Commission, Washington, D.C. 20207.

IRS and FTC: Less Fearsome Now

Of course, the arm of government most widely feared by small business is the Internal Revenue Service. Still, if you can't afford expert tax lawyers, or a tax-smart treasurer and controller, you can get pretty good information on how to stay on the sunny side of the tax collectors. Send for the SBA's Small Markets Aid No. 142, "Steps in Meeting Your Tax Obligations," and the IRS's own "Tax Guide for Small Businesses," published yearly. And if you want to dispute IRS for a sum up to $5,000, you can now go to tax court without any lawyer at all. (It used to be that this streamlined procedure for court reviews wasn't available if the amount was more than $1,500.) For more information, write to Clerk of the U.S. Tax Court, 400 Second St., N.W., Washington 20217.

Another dreaded agency is the Federal Trade Commission, which is charged with responsibility for curbing "unfair or deceptive" practices including false advertising, misbranding, and too-tough collection practices. Its cease-and-desist notices can put a mail-order firm out of business. It comes down hard on many other kinds of enterprise for misleading customers, substituting shipments without customer authorization, filling orders too slowly, and neglecting to offer refunds. If you run a retail or service business, and offer credit terms, you may get in hot water with the FTC under the Truth-in-Lending Act.

However, the FTC will now give you very sound legal advice in advance (at no charge) if you ask about something you're planning to do. The old rule was that such advice wasn't legally binding on the FTC, but that is changing. Congress recently amended the Truth-in-Lending and Equal Credit laws so that you're protected from liability for missteps under those statutes if you show that you were relying in good faith on advice received from appropriate federal employees.

Regulatory agencies will seldom certify the legality of past actions. You can only ask about something you *plan* to do, such as charging customers for making copies of lost sales slips, or asking for a copy of tax returns to verify their creditworthiness. (Both of these got FTC okays, incidentally.)

Many firms are afraid to ask, of course, because if the answer is no, they've called attention to themselves. But they can have a lawyer or accountant ask, without revealing their identity. Or they can look over advice the FTC gave other companies. FTC usually makes this available, sometimes with indexes that help find answers to specific questions.

For most small firms, a bigger worry than the legality of a proposed new procedure is the chance that their long-established procedures may break some newly made law they don't know about. The fastest way to check on this, without alerting inspectors, is to write or call the nearest FTC office and simply ask for copies of relevant federal and state laws. Or you can write Truth in Lending, Federal Trade Commission, Washington 20580.

The "Truth-in-Lending" Act

The "Truth-in-Lending" Act passed by Congress sets forth a code that governs the area of consumer credit-cost disclosure. The intent is to provide for "informed use of credit" by making consumers more aware of the cost of credit extended to them.

The code provides that the amount of the finance charge in connection with any consumer credit transaction shall be determined as the sum of all charges (paid directly or indirectly by the person to whom the credit is extended) imposed by the creditor. The finance charge includes:

   a. service or carrying charge;
   b. loan fee, finder's fee, or similar charge;
   c. fee for an investigation or credit report;
   d. interest, time-price differential, and any amount payable as a percentage, discount, or other mode, or as additional charges;

    e. premium or other charge for any guarantee or insurance protecting the creditor against the obligor's default or other credit loss.

The annual percentage rate (APR) applicable to any extension of consumer credit must be determined in accordance with regulations of the Board of Governors of the Federal Reserve System.

Free Legal Aid for Business

The government's armies of lawyers can give you powerful legal aid if you've been victimized in business dealings. Of course, you may want your own attorney involved too, to protect your interests; but if there's a valid case against someone, the government will undertake the main effort and will pay for it.

Let's say you're defrauded by a check floating or kiting scheme. Report it to the local federal or state prosecutor. Next get in touch with the regional office of the Federal Deposit Insurance Corporation, and then the state banking commission. All these offices have jurisdiction. They can coordinate enforcement action. Their threats of a criminal judgment, with possible fine and jail, may be enough to scare the cheater into making quick restitution.

Or suppose you're damaged by an illegal business maneuver such as a boycott, price-fixing, or unfair allocations by a supplier. The state and federal antitrust agencies are looking for business, so they'll be glad to hear from you. If your local phone company, for example, gives you static about using a Japanese switchboard, send your lawyer to the local office of the Justice Department's antitrust investigators.

Or maybe powerful patent holders push you around for "infringement" of patents that you believe don't apply. Here again, the Anti-Trust Division can give you free advice. You'll save money by getting the government to bring the first suit. Your lawyer can use that judgment as proof in a private triple-damage action.

Doing Business with the Government

The U.S. Government is the world's largest buyer. All over America it is constantly ordering big quantities of machinery, equipment, supplies, and services. As a buyer, Uncle Sam often seems no more cost-conscious than a Saudi prince in Beverly Hills. Instead of taking the lowest bid or best supplier, government agencies may be required by law to give a fixed percentage of their orders to small businesses.

Certain government orders are "set aside" for small business. Bigger companies aren't allowed to bid on them, so small companies are competing only among themselves for these contracts. Over the years, small business has won about one-fifth of the military's total dollar awards. It got $7 billion worth in one recent year. In addition, small firms make hefty sales to the Nuclear Regulatory Commission, the Department of Agriculture, and other big agencies. Lumber is a good example. The SBA persuaded the Department of Agriculture's Forest Service to set aside parts of the contracts for cutting federal timberland, and the little logging companies survive only through that program.

If you think you might be interested in government contracts, get in touch with the nearest Business Service Center of the General Services Administration. It will give you lists of items the GSA buys for all federal agencies. And it will sell you "The U.S. Government Purchasing and Sales Directory," a useful guide to doing business with the government.

The SBA will provide you with lists of military bases, laboratories, and other government installations that could be customers for your particular kind of work. If you meet certain standards, the SBA will also mail statements to the buyers at these installations, telling them that you are now an approved vendor for certain items. In addition, some SBA offices have salespeople who will peddle your product or service to government agencies. And you don't pay them any commission or fee.

Even if you don't think of yourself as a potential government contractor, it's not a bad idea to become listed with the SBA as a qualified source. It may bring you subcontracts from prime contractors who deal with the government. You can build up a good volume of work if you're known to big companies who need your production facilities. Subcontracting kept a lot of little shops busy during business recessions when private orders dried up. You may be able to rent idle government-owned machine tools if your prime contractor sponsors you. Subcontracting also qualifies you for financial assistance from the SBA.

Some small companies get so fat and happy with one government contract that they lose all interest in other customers. This is dangerous, of course. Congressional cutbacks can cause contract cancellations almost overnight.

Other companies get discouraged while pursuing government orders through mazes of red tape. Making a sale to Uncle Sam—especially the first sale—does take time, effort, and money. His massive demands tend to favor large enterprises. But if you feel you've been brushed off, you can seek redress through publicity. One small firm distributed a list of government contracts it believed it had been unfairly denied on suspicious technicalities—and was eventually awarded them.

In the long run, your company is probably better off if it spends no more than a minor fraction of its time on government contracts. You may win contracts but make no profits because competition forced you to shave your estimates to the bone. Government items are usually more costly to produce than the average civilian product, because the government (especially NASA and the military) sets rigid specifications for quality, grade, size, and other characteristics. A product that fails to meet some government standard—including delivery date—can be rejected. One mistake in planning your work can bring a hollow feeling to your bank account, and cast doubt on your ability to fulfill contracts.

Gardiner G. Greene, who has run several highly successful little companies, emphatically warns small entrepreneurs against government work:

> Mr. Small lands a government contract with some engineering involved, and gradually finds he has a new management problem. He hires engineers, technicians, increases his drafting department. The boys plugged into the government job punch out at 5 P.M. while Mr. Small and his older employees are used to ignoring the clock in order to get a job done. Friction builds up. Pay rates have to be adjusted, overhead goes up. Even before the contract is finished he is losing money on it. . . .
>
> His old staff (now going home promptly at 5) with new offices, secretaries and all the trimmings would never go back to the old days. Mr. Small's own salary and expenses are reviewed nearly every month by a government accountant. An overpaid civil servant knows all about his business and is telling him how he must run it. . . .
>
> Before you start courting the bureaucrats for government contracts, think it over carefully.

Free Consultants for You

In 1974 the SBA expanded its work of giving free analysis and advice. It now employs several hundred full-time Management Assistance Officers (MAO's) who counsel face-to-face with business owners in solving managerial problems. They have long experience at spotting and curing a firm's weaknesses.

In addition, the SBA's SCORE—Service Corps of Retired Executives —channels the volunteer services of about eight thousand older businessmen, many of whom were top executives in major corporations. At your request, the local SBA office will assign a SCORE member to meet regularly with you in your own office, or at home.

Whatever your difficulties, SCORE probably has people who understand them and can help you. They'll set up a bookkeeping system that gives you a clear idea of your costs and profits. They'll advise you on legal snags, insurance, marketing, inventory control, budgeting, personnel, or virtually any other area of business knowledge.

Some are sharper than others, of course. What to do with a weak counselor is a problem all SCORE chapters share. "He's a volunteer, so we can't fire him," says one chapter president. "But we don't send him to any more clients, and he soon drifts away." A retiree's advice is yours to ignore or follow, as you choose. But if you don't at least try out this source of help, you're passing up a potentially valuable asset.

KEEP THESE BASIC POINTS IN MIND:

- *The Economic Development Administration (EDA) can give financial help if you're hurt by imports.*
- *The Small Business Administration (SBA) and other agencies can give financial help when you hire "entry-level" people.*
- *SBA makes low-cost loans to small firms hurt by disaster, or by burdensome government rules.*
- *Experienced free consultants are available through SBA.*
- *Countless government agencies will give you valuable information and advice if you ask the right person. To find out who that is, start by asking a Federal Information Center. Next, write your congressman.*
- *To avoid trouble with the Occupational Safety and Health Administration (OSHA), get a free evaluation from the Department of Health and Human Resources' National Institute of Occupational Safety and Health, and seek advice from your suppliers.*
- *You can get free advice from the Federal Trade Commission (FTC) that will keep you out of trouble from its regulations.*
- *If you're victimized by unfair business dealings, the government's investigators and lawyers will help you at no charge.*
- *Many kinds of government contracts are available to small business, often with no competition from big business. The General Services Administration (GSA) and Small Business Administration (SBA) can give you information. But don't get too dependent on government orders.*

12
How Other People Can Help You

It's amazing how much valuable help—free or for pay—you can get from the vast world of outside experts.

Few small companies seek such help. The average owner-manager wants only a fast fix for today's troubles in his shop, and seldom looks outside for even that. If one of his men comes up with an idea—perhaps picked up from a competitor—the boss may try it. Or may not. His ego may prevent him from taking advice. "Well-balanced businessmen don't build companies," one consultant says. "Hyperthyroid take-charge guys, supersalesmen, or highly creative loners build companies. They also wreck companies sometimes, when they try to run everything themselves."

The average businessman who has owned his business for a reasonable period of time feels he knows it like the back of his hand and hates the idea of asking for—let alone paying for—advice from outsiders. He probably isn't curious about new information or new methods unless they offer an instant solution to a problem he's wrestling with.

Specialists to Help the Generalists

That's fine as far as it goes. Today's small independent, to be successful, must know a little about a lot of things—including when to seek outside help, when to tackle a job himself, and when to assign an employee to it.

We live amid ever-growing complexity. Even a hand laundry or a mom-and-pop trucking company may face such diverse tasks as inventory control, credit and collection, hiring and firing, buying insurance, budgeting, marketing, keeping up with certain fields of science or technology, and staying out of trouble with laws piled atop laws in a towering layer cake of confusion.

In some of these areas at least, you yourself can benefit from outside help, whether you're bossing hundreds of people or doing everything yourself. Let's scan the sectors where plenty of *free* expertise is available. Then we'll consider various kinds of *paid* consultants.

When you take a business trip, do you make your own reservations? Or do you ask someone in your office to do it? Either way, you're wrong. A good travel agent costs you nothing, and saves time and trouble.

A travel agent deals with more knowledgeable airline personnel than the clerks you tackle at counters and on phones. When flights are cancelled, or new ones suddenly open up, an agent's contacts and persistence can put clients onto the best available flights. Only an agent can get passengers on a priority waiting list.

An agent can buy your tickets far in advance, but pay for them only around trip time. Most agents accept major credit cards. If you travel to the same destinations often, your agent may be able to set up a series of discount flights. And of course, your agent can do all the necessary phoning to reserve hotel rooms.

How to Get Better Phone Service

If your firm has a telephone switchboard, you may be overpaying for it. Many companies are charged for equipment they don't need or don't have. And many lose business because would-be customers can't get through to them. You can dodge such losses by using free services that all the Bell System companies of AT&T provide.

Begin by asking your telephone-company marketing representative for a "busy study." It will show how many calls to your office are blocked by busy signals. If they are more than 3 percent of your total calls, consider a change. You may need more trunk lines. Or maybe you can use different numbers and private business lines for outgoing calls, leaving more of your regular switchboard free for incoming calls.

If the study shows no "busy" problems, maybe you have more trunk lines than you need, and can save by eliminating some. Sometimes a study seems to indicate enough trunks, yet customers still complain about busy signals. This means that your phone company's central office is probably overloaded. See if you can get service moved to another office with more capacity.

Of course, repair service is free when any phones are out of order. But repairmen may be slow in coming, if you're in a city that's growing fast. To speed up repairs, first call the service or business office. If you don't get satisfaction, ask to speak to the local division manager or vice president. (It's a good idea to get his name in advance, for future use.) Tell him your phones are "out of service." These are the magic words that galvanize telephone executives. Point out that the dead phones are more than an inconvenience; they're causing financial losses. For that, the phone company will probably pay for overtime work if need be.

If you have chronic trouble, you can complain to the state utility commission. The complaint—best made by letter, with copy to the phone company—won't speed up current repairs, but will probably get you better service in the future.

Another free Bell service is a "traffic survey." Observers will watch your switchboard operators to see if their efficiency is up to par. They'll tell you whether the volume of calls justifies another switchboard position, or perhaps just additional part-time operators for peak hours.

If some of your employees make sales via telephone, Bell has free programs to train them in selling techniques. Ask the business office.

You might also ask for a complete free audit of your telephone setup. Bell will itemize services and equipment, and what you're paying for them. You may discover charges for things you thought were discontinued. If your company changes equipment often, Bell will make regular monthly audits at your request, and do a physical check of your equipment too.

Does your office handle a heavy volume of long-distance calls? Ask Bell to run a cost analysis (also free) to determine whether you'd save money with wide-area telephone service (WATS). Bell won't mislead you on this. But keep in mind that your company's outgoing calls may jump sharply, with a consequent rise in your phone bills, after WATS is installed. One reason for this is that your people will do more phoning to faraway places ("After all, it's 'free' now") and talk longer, asking about wife and family. Business that used to be handled by mail will be taken up by telephone.

Another reason is that when your people find WATS lines busy, and are faced with delays, they may use toll lines in frustration. So unless your current long-distance charges are at least 25 percent higher than the estimated WATS cost—50 percent would be better—you shouldn't consider an outgoing WATS line. Just IWATS (incoming service) alone is often enough, to encourage your customers and salesmen to call in.

The phone company does have a good suggestion for keeping WATS costs down: Instead of a "dial-access" system which enables employees to dial a code to make a WATS call, use a system that requires all requests for long distance to go through your company operator.

Still another free service: Bell will study your whole phone system and suggest possible economies. Of course, the Bell expert doesn't know much about your possible future needs. So he might advise you to change to a smaller, cheaper switchboard, for example—and a year later you might find you need the bigger board you got rid of. Reinstalling it will cost more. So it would not be economical to make a downward change if it would be practical only for a limited time.

If you're choosing a switchboard, check the phone company's rates. A new model can cost three times as much as a reconditioned older board which might meet your needs equally well.

Do-It-Yourself Advertising

Maybe you prepare your own advertising, publicity, store displays, promotion circulars, or other sales-building materials. Your firm's promotion budget may not be big enough to interest a professional advertising or public relations agency. Here's another field where free help can be valuable. Homemade advertising is likely to be amateurish and unproductive. Newspapers, radio stations, and billboard companies soliciting your advertising will gladly help you write, design, and produce whatever you want. Don't be afraid to ask salesmen for free assistance. Newspapers can provide layouts and (sometimes) illustrations at no charge, and even help with general merchandising and sales-promotion plans. A really bright young media salesman might even dream up a campaign theme or slogan for you, or write a radio jingle.

If you're a retailer, you should be aware that companies that put merchandise on your shelves may also provide advertising materials free of charge. Their point-of-sale displays in windows and on counters can set your cash registers ringing. Many manufacturers, in their desire to cement relationships with customers, often cooperate with the retailer in the cost of advertising their brand products.

Maybe direct mail can build sales for you. Direct-mail agencies will help write your sales letters and booklets. And they'll help obtain lists of hundreds or thousands of prospective customers in your market area.

If you're in an industrial enterprise and are overstocked with inventory, you may be able to unload inexpensively by listing your surplus items in *Industrial Surplus Locator,* published by Water-Gard Publishing, Box GG, Gainesville, Georgia 30501. Or you can sell your obsolete machines and equipment through the *McGraw-Hill Equipment Bulletin,* Box 900, New York City 10020. Or you can get a comprehensive list of 385 used-machinery dealers free from the Machinery Dealers National Association, Box 19128, Washington, D.C. 20036.

Suppliers Will Help You

"I don't know what the little manufacturer would do without top-notch assistance from his suppliers," says one small Dallas manufacturer. But you needn't be a manufacturer to get help from salesmen. In your office, laboratory, or retail store, or on your delivery routes or service calls, you undoubtedly use many kinds of supplies and equipment. Companies that sell you these, especially if they are big companies, are probably glad to provide unlimited free consulting service on anything you're doing, if it involves or could involve what they sell. Large corporations often maintain internal consulting staffs just to help customers.

You can tap this free help through the salesmen who approach you—even those from whom you buy nothing. If you're friendly, that is.

Unfriendliness to salesmen calling on him is the mark of a stupid businessman. Salesmen soliciting business can be gold mines of information about prices, new products, competitive developments, money-saving methods, or whatever. No matter how closely you study your market and industry, you can't get inside your competitors' companies the way these salesmen can. Listen to them. Ask questions. Talk about your problems; salesmen often know how someone else solved similar problems. A salesman may even call a technician or troubleshooter from his own company who'll counsel you at no charge.

It's also worthwhile for you and your people to exert salesmanship on the salesmen who solicit you. Sell your company to them. If they hear about new orders, new plans, growth, and feel confident whenever they're in your place of business, they'll tell their credit department that you're an up-and-coming outfit. This can ease credit terms to you, thereby stretching your working capital.

Friendship with vendors is a form of public relations that costs you nothing and can help tremendously when you're in a tight spot. Salesmen can persuade their production crews to speed up deliveries to you. On the other hand, if you wrangle with salesmen about every bill, if you keep trying to shave their prices, if you put them into fiercely competitive bidding contests on every order, if you're slow in paying bills, if you badger them repeatedly about service or quality, then don't expect sympathy from them in your hour of need.

Of course, business is business. As a businessman, you should look for the best deals possible in the long run. Be firm, frank, but pleasant with your suppliers. Tell them what you need, and when. Have at least an approximate understanding about total cost. Expect them to deliver on schedule. Then pay them on schedule. They'll throw in countless bits of free information and guidance, for nothing.

You Needn't Go It Alone

Some small-business men join the Chamber of Commerce, a service club, and every possible trade group. Others think that all such cooperative efforts are a drain on their time and money. But a middle course may be best.

Sometimes competitors can teach you plenty—at little or no cost. You should at least watch their advertising and displays. Generally people are willing to help newcomers in their own line of business. Chatting with them at clubs or trade meetings can be a way to find out what's happening. And learning how some leaders in your field get results can give you useful ideas. (Keep in mind, however, that when a big majority of companies are in agreement on some practice or policy, you can be fairly sure it's out-of-date.)

J. S. Simmons, who runs a foundry and machine company in Atlanta, is one of those who deliberately keep looking for outside ideas. He spends up to six weeks a year visiting other foundries and machine companies, and he and his key men meet daily over coffee and doughnuts to discuss new ideas. Another enterprise that learned from competitors was a wallpaper outlet called The Wall-Nuts. Its three young owners, new in the business and open to ideas from everywhere, thoroughly checked other wallpaper merchants in their area and then proceeded to order copies of the most worn sample books they spotted in the stores. Thus stocked with the most popular lines, The Wall-Nuts were soon meeting all expenses and providing good income for the owners.

Local, regional, and national trade associations can be valuable, or time-wasters. Several different organizations may serve your line of work. Check each out, weigh the benefits, and decide which are justifiable for you. Some trade groups collect and distribute valuable facts on wages, sales, and prices. Some arrange for savings on insurance or supplies. Most maintain credit-reporting services that can save you from costly mistakes. A few offer training courses for employees, or for owners.

Almost all big ones gather specialized technical knowledge that no members, individually, could afford. Some offer individual advice worth many times what they charge. Others publish useful newsletters or magazines; maybe you can subscribe without being a member. Take a look at all available trade papers.

If your business sells to other local businesses, then any organization through which you get to know prospective customers should be worthwhile. But don't expect to hold business just because you belong. Belonging can open doors, but it's still up to you to provide good service at reasonable prices, and to make this well known.

Help with Your Main Task

The name of your game is marketing. Any organization that doesn't give priority to marketing isn't a business, and shouldn't be run as if it were.

America's economic revolution since 1900 has been mostly a marketing revolution. At the turn of the century, the typical businessman's idea of marketing was "I'll build a better mousetrap, and the world will beat a path to my door." Today, at least among successful enterprises, the attitude is "Our job is to produce what the market needs and wants."

Marketing is so basic that you can't turn it over to a sales manager and forget it. It shouldn't ask "What do *we* want to *sell?*" Marketing is much broader than selling. It is the whole business seen from the point of view of its final result—that is, from the customers' point of view.

This is why you'll find three entire chapters of this book devoted to techniques of marketing. Before you use these techniques, you and your top associates—and maybe a consultant or two—should spend some time rethinking your business, asking unaskable questions (What are we really selling? Who are our prospects? Where are they? How do they buy? What are their unsatisfied wants?) and designing your business operations to fit the answers.

At the very first stage, a man who starts a business may not need to ask "What is my business?" If he concocts a cleaning compound in his garage and starts peddling it from door to door, he need know only that he is selling a way of removing stains. But when the product catches on, when he must hire people to mix it and sell it, when he must decide whether to keep selling directly or through department stores or supermarkets or hardwares, when he must think about adding other products —then he must ask and answer the question "What is my business?" or he'll soon be back ringing doorbells.

You need to keep adjusting to changes in the economy and the population; to changes in fashion or taste; to competition. To adjust, you need market data.

How do you get market data? Usually from outsiders of one kind or another. Government organizations, as we saw in Chapter 11, can give you oceans of information.

Occasionally your own organization can dig out facts you need. Here's how one small company used its salesmen to ascertain the market for a new product to be sold to the steel industry.

The owner-manager needed to estimate possible sales so that he could figure how much working capital he would need. Any steel plant's use of the new product would be proportionate to the amount of water used for cooling purposes in the plant. So the salesmen asked, "How much water do you use?" during their calls at steel plants.

Next the owner-manager compared these water-use figures with each plant's known capacity for producing steel, pig iron, and coke. He figures the ratio between water use and production capacity. Then he computed the total amount of cooling water used by the steel industry, based on production figures from the American Iron and Steel Institute. This gave him an estimate of his nationwide market for the new product, accurate enough for borrowing purposes. Better yet, the Institute's figures enabled him to aim at plants that offered the best sales potential.

Finding market information can be frustrating. Your marketing needs may range from minor questions (How much does our competitor charge for his product in Reno? The company that made our valves ten years ago changed its name—how can I find it now?) to major problems (We're investigating additional product lines—where is the least competition? We need a list of plants in Utah that might buy Product B because we're thinking of expanding into that territory).

Such information may be available if you know where to look. Basic statistics on any industry can be obtained free from the libraries of the Commerce Department, the SBA, the larger stockbrokers, banks, and college and public libraries.

If you're near a big city, phone the reference department at its main public library. The researchers there provide free service and will gather in-depth information quickly. The chief problem in using them is that you can't say, "Tell me all about ABC Corporation," or "I want everything you have on the ketchup business." Instead you must ask, "How many female dogs are there in Ohio? How many veterinarians? Who are the primary pet-supply manufacturers in the United States and what are their addresses?" Be as specific as you can. The more focused your questions, the faster the search, and the less useless data you'll be burdened with. In a week, say, you can get a list of forty questions answered by the library, whereas the same list might take three weeks if you turned it over to someone in your company or even to a professional outside researcher. You see, these library researchers use government information, university information, authors' books and articles, stockbrokers' research, and other sources.

If you're too far from a big library, or if your questions are so off-trail that librarians can't find answers, you have several alternatives. They all cost money, but not big money.

1. You can hire a professional researcher. A young person trained in library science earns about $25,000 a year, so a per diem fee might be about $100. Make sure you explain precisely what you need—and why. This will help screen out irrelevancies—but more important, a researcher who knows "why" may pick up useful sidelights you hadn't asked for.

2. You can use a professional information-gathering service. There are firms that specialize in getting information for business either on a one-shot basis or for a retainer fee. They're useful if you want to stay anonymous while obtaining product samples, catalogues, and the like.

3. You can approach a college or university. It may refer you to a faculty member who already knows a lot about the field you're researching. He may take the assignment on a consulting basis.

4. You can set up your own data base, if your information needs are multitudinous. A company can establish a library shaped to its own needs, containing industry handbooks, catalogues, trade magazines, directories, annual reports (including 10-K reports for the SEC) of your customers, suppliers, competitors. Put someone in charge who has a broad understanding of your business and its potential.

If you have a really big idea, calling for an elaborate research job, the National Science Foundation might put up as much as $25,000 for a six-month study—provided the research will be in some area considered important to the public good, such as chemical threats, waste reclamation, help for the handicapped, or the like.

Companies like Dun & Bradstreet can make available business data, a great deal of information invaluable to the business community in many fields of research, and mailing lists as well as their better-known credit reporting.

What's Your Problem?

Maybe your business isn't thriving, and you wonder why. Would you like to have a nearby university send in a team of top-grade students to diagnose your trouble and help you overcome it?

Universities and community colleges in various states are doing this, with funding of $15 million a year voted by Congress in 1977. Analysis and advice in all phases of business operations can be yours for the asking.

Testifying in Senate hearings that led to the 1977 Small Business Development Center Act, Dr. Reed Powell said on behalf of California's nineteen-campus California State University and College system:

Many small-business men complain that they need more capital. In most cases our investigations reveal that the deficiency lies in the management of the capital, and in their lack of overall knowledge of how to run a business.

All the kinds of knowledge required to help a small business [exist] within a full-service university or college. . . .

Practically all small-business product lines are on dead-end streets. Companies simply do not have the resources to do the research and development necessary to modify, update, and change their product lines.

Business-school students have taken the initiative in going to their friends in engineering school for assistance in product redesign and other forms of technological modifications.

Students get valuable experience by applying classroom knowledge to actual business problems. Often they transform small firms' red ink into black by analyzing the bookkeeping, setting up cost-accounting systems, and showing owners how to manage cash flow. Sometimes they help with marketing surveys and plans for expansion.

More than three hundred universities and colleges are members of the Small Business Institute, partially funded by the SBA. The SBA contracts with an institution to provide free consulting service for small enterprises that want it. A faculty coordinator guides the different students working with one owner-manager.

Sometimes students just walk in and offer their help. Bob Bell, a Stanford graduate student, happened to eat at John Carter's 25-seat barbecue restaurant, and made suggestions that helped Carter increase average daily receipts by half. Then he got a faculty okay to work continuously with Carter as his term project for the Small Business Management class. He made marketing studies, overhauled bookkeeping, helped develop a regular dinner service, launched promotion to draw more customers, and changed menu planning from day-to-day to two weeks in advance. This led to expansion into a 125-seat restaurant with a cocktail lounge and game room. Bell was so enthusiastic that he stayed on to advise (still free) after the course was over.

There are other sources of special guidance for small firms. One is the Center for Small Business, sponsored by the U.S. Chamber of Commerce. It can provide struggling tradesmen with expert counseling free of charge. To find out more, write to it at 1615 H Street, N.W., Washington 20062.

Another is the Bank of America, the world's largest bank, which for decades has made a specialty of small-business advice. It publishes meaty, chatty, how-to-do-it "profiles" of almost every imaginable small business—starting with apparel stores, going on through bars and bicycle shops and bookstores, perhaps ending with (we're guessing) zipper-repair services. These big pamphlets are free at some Bank of America branches —which doesn't help if you're in any state except California, but you can get one by mail if you send $2 each to the bank's Department 3120, P.O. Box 37000, San Francisco 94137.

The bank also publishes free "Business Operations" handbooks, from 20 to 36 pages, about problems common to many small businesses. Some of the titles are "Beating the Cash Crisis," "Marketing New Product Ideas," "Advertising Small Business," "Exporting," "Personnel for the Small Business," and "Crime Prevention for Small Business." You can buy a complete set for $15. Several times a year a new booklet is published, and $8.50 will get you a subscription for ten future issues as published.

Free Information About Credit

Your own bank probably provides free services of its own. One vital service is credit reporting. In small business ventures, one credit loss can wipe out the profits from weeks of sales, or even wipe out the company. Most owner-managers are credit-wise enough to run checks on their big customers—but sometimes they don't know that it's also important to make sure about the financial soundness of suppliers and vendors. If a supplier runs short of cash, he can fall behind on deliveries.

Consider this story of a small company that manufactured a kitchen-ware article. Sales came slowly, and the owner-manager was getting discouraged. Then one day he called on a company that was selling products door-to-door. Its products were compatible with his, but not competitive. It was eager to expand. So it offered to take a high volume of the manufacturer's wares, and peddle them on its sales routes. The jubilant manufacturer worked hard to churn out the volume ordered by the selling organization.

In February he shipped the first orders—three times as big as all his other accounts. He hired more people, went on two shifts, and sent even bigger shipments in March and April.

At the end of April he had yet to receive the first payment from the door-to-door company. In May he ran out of cash. He then made his first real investigation of his customer. He found that the operators had a history of very sharp trading, and had stuck previous creditors for big sums. Now they were in bankruptcy, and the manufacturer had no chance of collecting a dime. He had to declare himself bankrupt. (However, in three years he worked out of the hole and paid all his debts.)

The moral, of course, is to check the credit of everyone with whom you have big dealings. Most small firms can't afford to subscribe to Dun & Bradstreet or other credit-reporting services—and don't need to, because banks do subscribe, and as part of their service will get reports for you. They'll do it either free or at their cost. You should arrange with a vice president to use your bank's D&B service, so that he'll know you follow sound purchasing and credit policies. But ask him to provide it through a clerk, so that he won't be involved every time.

Sometimes you can get invaluable business advice in a casual chat with a banker. For example, Ralph E. Merritt of Livermore, California, ran a company that made only safety fuses. He wanted to diversify. He asked a banker friend at lunch to name the most promising of all markets for manufacturers, and the banker picked plastics, especially glass-fiber products. So Merritt visited two Owens-Corning plants and several representatives, and decided to make Fiberglas-coated fabrics. In seven years he acquired new machinery and technical personnel with Owens-Corning's help, and increased his company's sales sixfold, to more than $3 million.

Better Ways Through the Maze

We showed you how the SBA can help you fight back against oppressive government agencies. Other kinds of free help are available when an agency gives you a runaround rather than an iron fist. This happens often. "People move within these agencies so frequently that there's no continuity, no accountability," says Herbert Liebenson, vice president of the National Small Business Association. "One fellow filed three times with one agency because his applications got lost. You hear this all the time."

If it happens to you, one thing you can do is write to Office of the Ombudsman, Department of Commerce, 14th Street and Constitution Avenue, N.W., Washington, D.C. 20230. This office goes to bat for businesses lost in labyrinths of government clerkdom.

You can also write your congressmen, of course, but in cases of lost papers or clerical errors he can't help much. A better bet is to find out which congressional committee or subcommittee has authority over the agency that's stalling you, and complain to the chairman or ask your senator or congressman to do so. Donald Ubben, a U.S. Chamber of Commerce director, says "The only time you get really quick action is when a chairman complains. It's amazing how fast things get done. Some agencies have a forty-eight-hour rule to reply to their congressional committee, but not to the average citizen."

A still better bet, in many cases, is to tackle your local or county federal office. Most of the Washington bureaus are out of touch with their operatives in the field. Suppose you complain about an allotment check from the Department of Agriculture. The USDA sends it down to the regional office, then to the state office, then to the county where it will be handled. This takes time, during which there are plenty of chances for your papers to get pigeonholed. But if you start with a visit or phone call to the county office, you may find a friendly human being who knows how to check back along the chain and get action.

Experts in Exporting

If you have a well-established small manufacturing business, maybe you should think about selling to foreign markets. Plenty of free expertise is available, especially if you're in a big industrial state such as New York, Massachusetts, Illinois, California, or a few others. They maintain state-sponsored offices, usually called the Office of International Trade or something similar, which can give you quick answers to questions about quotas, customs duties, freight forwarders, foreign loan programs, and marketing services in many parts of the world. Better still, enroll in the E. Joseph Cossman Seminar (See Chapter 1).

One of the best such services is in Los Angeles, at its World Trade Center. In 1978 it opened an "export hot line" manned by seven staff members who have spent most of their lives in international business. Richard King, director of the service, says "We use the term 'exports' loosely. It could mean licensing, joint ventures, even manufacturing abroad. . . . There are many, many small businesses which should be exporting but aren't. Often they're frightened off because they don't know enough. For instance, if a firm hears of a minimum that must be shipped, they might not know that their goods could be part of a larger shipment."

King has dozens of hot-line success stories. Here's one. A lubricant maker, with annual sales between $2 and $3 million, had never exported. He became interested in Japan and called the hot line. "We put him in touch with a Japanese distributing company and Japanese customers," King recalls. "We also talked about his firm at the Japanese trade mission in Los Angeles. He never had to leave the country. He wound up with an order equal to his annual sales."

Uncle Sam too wants to help small companies sell—or buy—abroad. He maintains an independent federal agency, the Export-Import Bank, at 8111 Vermont Avenue, N.W., Washington D.C. 20531. Eximbank, as it's known for short, will send free details of its services if you write and ask. Its work includes helping you get commercial bank financing by guaranteeing to reimburse the lender if one of your foreign customers turns out to be a deadbeat, and arranging credit insurance to protect exporters directly against default.

Outsiders Can Sell for You

Your U.S. sales might also grow with expert help from various professional people. We've already considered marketing research and marketing assistance. The actual face-to-face selling job can also be handled, anywhere in America, by people you pay to do so (at attractive low rates). These are called sales agents or manufacturers' representatives. They'll add your wares to the line they show their established customers.

How do you find such salesmen? There are at least three good sources.

Rep Information Service, Box L, Tarzana, California 91356, has a free listing service for companies seeking manufacturers' representatives and sales agents. Your first step can be to get listed, and await nibbles.

Your second step can be to buy a $54 book that gives information on reps in all areas. It includes addresses, size of staff, territories, products represented, markets served. It's called *National Directory of Manufacturers' Representatives*. It's sold by McGraw-Hill, 1221 Avenue of the Americas, New York 10020.

And for advice on how to get results from such a service, you can send for a free publication called *How to Succeed with Manufacturers' Representatives*. It's available from the United Association of Manufacturers' Representatives, 808 Broadway, Kansas City, Missouri 64105.

Assorted Healers for Hire

Some owner-managers resist spending money for outside help. They think they don't need it or can't afford it. And they don't realize that expertise can be worth many times what it costs.

For proof, consider Z. M. Roehr, a Polish refugee who started a one-man business making hypodermic needles in Waterbury, Connecticut. In his first three years of business he used four consultants to improve the company's techniques of quality control, work measurement, cost accounting, and metal finishing. When he retired, his company was one of the three largest in its line and employed two hundred people.

Or consider a similar story from Robert Kahn, retailing consultant:

"One of the smartest businessmen I knew, even when his company was small, used a major accounting firm and a good law firm. His advertising was handled by a creative agency geared to small business as well as large. And he frequently used business consultants—including a man who periodically evaluated his merchandising efforts. These advisers helped him grow. Ten years ago he belonged to a small retailers' association. Today he does more business than all the retailers in that group combined.''

Thirty years ago there were about 8,000 individuals and firms in the United States offering advice on new methods. By 1979 the number was about 40,000. Any big city shows hundreds of listings under ''Management Consultants'' in the Yellow Pages, and many more under ''Business Counselors.'' The growth of the profession would seem to indicate that clients find it valuable. Consultants grow through referrals and repeat business, since it is considered beneath their dignity to advertise.

You can buy counsel in countless highly specialized fields. If you want to improve your door-to-door sales routes, Know Associates is a specialist at it. If you want to build a new plant or relocate an old one, you can call on The Fantus Company. The big Alexander Proudfoot Company concentrates on techniques for cost-cutting and doing more with less. Kai Yamato, president of the International Business Management Company, specializes in helping American companies mate with potential subsidiaries in the Far East. Jerry Verlen, a New York consultant, will walk in the door of a failing men's retail store, manage it for weeks or months, and get it running profitably. If you need something in Washington and can't find out how to get it (after trying all the free guides through the swarms of clerks described earlier in this chapter and the previous one), Matthew Lesko will try to solve your problem through his firm, Washington Researchers, Inc. Whatever your weakness in marketing or production or office routines or anything else, some consultant probably specializes in healing it.

If you decide to get a consultant, make sure he really has the expertise you need. He should know more about a certain phase of your operations than you do. Never sign with a firm because of a convincing line of talk from its top man or its ''contact'' people. Find out who would actually be working with you, and judge him as you would a prospective executive. Don't take him if he'll need to spend days and days familiarizing himself with your operations, because the meter will be running and the rate will probably be $50 an hour or more.

Some consultants specialize in serving small businesses. They know you won't have much money to spend, so they won't regale you with a $15,000 or $20,000 proposal, which is about the minimum from a top consulting firm like Booz-Allen or McKinsey.

Charles S. Colman of 9201 Charleville Boulevard, Beverly Hills, California, is one of the leading Certified Business Counselors in the country. He works in small and medium-size firms at fees ranging from $550 to $800 a day. In a typical week he spends time in four or five different companies, many of them real-estate firms. "I can generate enough activity in a day to keep a client hopping for a week," he says.

How to Hunt for Consultants

To locate a good consultant you might begin by checking with your banker, with business friends, with your trade association. Almost everyone has a strong opinion about a consultant or two, and you'll get grim warnings as well as warm recommendations.

If you need to look further, there is a guide to hundreds of experts listing their special skills by category, plus names and addresses. It's called *Directory of Management Consultants*. You can buy it for $37.50 from Consultants News, 17 Templeton Road, Fitzwilliam, New Hampshire 03447. Another possible source of names is the Association of Consulting Management Engineers, 347 Madison Avenue, New York 10017.

Pick three or four likely-looking consultants, and try to get well acquainted. Ask for a list of clients for whom they've done work similar to what you need. Then follow up the references. Find out how past and present clients evaluate what was done for (or to) them.

Another way to evaluate consultants is to attend one of the trade shows, conventions, or conferences where droves of experts congregate. These meetings often feature consultants as guest speakers or discussion leaders. Pick out sessions that will attract experts whose know-how might help you, so that you can "preview" them and ask questions without being treated as a hot prospect.

Sometimes you can do even more at such seminars. A number of your people can "jam" a session in such a way that experts tell what they know without realizing that you're getting advice you'd otherwise have to pay for. Your team can steer the seminar toward the topic you want covered. One of you asks a question close to the speaker's subject, then another follows with a related question closer to your own field of interest, and a third finds a way to build on the previous questions and draw the whole audience into a brainstorming session in your own research area. In two hours you might collect several years' worth of research.

When You Sign Up

It's customary—and important—to have a specific written understanding with a consultant before he starts any work for which he'll charge. (Some firms, especially the big ones, will spend a couple of days studying a firm's internal operations at no charge, as a preliminary to a proposal for a major project.) One way to cut consultants' costs is to contract for only an oral report on the study, backed by a written summary. This can save you the substantial costs of a voluminous report clogged with data. Consultants' recommendations are usually more important than how they were arrived at. And a final question-and-answer session with them is more enlightening than hours spent pondering their typewritten sheets.

Here are points that should be covered in a consulting agreement:

1. The scope of the project, clearly and completely defined.

2. Reporting dates for various stages of the study.

3. Results expected—that is, ways in which your company should benefit from the project. The benefits ought to be measurable, not just vague "improvement."

4. What material generated by the study—such as lists, charts, and samples—will remain your property.

5. Overall fee. Most consultants can provide fairly accurate estimates before they start work. If this is impossible because of the nature of the project, they should at least specify names and pay rates for consulting staff members, plus allowances for travel, hotel, and clerical-support expenses.

Always remember, though, that the caliber of the work is what you should be most concerned about. Even at high fees, good advice usually saves money or boosts profits. Even at low fees, poor advice can cost more in lost profits than what you save on consultants' compensation.

Lawyers and You

As we saw earlier in this book, you need a competent attorney when you are buying a business, signing an important contract, or setting up a partnership or corporation. Maybe you think you'll have no other need for a lawyer in your business.

Nevertheless, you'll be smart to stay on such friendly terms with a good law firm that you can telephone at any moment and get prompt service. There are more ways than you can imagine of getting into costly litigation. Here are some of the things that can happen:

- You receive a shipment of the wrong goods and send it back, refusing payment. The vendor sues you for breach of contract.
- One of your customers returns a big shipment, claiming it doesn't conform to specifications (which weren't in his purchase order). You'll have to take him to court.
- You buy tickets to a testimonial dinner for a union leader. It turns out that some of the money went into his pocket. You're charged with a

violation of the Labor Relations Act, which makes it a crime for an employer "to pay any money to any representative of his employees."

- A woman who has been on your payroll for years, and never sought a promotion or even a raise, sues you for discriminating against her because of her sex.
- Your advertisements use the phrase "satisfaction guaranteed." A buyer says he wasn't satisfied at all, and complains to the Better Business Bureau, which threatens legal action for misleading advertising. The buyer also sues you for breach of contract. Or maybe a consumer group sues, saying your product is dangerous.
- One of your truck drivers earns less than $10,000 a year, and has a dependent child. The government tells you that you're breaking a federal law called Earned Income Credit, which took effect July 1, 1979.
- You have lunch with a couple of your competitors. They mention a certain customer of theirs who is unpleasant to deal with. Later this customer offers you an order, but you refuse to do business. You're charged with a conspiracy in restraint of trade.
- You fire an employee. His lawyer claims that you defamed his character, or that you violated the Age Discrimination Employment Act or the Equal Employment Opportunity Act.
- You have a suggestion box in your plant. Several workers suggest an idea which you had already thought of and had decided to put into effect. When the employees see the idea used with no credit or payment to them, they sue.
- You send around a memo with some loose, glowing language about great opportunities in your firm. Later you have a bad year so you give no raises or promotions, and even lay off a few people. Your employees aren't unionized, but they sue because your memo made "false promises."

In emergencies such as these, especially if government prosecutors are knocking at your door, you won't want to trust blindly in a lawyer you barely know—nor will you want to waste time shopping for a good one. Why not find a good one now, before you need him?

It's a sad fact that most people postpone choosing a lawyer until they're in serious trouble. Ideally, a lawyer should be a continuous adviser similar to a doctor. He should be thoroughly familiar with his client's history in order to do the best possible job in an emergency. At other times, he can prevent a client from taking serious risks, if he's kept informed about what the client is planning.

You may want to be advised by the biggest and most glamorous law firm in your city. But unless you're very wealthy or very well known, the firm will assign your work to junior partners.

You may well want different lawyers to handle different matters. The one most experienced in contract law may not be best against someone who has damaged your property. But in the long run you're probably better off with one good attorney whose practice covers a wide range of business matters, and whose astuteness and expertise are up to your needs. He should be willing and able to sit down and talk, or answer questions on the telephone, when you need him. If he is consistently slow in returning your calls, or if your law work seems to get sidetracked in his office, you need another lawyer.

Often the best is a young lawyer-on-the-rise. Look for an about-to-be-partner who hasn't yet brought in many clients. His partners can help him in fields that are unfamiliar to him. A good lawyer will give you his home phone, will work nights and travel weekends when it's needed, and will talk for you in negotiations and disputes more intelligently than you yourself could.

When he serves you well, pay his bill without quibbling, for he can be a great comfort in a crunch. However, he shouldn't charge heavily for run-of-the-office legal chores—and won't, if you reach an advance understanding with him. Try not to let him charge a fixed hourly rate regardless of the task. Reviewing a file should cost less per hour than going to court. Handling an emergency that means dropping everything else should be worth more than doing research under no time pressure.

Like you or any other businessman, a lawyer sells services and know-how. He should be paid for every hour worked, even when he gives a fast answer on the phone. But don't settle for a slip of paper that says "For services rendered in May." Ask that bills be accompanied by an itemization of work done.

Getting the Best out of Your Accountant

Accounting is said to be the "universal language of business." But few owner-managers are fluent in the language. Most started as salesmen or technicians. So they're likely to be weak in financial planning.

A typical problem in small business is keeping income balanced with outgo. Cash to pay bills isn't provided by profits tied up in machinery or inventory. When a company has an out-of-balance accounts-receivable position, with a big percentage of debts that have run 90 or 120 days, it has a serious financial management problem—which it may not understand until too late.

Just knowing how to stay out of this predicament takes financial background. You need somebody who'll keep an eye on the cash budget and other financial variables that can spell trouble. You may not have anyone in your organization capable of this.

As a rule, until a company has several million dollars' worth of sales it can't afford to employ a competent treasurer or controller. Such men command higher salaries than small companies can afford. So small companies usually rely on an outside public accountant. Even a tiny business needs an accountant once a year, at tax time.

A good accountant is the most important single outside adviser a small business has. Over the years, he'll play a bigger role in its success or failure than any other outside expert.

How can an accountant help you? Mainly, as suggested a moment ago, by keeping you aware of how your business is doing financially and what can be expected in the future. John Clow, president of San Francisco's society of CPA's, recalls:

> We recently took over the accounting for an equipment-repair business. They had yearly maintenance contracts for which they were paid in advance, and believed they were doing fine on the basis of this immediate cash flow. However, when those cash receipts were spread over the year in which the services were performed, the business was operating at a loss. Its rates weren't realistic. Survival prospects were poor unless changes were made.

Listen carefully to your CPA's advice. Many accountants think that dropping hints will put their message across. They don't realize that clients have a habit of hearing what they want to hear, and ignoring gentle warnings. This is especially true among entrepreneurs, who prefer to think about the new rather than try to fix the old.

Quite a few accountants don't even give warnings, unless they're asked directly. Essentially, accountants do the work they're hired to do. If this is just to file tax returns and perform specified bookkeeping tasks, that's fine with them. But it means that they aren't accountants at all, only bookkeepers. You aren't getting much for your money unless the accountants at least make your records easy for you to use and understand.

Get to know the accounting firm's top people, and how the firm works. Smaller clients often don't realize that they can talk with the top partners simply by asking to. You should needle the senior partner if you're not getting the service you need. This can also lead to enlightening chats with the partner about trends and methods in businesses similar to yours.

Quiz for CPAs

Your top management must train itself to ask your CPA the right questions on how to save money and make the business run better. For example, a CPA should be asked about tax shelters. State taxes are getting to be a bigger headache, and the states as well as IRS have closed many loopholes. Your accountant might help assess the soundness of new tax angles, and certainly can discuss various possible tax treatments of depreciation and inventory valuation.

If you have a pension or profit-sharing plan, your CPA should be asked how to maximize tax benefits for individuals and the company, in view of complications caused by ERISA.

He should be asked about your reserves and your long-term debt. Cash-flow projections, budgets, all the various spending and investing options should be run past his skeptical eye.

Your CPA should also be asking *you* questions beyond his audit function. Is he triggering you to look at cost savings? Is he prompting you to look into the efficiency of an operation? Is he urging you to work up numbers for a cash-flow projection? Probably not, so that you won't think him pushy. Yet these are questions you should be asked, especially if you lack the staff to do that kind of fiscal thinking.

Keep Them Informed

A company had an independent CPA prepare its income-tax returns. He used the familiar bank-deposit method to show corporate income. The owners never told him that some receipts went into other bank accounts. So their tax return omitted some income, and a court ruled it fraudulent.

From management's side, the important thing about getting the most out of any consultant—accountant or lawyer or whomever—is to tell him about plans in advance, so that he can help shape them wisely. CPAs and other consultants are professionals. They never gossip, being keenly aware of possible conflicts of interest due to other clients who might want to know something about your business. Treat them as full members of the inner circle. Give them a good look at all new ideas.

Get your attorney tuned in on your hiring and firing, your promotions and raises, your sales literature and internal communications, your dealings with big customers. Tell your admen and sales reps about possible new products, or new markets you're thinking of invading. Keep your accounting and banking advisers informed of your plans. The more you tell your outside experts, the more they can help you.

Too often the small independent businessman resists advice he might profitably utilize because of his own personality shortcomings. Ego, as we have said earlier, is a real stumbling block for some; fear of someone else's advice being inferior to his own judgment is another personal hurdle.

He may envision himself as a general, but all too often he spends his valuable time in menial tasks which should be assigned to a sergeant or a private.

This do-it-yourself syndrome can be the one factor that impedes his growth and progress.

Help Others to Help You

In the constantly changing climate of today's complex business structure, it is only the strong who will survive. To be strong requires continuous vigilance and continuing study of the external forces that contribute to or perhaps even control the degree of success enjoyed by a business owner.

In addition to the need for belonging to a trade organization, it is advisable to attend lectures and seminars on business topics that have to do with a more ordered operation of your business. Such a seminar is available on Business Opportunities; it gives businessmen a thorough insight into the interplay of buyers and sellers, negotiations, understanding financial statements, cash flow, government regulations, tax implications, and dozens of other vital topics. These seminars (2½ days of study and workshop) are given periodically throughout the United States. Scheduled dates and other information on these seminars can be obtained from the Education Advancement Institute, 50 Washington St., Reno, Nevada 89503.

Additionally, a comprehensive manual is available to businessmen from the same source. Entitled *Business Opportunities—Guide for the Professional,* it is coauthored by Albert J. Lowry, Ph.D., and Charles C. Colman, C.B.C. and is priced at $49.95.

KEEP THESE BASIC POINTS IN MIND:

- *When you travel, a travel agent costs you nothing and saves you time and trouble.*
- *Use the telephone company's free services to get maximum economy and efficiency from your company's telephoning.*
- *Advertising media salesmen will help you create and polish your advertising, at no charge.*
- *Salesmen for your suppliers are valuable sources of information and advice.*
- *Marketing is your most important operation. Many outside resources can help with it.*
- *Students and faculty of a nearby university are probably providing free*

counseling to small business, through the Small Business Institute or individual institutional programs. You'll find them worth investigating.

- Always check the financial soundness of your big customers, suppliers, and vendors. Your bank can do this for you.
- If your products can be sold in foreign markets, ask advice from your state government and the Export-Import Bank.
- Consider using sales representatives, instead of your own full-time salesmen, in expanding your market.
- Paid consultants have been tremendously valuable to many small businesses. If you have a special problem, look around for a consultant with expertise in that field.
- Get on friendly terms with a good law firm before you need them.
- Your CPA is your most important outside adviser. Keep him fully informed, and ask him to warn you of any financial problems he sees ahead. Let him know that you want him to ask you questions to clarify your own financial thinking.
- Treat all your outside advisers as members of your inner circle. The more you tell them, the more they can help you.

13
Winning the Paperwork War

Papers, letters, bits of half-finished jobs were scattered on his desk. People came in at all hours and dumped more papers on the desk. Elbow room was out of the question, so the man had to be a contortionist to do his work. When a certain paper was wanted, the only way to get it was to search through the desk. Hunting for lost articles took so much time that the man didn't have a chance to make a living. He never caught up with his work. When a client or customer wanted immediate action or information, everybody in the office was in consternation. Among the total impossibilities of life was an exact knowledge of how the business was going.

This description, written in 1919 by Edward Earle Purinton, was supposed to depict an old-fashioned businessman who hadn't yet discovered "the new science of efficiency engineering." Yet it might apply to many of today's desks, especially those belonging to heads of small businesses.

Our civilization suffers from a superstitious belief in the magical powers of pieces of paper—letters, memos, reports, printed forms, purchase orders, price quotations, invoices, waybills, computer printouts, news clippings, expense vouchers, et cetera ad nauseam. Most of us in business yearn wistfully for a clean desk, which is supposed to signify an efficient executive (but doesn't necessarily do so, as we'll see), and wonder how to cope with the paper engulfing our desks and file cabinets and briefcases.

Well, there are ways to cope. That's what this chapter is about.

Money in the Wastebasket

The first step is to realize that we don't need most of the paper in our offices.

Business does move on floods of paper, but "paperwork remains undoubtedly the least efficient operation in U.S. industry," according to *Fortune* magazine. A full wastebasket is likely to mean an efficient office. This isn't just somebody's opinion; it has been proved repeatedly by businesses that studied themselves.

Back in the 1950s, when a shortage of office space made many companies realize how much their offices and filing systems were costing, managers began to discover that they could cut down their office files by two-thirds or more without any loss of efficiency, simply by destroying old papers. Equitable Life threw out enough papers to make a pile twenty times as high as New York's tallest skyscraper. Monsanto Chemical not only recovered thousands of cubic feet of office space, but cut its normal expenditures for file cabinets from $12,500 to zero the first year, and in addition abolished a $30,000 photocopying operation.

Some companies hired experts from Remington Rand, Shaw-Walker, and other office-equipment makers to show them how to streamline their paperwork. And some turned their problems over to an organization called National Records Management Council, which specialized in slicing the deadwood out of office files. More recently a national temporary-help firm, Olsten Corporation of Westbury, New York, began presenting an annual award to companies for excellence in record-keeping.

Olsten found, just as NRMC and the others had a generation earlier, that the beginning of efficient paperwork is to clean out the files and stop putting so much into them. Olsten says that 65 cents of every dollar the average company spends on record-keeping is wasted; typical firms file 70 percent more documents than they really need—and in fact, never refer to 85 percent of the letters and forms they file.

Such a statement is hard to believe. But Procter & Gamble, the giant soap company, proved it through its own slow, safe tests. It began with one type of record which it had been keeping for six years (and which filled several hundred file cabinets). It reduced the holding period first to three years, then to one year, then to six months. Finally it cut the period down to three months, and still didn't notice any inconvenience or loss. One P&G executive said, "We'll never know whether or not we've gone far enough with our program until we are hurt. We haven't been hurt yet."

Such examples showed big business that it could solve some of its paperwork problems—and enhance its profits—with some calculated risk-taking. The profits came because salvage companies paid as much as $20 per ton for bundles of paper that could be recycled. Pan American World Airways sold about 100 tons by clearing out more than half its files. Westinghouse unloaded 120 carloads of miscellaneous papers, and moved another 300 carloads to a five-story archives building. Worthington Corporation discarded and sold 154 tons of paperwork.

If these giant companies, with their complexities and ramifications, can simplify their paperwork so drastically, shouldn't a small business be able to do likewise?

Of course, every business must make and keep certain records because the government requires them, or because they give protection against possible lawsuits. But the records needn't be kept forever. For free detailed information on how long to keep invoices, expense reports, financial statements, bank statements and other records, ask for a copy of "Records Retention Timetable" from Electric Wastebasket Corporation, 145 West 45th Street, New York 10036.

Don't save information you're unlikely to need. You probably carry the most important data in your head anyway.

To avoid needless filing, never say, "We'll keep this just in case," and never ask, "Is it possible we'll ever need this?"

Instead ask, "What would happen if we needed this and it wasn't there?" The answer in most cases is that it wouldn't matter many dollars' worth.

Think about your expense for cabinets needed to file the stuff you're keeping—in addition to the value of the time wasted in filing. At an estimated 1,500 pieces of paper per file drawer, the average cost of maintaining a four-drawer file cabinet could be hundreds of dollars yearly.

Birth Control in the Office

Purging your files is only the first step toward conquering paperwork. The second step is to establish a "birth control" program. Probably most papers in your files needn't have been created in the first place. Maybe you can quit compiling certain kinds of records.

Sears, Roebuck & Company has for sixty-five years been sending the customer's original order and the company's bill right back with the goods asked for. Keeping only a record of the total bill, Sears takes the risk of having to refill orders for customers who claim they didn't receive shipments. Obviously the risk isn't very big, or Sears wouldn't have kept taking it for all these years.

United Parcel Service ducks paperwork by using the phone whenever possible. One of the company's local managers says, "We don't get as many as 375 letters from our customers in a year, but we do make twenty times that many personal contacts."

The savings are evident when you see that a small clump of file cabinets suffices for United Parcel. For example, its complete correspondence file on one of its biggest department-store customers is less than three inches thick—although it has done business with the store for the past two decades. Further evidence of the company's savings on paperwork is the fact that only four secretaries serve its entire New York management staff of forty people, dealing with more than four hundred stores!

Telephoning costs money. But it often costs more to write and mail a letter, to say nothing of filing the carbon copy and the eventual reply. Phoning may save exchanging three or four letters. So unless you're sure you need a formal record of what you say, consider telephoning.

And when you receive a letter that needs a written reply, consider writing a brief message in longhand on the face of the original letter, which can then be returned to the sender. This is what Procter & Gamble does. If a longer reply is required, it is simply typed at the bottom or on the back of the original. A photocopy is made for the files, if necessary —but P&G stenographers have standing orders not to make any copies unless their boss specifically asks them to do so.

The company deters executives from piling up paperwork by limiting each correspondence "dictator" to one file drawer. Yearly audits of correspondence files, and tight control over requisitions for filing cabinets, have so changed P&G management's habits that on the average, one drawer holds the paperwork of four dictators. Executives keep only "suspense" files—that is, papers on matters being handled. "As soon as a final letter winds up the matter, we consign the entire file to the wastebasket," a P&G man says.

More and more companies answer letters by a note on the face of the original letter. You could give this system your personal touch by having small self-adhesive stickers made. They might be headed LETTER SAVER or SPEED-REPLY, and continue:

> In order to give you the fastest possible reponse, we have made these marginal notes on your letter. In this case, we think you'll prefer speed to formality.

Then your company name and address can be at the bottom of the sticker. An attractive sticker can be as small as 3½ inches by 1½.

Similarly, when you do originate a letter to someone you know, maybe it can be a handwritten note instead of a formal typed letter. You (and your secretary, if you have one) can save a lot of time that way, and give an impression of informal friendliness.

Which Papers Should You Handle?

However, weeding out correspondence files is much easier than cutting down the daily paper-shuffling. As we all know, business paper comes in many forms besides correspondence. You can be buried in paperwork without ever handling a letter. But you'd better not be. That way lies bankruptcy.

In many small businesses, the top man is criticized by those beneath for spending his time on the wrong things. Their criticism is valid if it means that the key activities of the business aren't being taken care of, and this is often the case.

But sometimes it merely means that he is tackling the activities he is good at. He is using the talents that led him into the business in the first place. So far, so good—but if other key activities are being neglected, then he's doing only part of what he should. For example, if he's gifted at finance and is spending most of his time on it, the answer isn't to turn over money matters to the controller while he himself cultivates customers and keeps watch over production work. The answer is to realize that an owner talented in manipulating money and making it grow is a rare asset—and that he should keep on doing so, but should also make sure that someone else looks after the customers and the quality control, which also are keys to success.

By the same token, a restaurant owner who is a great cook ought to be in the kitchen more than at a desk; a retailer who knows merchandise and knows people should spend most of his time buying and selling, not perspiring over tax returns. But in all such cases the owners need to *manage,* in addition to using their special talents.

All heads of businesses must manage. This principle can help you plan your personal strategy for staying on top of paperwork. Let's see what it means.

Less Paperwork Means Smarter Management

There used to be a widespread notion that small-business men needed little or no expertise in "business administration"—that is, in management. Management was supposed to be for big companies. Even now you sometimes hear an owner say, "I don't need anybody from a school of business administration. That's for General Motors. My business is small and simple." But he's fooling himself. To make a profit, a hamburger stand needs systematic management even more than a corporation does.

Managing a small firm systematically doesn't call for a sea of desks, or fancy procedures. Systematic management means organizing the work of whoever runs the business, getting him the right information, keeping him in control of the right activities.

A small business, for our purposes here, can be defined as a business that requires *one full-time top executive.* In most small firms, that top person also does certain specialized work in which he's expert; and this is as it should be. But this makes it all the more necessary for him to identify the other key activities on which the business depends, and to make sure that they are assigned to some qualified lieutenants. Otherwise they won't get done.

Heads of most small firms think they know what the key activities are, and think these activities are taken care of. But they're probably fooling themselves. Everybody is probably talking about the key activities while nobody does much about them. A business seldom needs more staff. What it needs is more commonsense planning, and a simple reporting and control system—maybe only a checklist—to make sure that the work is really being done.

The top person in a small business (even if he's the only person) must structure his work so as to make time for two tasks nobody else can do. One is keeping in touch with all the key operations—usually the key people—in the enterprise. The other is spending time on "the outside" —the market, the customers, the competition, the technologies. He dare not let himself become deskbound. And if his wife is his only helper, she shouldn't be deskbound either.

Most top people think they already spend too much time away from the desk. They're forever out in the shop or behind the counter or on the road. They themselves often handle the big accounts. They usually have to negotiate whatever loans they need from the bank or from other sources.

But they need a different kind of outside time. They need time to keep informed on their market, on new opportunities, on changes that affect the business. If information about these matters is available in certain trade journals or newsletters, then they should get read, or at least skimmed with a sharp eye for significant news.

As mentioned a few paragraphs ago, a small business needs its own control and information system. Its resources are limited, both in money and in people. So it must apportion its resources where they'll do the most good. It must think about questions like "Where are the markets?

What are the right things to do, and the right things to stop doing? How can we waste less of our resources, and make them more productive?"

Furthermore, a small business hasn't much power to get additional resources. So it must make sure it won't outrun its financial base. It must know well in advance when and where its financial needs will increase. A small company can't let itself get caught in a liquidity squeeze, facing a sudden demand for more money. Even if the business is prosperous, getting more financing usually takes time, as we'll see in Chapters 20, 21, and 22.

Probably your business has the usual accounting figures. But do you know your cash flow? Can you forecast next month's or next season's cash needs? If not, take a look ahead at Chapter 14, and work out a system that will put the right figures on your desk, or on the desk of a top associate who is astute about money management. (Or at least knowledgeable about money management; really astute money managers are rare.)

Probably you know your receivables. But do you know whether your customers—your distributors or dealers—are piling up unsold inventories of your wares? If not, you need information about the final market for your goods—that is, consumer purchases from dealers. Without this information, you'll be in trouble sooner or later.

A small business needs few figures. And most of the figures it needs are easy to get, since they needn't be precise. But these aren't the figures likely to be provided by the ordinary accounting setup. They are figures that relate the company's present condition, and its deployment of its key resources, to the shape of things to come—so that the company can identify opportunities and ward off dangers.

A small business has to be better at management because it can't afford a big central office, or a string of specialists. It doesn't need elaborate procedures. But it needs to structure the top job or jobs, precisely because the few people at the top must know everything important about their business, and must make sure that the key activities are carried on well. Since there are so few people at the top, they need to focus and concentrate their energies much more.

Without information that shows him clearly where his business is heading, a businessman is in the dark—and worse yet, he tends to do the wrong things. He gets stuck in trivia. He handles whatever hits his desk, unscreened. Instead of planning, he only reacts.

Very well. With these principles in mind, why not get off by yourself for a few quiet hours and make a list of the key activities and key kinds of information, whatever they are, in your business?

Pinpoint what you should be doing, and what your key helpers should be doing, and what should be shunted aside to low-level people. Once you've mapped this out, you'll be ready to clear away the clutter from your desk by eliminating whatever paperwork shouldn't be part of your job.

The Trouble with Reports

"Putting it very bluntly, I don't believe that one can manage a business by reports," writes Peter F. Drucker, one of the world's most respected management consultants. "I am a figures man, and a quantifier, and one of those people to whom figures talk. I also know that reports are abstractions, and they they can tell us only what we've determined to ask. . . . One must spend a great deal of time outside, where the results are. Inside a business, one has only costs. One looks at markets, at customers, at society, and at knowledge—all of which are outside the business—to see what is really happening. That, reports will never tell you. . . . Reports are comforting to me; they tell me a great deal. But they have also misled me often enough to make me realize that unless I go out and gain understanding, I may be acting on yesterday, even though the information is up to date."

Reports can be dangerous time-wasters. Let's suppose that three people in your firm give you weekly summaries of certain operations. An outside consultant like Drucker might ask you, "Aren't these a waste of time?" You might smile and retort, "No indeed. The three guys boil everything down to one page each, and I just glance over it. Takes a few minutes."

"What do you get out of it?" Drucker would certainly ask.

"Usually not much. Now and then I see something that needs a follow-up. But it's no big deal. I don't spend much time on it."

"I wasn't talking about just *your* time being wasted," Drucker would murmur. "You don't spend much time on it. But how much time do these key people spend summarizing and boiling down something that you don't consider a big deal?"

Keep reports and procedures and "controls" down to the bare minimum. Use them only when they save time and trouble. To illustrate this point, one of America's major company presidents tells a story on himself:

"Some years ago I bought for my company a small independent plant in Los Angeles. I bought it because it had been making a profit of a quarter-million dollars a year. When I went through the plant with the owner—who stayed on as plant manager—I asked, 'How do you determine your pricing?' The former owner answered, 'That's easy. We just quote ten cents per thousand less than your company does.'

" 'And how do you control your costs?' was my next question.

" 'That's easy,' was the answer. "We know what we pay for raw materials and labor, and what production we should get for the money.'

" 'And how do you control your overhead?' was my final question.

" 'We don't bother about it.'

"Well, I thought to myself, we can certainly save a lot of money here by putting in systematic controls. But a year later the profit of the plant was down to $125,000. Sales had remained the same and prices had remained the same. But the introduction of complex procedures had eaten up half the profits.''

What Information Do You Need?

Every business should periodically ask, ''Do we need all the reports and procedures we use? How do we use them? What would we lose if we didn't use them?''

Your business may need information for some or all of the following purposes:

1. To plan ahead. Past information can sometimes help you in planning: past sales trends, sales per salesperson, the output of a machine, the delivery time for a purchase, payment experience with a customer, the demand for a particular item at a given time, or (maybe) the quality of an employee's work. Be very careful in judging employees by reports; in a moment we'll see why.

2. To meet obligations. Money is borrowed, supplies are ordered on credit, delivery is promised for a certain day at a given price, taxes fall due. You need a simple system to make sure such obligations are met.

3. To meet government requirements. Tax returns aren't the only example. You may be legally obligated to make reports on your hiring practices, your pricing, your quality-control standards, your safety equipment. There may be investigations of your business ethics. If people in your organization are taking kickbacks, or trying to bribe somebody, you can be held responsible. (But don't expect that reports will reveal secret dealings. The best way to pick up clues is by developing alertness for them when you're circulating inside and outside your organization.)

4. To control routine activities. Normally this kind of information should be monitored by an intelligent clerk, not by you. For example, supplies ordered haven't arrived; inventory is too low; material is being

spoiled; output is dwindling. Set up guidelines and warning signals. Make sure that a clerk understands the importance of watching them.

Your office files should probably contain other important information: lists of vendors, lists of customers and prospects, specifications for products, perhaps notations about special aptitudes of employees you don't know well. Every type of business has different needs for information, and you must decide what your needs are. Just don't clog your files or desks with what you don't need.

Don't Judge Employees by Reports

A worker should be judged on his performance, not on reports by him or about him. Reports can be snow jobs or smear jobs.

Strange as it seems until you study it, a report should be the tool of the person who compiles it. If he needs it to help him direct his own efforts toward results he can control, fine. But don't have him fill out any forms, or make any reports, except those he himself needs to achieve performance.

An exception—in a way—to this rule would be the quick news-bulletin report that takes only a few words. Maybe you need to know any new accounts that came in, old accounts lost, dormant accounts activated. Maybe you need to know if any machines get out of kilter, or if there are an unusual number of customer complaints or inquiries—or whatever. Vital information should flow to you immediately on slips of paper, so you won't have to go out and talk to different people in order to keep abreast of important developments in your own organization. You'll save time for everyone concerned.

But you'll kill morale by demanding that people compile reports for "the boss" filled with information they themselves don't need. It directs their attention away from their own work. Instead of trying to do good work, they try to "make a good showing."

Whatever they're asked to report on is assumed to be a reflection of what the boss wants; so the idea spreads that the people who turn in impressive reports are the people who'll get ahead. Although resentful, people will tend to put effort into reporting rather than into their own work. Soon the boss too is misled, if not hypnotized, by the reporting procedure.

The kind of work most bogged down by reporting is sales work. A 1978 study by the University of Virginia assertedly shows that "the more detailed the call reports, the better performance by the sales personnel." But experienced sales consultants challenge this. One of them says, "Sales managers are now so snowed under with all kinds of paper that they don't know who the customers are, they don't train the sales force. They've never been out. Good salesmen are poor paper handlers; there's almost an inverse relationship between the ability of a salesman to sell and his handwriting legibility. . . . A salesman's chief resource is time. If you find that half of your salesmen's time is spent on paperwork, you'll get more sales by simplifying or eliminating the report system.''

Keep in mind that control isn't a flood of facts, but knowing what facts you need and what they mean. The information you receive should enable you to spend less time controlling, more time doing the important things. Your system should liberate you from routine—give you time for people and for the outside, where the money is.

Certain forms can save you and your people a lot of time, instead of wasting it. For example, if you're in a business that does some kind of custom work, you can hardly get along without an estimating sheet that lists all the possible operations to be performed, with a space to put a dollar figure by each. If you don't use such a sheet, you'll often miss some cost items while figuring estimates.

Also, you may need some kind of master job log in which you can give each incoming job a number, description, date in, due date, and any other essential information such as the worker or foreman who is handling it. The same information, perhaps on a job envelope containing more detailed instructions, can be placed with the job itself as it goes through. This simple system can bring order out of chaos in a busy shop.

Another helpful form: a list (on a blackboard or on somebody's clipboard) of priorities, updated daily, for work in process. This lets employees know which work should get first attention that day.

Keeping Score

Much of the information that comes to your desk will probably be financial information. If you're a sophisticated financial type, or if you've taken courses in accounting, you may be able to spot some significant numbers in this information, and they may guide you in planning. On the other hand, if you have no financial background, you may spend hours dutifully plodding through the figures without getting any clear idea of how your business is doing. That's where your accountants should come in. If they only keep records, without making them easy for you to use, you aren't getting what you pay for. To some accountants, keeping the records is an end in itself. They aren't accountants at all, but bookkeepers.

Assuming that you have no financial background, here's a capsule summary of the way a business should keep score. We'll begin with the most basic of basics, the famous "bottom line."

When people talk about the bottom line, they usually mean the last line of an income statement. The line says "Net profit after taxes," or "Net income." This is the amount of cash a business has to spend—right? Wrong.

The bottom line, net profits, is just a score. The business may have much more cash to spend than the bottom line shows—or much less. Confusing the bottom line with actual cash can lead to stupid mistakes. Get your accountant to help you figure out how many spendable dollars your business has, or is likely to have in the future.

Let's carry this further. You get a sales report. It shows the dollar volume of sales. Can the dollars from these sales be spent? No. In most businesses, sales figures are scores. The actual money won't be available until the customers pay their bills.

Or you get a purchasing report. It shows that so many dollars' worth of goods have been bought and put into inventory. Does it mean those dollars are spent and gone? Not quite. The figure is just another score. The dollars won't be paid to the suppliers until later.

And so it goes with standard financial reports. They show scores. Scores aren't the same as spendable dollars. But they can be important. Loans are made, companies are bought and sold on the basis of financial scores. Good scores are likely to indicate that your business is doing well.

On the other hand, scores can be deceptive unless you know what's behind them. For example, most statistics on sales performance, whether by an individual salesman or by the whole sales staff, report sales in total dollars. But in many businesses this is misleading. The same dollar volume of sales may mean a big profit, no profit, or a loss—depending on the product mix sold. Some products are more profitable than others.

Take a sadder example. The owner of a small factory was delighted because the total score on labor grievances showed "only five grievances per thousand employees per month." If these had been scattered evenly or randomly through the plant, he could rightfully have been happy. He was smart enough to check a little further, and found that there wasn't even one grievance per year in the departments that employed 95 percent of his work force. This contented him. But he hadn't checked deeply enough. If he'd been smarter yet, he would have asked, "Just where *are* these five grievances per month?" Then he would have found that they were almost all in the same department, where only a half-dozen people worked.

This department happened to be Final Assembly, through which all production had to pass. The total of "only five" grievances per month really meant about ten major grievances per person per year in Final

Assembly. So when Final Assembly went on strike because its grievances were neglected by a management misled by its own statistics, it bankrupted the company, which no longer exists.

Perhaps many of these grievances could have been avoided or, at best, attended to before they festered by the use of an employee "suggestion box" in each department, with cash bonuses paid for each suggestion found viable. A notice should be posted above the suggestion box stating that each grievance or positive suggestion will be placed on the top executive's desk and not on the foreman's (fear by the employee of the foreman's reaction).

It's up to you to analyze what kind of scores can give a revealing picture of your company. Probably you'll come to the conclusion that "approximately" is more helpful to you than a firm-looking figure worked out to six decimal places. You'll find there are situations in which a range tells you more than even an approximate single figure. You'll come to understand that "larger" and "smaller," "earlier" and "later," "up" and "down" can usually tell you all you need to know.

Your Desk Can Be Clutterproof

How can you keep on top of the mass of details that never stop coming? And how can you simultaneously push ahead on the main tasks, each of which may take days of investigating and conferring and planning?

Moving papers off your desk is a matter of system. You'll be surprised how two simple techniques will enable you to keep your desk load to a minimum.

The first technique is preliminary screening. The other is classifying your paperwork with "must do" items on top, then "should do," and then "do if time."

There are only three useful ways you can handle a piece of paper, whether it's a memo, a phone message, or a publication: 1. You can throw it away; 2. you can act on it as required (make a call, send a reply, refer it to someone better able to handle it, or take other indicated action; 3. you can save it for consideration at a better time.

Of course there's also a fourth option, which isn't useful and must be eliminated; you can shuffle it from pile to pile with no action. Too many people take this option almost by reflex, because they unconsciously dread making decisions. So they feel harassed, and they're slow and inefficient—especially at finding a paper when they need it.

Get into the habit of making a decision every time you touch a piece of paper. Soon you'll develop a rhythm. You'll throw away the trivial stuff fast. You'll move along from problem to problem without tension or confusion. And you'll find that you've broken yourself of postponing actions that could just as easily be taken at once.

Some efficiency experts preach that you should never handle an incoming piece of paper twice—or that you should at least do as much as feasible about it immediately. The theory is that once you pick up a paper, you have an investment of time in reading it; therefore if you put it aside without action, you lose the duplicate pickup time. Accordingly, you should preserve your original investment and avoid rehandling time by carrying the matter through to completion.

But this can mean that you get stuck on one piece of paper for hours while others pile up. Under the screening system you dispose of some papers at first glance, but you classify the others for attention after completion of the screening. This seems better for most people.

If you have a secretary, you can use her to screen and sort your incoming mail and other paperwork. She'll find many items that needn't cross your desk. Everything she does put on your desk can be divided into piles (or into separate folders) according to any system of classification that works well for you. One system might be:

A. Urgent matters for prompt action.
B. Other matters that call for action soon.
C. Long-range problems that will need investigation or study.
D. Information for reading.

Schedule your work to establish whatever sequence of activities will best bring big projects to early completion, or implement new decisions most smoothly. Never try to get all the little jobs out of the way before you start a big one. Many small tasks take care of themselves if you put them aside.

You can use this same principle in handling phone messages. Don't return all calls immediately. Spot the crucial ones. Half the rest will be from people who've already solved their problems; others will call you again soon enough.

Here is where a good secretary is worth her weight in gold. She knows your priorities, and is able to act as a buffer to shield you from time-wasting phone calls. She may be able to direct many of the calls to others who can handle them without "bothering" you.

Stick with top-priority problems until you've done as much as you can with them. Set a time limit for the process—and when you can't find a solution to a problem, don't continue to waste time on it. Drop it, and come back to it later. You may discover that the "fireless cooker" in your subconscious has worked out a solution.

Keep Yourself Reminded

You and your secretary might arrange a "bring-up" system by which she keeps a list of matters you want referred back to you at certain future times. Instead of keeping things on your desk or in your desk drawers, you can give them to the secretary with a note saying, "Bring up after we get a reply," or "Bring up the next time Bob is in the office."

If you don't have a secretary, you can set up your own tickler file. Number manila folders for each day of the month. Anything you can't dispose of immediately goes into one of these future folders, according to whichever day you want to handle it again. Each day, as part of your regular routine, you go through the folder for that day. When it's empty, move it to the back of the row, so that the next day's file is in front. Similarly, there can be special folders for matters you want to discuss with particular people when they're available.

Systems technicians have developed various other kinds of memory-ticklers. These range from the very simple, such as a desk pad for jotting down "must do" items, to complex visible control systems and even electronic signals. A desk calendar is an obvious and universal tool for keeping track of commitments. The week-at-a-glance and month-at-a-glance calendars are especially helpful—not only in saving the turning of pages while you're working out an appointment with someone, but also in showing the general configuration of your activities for a week or month—making visual all the things you must do over a span greater than one day.

Control-board systems are useful in much the same way. They can show you the full array of activities you must monitor. The simplest control boards, such as blackboards and bulletin boards on the wall, are mere visual inventories and reminders of things to do, although you can arrange for other people in your organization to post daily or weekly updates or "red flag" items there—cash receipts, shop workload, equipment-maintenance reminders, or whatever information you urgently need in planning your own activities.

As you get into specific control of target schedules, you may turn to systems that use boards with date columns, colored pins or buttons, and colored tapes to chart progress toward previously set milestones. But don't get carried away. Keep your reminder systems simple, or you'll need a full-time employee to handle them. And keep them current, or they'll be worse than useless. An elaborate control board is best suited to massive clerical or production work which can pile up at bottlenecks unless someone controls it.

Colored signals can keep you aware of important unfinished matters. A colored tab or a colored folder can serve as a reminder by making something stand out among other papers that cross your desk. Just remember that too many colors will nullify one another's usefulness.

Bunching for Efficiency

Another point about sorting out paperwork instead of tackling it in whatever order it hits your desk: if you'll group similar items, and handle them as a group, you'll finish them much faster.

For example, let's say you're a one-man organization. You write your own letters, pay your own bills, do your filing and bookkeeping, make and receive all phone calls. In the whole world of business, you're the one type of enterprise most in need of efficient organization.

If you're not well organized, you may handle the morning's mail item by item. The first letter asks for information. So you walk over to a file and look up the information. Back at your desk you write the reply, address and stamp the envelope, then go back to the cabinet to file the letter and a carbon copy of your answer. The next envelope contains a bill. So you get out your checkbook, write a check, fill in the stub, and stamp the return envelope. Next you find a request that you make a sales call. You grab the phone and make the call. Next letter asks for information. Back to the file cabinet—and so on, back and forth, doing each kind of task repeatedly but interspersed with other kinds. Your morning is full of waste motion.

Visualize how much more efficient it is to go through the whole pile of mail first, sorting as you go—bills in one pile, information requests in another, matters to be handled with phone calls in another. Some piles can be put aside and allowed to grow for several days. When a pile is big enough to take an hour or more of your time, handle it in one continuous operation. For example, you can look up information to answer a dozen queries in one trip to the filing cabinet or reference shelf, saving many steps and repetitious handlings. Likewise, do a big batch of filing at one time; it may enable you to open a file drawer just once instead of ten times.

The bulk of your month's check-writing should be done at a single sitting. First write all the checks—using a typewriter if you're an adequate typist, so that you can insert a sheet of three checks in the roller and hammer them out in one quick series. Then record all the checks in another single operation. Next, put them all into envelopes, and seal and stamp the envelopes. Finally, file the bills if you think you need them.

Incidentally, if you're spending much time on clerical work, you're not doing other work that could make your business grow. An expenditure of enough money to pay a secretary—even a part-time one—may be the best investment you can make.

If you do have a secretary, make sure she does chores in batches. And if you give her dictation, save it up until you can dictate a bunch of letters and memos in one sitting; don't keep calling her in for short takes. (Better yet, dictate into a machine—preferably a lightweight recorder that you can use while driving to work or waiting at an airport or even shaving and dressing.)

Accumulate quick, easy, yes/no-type work in a special "captured minutes" folder. Work on it during odd moments—while traveling, perhaps, or at your desk while waiting for a phone call to go through or for a meeting to start.

Similarly, if you work with other people, save up the matters you want to discuss with them. It's better to ask a department manager five questions in one session than to interrupt him five different times. And when you make phone calls to customers or suppliers, your brain will function better—get warmed up, so to speak—through similar calls in quick succession.

Likewise, most problems can wait a few hours or days. When you bunch them, you'll find that similar ones can be handled with one trip or one phone call or memo—while others will disappear altogether, as someone else takes care of them or they just resolve themselves. Keep asking, "Am I doing work that someone else could do just as well?"

How to Arrange a Desk

The untidy desk is an old joke. The clean desk is thought to be a symbol of efficiency. It implies "doing today's work today."

The clean-desk fetish has been carried so far that some image-minded executives make a point of not using any desk. They sit in an easy chair, where they work on a small lap board. This may be fine if somebody else sorts all their work, and feeds them the important stuff bit by bit. Otherwise, how does the executive without a desk ever go through his mail and messages?

The trouble with the clean-desk fetish is that we confuse the symbol with the real thing. That is, we confuse barren neatness with efficiency. A clean desk may be the habitat of someone with too little work; or it may mean that drawers and cabinets are stuffed with unfinished work.

Lots of efficient people prefer to see many current papers on the desk, where they serve as reminders of things to do or questions to mull over. Whether you like lots of papers or a bare desk, think of your desk as a work station, not a storage bin. Have a place for everything you need. And make sure it's the best place. For instance, is your telephone handy, or must you reach and swing away from your desk, without a good place to write as you talk? A pad by your telephone is a must.

Another must is an alphabetical telephone-number reference book or device with all of the numbers written down for easy, fast access, rather than on the walls or on business cards thumbtacked all over the office.

There could even be a cross-reference on this phone-number device, listing frequently called numbers by classification—say, like Escrow Companies, Freight Forwarders, and so on—with the names listed below those titles.

Do you keep reference materials you often consult within easy reach, or do you have to get up and go to another office whenever you need to look up something important? Are small supplies handy enough? You can lose minutes a day—a whole week every year—if you must leave your work area every time you need paper clips, staples, a stamp, a phone number.

How about a pencil sharpener next to your desk instead of in the outer office? Any reason why those files you consult so often shouldn't be yards closer to you? If you're likely to need a certain paper soon, will you know where to find it? (Seconds spent hunting for something during a long-distance call can mean the difference of a minute in the time charges —to say nothing of the irritation caused by the delay.)

Many efficient executives work at a double desk—that is, a long work-table behind them, a desk with several handy drawers in front, and a swivel chair in between. Others have an L-shaped desk extension—or even an L-desk plus a back table. All these arrangements provide plenty of top area within easy reach as the executive swings around in his chair. There is room for papers which must tarry until other information is assembled for use in working with them.

Maybe you need some such arrangement. If you perform a variety of tasks, or if they are complex, you're likely to need many papers at your fingertips.

The top of your desk should be laid out for the convenience of secretaries and messengers as well as for your own ease of operation. There should be one place for incoming papers and another for outgoing. If your work is sorted before it comes to you, you might need two or more boxes or desk folders in which different priorities of work are put.

One manufacturer who caters to the efficient organization of executive desks is Shaw-Walker, with its Carlyle line of desks. Carlyle desks are dedicated to the clean-desktop look. Drawer space is provided for just about everything: the telephone, letter trays, paper files, card files. There are reference pull-out shelves and side utility drawers in place of the center drawer—to do away with the need for backing away from the desk when you need a rubber band or a ruler. These desks even contain hidden wastebaskets.

Another desk manufacturer, Globe-Wernicke, made a time-and-motion study which showed variations of as much as two seconds in laying hands on materials, depending on where they were stored in the desk. The time needed to open the drawer, extract the item, and close the drawer was shortest when it was located at the top right, and greatest at the bottom left (assuming in both cases that the executive already knew where to reach for the material). You might take this into account in deciding where to store things in your desk, so that those most often used will be most quickly reached.

A third student of office efficiency, the Art Metal Construction Company, reported: "Modern office technique demands that the desk, the chair, the light, and the worker should be considered as a single operating unit, and each component should be carefully fitted to the others to produce the maximum possible efficiency and comfort."

Make sure your lighting is adequate. It should come over your left shoulder (if you're right-handed) or should be evenly distributed.

Buy the best furniture you can afford, to cut down time-wasting repairs or faulty operation or downright discomfort and inefficiency. Art Metal says, "Fatigue is responsible for more errors and slow-ups than any other cause. Correct-posture seating reduces fatigue and helps to increase efficiency. . . . The weight should be on the bottom of the thighs and not on the base of the spine. The seat height is usually correct when the weight at the knees is supported by the feet and there is no pressure on the under part of the upper leg at the front edge of the seat."

KEEP THESE BASIC POINTS IN MIND:

- *Most of the paper in our offices should be thrown away.*
- *Most of the paper needn't be created in the first place. See if you can quit compiling certain kinds of records. Answer letters by phoning, or by writing a reply on the face of the original letter.*
- *Try to spend most of your time on whatever you're good at. But make sure that other key activities are well handled, and keep in touch with them.*
- *Make time to keep informed on your market, on new opportunities, on changes that affect your business. Think about "What are the right things to do, and the right things to stop doing?"*
- *Don't try to manage your business by reports. Only reports that save time or trouble should be used.*

- *Any detailed reports compiled by employees should be for their own use, not to impress superiors. Don't judge employees by reports.*
- *Sort paperwork into separate piles for handling as groups.*
- *Set up a system to keep yourself reminded of important matters.*
- *Arrange your desk to minimize waste motion.*

14

What You Should Know About Money Management

Look at any small business that grows and thrives and pays its bills promptly, and somewhere inside it you'll find a capable financial man keeping a cold eye on operations. Sometimes he's called the controller, sometimes the treasurer, sometimes just the accountant or bookkeeper or office manager. Often he's the boss himself. Whoever he is, whatever his title, he's shrewd and thrifty. He's a detail hound. Otherwise his company wouldn't be so strong.

If you don't have such a person in your firm, you'd better get one. Meanwhile you, as owner-manager, may have to be watchdog of the dollars yourself. How to do the best job at it is the subject of this chapter.

Better Buying

Let's start with buying, since that's the first step in business operations. Or almost the first. Before any important purchase, there should be considerable shopping, thinking, and maybe dickering. Once there was a cartoon strip in which a little-girl brat was holding a sign that offered "Interesting and Educational Tour into the Woods—Only 10¢." In the second picture a customer said, "That seems reasonable enough," and accepted. In the last picture, they were on their way into the forest together as the girl murmured casually, "Later we'll discuss the fee for bringing you *out* of the woods." That's the way with purchasing. What seems like a good cheap buy may get you deep into trouble and cost you a fearsome price later.

Before you buy, you need to know not only price but also details about delivery, service, quality, durability, and perhaps other elements of total cost such as storage and upkeep.

When you figure that any company's purchases can drain away 50 cents or more of every dollar that comes in, you can see that thrifty buying is a big part of profits. If you save just 1 percent of the cost of purchased goods and services, you make as much profit as by increasing sales 6 or 8 percent.

Whether you're purchasing paper clips or a printing press, you ought to look at several sources. Establish two or three vendors for every item of supply or service if you can. Then you're in better shape if your normal supply is cut off for any reason and you must find an alternative source. Furthermore, a supplier is likely to give better service and better prices if he knows competitors can easily get your business.

Of course you can carry the shopping-around concept too far when you're small. If you order from too many vendors and your orders are relatively small, you won't be on especially friendly terms with any. A small firm is often at a disadvantage in dealing with suppliers. When supplies get tight or times are hard, manufacturers tend to favor a big buyer who can take virtually their whole output with one order. So you'd better make special efforts to cultivate your sources.

Invite salesmen to call on you even if you don't plan to buy from them immediately. Put your cards on the table. Explain that you have a supplier but want to keep in touch since you may make a change. Instead of asking them about their products, tell them about your needs. Let them know about your budget limitations and cost comparisons. They'll respond with better prices and show you how to save. They may be able to arrange quick repair services on their product, persuade their company to grant better credit terms, and alert you to discounts and promotional offers.

There are several ways to buy supplies, or merchandise for resale. You can buy directly from producers, from wholesalers or distributors who may carry several competing lines, or through manufacturers' representatives who may represent many different product lines and simply take your orders. Each has advantages.

Wholesale houses give special discounts. Sometimes by combining small orders for different items, you actually pay less than by buying direct from manufacturers. For example, if you're running a bookstore, you can't get a 40-percent discount from a publisher unless you order five or more books at a time—but a book wholesaler will give you the 40-percent reduction if you order one book from each of fifty publishers through him. The same rule applies in many industries. So if you need only a few items from many sources, you may find it profitable to buy from a distributor or a rep.

If you're buying supplies—say, file folders and pencils and other standard office items—it may be better to buy them all at retail from an office-supply store. The store will probably let you buy on open account, or use a credit card or some other form of credit, while distributors are demanding cash.

Big orders, direct to a manufacturer, usually get you the lowest price. But in order to get this price, or to avoid heavy express charges on small shipments, you may have to order a bigger quantity than you really want. Can you afford to pad an order beyond your short-term needs for the sake of the low price? Balance your saving against the cash that will be tied up in inventory.

Keeping too much stock on hand is expensive and uses up valuable selling space or storage room. Inventory can be a big cash trap. Each $100 in material on the shelves costs between $15 and $25 per year in handling, storage space, debt service, deterioration, obsolescence, and "shrinkage" through employees' helping themselves.

Therefore, try to plan for fast turnover of whatever you buy. If space is limited, buy from firms that deliver often and carry a fairly complete stock. For some expendables that you buy often, let the salesmen check your inventory and order what you need; they can also fill out the order forms, saving valuable time in your office. Even on bigger orders, you can do this through a systems contract, as it's called. Instead of your company's maintaining inventory, the supplier maintains the inventory for you, automatically replenishing your stock according to a schedule agreed on in advance. This earns you a bonus discount, yet you're not billed until you receive the goods. Give the vendor the responsibility of checking and delivering on time—but run spot checks on his accuracy.

Look for Substitutes

Did you ever hear how Henry Ford used his ingenuity to hold down the cost of his early Model T autos? After he froze this car's design and production, his vendors supplied the same components year after year, and could afford to quote very low prices. But one year Henry announced that he wanted his engines shipped in special crates. Each crate must be a perfect cube made of prime wood with no flaws. He specified the crate's dimensions to $\frac{1}{16}$-inch. And he warned engine vendors that if one side of a crate was even slightly damaged in shipment, it would go back unopened and unpaid-for.

Henry was known for eccentricity, so everyone shrugged. But when the bids came in, his controller summoned up courage to protest: "Mr. Ford, do you realize that you'll pay fifty cents per engine more because of these costly crates?" Henry ignored him.

When the engines arrived, Henry personally supervised the crew that uncrated them. "I'll fire any man who so much as marks any side of these crates," he threatened. At last, when his production line began to roll, everyone understood. The wood from the crates became the Model T floorboards.

Maybe you can be just as ingenious in some of your purchasing. At least you can scratch around for alternatives, instead of using the obvious suppliers. Take telephones, for example. Do you know that Bell no longer has a monopoly on them? Instead of renting instruments as we've always done, we can now buy them, new or used, either at retail stores or from the phone company itself. Competition is pushing prices down. At this writing, a plain rotary-dial instrument costs about $20. A phone with "hold" button and five line buttons is about $100.

To know whether you'd save by buying, figure how long it will take to get back your capital investment. The capital expense includes not only the cost of the phones but also a one-time installation charge, coupler rentals, extension-line charges, and extra-cost services. The payback period on capital cost vs. the former rental cost should be less than three years. If it's longer, you would probably be tying up too much money.

Capital Investment? Be Cautious!

When you buy big-ticket items from big companies, you probably pay more than you need to. Any company that keeps full-time salesmen roaming the territory must sell its products at a higher price because its price must include high sales commissions and maintenance and service facilities as well as a flock of sales managers and other help who add nothing to the value of the equipment. You're better off to buy the equipment used from a local dealer who can service it. In the Sunday classified pages of big-city newspapers you'll find all kinds of used furniture and equipment bargains. Also, new office furniture and other fixtures are now available at discount stores for surprisingly low prices.

There's another source of bargains you may not know about. It's called Support Services Alliance, Inc. It's a nonprofit outfit started in 1977 by Herbert Heaton (comptroller of the Rockefeller Foundation) to provide buying services for businesses with fewer than twenty employees. The only requirements for membership are a checking account and a $10 initial fee. When you buy something through SSA, you pay it a fraction of the savings you make on the purchase. For example, if Xerox offers a 15-

percent discount on the cost of renting one of its machines, SSA may take a 2-percent cut, leaving you with a substantial 13-percent reduction.

Think especially hard before you invest capital in anything new. Many young entrepreneurs get carried away simply by the image of its newness. They sink $30,000 into equipment which could easily cost no more than $6,000 or $7,000 secondhand—and which they won't need anyway until a year or two later. Lack of experience makes them easy targets for salesmen whose legitimate mission is to sell new equipment.

As mentioned in Chapter 4, almost any large machinery can be bought used for about a quarter of what it would cost new. Buying secondhand may also enable you to shortcut a long wait for the new machine. There are three main sources for used machinery.

One source: industrial auctions. They are a big business in many parts of the country. But don't bid unless you really know machinery. All sales are "as is," with no warranties or refunds. The machine may have been tricked up for the auction, and the auctioneer may not let bidders examine it or even listen to it running.

Another source: big companies that use the kind of equipment you're looking for. They may have systematic programs for selling unneeded stuff. Some of them keep mailing lists and send out fliers. Du Pont, International Paper, and others publish catalogues several times a year.

The third source: dealers in industrial surplus. The Machinery Dealers National Association, Box 19128, Washington, D.C. 20036, will send you a free list of surplus and salvage dealers all over the country.

Whatever the source, buying secondhand machinery is a game for experts. The machine may turn out to be not quite the right size or pressure. Parts may be hard to get, or even impossible. The cost of rejiggering nozzles or feeders or whatnot may wipe out the savings. Then too, an older machine may not meet current standards stipulated by the Occupational Safety and Health Administration. If you get socked with a penalty, whoever sells it to you is liable, but collecting from him isn't easy.

Avoid buying any capital equipment, new or used, before you need it. Some people say you should buy now to beat inflation. Not necessarily. Although the prices may keep climbing as inflation heats up, the prices of electronic gear like computers and telephones have kept dropping. And anyway, you may be in a better position to pay later on, which is important.

Of course, major investments in new hardware or buildings sometimes *must* be made. But be sure about that "must." Will the new investment pay for itself within a reasonable time? If not, can you do without it for a while longer? Can you find a cheaper substitute? Or can you at least arrange to stretch out the payment?

If you desperately need a new major facility, but think you just can't afford it because it will wreck your capital budget, or because the return on investment will be too low, ask the vendors to itemize the total cost. This "unbundling" may show that you've put too much of the cost on your capital budget. An itemized bid will show you what fractions of the total expenditure can be treated as *current expense* (for example, software in computer controls), and the return on the smaller actual *capital investment* may look better.

Vendors may balk at unbundling unless you're close to making a deal. They're afraid you'll use the itemized list as a shopping guide to work out a better deal with a competitor. But most of them can give you a good idea of what the ratio between expenses and capital costs will be. And they should agree to give you a detailed breakdown when they see that this may clinch the sale.

Unless you're extremely cash-heavy, try to buy on installment terms. Get the best financing you can. Before accepting a deal offered by a sales rep, see if your bank will lend your company the money, perhaps by taking a chattel mortgage on the equipment. The bank rate might be 13 percent while the vendor might want 15 or 18 percent.

Leasing Can Liberate Cash

If you're painfully short of cash but need new equipment badly, look into the possibilities of leasing instead of buying. Leasing as a substitute for direct ownership has expanded fast in recent years. Autos, trucks, computers, machine tools, and umpteen kinds of equipment can be leased. Your long-run out-of-pocket costs will be greater—but it's a way to get equipment immediately without forking over a big bundle of bucks, and without using your all-important borrowing power. Your lease charges are tax-deductible (just as financing charges are, of course) and may give you a faster and fuller tax write-off.

The equipment-leasing business is hotly competitive, so you can bargain on price and other terms. But watch out for lowballing—the old auto-dealer trick. A vendor may quote a rental price sharply below his competitors'. After you sign with him and inform the losing bidders, he stalls. He speaks of vague trouble with his financing source. As the date for installation of the equipment nears, and you get twitchy, the vendor demands that you renegotiate the lease at a higher price.

To protect yourself, if any vendor or broker quotes an unusually low price, insist on knowing who is financing the lease. Then go to this person or institution, explain your position, and ask for written confirmation of the vendor's lease proposal before you sign.

During the negotiations, try for these concessions:

1. No security deposit from you. The lessor's interest is amply protected by his retaining title to the equipment. He can always repossess.

2. No unconditional guarantee of payments. No commitment that you will assume the lessor's debt to the manufacturer or the lending institution.

3. No tie-in clauses that force you to buy supplies, services, or insurance from the lessor.

4. No "separate agreement" that the lease is void unless satisfactory equipment is delivered. This should be in the lease itself. If you do sign such a separate agreement, make sure you don't waive claims or defenses against assignees. Otherwise, here's what can happen: You take delivery and begin making payments. Meanwhile the lessor assigns the lease to a bank, giving the bank an "equipment acceptance notice." You find that the equipment is shoddy, so you stop paying. The bank sues for its money, and wins, because the separate agreement had no effect on your obligation to the bank. You still have a claim against the bank as lessor-assignee, but you'll be a long time collecting. Meanwhile you're stuck with inferior equipment and a court-upheld obligation to keep paying for it.

5. Any clause that escalates payments to keep pace with inflation should apply only to maintenance costs. The lessor's basic capital cost isn't raised by inflation, so why raise the basic rental?

6. If the lease is renewable, payments after the renewal should be smaller. Your payments on that first lease covered most of the lessor's capital costs. Only the residual value of the equipment should carry over into a renewed lease.

What about servicing of the equipment? The vendor's rep will probably offer you a service contract. Service contracts are a form of insurance—and as we'll see in Chapter 16, it's often smarter to set up your own reserve fund (called self-insuring) than to buy insurance. Service contracts seldom cover all costs, and never guarantee better service. In fact, they limit you to one service source when you may prefer to have several. Then too, service contracts are dead losses if the equipment needs no service—or if the service firm goes out of business.

Here's one more possibility for a capital investment at low cost. Suppose you've owned a business building a long time. It cost $20,000 and is now worth $80,000. You want to sell to relocate, but you can't afford to pay tax on a $60,000 capital gain. An answer is to get the prospective buyer of your old building to purchase the newer building you want. Then you swap buildings with a cash adjustment, partly tax-free.

So much for purchasing. Now let's consider what else you do with company money.

You pay out some on overhead. Some on people—wages, salaries, fees, commissions. Some on taxes.

These are more or less fixed, unavoidable costs. But you may be able to pare them down, so we'll look at all of them later. But first let's consider something else you do with company money.

Where do you put it when you don't have to spend it for a while?

How to Avoid Tax Trouble with Surpluses

Most small businesses have uneven cash flows. Their revenues are heaviest at one end of the month, or in one particular quarter, while expenses tend to bunch up somewhere else. Consequently, they often operate during much of the year with more cash than they need.

What should you do with your surplus? Let's assume that, as often happens, the owners don't want it paid out in dividends.

No doubt you try to tuck it away in readiness for taxes, for absorbing unexpected losses, for carrying the company through a slump, or for future expansion. But reserves can be pitfalls. Here are considerations to keep in mind.

A reserve for tax payments isn't tax-deductible, of course. But if an IRS auditor sees it on your books and notices that it wasn't all used up when you paid taxes, he'll want to know how it was computed. If he finds a worksheet in your file, listing deductions on the return which *might* be disallowed and their tax cost, he'll naturally go back and disallow them. So why give hints to the IRS about questionable items? Keep your tax reserve under some other label.

What about a reserve for bad debts? It is nontaxable unless tax men regard it as a device for sheltering income from taxation. They probably won't question it unless there's an unusually large contribution in any one year, or unless you can't show how you computed the amount of reserve needed. Your bad-debt experience in past years would be a reasonable yardstick. Another standard way to calculate it would be a fixed percentage—say, 5 percent—of your accounts receivable. A more accurate way is a percentage that goes up as your delinquent accounts get older. The reserve for accounts six to nine months overdue might be 25 percent, and so on up to 100 percent for those more than a year old.

Of course, you can take tax deductions for bad debts as they occur. But putting money aside for them in advance gives you more flexibility in managing your surplus. It can give you a predictable tax deduction, and can avoid sharp fluctuations in losses from year to year, cushioning bad years with surplus contributions in good. This is just about the only "estimated item" the IRS allows.

What about another reserve just for whatever needs may arise? In some instances this might prove to be prudent. But if you pile up unspent money, the IRS will cast suspicious eyes on it, and try to assess an accumulated-earnings tax.

Sometimes you can fend off such a challenge by borrowing money from the bank, to be used in case your sales sag. Then the IRS will probably concede that you can't very well pay dividends when you're burdened with debt.

Or you can say that your reserve is for expansion, modernization, new-product development, or other expenditures you may want to make in the future. That's okay if you can be specific. Put something on paper. The T-men will insist on seeing plans in your file, with cost estimates, to justify the reserve.

Here's still another way to explain your reserve. A company can legally hold on to earnings simply for the "reasonable needs" of the business. These needs aren't necessarily limited to meeting cash-flow requirements or financing future growth. You're equally entitled to put away money as protection against hazards, provided you specify the hazards.

Put a dollar amount on each hazard. How much can it cost you if environmentalists pass laws that force you to make changes? How much might the next union contract cost you? How much extra interest will you have to pay if your credit rating sags, or if bank interest rates rise? How much will you need if your insurance is cancelled, or if you suffer certain types of loss not covered by your insurance? (We'll get into insurance and self-insurance in Chapter 16.) All these add up and can legitimately be provided for.

Where do you keep your reserve? Most small companies just leave it on deposit at the bank. This isn't brilliant, in view of the low interest rates paid by banks. Your money should be working hard. Why not park the surplus in investments such as short-term government securities, commercial paper, money-market funds, or stocks and bonds recommended by a good investment adviser? When you consider that a corporation's investment income is 85-percent tax-sheltered, the return on some of the safest investments is juicy. It can fatten the company's net worth faster (at least, in the short run) than plowing the reserve back into the business.

For this same reason, any stocks you own personally might be transferred into your corporation. The dividends will be taxed much less, and you can take them out later as capital gain.

Down with Overhead!

"Overhead" usually means fixed costs, including rent, utilities, and other expenses, that a business faces just to be open and ready for its customers. It may also include amenities such as wall-to-wall carpeting, impressive oak desks, and beautiful receptionists (although we'll put all personnel costs in a different category and consider them next).

Overhead costs don't rise because of increased production or sales. This is why your cost per unit goes down as your volume goes up. On the other hand, you can't make a profit until you've met your overhead. So if volume declines, you must move quickly to cut expenses. An accountant can work out a break-even chart to show your profit margin at given levels of production or pricing.

Of every $100 the average retailer rings up on his cash register, about $65 goes to pay for the merchandise he just sold, since he works on approximately a 35-percent profit margin. Some of the remaining $35 pays overhead—and some is left over for profit, if he's a good businessman. Control of overhead is a key to profit.

One way to minimize overhead is to start small. Instead of taking space in a high-rent downtown area, maybe you can operate at home, or in a low-rent district. (However, if you're a retailer, remember that a good location is more important than any other single factor—although a well-located store needn't be big.)

Elegant offices for small firms may awe a few visitors. But the shrewder visitors are likely to be more favorably impressed by simple quarters and a shirt-sleeves atmosphere. Anyhow, if you do most of your business by phone or mail, or away from your office, why spend a nickel more than necessary for rent, furnishings, and utilities?

It might seem hard to economize on utilities—water, heat, electricity—without discomfort. But there are ways. You'll find many in an earlier book of mine, *How to Manage Real Estate Successfully—in Your Spare Time*. Look in Chapter 16, "Keeping Down Upkeep." There's no need to duplicate that material here. But there is more to be said about electricity. It isn't going to get cheaper. Here are ways to save it in your office or workrooms.

Electrical Economies

You'll need less air conditioning if you install reflective solar film, or sun screens or awnings, on windows exposed to the sun. They can keep out as much as 80 percent of the heat entering through windows.

You can install timers on air conditioning to shut down during lunch, shortly before closing, and on weekends. Heating can also be changed at preselected times, with a little gadget attached to a timer plugged into a wall outlet. You can get details from Fuel Sentry, 79 Putnam Street, Mount Vernon, New York 10550.

Consider removing or dimming your conventional overhead lighting fixtures (called "ambient lighting" by architects) and substituting "task lighting," which a) concentrates light where people need it, b) reduces glare and reflections on work surfaces, c) puts less burden on cooling equipment. Task lighting usually takes about two watts per square foot, while ambient lighting uses five watts. Ask an architect for details.

Are lights burning continuously in some parts of your premises, such as hallways, where less illumination would do just as well? If so, you can remove some bulbs, or substitute lower-watt ones. And if there are vending machines in the hall, they work just as well with their lights off.

It's a myth that incandescent lights should be kept on continuously because turning them on and off wastes energy. On the contrary, you save energy and money each time you turn off an unneeded incandescent light. On the other hand, fluorescent lamps do wear out when turned on and off often. But if you're going out for an hour or more, you save by turning off fluorescents in an empty office.

If your company has its own building, even a small one, maybe you light up its exterior at night, for security. Low-pressure sodium lamps are the cheapest outdoor industrial lighting. One big company used twenty-two of them around its plant, and found that they gave as much light as needed for an annual cost of about $832, compared with $1,358 for high-pressure sodium and $1,971 for mercury vapor.

Electric-power companies all over the country are gradually moving to "time-of-day" rates, which mean highest rates at peak daytime hours, lowest rates at night. Few give any discount to volume users—and in fact may charge a penalty. So if you run a job shop or manufacturing business, consider spreading out your work, maybe putting on a night shift.

Simple Office Economies

Behold the humble postage stamp. Would you believe it can cost you hundreds of wasted dollars each year? Use these little-known ways to cut postal costs:

Test your postage scale's accuracy. Nine pennies should weigh exactly one ounce. Test it often if there are frequent temperature changes in your office.

Your postage meter is cranking out money. Train anyone who'll be using it. Lock it each night to prevent unauthorized use after hours. And get a rebate from the post office on spoiled or unused metered tapes and envelopes.

If your company mails bulletins or newsletters, second class will be only a fraction of first or third class.

Don't always send parcels, freight, or mail by the fastest and easiest way. When speed isn't important, use one of the less costly methods. A customer-service representative from the post office can give you free advice.

If you send large bulk mailings, use the post office's special equipment, which it will provide at no charge: canvas bags, steel racks to hold the bags, large canvas carts on wheels, trays. They'll save time in your office and in the post office.

Never affix uncancelled stamps to return envelopes enclosed; this is an invitation to the recipient to tear off the unused stamp and use it on his own mail. Use a postage-free-permit print on your return mail. Then if the envelope is never used, at least you have saved the extra expense of a "gift" stamp.

Make your mail department off-limits to employees from elsewhere in the company. Require that all requests for personal postage be cleared through the bookkeeper, or whoever is in charge of mailing. In fact, it's a good idea to keep all office supplies in a locked room or cabinet.

Reuse large envelopes received in the mail. Use the clean side of old forms. Cover old file-folder tabs with new labels.

Eliminate telephone extensions and lines that get little use. Log all long-distance calls. And check your phone bills; they often contain errors.

Savings in Salvage

If your business has any manual-labor facilities, you can push down overhead by regular walk-through inspections. Even if you don't find much, the fact that you're looking will make employees more thrifty.

Look for little things. Are small parts, like washers or bolts, lying around? They cost money. What about cleaning rags? Too many in sight may mean they're used carelessly. Are there leaky taps or hoses? A slowly dripping faucet drains off 15 gallons of solvent or fuel per day. A $\frac{1}{16}$-inch-diameter hole dribbles out a hundred gallons.

Check the wastebaskets and scrap heap for salvageable material or too much spoilage. What does your shop do with scrapped material? Maybe you can recycle it, use it for something else, or sell it. Don't let it pile up for disposal once a year; take advantage of fluctuating salvage prices.

You should find out about waste exchanges, if you have lots of material left over from industrial processes. Maybe you can sell your waste, or swap it for other excess supplies that can be used in your own operations. Ask the St. Louis Industrial Waste Exchange, 10 Broadway, St. Louis, Missouri 63102.

Space Is Money

It's worthwhile to review your space layout occasionally. Should it be changed to save steps or smooth the work flow? What proportion of total space is used for administration, production, aisles and hallways, active files, dead storage? Maybe you're using more space than you need, or using it less profitably than you might.

If you do have extra space, can it pay for itself in some way? Maybe you can sublet it—that is, rent the space to another tenant. Your lease probably permits this on condition that the landlord approve the prospective tenant. If the landlord gets sticky about it, you may be able to claim that he is acting in an arbitrary way, and that therefore you have "just cause" to terminate your lease. You can then prepare to move. At this point the landlord is likely to accept the sublet tenant, rather than lose you and go into litigation. Sometimes when a bank or insurance company owns a building, the lease sounds tough and inflexible, but don't let that deter you. By and large, institutions are the most sensible and flexible landlords. They seldom try to enforce harsh clauses.

Maybe you own a factory, warehouse, or office building that's part of your business. Do you realize that it's a ready source of cash? Of course, you can take out a mortgage loan on it, but often there's a better way. If it's fairly modern, you can probably sell it to some investor for a premium over depreciated book value, and then rent it back in a sale–lease-back arrangement. Your rent is fully tax-deductible. Pension funds, insurance companies, and other big-buck investors are constantly looking for safe, high-yield investments such as buildings with good long-term tenants.

Profits Through People

As a small business grows, the lengthening payroll usually threatens profits. Personnel costs may eat up 65 percent of a firm's income—which is too much. Some well-run small companies keep their "people costs" below 40 percent of gross.

Without playing Scrooge or Simon Legree, you can probably get good service from good people for less than you're paying now. Here are some possibilities.

Think about whether you can get along with fewer employees. If so, you may not need to fire anyone; just wait until someone quits, then don't hire a replacement. Maybe some of your top people can answer their own phones, even do their own filing or typing. Maybe you should "rent" part-time or temporary clerks and typists through an agency. Outside accounting services or a computer service bureau can keep books for you.

Without paying any fee to a service, you can engage individual outside help through want ads or just through personal contacts. Many women are eager to work part-time while their children are in school. Lots of people "moonlight" at hourly rates. There are free-lance bookkeepers who work full time but divide their services among several firms. There are free-lance artists and writers who do pamphlets and sales literature; free-lance draftsmen, engineers, and designers; even free-lance truck drivers who'll haul and deliver for you. Consultants are additional possibilities, as we saw in Chapters 11 and 12.

You can pay outside people more per hour or day than those on your regular payroll and still save 12 to 15 percent—because you won't have to pay Social Security or unemployment taxes, medical insurance, vacations, sick pay, or other fringe benefits. You pay them only for the days they work, or the tasks they perform.

But be careful. When you bring in outsiders and don't put them on your payroll, the Treasury Department may regard this as a tax dodge and claim that they are really employees. In that case you could be liable for the withholding taxes you didn't deduct, and for other payroll taxes, plus interest and penalties.

If your firm closely controls what an outsider does, and how and when it's done, then that person is your employee in the eyes of the law. But if the person does piecework on his own schedule, and you're concerned for results only, then he's probably a legitimate independent. It helps if the work is done off your premises, and if the worker provides tools and equipment. But if someone on your payroll is shifted to "independent" status, you're asking for trouble. In borderline cases, you'd better ask the IRS for a ruling. It might be to your advantage to put your outside commission salespeople on an independent contractor's contract (signed by both you and the second party) rather than show them on the company payroll.

Sales Reps: A Necessary Evil?

Should your business sell through full-time salesmen? Or commission agents? A new company often makes a serious blunder by hiring salesmen directly; it may not be able to afford their commissions and salaries and expenses. Usually you're better off, in the early stages, to employ manufacturers' representatives or wholesalers' salesmen to dig up customers until you can afford your own sales force.

Such agents are paid only on sales they bring in, so they represent almost no overhead. This system enables countless small companies to sell their products regionally or nationally. But reps can get too powerful. They stand between a company and its customers. Because they are the source of the orders, they sometimes think they should decide company policy, prices, and personnel. There are cases of reps' conspiring in a smoke-filled room to get a sales manager or production manager fired.

Some reps divide their sales efforts among fifty or a hundred product lines. They get to be pals with their customers, and just coast along, taking orders. If real salesmanship is needed to introduce your products, they may not bother. It's simpler just to drop your account. Then back for credit comes a load of stuff they "sold" and collected commissions on, and you're holding the bag. Reps don't guarantee the credit of customers. You take all the credit risk in filling their orders.

One way of sizing up a sales agency is by what it demands before it signs up to represent you. The best sales-rep firms are the most demanding—and are usually worth what they ask. They'll want your guarantees of prompt, accurate shipments; evidence of your reliability and good repute; a detailed sales story for your products, and adequate supplies of sales literature; information on whom to call if there are complaints by buyers, on how to get questions answered, and how to straighten out problems quickly.

A rep costs less—and sells less—than your own company salesman. If you don't expect big-volume sales, an agent is more profitable than a salesman. But as your sales increase, you'll reach a point at which it becomes more profitable to hire and train your own sales force.

In the meantime, have you thought about telephone selling?

This type of sales operation is growing fast because it works. Oregon Marine Supply Company increased profits by one-fifth with a planned telephone selling program. Lakeside Manufacturing, which has 2,200 dealers for its product line, has no salesmen or reps in the field because it sells only by phone, nationwide. Lakeside's president says the system cut the cost of an average sales call from $30 to only $1.50.

Now that the national average cost of a face-to-face industrial sales call is about $80, the advantages of telephone selling can make a big difference. Telephone salespeople needn't be in your office. They can call from their homes, or from field offices. They can follow up on leads generated by your advertising; can reopen inactive accounts; can make routine contacts with customers; can canvass to locate good prospects for later direct selling; can reach busy people who won't let a salesman get past the receptionist. And of course they lose no time in waiting rooms, or in travel, or at expense-account lunches.

Most products and services can be sold by phone. How about yours?

There's only one way to be sure: by testing. Reuben H. Donnelley Corporation, one of the nation's biggest telephone-selling organizations, has developed a program to teach other companies to sell by phone. It will recommend a specialist to run your test. The Donnelley organization is at 825 Third Avenue, New York 10022.

Now let's consider your regular full-time payroll. Money management is important here too.

By switching paydays you may conserve cash. Employers paying on the 15th of the month must pay the FICA (Social Security) and federal withholding taxes on payroll by the 18th—but if payday is on the 16th, taxes aren't due until the 25th. Either way, only 90 percent is due immediately. You can hold back 10 percent of the tax bill for as long as seventy days. It's surprising how few firms know this.

Another economy tip: If you hire continuously through an employment agency, and some new hires don't stay, keep a record of them, and get refunds on the fees you paid the agency. Refunds add up if your turnover is high.

Thrifty Ways with Giveaways

There are other ways of making more by giving more away. Sometimes it's profitable to make your employees part owners; about a thousand U.S. firms have some form of employee ownership. According to one study, there are sixteen worker-owned plywood firms in the Pacific Northwest, and they are 26 to 43 percent more productive than conventionally owned mills.

As long as an enterprise makes big profits so that employees get big bonuses or dividends, profit-sharing plans seem to work. But as a business gets bigger, profit-per-employee usually shrinks; then it's hard to convince employees that there's an ever-present danger of loss—and to convince them that the way they themselves perform has something to do with the size of profits. So don't commit yourself too far.

Sometimes it's simpler and more profitable just to encourage your non-production people to take on small production tasks, and reward them accordingly. For instance, many organizations consider good housekeeping valuable, and offer to pay their regular employees a bonus of a janitor's wage if they'll keep the facilities neat. It's impressive how many office people are glad to grab brooms, mops, and dustcloths, and clean up after work. Likewise, when the premises need painting, a company may offer the painting contractor's fee to its own people if they'll come in on weekends and paint.

Occasionally a small-business owner is under pressure to lend money

your inventory contains damaged or obsolete supplies, or merc
that you can't sell for enough to recover its cost, you can cut ta
riting down (or writing off) this year-end inventory. But if you wr
f, it has to be dumped. And if you write it down to what it might brin
rap or in a distress sale, you can't take the deduction unless and until
really liquidate it that way.

hen your company acquires new or used equipment, you can proba-
ake the investment credit under the Revenue Act of 1978. Many firms
look the big tax savings this makes possible.

e investment tax credit is a direct, dollar-for-dollar offset against tax
ity. Because it is deducted directly from your tax bill, it is worth
t twice as much as an income-tax deduction of the same amount,
ming that your company is in the 46-percent bracket (taxable income
$100,000).

e investment tax credit doesn't apply to buildings. But it includes
st any asset used in business that moves and has a useful life of three
s or more: office equipment, machinery, company cars and trucks,
ay racks and shelves, wall-to-wall carpeting, movable partitions,
cases, signs, individual air conditioners, and so on.

e credit also applies to some building components, and may apply to
y spent modernizing or repairing an asset more than twenty years
So if your firm has spent much on facilities this year, you should
ably retain a tax expert to go through and pick out everything that
fies for the credit.

re's another way to shelter income from taxes: go into the leasing
ess. Buy equipment and rent it to a lessee with a triple-A credit
g. The lease secures the recourse liability you've incurred in buying
quipment. Then you can take full advantage of the investment tax
t and accelerated depreciation. In addition to the pure tax savings,
eal postpones taxes for a few years, giving your company the use of
oney. So it works best when you expect lower income (and a lower
racket) in following years.

the other hand, if you expect to be in a higher bracket soon, when
uy business equipment you'll probably gain by writing off the sales
ver the life of equipment instead of deducting it immediately. Post-
g deductions probably isn't good if you expect to be in the same
et for years to come. Better get advice from a tax expert, if thou-
of dollars in taxes are involved.

to a brother-in-law or uncle who needs extra cash fo⟩
you're caught in this position, and can't buck the fam⟩
a way to help your relative with a minimum of stress⟩
for a loan that you guarantee. Then if he misses a pa⟩
you, does the dunning. If he defaults, you'll have⟩
bank, but you can deduct the full loss on your con⟩
you handed him the money outright, you'd have had⟩
bad-debt deduction, which must be reported as a sl⟩
at 50 cents on the dollar.

Does your business make charitable donations?⟩
enables you to borrow money from Uncle Sam, inter⟩
the money—get it authorized by your board of direc⟩
year and add it to business expenses on your tax ret⟩
as long as 142 months to actually hand over the don⟩
170 of the IRS Code.

If you have a high profit margin but are stuck⟩
warehouse or stockroom, consider donating them t⟩
tions, and taking full value—including your high ma⟩
tion. Suppose your business is in the 46 percent tax⟩
percent gross-profit figure. Then your net cost of c⟩
of goods is only $276. If you gave the charity $1,0⟩
would be $540.

More Tax-saving Ideas

While we're on taxes, let's examine other chance⟩
Whoever prepares your tax return can invoke S⟩
Code to take a "bonus depreciation" of as much⟩
$10,000 of property acquired by your company ir⟩
then depreciate the rest in any particular year. T⟩
reported specifically as Section 179 property. But ⟨
profit year, because you'll be better off to deduct⟩
against higher tax rates in the years to come.

You may be able to change a depreciation deduc⟩
cutting taxes, if you can show that—

- new and better equipment is now available, and b⟩
  petitor, so you'll scrap and replace your equipme⟩
  out; or—
- because of changes in the market for secondhand⟩
  the estimated salvage value will be less than you p⟩
  or—
- a piece of equipment is wearing out faster than ex⟩

How to Unfreeze Corporate Cash

Every business is likely to find itself short of cash occasionally, especially when it's growing and sales outrun payments by customers. In many fields of business, a really good account is one that pays in thirty days. It's not uncommon to wait sixty or ninety days. At the same time, your suppliers probably expect cash up front, especially if you're a new account. So your incoming money lags behind outgo. You're caught in a "cash flow" shortage. Accountants call it a "lack of liquidity" or a need for more "working capital."

The problem can be serious or even fatal, if your accounts receivable get too old or too big. Suppliers and lenders can put you out of business if they're unwilling to wait until you've collected payment from those who owe you.

Maybe your shortage can be eased by a short-term loan from your bank. But the loan must be repaid, and the cash-flow problem may persist. The best long-term remedy is to get your customers into the habit of paying faster, and in a moment we'll look at ways of doing this.

But first let's see how you can release cash that's at hand within your own organization, to keep you as liquid as possible without borrowing.

Most companies underestimate their checking-account balances by at least 30 percent, because they never know which checks have cleared. They probably have an extra ten days' dollars which could be working profitably elsewhere. You can easily monitor and analyze the float. Ask a bookkeeper to make a study of your outgoing checks to big creditors. Chart each one's float time. Then you can estimate how long your new checks will take to clear, and keep only as much money in the checking account as you really need.

Instead of mailing all your checks on the same date each month, regulate payment dates to your own advantage. You can still write them in one batch to save time, but store them by release dates. If Vendor A bills you on the 10th of the month and Vendor B on the 20th, and each offers a discount on bills paid within ten days, then you can pay A on the 20th and B on the 30th. You get free use of B's money for an extra ten days.

You can convert incoming checks to cash faster by using bank lockboxes. On the average, for every $100,000 your company grosses, this system will keep an extra $270 in your daily bank balance. But the bank will charge you about 25 cents per check, so the service is worthwhile only if the extra cash is important. Ask your bank for details.

Another possibility for stretching your cash is to ask your bank, or others to whom you owe money, to refinance your debt. Often a creditor will do this if he understands your problem, and is sure you're making honest efforts to pay him. But don't delay your plea. Call him before he calls you.

KEEP THESE BASIC POINTS IN MIND:

- *When you buy, consider not only the price but total ongoing costs. Look at several sources, and cultivate them, so that you'll never be at the mercy of one supplier.*
- *Keep inventory as light as possible. Try to plan for fast consumption or turnover of whatever you buy.*
- *Before you make any important capital investment, consider carefully whether you really need it yet. Then explore the possibilities of buying secondhand, or leasing.*
- *Invest the company's cash reserves; its investment income is 85-percent tax-sheltered. If the reserve is so big that the IRS might tax it as accumulated earnings, build up documentation on specific purposes for which the reserve may be needed.*
- *Minimize overhead by limiting your facilities to what you really need. Check your office, workrooms, and personnel to make sure these resources are used as productively as possible. Turn your salvage into cash when you can. Sublet extra space. Use part-time help.*
- *Sales reps are probably necessary when your business is small, but telephone selling may be your best bet.*
- *You can save money by making charitable donations in tax-wise ways.*
- *Be sure you make full use of the investment tax credit.*

15
Giving Credit:
The Risky Necessity

Debtors Cost You Money

A past-due account means your customer is borrowing money from you, interest-free. You're also being hurt in other ways. Your time, and the time of other top people, may be taken up trying to collect from key accounts. Meanwhile, you may lose sales; your slow-paying customer may buy from your competitor because he hasn't paid you.

In the end, if the debt can't be collected, the loss can be as bad as a major theft. Figure it this way. Suppose you sell a thousand dollars' worth of gismos on credit to the Gyppo Company. Months pass with no payment. Finally you learn that Gyppo has gone out of business. If your profit margin on gismos is 5 percent, you must sell $20,000 worth to offset the $1,000 you can't collect.

A small business may find itself needing many thousands of dollars of working capital in order to finance honest but slow-paying accounts. As it expands, it can easily expand itself to death. That's why you must try to limit yourself to customers or clients who pay promptly. No small business can be very heavy-handed in collection procedures—so it simply can't afford many unreliable customers.

If you can do business on a cash-and-carry or COD basis, you're in the best possible position. Some job shops and service businesses even ask payment in advance if they estimate that the total price of the work will be under $150. For bigger work, they require half in advance.

Many retailers dodge the dangers of setting up charge accounts for customers by accepting national credit cards. Then they get paid by the card issuer, although at a discount of about 7 percent—which they figure into their price schedule.

The next-best plan, which some manufacturers and wholesalers use, is to ship on consignment, with title to the goods remaining in their hands until the customer uses and pays. And if they ship to a field warehouse instead of direct to a customer, the warehouse agent can issue warehouse receipts, creating negotiable instruments which the customer can use for bank credit so that he can pay. If the customer does go broke, the supplier can recover the goods instead of standing in line with other creditors.

If you can use this system with a hard-pressed customer, you keep him in business, and encourage large orders from him instead of the string of small ones that cost you more to service. At the same time, you turn over your inventory faster—which saves you money, and limits the risks of obsolescence.

Maybe none of these procedures are possible for you. Then you must be careful about the credit-worthiness of all prospective—and current—customers. No sale is complete until the money is paid. A sale beyond the customer's ability (or willingness) to pay means the beginning of a bad collection problem.

Beware These Credit Frauds

It's not uncommon for a prosperous-looking, pleasant-mannered person to walk in off the street, buy on credit, then simply ignore the bills. Some famous figures in sports and show business are shameless deadbeats. It's best to ask all new customers, even famous ones, to fill out a credit application, which you can check with the credit bureau before handing over any valuable merchandise, or before doing any big service job.

More dangerous is the business customer who pays promptly for his first, second, and third purchases—small ones—and hints about bigger orders if you please him. Then he makes a whopping buy, on credit. By the time you realize he isn't going to pay, he has left town, leaving no forwarding address. You should have asked for credit references, and made sure they weren't faked.

The woods are full of fast-moving fly-by-night organizations that systematically buy big loads of merchandise on credit, resell it, and disappear before the shippers can collect. Look out for any obscure company that places a small "trial" order, follows up with an enthusiastic call or letter, and orders a big shipment. Look out for a company whose name is deceptively similar to that of a well-rated firm, and has an address on the same street. Look out for the rush telephone order from someone whose name sounds familiar, but whose address is different.

There are operators who place COD orders with dozens of suppliers in distant cities, then telephone with a tale of being temporarily short of cash. Because of the distance, a return shipment would cost the supplier too much, so he accepts a temporary part payment—which is all he gets.

Bigger operators, often Mafia-connected, have enough capital to buy out and operate some middle-size firm whose credit rating is rock-solid. One such gang bilked the firm's longtime suppliers for a million dollars' worth of goods in two months. The gang resold the merchandise and skipped before the suppliers realized what was happening.

Any major order, even from a well-known company, should be your signal to investigate whether the company's credit is still sound. If its stock is listed, ask your friendly stockbroker about its financial condition. Watch the financial and trade press (or pay a clipping bureau to do so if you haven't time) for news such as annual statements, quarterly reports, changes of ownership, industry slumps, fires, strikes, or any other inklings that your customer is in trouble.

Several other avenues are also open to the businessman for information on the credit-worthiness of a customer. He can seek information from Dun & Bradstreet's credit information service, from the Retailers Commercial Agency, from the consumer-credit division of TRW, or from one of the many credit managers' associations in the major cities across this nation.

One special warning about your advertising agency, if you use one. Newspapers and other advertising media bill the agency for your ads. The agency bills you, and deducts its commission before passing along your payments to the media. But if an agency gets cash-hungry—as several have in recent years—it may be tempted to overbill you, or to divert your money to pay its older debts. The media can hold you responsible for payment if your agency defaults. So you ought to audit your agency's financial condition from time to time.

The audit can be a simple spot-check questionnaire that the agency fills in and sends back to you. Your form should list a few recent media purchases, and ask for the dates when the agency received the bills and paid them, also get tear sheets of ads run for proof of insertion. Ask the agency to send photocopies of invoices and statements along with the completed form, and to list the check numbers of payments. Be sure to ask for the completed package back within three days. If there's a delay, this is a danger signal. And if you're not satisfied, check directly with publications that ran your ads.

By approaching a bank discreetly, explaining your relationship with a business firm and things you've noticed about it, you can probably get an idea as to whether the firm is profitable, whether it shows any change in business patterns, whether there are secured liens or lawsuits against it. Bankers won't give out confidential information, but their nonconfidential data and rough estimates can help you a lot.

At least you can get a Dun & Bradstreet rating, if there is one, and perhaps a report from a credit bureau when you're doubtful about granting credit. One further protection, as we'll see in Chapter 16, is to carry business credit insurance.

The Art of Collecting Accounts Receivable

Even though you're cautious about credit, you'll have trouble collecting unless you follow up systematically and persistently. Good retail customers often slow down payments for personal reasons. Many businesses delay paying bills when money is tight. Your defense begins at shipping and invoicing.

Process orders as fast as you possibly can (which may also help you win more orders), and mail the invoice the very day the goods are shipped or delivered. Make sure orders or bills that are hard to write up aren't buried at the bottom of your pile. Any slowness at your end encourages slow payment. Make sure that orders are filled as they are received.

Make your invoices clear and easy to read. Customers who have any doubt about a bill often postpone payment until the problem has been clarified to their satisfaction. You should show the date ordered, the person who placed the order, the date it was shipped or delivered, a description of the goods, the unit price, the total amount, and the terms. Underline—maybe in bright ink—any discount for prompt payment. Unusual bills (or credits) should carry an explanation.

Also, make it easy for your customer to respond. Print your phone number and your bookkeeper's name conspicuously on the invoice. Enclose a return envelope—maybe postpaid, if the customer's good will is important to you. If the customer sends a question or complaint, answer immediately, and speed up any adjustment needed.

Then comes the follow-up. It must be consistent. Your customers must learn what to expect from you. Just because a customer is big, don't be bashful about pressing for prompt payment, unless you've negotiated special terms. The customer will respect you rather than resent you. And small accounts should get the same follow-up. Here's one possible system.

First, "squeak the wheel" in a nice, firm way. Send a memory jogger on the tenth day after payment is due. ("Payment crossed in the mails?" or "Did you overlook our statement?") This first approach should be low-key, especially in a consumer business. The customer may be ill, or away on a trip, or dealing with urgent family or business matters.

Second should come a series of polite weekly letters, triggered by computer if possible, and pleasant calls that get made automatically when payment is late. Calls are cheaper than letters, and more effective. If you have salesmen in the area, instruct them to pick up a check and write an order in one visit. They don't like to be bill collectors, but they can be, if necessary. They should be willing to follow up their own customers, if you tie their compensation to payments rather than orders shipped. This may cure them of the habit, common among salesmen, of recommending their customers for liberal credit.

Third: When a payment is six weeks overdue, telephone the customer and diplomatically but firmly ask for immediate payment. If your firm is so small that you have to do this personally, you'll probably be reluctant. It's embarrassing to remind a personal customer that he hasn't paid and, by implication at least, that you need the money. But you definitely will need it soon, as we've seen, if you let these unpleasant matters slide.

Here's a telephone tactic that often works well. You or your collector identifies your firm, explains that the bill is forty-five days old—and pauses. There's a silence. The customer is forced to explain his delinquency. If he says he can't pay just now, your collector asks when he will pay. The goal of the call is to get the customer to make a commitment, set a date.

If you get the commitment, record it on a calendar and phone again on that date if the payment isn't in. Don't wait even twenty-four hours. You'll build credibility and establish yourself as a no-nonsense type by your immediate action. (Likewise, call to say thanks whenever a customer comes through on schedule.)

But maybe your customer is evasive. Maybe he pours out a tale of woe. Evaluate it carefully—but sympathetically. Don't lecture, or threaten, or question his integrity. Be ready to meet him halfway. Offer to work out a plan for taking partial payments over time. Collecting small sums regularly is better than not collecting large sums at all. Set up an agreement in writing and have the customer sign it.

Meanwhile, you should keep a record of progress—or lack of it—on the customer's ledger card. You'll have a permanent credit profile which will alert you in future.

Your card file should make overdue accounts stand out at a glance; if you don't know who owes what and for how long, you may be doing too much business with slow payers. Use filing stickers, the kind that can protrude above the card. Use different stickers for 30 days overdue, 45, and so on—perhaps with a color-coded system, such as blue for 30 days overdue, yellow for 45, and red for anything over 60 days. Instead of replacing one sticker with another, attach the new atop the old. This makes your oldest receivables stand highest in the file.

Incidentally, make sure that your sales to a chain are totaled. Some accounting and computer systems list sales to branches separately, which leaves the company unaware how much credit has been granted to one customer.

Danger Signals

Watch for trouble signs on your ledger cards. If a company stops taking available cash discounts, then stretches out payments, or blames its slowness on slow mail, you may want to drop the business and leave it to your competition, rather than keep on making sales that won't bring back cash for a long time.

On the other hand, if a customer contributes enough profit to justify waiting for payments, you may want to experiment—either by offering a bigger discount for cash on the next sale, or by notifying the customer that you charge 12 or 18 percent interest on past-due accounts.

When pressing for a big payment, go to your customer's top decision-maker. Unless he gives special instructions to a clerk, your invoice may stay buried in a clerk's pile. If he stalls, you know there's real trouble.

Some companies play tricks to delay payments. After waiting some weeks, they write up a bill of particulars about why they are dissatisfied with a shipment or service, and why they want an adjustment on the invoice. They try to draw you into a long dispute.

Sometimes they send a check in partial payment, typing on the back of the check, "Payment in full of all obligations due." If you're careless enough to cash it, that's probably all you'll ever get. If you return the check, the sender may just sit back and wait until your attorney or collection agency finally forces a settlement.

Other companies "carelessly" send unsigned checks, or checks with a discrepancy between the numerals and the written amount, or checks with the name of your company so garbled you can't cash it. Or they may stop payment on a check, and when you phone to ask why, they'll say, "Oh, that dumb bookkeeper of mine. I told her to stop payment to the XYZ Company, not you." You deposit the check again. The bank again rejects it. Your creditor curses the stupid bank. And so it goes.

Such games are ways of buying time. One defense is to send someone in to pick up payment personally. Even a plane trip to pick up a check for several thousand dollars may be worthwhile. It usually works.

If you don't want to do this, any clues that a customer is evading payment should prompt you to make a business-risk decision immediately. How much longer should you wait in the hope of keeping the customer? Does he have other sources of supply, or will he be brought to heel if you stop shipments? Will he be worried by the danger of damage to his reputation?

If your customer is a distributor, maybe you shouldn't crack down too quickly, especially if your products are in a competitive industry where your brand doesn't mean much. You may need the distributor's best efforts when business slows down.

Or if your customer's business is in serious danger, decide whether you can give sympathetic help that might let him save face. His financial pinch may be only temporary, and he could become a good customer in the future. A credit extension may spur his efforts to repay you, especially if your competitors are making life hard for him.

One company often gives special terms to another company in a squeeze, if the problem is honestly explained. But if you go this route, be sure to get collateral security, notes, postdated checks, sureties, or other legal assurances of payment. And make sure a schedule of future payments is set up at the same time. Follow up to see that the payments are made.

Tactics with Tough Debtors

Stay in touch with any company whose bill is seriously overdue. It has other creditors too, and you're competing with them. One common cause of collection problems is lack of contact with the debtor. If you're pressing someone who refuses to be available to you, don't give up. Use different envelopes without return addresses. Vary the letters; the same old dunning letter loses attention. Try sending a Mailgram urging payment. Have your secretary place a call. Call person-to-person from out of town. Go to see the president. He can be unstrung by a confrontation at his home or on the golf course.

With help from your bank, there's one strong move you can make to collect a trade bill. Banks don't like to do it, so save it for special crises. Here's what you do. Find out where your customer banks. Then tell your own bank you want to draw a draft against his account. Explain that you're trying to speed up a delinquent payer. Your bank can send a draft to his bank, with your invoice attached. His bank will call yours to find out what's going on.

This corners your customer. If he refuses to pay the draft, he'll be admitting to his bank that he's not paying his trade bills. Rather than broadcast this—especially to a bank that may also be his creditor—he'll probably pay the draft. But don't expect any more business from him.

A softer strategy is to offer a compromise. Suggest that he send back your unused goods; or better still, try a quick discount of 10 or 15 percent off the bill for immediate payment; this is probably cheaper than a lawyer or collection agency.

If these efforts fail, don't delay. The longer your debtor stalls, the more it costs you. Close the account and turn it over to a lawyer or collection agency.

It's foolish to threaten action unless you mean it. If you bluff, your customers will get wise and you'll have more trouble. Also, any threat other than a threat to bring civil suit to collect a just debt may leave you open to prosecution or blackmail.

Keep in mind that deadbeats often counterclaim when a case goes to court, and wangle a costly settlement. Ask your lawyer about third-party proceedings, by which money or property due your debtor can be applied on your claim. Avoid putting your debtor into bankruptcy if you can find any better, faster remedy. And don't even think of filing criminal charges if the debt is in dispute.

Negotiate the fee with the lawyer or collection agency. You'll be told that a certain percentage of collections is standard, but most will accept less, especially if the claim is big. For instance, you shouldn't pay more than 10 percent for collections over $25,000. On smaller amounts, agency charges average around 25 percent on business debts, up to 50 percent for retail accounts.

If your enterprise is big enough—and foolish enough in extending credit—to use a collection agency often, you'd better investigate why a particular agency is being used. You may find that it is giving kickbacks to your credit manager. Or if your lawyer is routinely collecting debts, he may be charging fat fees for merely sending a couple of letters.

The Fair Debt Collection Protection Act

From the consumer's standpoint, there has been drastic improvement in credit-collection practices since the passage in October 1979 of the Fair Debt Collection Protection Act. This set of laws lays down fairly rigid guidelines for business methods when collection agencies are employed on delinquent accounts.

The consumer, prior to its enactment, was subjected to many and various forms of abuse, harassment, and threats with the intent of intimidation. It was not unusual for an individual somewhat delinquent in the payment of his installment purchase to receive a phone call from the collection agency at two o'clock in the morning, accompanied by a veiled or actual threat to life and limb if the bill was not settled promptly.

Now that is no longer an accepted practice. Phone calls, for example, must be made within reasonable hours, and never before 8 A.M. Too, if the debtor has written to his creditor or the collection agency requesting that he not be subjected to harassment, one, and only one, collection call may be made to him. From that point on, attempts to collect must be made by letter. The debtor now may also request that no communication, other than to try to locate him, be attempted by the collection agency to any friend or relative. Furthermore, if the debtor brings an attorney into the action, further communications must be directed to the attorney and not to the debtor directly.

This act also provides for other protection for the consumer. Information regarding it is set forth in a pamphlet available from the Federal Trade Commission in your area or in Washington, D.C.

A rather detailed explanation of the workings of the act is given in a book by Lipman G. Seld entitled *Harassment and Other Collection Taboos.* It is obtainable for $6.25 from the National Association of Credit Managers, 475 Park Avenue, New York 10016.

According to Joseph Newmark, general manager of the large Trade Paper Products Company of Los Angeles, "The consumer has been liberated from the threat of bodily harm, harassment, or debtor's prison. He is to be treated and dealt with in a businesslike manner when pressed for payment of a bill. The businessman, working through either his own collection department or a collection agency, must try to negotiate an orderly settlement in a totally reasonable mood and manner."

The Last Resort

Finally, should all other methods of collection prove fruitless, there is always the option of litigation by the business owner. In California, if the amount of the suit is less than $1,000 he can take his case to the Small Claims Court for adjudication. Parenthetically, even though he is successful in winning a judgment, that is no guarantee that the debt will be paid; he still has to face the exercise of collecting against the judgment.

As old Casey Stengel said after his team had come home from a road trip losing 11 of the 12 games played, "You can't win 'em all."

KEEP THESE BASIC POINTS IN MIND:

- *Whenever possible, do business COD or cash-and-carry, or through credit cards, or on consignment. Credit costs you money in many ways.*
- *When you extend credit, be on guard for frauds. Even your biggest*

customers may get into trouble, or fall into the hands of crooks. Get credit ratings whenever possible.
- Remember, if sales are the lifeblood of your business, credit could be its life support.
- Follow up all credit accounts systematically and persistently.
- Begin by doing your shipping and invoicing as speedily and clearly as you can. Send a memory jogger on the tenth day after payment is due.
- Set up a series of polite letters or phone calls as part of your office routine.
- When a bill is long overdue, offer to work out a plan for taking part payment, if you want to keep the customer's business.
- Your record system should show the status of all past-due accounts at a glance. Stay in touch with big delinquents.
- Keep close watch for news about changes in the credit-worthiness of big customers. Sometimes it's better to help them, sometimes to push them hard. You need information to decide.
- Never threaten action unless you're ready to follow through.
- Negotiate collection fees with an attorney or collection agency. And be alert for under-the-table deals.

16
Insuring Your Business

By skimming a few dollars from petty cash daily, an office worker stole $40,000 over a period of years. When he was finally caught, the business carried no dishonesty insurance that would reimburse it.

Another firm's biggest customer filed for bankruptcy, leaving the firm stuck with a pile of uncollectible receivables. It had no business-credit insurance and couldn't sustain the loss, so it followed its customer into bankruptcy.

A heart attack hospitalized an owner-manager. His business had no key-person insurance, and collapsed.

A little manufacturer carried business-interruption insurance and thought it would pay off when his warehouse burned down, leaving him without raw materials to continue production. But destruction of the warehouse wasn't covered in the business-interruption policy. "For that, you should have had a contents policy," his insurance man said.

A merchant likewise found his business-interruption policy useless when a flood wiped out most of the shopping mall where his store was located, including the only entrance road. His store was untouched by the flood, so he got nothing, although no customers came for weeks.

Another firm's truck had a crash while the owner-manager was away on a trip. Ten days later he returned, and reported it. His insurance company sent a form letter brusquely refusing to handle the case, since he hadn't reported it within the twenty-four hours stipulated in his policy.

A run-of-the-block insurance agent assured a manufacturer that he had all the coverage he needed against accidents—which was, typically, automobile liability, comprehensive liability, and a workmen's-compensation policy. It sounded like good protection. But an infant in Brussels got hold of his product—a 29-cent ball-point pen—and fell. The pen jabbed into the baby's eye. The baby died. The parents sued the manufacturer.

His insurance agent told him, "Your policy doesn't cover you when your product is distributed overseas."

Watch Those Loopholes

The moral of these sad tales is, of course, that you should read your insurance policies, study the exclusions, and make sure you're protected.

Post your insurance policies (or copies) within easy view of employees. Mark in red all clauses that might nullify or reduce your coverage, and circulate them throughout your organization. Be watchful to prevent anyone from violating those clauses—because if you file a big claim, your insurer will look hard for a loophole.

Neglecting to report a loss promptly is a common mistake that leads to an uninsured loss. It happens because the boss is usually the last to hear about anything bad within the company, and subordinates aren't authorized to file insurance claims.

Equally common and disastrous mistakes are forgetting to report to an insurer that you've acquired new property or expanded your operations, and forgetting to renew a policy before expiration. So here we find another moral: an alert, conscientious executive in your organization should carry clear responsibility for all insurance matters. You might have the executive read this chapter as his introduction to the work.

You Need an In-house Specialist

It's startling to see how many companies spend freely to build up sales, yet risk bankruptcy by delegating insurance to an untrained low-echelon desk worker who is burdened with ten other duties and is glad to leave the insurance to a half-baked insurance salesman. Insurance can't build profits, so owners seldom give it much thought.

If your firm consists of only a few people, insurance should be the responsibility of the highest or second-highest executive, who should be fully aware that one error could wreck the business. As the firm grows, somebody ought to specialize in the subject as soon as insurance premiums amount to twice his salary—or sooner, if the company's operations are growing fast or are getting complicated.

Your in-house specialist, whether part-time or full-time, should understand certain information which will be summarized in this chapter— except for a few topics already covered in detail in one of my previous Simon and Schuster handbooks, *How to Manage Real Estate Successfully—in Your Spare Time*. There, on pages 29–31 and 237–44, you'll find the facts that any owner (whether of an apartment building or of some other business premises) should know about insuring buildings and insuring employees, together with tips about the best ways to buy any insurance. That ground needn't be covered again here, but a telegraphic summary of it may help:

1. If you buy a building—or a business—from someone, don't rely on his assertion that the existing insurance covers you. Even though he transfers the policies, an insurance company has no obligation to honor that transfer until the company's representative signs the assignment.
2. Make sure you carry workmen's compensation, even if you don't think you have any employees. Anyone who does part-time chores for you may be an employee in the eyes of the law. The same holds true for employees of a service company, if the service company doesn't carry workmen's compensation, and many small outfits don't.
3. You're liable for auto accidents of employees when they're on errands for you, driving their own cars. Coverage for "non-owned auto" is so inexpensive that agents seldom bother to solicit it, but you should carry it.
4. Buy insurance by comparative shopping. Look for policies with the broadest coverage and fewest exclusions. Beware of unusually low premiums.
5. Make sure you understand the co-insurance penalty. Have your broker keep checking to make sure your property isn't underinsured as costs rise.
6. Insist on an inspection of the premises before agreeing to any insurance program. Insurance inspectors will point out hazards, and tell you how to get lower rates by correcting these hazards.
7. If an old building is damaged and must be rebuilt, you'll have to pay today's higher building prices. Protect yourself by getting policies that pay for actual replacement cost.

What Coverage Does Your Firm Need?

There are a dozen or more types of commercial insurance that you should consider, depending on your line of business. As soon as you open your doors, a sizable percentage of the people entering will want to sell you insurance; these are *not* the ones whose advice you should seek. They're trained in sales tactics, not in insurance. Decide what coverage you need, then seek out experts in such coverage.

Despite the many different types of insurance, they fall into three categories: Must, Optional, and Frill.

Must-carry insurance includes fire, extended coverage, all aspects of liability (products, premises, vehicles) and workmen's compensation. Fidelity bonds are also a must, for any employee who might embezzle from or defraud you.

Optional insurance might be business credit and business interruption, which are vital for some enterprises and needless for others; crime coverage; various kinds of insurance on partners and key people; and auto property damage.

Frills would include plate-glass insurance, for example, where you'll probably find that replacing *all* your windows would cost about as much as your premium. Other frills would be special insurance for that cherished painting in your reception room, or the beautiful exterior of your building. Debris removal is a frill. So are most of the additional features of automobile coverage.

You Can Afford Some Self-insurance

It would be prohibitively expensive to insure against every mishap that might cost you money. You can cover small risks adequately by loss-prevention programs, or by setting aside a financial reserve to pay for them when they happen, which is called self-insurance.

The key is to insure against catastrophes. A burglary would be bothersome but wouldn't break you. On the other hand, an accident caused (in a court's opinion) by your product or your premises or your representative might mean paying a five-figure or even six-figure judgment.

Insurance should reflect the life-cycle of your business. A new venture with delicately balanced budget should have as much protection as it can afford. As it grows in assets and stability, makes fewer mistakes, it becomes able to absorb some losses instead of insuring against them. Ultimately it needs little or no insurance against most kinds of loss, because its resources are ample. It does a lot of self-insurance.

In family life, an example of self-insurance is a decision not to buy coverage of the damage to one's own auto in an accident. The family may realize that the cost of collision coverage is a frill, especially since nobody in the family has incurred anything worse than a scratched fender in years —so it accepts the risk of having to pay for repairs. Or maybe it gets a low premium by opting for a high deductible, so that insurance will pay only for collision costs over $1,000, say.

In business, self-insurance may be a foolish trust in luck; or it may mean surplus funds loosely earmarked as an umbrella against a rainy day; or it may mean analyzing risks, setting up safeguards, and finding that coverage against a particular risk isn't worth what it costs.

Every company should consider some degree of self-insurance, to keep rising insurance costs in line. Of course, a fully funded self-insurance program against all risks isn't practical. But higher deductibles are.

Every business insurance policy should have a deductible. Complete coverage from the first dollar of loss is the most costly coverage there is. The more self-insuring you do, the bigger your cash resources are likely to become, since you spend less on premiums, fees, and commissions. Money in your self-insurance fund keeps drawing interest for you. Also, there's stronger motivation for loss prevention within your organization.

The size of a possible loss is more important than its likelihood. The more likely the loss, the less likely that you should insure against it, because the premiums will run almost as high as the loss itself.

Generally speaking, frequent losses tend to be smaller losses, easily absorbed. Even if they're not, and you insure against them, the insurance company may cancel as soon as it sees how many claims you're filing.

Self-insurance works best when risks are spread among a large number of objects, places, or people; when no single item is precious; and when your assets are geographically distributed, so that only a few would be affected by one mischance. Thus a business with numerous buildings, well separated, is best suited for self-insurance. A small one-site business would be least suitable.

Insurance makes sense only when it protects against crippling calamities. Even a tiny enterprise can get along without protection against minor losses. The rule should be to insure the worst exposure first, then the less likely losses as your budget permits. Too many small companies insure their cars against collision damage but skimp on liability coverage. It's the liability judgments that bankrupt businesses.

After expert analysis with the help of one or more insurance brokers, your company should decide the maximum loss it can afford. Then buy blanket or umbrella coverage (an excess-loss policy) at very low cost for everything over that. You can change the limits of this protection (thereby cutting the premiums) as the company becomes able to withstand bigger losses.

A broker may try to discourage you from self-insurance or high deductibles, since they mean less income for him at the outset. If so, consult other brokers. (A casualty agent earns considerably less than an agent for life or accident and health insurance when the policy is first written. But his commission stays level as the policy is renewed, while the others' commissions taper off after the first year. So your broker, if he's good, will prosper by staying in close touch with his clients as the years go by.)

You may also want to send for a free booklet full of tips on how much risk a company can afford to carry itself. It's called "Risk Management," and you can get it from INA (Insurance Company of North America), one of the oldest and biggest groups of insurance and financial service companies, at 1600 Arch Street, Philadelphia 19101.

Another form of self-insurance that's growing fast is the program whereby a group of companies in one industry pool some of their reserves and draw from the pool to cover losses, thus sharing their risks. Sometimes a trade association arranges this.

You might also look into "risk transfer" as still another way of avoiding insurance costs. It involves getting someone else to carry the insurance for facilities or workmen you're using. For example, you might lease vehicles under a contract whereby the lessor buys the accident insurance. Instead of hiring personnel, use outside services to do work. This way you fix the supplier of the service with responsibility for loss or liability —but check to be sure your supplier has adequate insurance. Similarly, you can shift the cost of insuring inventory to manufacturers or wholesalers by "hand-to-mouth buying" through which you avoid storing supplies or merchandise.

However—speaking of goods in transit—you'd better insure them yourself if they're valuable and a single shipment involves several carriers, because each might claim some other carrier did the damage. Likewise, you need your own insurance if damage might not be evident right away, as in a complex piece of machinery.

Who Can Sue You?

One of every four people will get hurt in some sort of accident this year. That means 50 million potential lawsuits. Next year, and every year after, there'll be 50 million more. Accident victims or their relatives can sue not only for their medical costs but also for "loss of income" caused by the injury, and even for punitive damages.

Laws have stretched the rules of liability to a point at which just about any accident can be blamed on some business or individual. It's common knowledge that business is covered by insurance. So judges and juries seem to find it easy to rule against a business accused of negligence, assuming that some billion-dollar insurance company, rather than the business, will pick up the tab.

The size of jury verdicts isn't as high as the insurance industry would like everyone to believe. According to the Association of Trial Lawyers (which of course would like everyone to believe that damage suits are a fine thing), 1973–76 statistics showed that jury verdicts increased at less than 7½ percent a year, which didn't even keep up with inflation. The lawyers say that despite the many product-liability suits, only three punitive-damage judgments were upheld on appeal in ten years. Another study found only one case out of 24,000 in which punitive damages were actually collected. The average payment made on all bodily-injury claims was said to be just over $3,500.

Some companies that had trouble getting any liability coverage at all are now finding several carriers competing for their business. This is because many giant companies either are self-insuring or are setting up their own subsidiary insurance carriers—which leaves more insurance-underwriting capacity available to smaller companies. So when you shop for liability insurance, keep in mind that you're in a buyer's market.

Anyhow, there's no question whatever that a business should carry hefty liability insurance. The only question is, how much?

In this age of litigation, malpractice, and me-first morality, claims can happen anytime. Someone can slip on mud near your front door. A chair can break. A workman can cause costly damage to water mains, walls, machines. Cables snap, wood splinters, mortar falls. Trash or a ditch can contribute to serious injuries. Any bystander or passerby, any salesman or delivery boy, is a prospective claimant if there's some way of blaming your company for an injury.

Far from your premises, your own workmen, salesmen, and executives can get you into trouble for what they do—even in off hours, sometimes. An executive of one company got lonesome away from home and picked up a redhead. In his hotel room, a cigarette started a fire that burned them to death. Whom could the executive's widow sue? The company. It was forced to pay death benefits to her, because the Supreme Court of California held that her husband's death was work-connected. It ruled in effect:

> As a general rule, a commercial traveler is regarded as acting within the course of his employment during the entire period of his travel upon his employer's business. His acts in traveling are all incidents of the employment. Where injuries are sustained during such activities, the Workmen's Compensation Act applies.

Million-dollar judgments are still rare enough to make the newspapers, but $100,000 claims aren't news anymore. So a million-dollar insurance policy is too high, but $300,000 may be low. A safe limit is probably $500,000 per accident.

You might think that the maximum which could be assessed against you is the value of your business, but this isn't necessarily true. All the company's assets could be attached too. On the other hand, even if your business is worth far more than a half-million, it's extremely unlikely that a judgment against you would be so big. First, what accident would do

$500,000 worth of damage? Probably only the rare kind that dooms a victim to nursing care for a lifetime. Second, if you're insured, your insurance company will put up a stiff court fight against any six-figure claim. This is the real advantage of carrying substantial liability insurance.

Only 3 percent of all liability cases ever get to court. The rest are settled outside, for much less than the claim. Competent claims lawyers always settle with the insurance limit in mind, and they'll advise a claimant to take immediate cash instead of waiting five or more years for an unpredictable verdict in court.

Are You Covered?

When someone sues your company for personal or property damage, the worst development is to find that your insurance policy doesn't cover that particular kind of claim. Then your insurer will refuse to defend you. You'll have to retain a lawyer on your own, and he won't come cheap.

So a comprehensive liability policy, which is generally the best package on the market, may not be quite enough protection against peculiar hazards in your own business. Here are some gaps in the normal liability coverage:

There's no coverage against a charge of false arrest. If one of your clerks nabs a suspected thief and fails to prove the charge, you're liable. Nor is there protection against suits for invasion of privacy, defamation, libel, slander. These aren't far-out contingencies. It takes only one office busybody whispering the "real" story about someone's firing, and you could lose a defamation case.

As indicated early in this chapter, foreign operations aren't insured by U.S. companies.

And there's the minefield of medical malpractice. If you refer one of your employees to a practitioner who injures him through negligence or bungling, the employee can sue you, and your regular liability policy won't protect you.

You may sign some business contract (particularly with a municipality) which contains a hold-harmless clause. This clause shifts responsibility onto you, without the protection of insurance coverage.

Policies exclude "occurrences" that aren't accidents. So if a water leak gradually ruins the office below yours, you can be solely responsible.

And of course insurance won't pay off for intentional acts by an insured. Interpretations of intent can be farfetched. One boss told a crew, "Clear everything fifteen feet from these markers," but didn't specify in which direction. His workmen tore out magnolias, shrubbery, and a fancy antique doorway to the adjoining property. The insurer wouldn't pay because, it said, the boss intentionally caused the damage. A court upheld it. The boss paid for the loss.

These are just some of the risks that insurance companies don't cover in standard policies. So the burden of buying adequate liability and casualty coverage is on you. The way to share the burden is to find that rarity, an insurance broker who understands your business and will go to as many insurance companies as necessary to get you the protection you need.

How to Deal with Insurance Brokers

Brokers are the insurance men most interested in small business, being small-business men themselves and sometimes finding it hard to compete with big companies and big agencies. Even so, most of them have only vague notions of the inner workings of any business except their own. Because there are hundreds of complex insurance contracts and special lines on the market, no broker's knowledge can be complete. Therefore you should look for a broker (not for an agent, representing just one company) who has handled several accounts in your particular line of business, and thus knows specific kinds of coverage you need. He also should be noted for serving his clients well in time of loss.

If an insurance man gives you a high-pressure sales talk, steer clear. Anyone pressing you to buy business insurance is probably hoping to sell coverage you don't need or can never collect on. Many a low-grade insurance company tries to push a profitable gimmick, insure against nonexistent perils, and avoid risky parts of its policyholders' operations.

A hungry salesman may spot certain dangers in your way of doing business that would cause insurance companies either to reject you as "uninsurable" or to set the premiums too high for you to pay. So what does this salesman do? He clean-sheets you, as it's called. He sells you a policy and doesn't tell the company about the dangers that will void the policy. So if you eventually make a claim, his lie comes to light and the company refuses to pay.

Other high-pressure tactics are the "buy now because you may not be able to get insurance later" pitch, the churn (urging you to drop older policies and buy new ones), the old-pal appeal, and glib doubletalk when you ask what is excluded from coverage he's urging on you.

Contrariwise, most good brokers for business insurance are scarcely salesmen at all. Since they offer negative products, they tend to be negative personalities instead of the extrovert types common in other sales work. Most businesses really have to sell their products; insurance men don't, because everyone has to have some. If a client seems to know what he wants, they may content themselves with mere order-taking.

So when you find a broker who's familiar with your type of business, bear in mind that he isn't a salesman and won't keep after you the way other salesmen do. Be sure he understands what you expect of him: a thorough inspection of your business and a written report to you, specifying what coverage he recommends and listing the exclusions in clear language. Ask him to mail the report. You'll need to study it privately, undistracted by his conversation.

A good broker should show you how to reduce your premiums by low-cost safety engineering to minimize the chance of accidents. He may help you classify your employees more accurately for workmen's compensation; premium rates are 250 times as high for "dangerous" jobs as for "safe" ones.

There are special policies or endorsements for contractors, store-keepers, restaurateurs, beauty-parlor operators, ranchers, and others. At a broker's request, insurers sometimes design special contracts to cover a particular risk in a business. If you own your building or machinery, power-plant insurance is essential to cover boilers and machines. Explosions have caused property destruction, deaths, and lawsuits that have ruined many businesses. Insurers give plant owners extra protection by making periodic inspections to detect cracks, weakening, and vibrations that could cause explosions.

You also need a separate policy covering vehicles used by your business. However, to preclude a dispute in case of a liability, you'd better use the same insurance company for your comprehensive liability and automobile policies. Otherwise if there's an accident in the loading of your truck, for example, there'll be wrangling between companies over which should pay.

Your product-liability insurance ought to be written so that limits apply on a "per claim" basis, not "per occurrence." A recent decision from the U.S. Court of Appeals left manufacturers with far less protection than they thought they had. The court said that a flaw in the manufacturing process which causes hundreds of defective products is a single occurrence. So the insurance company's liability for all injuries caused by those products was limited to the "per occurrence" amount in the policy. A "per claim" basis would have guaranteed the manufacturers multiple payoffs.

You should discuss special endorsements, changes, and extra coverage with any broker you're considering. Two or three reports from different brokers, suggesting ways to reduce rates while buying better coverage, will give you a clearer picture of the insurance program you need. Naturally, you should return the reports you decide not to use. You may want to pay for these evaluations, but this may be illegal in your state. Check the law.

Your relationship with whatever broker you choose should be one of mutual trust. He should know everything. If you mislead him, and the untruth is uncovered later, the insurance company may cancel your policy or jack up the rates. And of course, it won't pay a claim if it can prove you lied.

Your broker, no matter how expert, probably doesn't understand your business thoroughly. Make sure he describes it accurately to any insurance companies with which he seeks to place your business. His description can make a big difference in the rating and, hence, in your premium. Insurers generally base the premium on the firm's risk category. This category may be askew in your case. If the premium is sizable, go with the broker to the underwriter and explain why your company has less exposure—perhaps because of your tight safety procedures, for example. (As a simple case in point, a night watchman can reduce the premium cost of fire insurance by one-fifth.) Or brief the broker on these details so that he can explain.

Remember, too, that the policy you buy is only as good as the underwriter behind it. Good protection means a solvent insurance company which offers broad coverage, liberal settlements, and expert assistance in preventing accidents. Dozens of casualty companies have gone broke in recent years, mainly owing to sharp practice by their owners. Firms insured with these companies were left facing the losses and lawsuits.

Investigate the Insurance Company

As with any other contract you negotiate, check out the other party—the insurance company, in this case. The state insurance commissioner or your lawyer can help. *Best's Insurance Reports,* published yearly by Alfred M. Best Company, Morristown, New Jersey, gives ratings for all insurance companies. The rating is based on financial soundness. It also shows underwriting results, claims paid, premiums collected, investment income, and gains and losses.

But what about the local or regional office that will handle your claims? Check with some nearby customers whom the company insures, especially those in your line of business. Ask about its efficiency, attitudes, and ways of doing business. Ask the Better Business Bureau too; it keeps a record of all complaints against specific companies.

V. P. Chernik says in *Consumers' Guide to Insurance:*

A good company is not always a century-old, traditional, solid institution with heavy premiums. Many companies are entrenched in old beliefs, in approaches which have hardly varied since the turn of the century. The proliferation of so many specialty-minded insurance companies shows, in a way, the apathy and lack of understanding of many of the insurance giants. . . .

The selection of an insurance company should closely follow your own personality. If you are conservative, seek a traditional company. If you are aggressive, go with a firebrand type of outfit—your needs would be better met.

Just about every insurance policy has a cancellation clause. The company doesn't need to give a reason for cancellation, and some clauses allow a carrier to stop the policy after only five days' notice!

When buying a policy, negotiate that clause. Demand as much as ninety days, but accept thirty if the carrier agrees to guarantee the first ninety. You'll need as much time as you can get to line up new insurance in the event of a mysterious cancellation, which is likeliest to occur when the policy is young.

Claims Strategy

You'll learn more about your insurance company and your broker when you submit your first claim. How fast do they react? What's their attitude? Are they fair in their evaluation of losses? Do they send up a smoke screen of legal jargon? If they quibble over a $300 loss, you can expect the worst in a serious case. So don't wait. Find another company and/or another broker before your policy is cancelled or you have to take your insurer to court.

To give you an idea what can happen, here's a true story told by Gardiner G. Greene, himself a successful operator of several small businesses, in his book *How to Start and Manage Your Own Business*. An owner bought a new building, and told his broker to get fire insurance on it. Several weeks later, the building caught fire. The broker came and watched the fire, which caused big damage. The next day, he delivered the insurance policy. After the fire!

Had the policy been made out before the fire? Or was it hastily drawn up afterward? The owner had left details of coverage to the broker. What coverage had he chosen? The broker represented several fire-insurance companies. Which one did he choose? And why? Did he pick a company that was about to drop him anyway, because it had suffered too many losses through him? Or one with a few losses, which might be more willing to pay promptly? Were his own best interests served by fighting for his client? Or by looking out for the underwriter?

This was an unusual situation, but it highlights some choices a broker may confront. You must try to make sure he's looking out for you, not himself or an underwriter. His reputation among businessmen who know him is probably your best guide.

In case you're wondering whether this particular owner was really insured, on the basis of a mere phone call to a broker—he was. Such calls are common in the insurance business. They're known as binders. The system is such a convenience to brokers and insurers that abuse is rare, even though there's no legal record that the client ordered the coverage. So be sure to phone your broker as soon as you acquire anything that needs coverage. If you don't know he's reliable, you can always have one or two people witness your call—and it's always a good idea to follow up with a letter confirming the conversation.

Anyhow, try not to leave many details to the broker. Obtain the new policy as soon as you can—and read it. Earlier, make sure the broker is ordering the coverage you want, from a company you approve.

When you first sign with a broker, insist that he provide you with a certificate of insurance—a type of "malpractice insurance" for brokers. Make your coverage through him contingent on the certificate. Then if he fails to follow through on a binder, or omits some critical detail about your company in reporting to the insurer, at least you can collect via his own insurance.

You vs. the Claims Adjustor

Each time you have a loss, you'll meet a supposedly independent claims adjustor. He's likely to be undertrained, underpaid, and uninformed about technicalities of your business. Who pays his salary (or maybe commission)? Is he really independent? Adjustors who prosper aren't liberal with claimants; they fight hard for insurance companies. They also tend to stall, telling a claimant that the only way to get his money quickly is to settle for the low payment they offer. Don't sign any paper an adjustor presents to you without an attorney's advice.

Many owners think that nothing should be touched after a fire or storm or some other casualty loss until an adjustor arrives to examine the damage. But there's a danger in keeping hands off: the damage may get worse if the company does nothing to protect what's left. An insurance company won't pay for additional damage caused by neglect.

It's up to your company, not the adjustor, to make an inventory of loss. Don't let him compute the claim. He doesn't know enough about your facilities. You should immediately summon a competent contractor, repair service, or the like, to provide expert estimates of work needed. At the same time, you should take inventory, with an insurance rep joining in the checking to avoid arguments later. Keep the adjustor at the site until a responsible company man thoroughly reviews the situation with him, and they reach some agreement on the facts.

It's hard to believe, but many firms can't accurately determine their losses, whether by damage or by theft. Their records are inadequate. In one case a theft loss amounted to $250,000 but the company could substantiate only $10,000 of it.

You need to plan ahead with your accountant and lay out the best procedures for proving what you own, should you have to make a claim. Save purchase receipts, expert appraisals, newspaper clippings, and anything else that will help document your casualty claim. Before and after photos can be a big help; you might consider taking periodic photos of your entire premises. All this material should be in one handy place—but not where damage to your property might destroy it too. You can have your attorney or CPA keep it, or you can put it in a safe-deposit vault.

As soon as you claim a loss, the insurance company's adjustor will ask you for an estimate of the damage—"just a rough guess," he'll say. But be careful. If your guess turns out to be much too low or too high, there'll be difficulties.

Suppose you underestimate. So the adjustor reports a number that's too low, and must go back later to the insurer and restate it much higher. He looks foolish. So do you. Those hurt feelings can complicate loss negotiations. So tell the adjustor about any problems in making your estimate. At this point it's a good idea to call in your accountants to be sure you don't leave out anything significant.

On the other hand, if you overstate a loss to the point at which your credibility seems questionable, the insurer will take a hard line. So it's important that even your preliminary estimate be in the right range. Usually when a claimant takes a fair position, the insurance people will still bargain over the claim but will be more reasonable. In a moment we'll see how you can get expert help with your estimate.

But first, another warning: don't turn over repair work to the insurance company's contractor unless your own builder okays the specifications. In the long run it makes no difference to you which contractor does the job, if it's done competently—but you're entitled to have your loss repaired or replaced in like kind and quality. Be sure to have your own expert check the work as it goes along.

One more warning: if you're told that your policy doesn't cover a loss you've reported, ask to speak to someone higher. Insurance brokers and claims investigators are sometimes unaware of a policy's full coverage. If unassailable authorities still say no, there's plenty of time to have your lawyer check the policy.

You Can Have Your Own Adjustor

Because there's incessant turnover of insurance adjustors, there's always a chance that you'll have an important claim handled by a totally inept or unfair adjustor. But you can prevent this. In advance, line up one or several adjustors and get them familiar with your company's work. Have them meet regularly with your broker and your executives (and your safety engineer, if you have one) to exchange comments and criticisms.

In simple loss situations you won't need a public adjustor. But if a loss is big or complicated, he may be worth the extra cost. A public adjustor usually charges between 5 and 12 percent of the amount the client collects, depending on how much work is involved. The charge is negotiable. A few public adjustors charge a fixed rate based on time.

A public adjustor will bring in his own experts and will prepare your claim in detail. He knows how, and can probably do it much better than your own staff. Even at the outset, he can help with your preliminary estimate, and it's likely to be on target because of his expertise.

In looking for a good adjustor, get recommendations from people you trust. Keep in mind that an adjustor may pay a finder's fee to your insurance broker or your attorney for bringing him your business; this could work to your disadvantage in the long run.

Get Regular Checkups

Just as your physician should give you a thorough medical examination every year, so should your insurance broker and CPA check your insurance annually, seeking out unseen risks before it's too late.

If a cab company in Los Angeles had gotten such a checkup, it wouldn't have let its workmen's-compensation insurance lapse—and wouldn't have been shut down by the municipal board of transportation. By state law, when an employer is found not to be carrying this mandatory insurance, a stop order must be issued. The order forces the employer to send his workers home, pay regular wages while they are off because of the order, and recall them only when he has bought the proper coverage. He must also pay a penalty assessment of $100 per employee. In California a total of 1,208 such orders, mostly to small companies, were issued in 1978, with penalties totaling $924,950.

An insurance checkup may uncover possible savings for your company. One firm found it was paying fire insurance on a demolished building and auto insurance on a truck that didn't exist. The imaginary truck was created when someone inadvertently transposed an engine number on business records, and the insurance company assumed a new truck had been added.

Every business changes. Its risks keep changing. Laws change. So insurance policies should change too. Amounts should be upped or lowered. Deductibles and loss-sharing should be reconsidered. New safety measures may be needed as equipment is added, or new quality control as you lengthen your product line.

Your insurance needs will also change with the national economic cycle. During a slump, you need less insurance against business interruption—because when times are hard, it's easier to replace a damaged structure. Construction workers are plentiful. Machinery can be obtained faster. Employees are willing to take less pay. Meanwhile, you probably have high inventories available—and fewer customers for the business that was interrupted. So don't be shy about asking your insurance carrier for a rate reduction, based on a lesser amount of insurance during a recession. You'll get it.

Conversely, you need more business-interruption coverage when prices are soaring and people are flocking to buy. You'd lose more by having to stop business. Your annual insurance checkup should take this into account.

If your broker wants to keep your business, he should keep you abreast of new possibilities, other policies, ways to reduce your premiums. To keep him on his toes, consider changing brokers every two or three years. Get new bids, with new surveys of your requirements. Let your broker bid only if he has served you well. If no one else offers better coverage at lower prices, or can guarantee better service, then you're safe in sticking with your present broker.

Sometimes an even better idea is to divide your business among several brokers, if you can do so without duplicating any coverage. For example, one broker might handle your fire insurance, and another your workmen's compensation. You almost certainly should separate your health insurance from your liability and casualty coverage. These are entirely separate fields, with brokers who specialize in nothing else. Some brokers consider themselves experts in both lines, but most insurance professionals admit that they must concentrate on one or the other to do a good job for clients.

Never let your company's insurance program slide into a rut, with terms decided offhandedly by a broker. Keep your insurance dynamic and up-to-date, always based on analysis by experts. That way you'll sleep better.

KEEP THESE BASIC POINTS IN MIND:

- *Read your policies. Look out for loopholes. Make sure you're covered. Make sure your organization does nothing that would nullify coverage.*
- *Delegate insurance matters to one of the best people in your organization.*
- *Insurance salesmen who approach you are not the kind you need. Seek out a broker who handles clients similar to you—or several brokers. Buy insurance by comparison shopping.*
- *Insist on inspection of the premises before agreeing to any insurance program. Make it clear to your brokers that you want them to specify what coverage they recommend, listing exclusions in clear language.*
- *Consider covering smaller risks by self-insurance, or by taking higher deductibles.*
- *Liability insurance is your most important coverage. Get the broadest possible coverage in this category. But it will still contain gaps, so you must check closely to be sure special coverage is added where your kind of business needs it.*
- *Make sure your broker describes your business accurately to insurance companies with whom he seeks to place your coverage.*
- *Your policy is only as good as the company behind it. Investigate the company before buying its policy.*
- *Be alert in dealing with a claims adjustor. Don't let him compute the claim. Keep him at the site until he and a company man have gone over the damage together and reached some agreement on the facts.*
- *Work out advance plans for proving the extent of losses when you have to make a claim. Keep full records in a handy place away from your premises.*
- *Line up a few adjustors in advance and get them familiar with your operations. In case of a serious loss, consider retaining a public adjustor.*
- *Get a complete annual checkup of your insurance. And get new bids from brokers every few years.*

17
How to Manufacture Customers

A certain independent cabdriver gets calls from all over the city requesting his taxi. A certain shoe-repair shop has customers lined up along the sidewalk. A certain lunch counter draws patrons from miles away. Why? Because these little enterprises are run by natural showmen.

Once you get the knack, you too can be a showman. "My business is different. It can't be dramatized," some say.

They're wrong. Even industrial selling uses showmanship. A new manufacturer of conveyor furnaces puts certain sales-compelling words on each furnace, and outsells competitors even though he charges more. A valve manufacturer uses a paper clip to illustrate how to sell valves. A little brush manufacturer becomes biggest in the West by advertising nonexistent kinds of brushes as comparables.

Big-money sales can come without huge billboards or full-page ads. A canning company sold 24,462 cans of cranberry sauce with one small ad. A restaurant changed its name and multiplied its business tenfold. Variety stores sold thousands of clothespins by giving clerks three words to say.

Countless ideas that create customers are simple and inexpensive. This chapter and the next will show you 203 such ideas. Probably some of them can be adapted to your business. Others may stimulate you to a brainstorm of your own.

Call it marketing. Call it promotion. Call it public relations, or applied psychology, or creative advertising, or showmanship. In whatever guise, it's the art of wooing prospective buyers.

A Neglected Art

You've seen many a business of which people say, "They haven't had a bright idea in ten years." Along comes a competitor with just a few bright ideas, and the older company hits the skids. Business is now so competitive that owners and managers must innovate or decline.

Constant promotion is needed just to replace the customers who die, or move away, or change their buying habits. Good promotion can not only replace customers but add new ones, and sell more to current customers. It can be used at long range via radio or mail or newspapers or telephone. It can be used close up in window displays or packaging—or across a counter or desk.

Yet the average small-business man seldom thinks about cultivating customers, or expanding his market to attract new ones. He may advertise on the shirts of a Little League or bowling team he sponsors. He may get publicity when his name appears among contributors to a local charity auction. Some firms buy radio time and run the same dull spot over and over, expecting it to work like a Tibetan prayer wheel.

Few advertisers understand the importance of being attractively different. Even fewer think of small acts that can bring the best kind of free publicity to back up their paid advertising. The most common problems of small business arise from this ignorance, according to the SBA's new Business Development Centers.

Volumes can be written on the subjects of marketing, advertising, and selling. Book publishers find a ready market for their books dealing with these subjects. But books examining the specific subject of small-business promotion are almost nonexistent. You may have to be your own expert.

You may say, "I have no talent along those lines. So I'll just provide good products and good service, and the customers will come."

Good Work Isn't Everything

Well, you're right in feeling you must start with something that customers will like. Court files are crammed with sad examples of enterprises that tried to promote untruths—and ended in bankruptcy or with their operators going to jail. Aside from the ethical considerations, it is simply very unprofitable to promote most products or services with untruths, however alluring. To create a customer costs effort as well as time and money. The cost is too high to risk incurring the ill will of the new customer who finds he was bilked. He'll not only stop buying, but will bad-mouth the business.

But quality is only the first chapter in the long story of any successful business. Your business may offer quality for the lowest possible price and yet go broke, if nobody seeks you out. You can have the best products, you can have all the financing you'll ever need, you can have the most modern and best-equipped plant, you can have the world's most efficient people working for you, but until you get a customer, you haven't got a business. To date, the Taj Mahal hasn't made a cent; neither will you if you build a monument.

Five P's for Three B's

Let's anatomize this nebulous art of creating customers.

It can be done by (1) a good Product (2) in a good Place (3) at a believable Price, (4) with an attractive Personality or "image," (5) purveyed by the right kinds of People in sales and service.

Practically all ideas that boost sales can be classified under one of these P's. We'll consider the first three in this chapter, the other two in Chapters 18 and 19.

Sales ideas can also be grouped according to the type of business that can use them. Businesses are roughly divided into three levels according to the complexity of their relationships with their customers. Each level has different marketing problems. Let's glance at the three in turn.

First is the "job shop" level, in which the business does its work to order. Usually it is a service business such as a restaurant, a dry cleaner, a detective agency. When a customer brings in an order, the business starts up its apparatus or uses its skills to complete the work. This is the simplest type of business. If it does adequate work (Product) at reasonable Prices, and if its Place of business is fairly convenient, it can boost sales through its Personality or its People.

An example is the shop mentioned in the first paragraph of this chapter. Sam Forelnick sensed the possibilities of a shoe repair and shine shop in San Antonio. He opened his shop with a gala floral display and a three-piece band. From the first day he regaled patrons with the newest magazines and pleasant radio music. An advertising expert wrote, "I counted in his store thirteen different ways of interesting customers—from colored blazers on his workmen, embroidered with the shop's name, to free shine tickets with every repair. When the rubber heel came, its entire surface was embossed with an advertisement of his service. Most advertisers don't bother with these important little items so near home."

Sam wondered if people outside San Antonio also wanted something done for their shoes. Out went men to investigate whether Sam could do business by mail, how many had heard of him, and if not, why not? Soon as much business was coming from outside as from the town itself.

Then he wondered if his Product might be expanded. He established a "breaking in" service for new shoes. "People don't like new shoes because they generally don't fit comfortably," he explained. "They have their old shoes fixed because they are so comfortable. We can make money by making new shoes comfortable." No wonder customers stood in line.

Hearing of Sam's success, Joe Zinke opened a luxurious shoe-repair shop in downtown Los Angeles. There were velvet armchairs and a custom carpet with Z's worked into the pattern. The walls were hand-tooled leather. Joe started with ten employees, the latest machinery, and a big store. "The bigger the store, the easier it is to operate," he reasoned. "If you have only one person, what happens when that person isn't able to be at work? Besides, the more people I have, the better service I can give." He offered while-you-wait service, even for full soles and heels. Speed saved money for Joe, because it meant less handling and storing, as well as more customers who liked the convenience. In addition, the customers were made to feel at home and comfortable. One of his little tricks: each customer's feet were wrapped in a small blanket while their shoes were being repaired. Things like this became a Zinke trademark, and as a result, within a few years he was able to build a chain of shoe-repair parlors up and down the West Coast and as far east as Cleveland. They had neon signs, drive-in parking, and carhops in short skirts fetching shoes for customers. Joe Zinke had become a millionaire.

A cab company is also a job-shop type of business, even though it doesn't occupy any shop. People phone it for service, and each job is slightly different. But how can anybody in this business increase his clientele? Through Personality. A driver who owned his own cab fixed it up with a mirror on the back of the driver's seat, set at a convenient angle for lady fares. He offered passengers a complimentary cigarette of whichever brand they preferred, plus a book of matches—with his.phone number on it. He remembered the names of people who phoned for his cab, and spoke to them by name. (One of the sweetest sounds to our ears, psychologists say, is the sound of our own name.) So this cabbie got lots of calls, and good tips.

Add Something—and Multiply Sales

The second of the three business levels is the operation that puts together many component parts to make one or several end products. A small business at this level might manufacture power hand tools, or make a line of furniture, or package a line of foods. It might be a publisher or an apartment building or a chemical company.

At this level, the promotional effort usually proclaims the merits of the Product. But not always. There's a sales strategy known as the tie-in, or premium offer, which can sell your product by offering something extra to go along with it.

As an example, consider the cranberry canner in Hanson, Massachusetts. Somebody in the office thought up a cute little novelty: a cutter made of plastic. It could cut slices of cranberry jelly into the shape of a turkey. The company offered it to people who would send in a dime and a label from a can of its cranberry sauce. Wherever this little novelty was advertised, as many as 10,000 replies per day came in—each with dime and label. All those people had bought Ocean Spray cranberry sauce.

A simpler example is based on the fact that many women like pets. One hardware dealer found he could build up business by selling birdcages. From there it was an easy step to selling canaries at cost with the cages. When his ads shifted from selling cages to selling birds *with* cages, sales jumped 34 percent.

The secret of tie-in success is to link products that complement each other. A manufacturer of medium-price pens makes a deal with a luggage maker who wants to boost his medium-price attaché case. The latter promotes sales by "giving away" a premium (the pen). He buys the pens in huge quantity at a very good price. He advertises that anyone buying his case gets a free pen. His ads feature the pen, by name, as well as the attaché case. So the pen company makes a profit and gets advertising—at no cost to itself—through the attaché-case display ads. Its also gets widespread sampling of its product while unloading a heavy inventory.

This can be a better way to distribute some of your Products than by struggling to get them stocked and displayed in good Places—or by cutting Price and unloading them to discounters. Discounters may give a line an undesirable "cheap" Personality by selling it at cut rates, and may also upset your distribution system by undercutting your regular sales outlets. A promotional tie-in if you find a good match-up, *enhances* a Product's image.

And remember that the idea isn't limited to consumer products. It can work with industrial products, if they're sold through salesmen or manufacturers' representatives. You can develop a sales incentive program by rewarding good performance with gifts you obtain from companies looking for promotional outlets and/or ways to work down inventories.

Even if your "Product" is entertainment, you can sell more tickets with tie-ins. Most baseball clubs pull people into the park by announcing giveaways of club caps, or "free bats to the first thousand boys at the box office," and a wide range of other gifts, each on a special day. Similarly, back in the 1930s when times were hard and movie audiences dwindled, the theaters filled seats by advertising prize drawings for dinnerware. Balloon giveaways filled the house with enthusiastic children at Saturday matinees.

One college student earned tuition money by doing publicity for a local nightclub. But one Friday night his club was in competition with the college itself, which had scheduled a show that most students wanted to attend. He solved the problem with a tie-in. He bought space in the program of the college's show for an ad with coupon offering a special prize to students attending the nightclub after the show. He got an even bigger crowd than usual that night.

As you can see, a company with unchangeable Product has a narrower range of promotional opportunities than a job shop. Personality may not count for much. Still, a few small processors have helped sales by making their names well known.

What's in a Name? Plenty

A blacksmith named John Deere began making steel plows with three replaceable parts. He couldn't patent them, but he made himself and Moline, Illinois, famous by putting a stylized sketch of a deer on the plows and on all the signs that bore his name. A poor pun, but good business. Deere & Company expanded into a full line of farm equipment, and became a worldwide manufacturer.

A lumberyard near Salt Lake City offered pretty much the same lumber as its competitors. Not much chance to give itself Personality? The owner saw a chance. His name is Green. He painted the fence green, wore green socks, green suit and shirt and tie, green hat. He got the phone company to break a rule and put a "Green" prefix to his phone number. He used green ink on every piece of paper that left his office. And he advertised: "Green for lumber! When you think of lumber, think Green." His yard kept growing; the green stuff kept rolling in.

A rose by any other name may smell as sweet, but won't sell as well. Ladies buy twenty times more hosiery of a shade named "Desert Sand" than when it's called plain "beige." A paint maker, too bright himself to sell his product simply as "white enamel," named it "Barreled Sunlight" and added $250,000 to the value of his company.

A little restaurant in Michigan was selling only $20 to $30 worth of food daily. The name on its sign was "Tea Room." When this was changed to "Restaurant," the sales swelled tenfold.

Perfume manufacturers are well aware of the psychological value of catchy names. Such names as "My Sin," "Tigress," "Temptation," "Christmas Night" are examples of how they play on human emotions.

Decades ago, when movie studios were at the height of their glamour, the Los Angeles Chamber of Commerce sent Genevieve Staley to urge big New York stores to buy and promote Hollywood fashions. The stores said no. "They're too bizarre out there in Hollywood," they told Miss Staley. "New Yorkers won't go for Hollywood fashions." Thereupon, in a flash of creativity, she proposed "Let's call them California fashions." The stores stocked and displayed them under this name, and Los Angeles apparel makers using a "Manufactured in California" label were on their way to a bonanza.

Big business learned long ago that a name can be worth millions. According to a legend, the R. J. Reynolds Tobacco Company refused ten million for its "Camel" name. After Norton Simon, Inc., bought Avis Rent-a-Car, it spent a quarter-million dollars trying to stop Warren Avis from using his own name in a new business, Avis Flowers Worldwide. Maybe you can make your name comparably valuable in your own market.

Back to our three basic business levels. The third—and least flexible —is the operation that is geared to turn out a given amount of a given product in a given time. Examples would be a gasoline refinery, a bobby-pin manufacturer, a coal mine, a cotton plantation. Usually this kind of enterprise has virtually no chance of changing its Product.

Its marketing strategy may boil down to questions of market penetration, of supply and demand (and therefore of Price), of logistics. Sometimes it may find new uses for its Product, and thereby expand its market. More often it develops strategic business connections through its People and Personality. Executives and salesmen of such companies entertain tirelessly, and may try to do constant favors for customers and prospects. Meanwhile, such companies' marketing men pore over business statistics in search of more Places to find customers.

Dramatize a Difference

However, too many of these salesmen and "marketing specialists" overlook a fundamental, obvious axiom of marketing: Play up any difference that will give you a jump on competition. If no difference can be found, play up some attribute which the competition hasn't stressed, so that the attribute will *seem* different.

The valve manufacturer mentioned early in this chapter had rivals who made almost identical valves. But he won sales by showing that his Hancock valve could smash a paper clip without injury to the valve. His salesmen would set a loosely assembled valve on a prospect's desk, and say, "Here's a paper clip. Push it in between the seat and disk, anywhere you like. . . . Now tighten the valve." When it was taken apart again, the clip was mangled, but no mark was left anywhere on the valve. Purchasing agents were impressed.

Similarly, the Michigan Ladder Company put a Ford onto a ladder and photographed it. The sales manager himself didn't believe any ladder could support the weight of an automobile, and wouldn't let his car be used for the test. Another car was used—and prospects were just as amazed as the sales manager.

Other companies follow the same principle by putting an elephant atop their product, or by dropping it from a tower, or by firing guns at it. Timex Watch Company's promotion manager must sit up nights thinking of new torture tests for his products. Many of these tests look pretty silly, but their impact is tremendous.

What are *your* product's marketable differences? A laundry decided that the cleanliness of its seven-rinse process was a difference. Facts about the bacteria tests of the rinse water seemed dull—but the laundry dramatized them. Its salesman called on prospects with a jar of water in his hand, and a big button on his lapel reading CAN YOU DRINK IT? He said, "When we rinse your laundry the seventh time, the water is so clean you can drink it. Do you think that when laundry is done elsewhere the water is really clean enough to drink?" With that as a start, the salesman told his scientific story, backed with the authority of a state university's chemistry department. Sure it was dull, but the jar of water dramatized it.

Use Eye-catchers

Movie and stage people say, "The eye remembers what the ear forgets." Action catches the eye—especially if the action involves some interesting object, called a "property" or "prop" in show business.

That's why a good salesman shows you pictures, gives you something to handle, keeps moving. He pulls out a pencil if he has nothing better. He uses it as a pointer. He waves it in the air. Maybe he even breaks it in two or throws it away to illustrate a statement like "Figuring won't support your family if you die tomorrow." A moment later something else is in his hand. He keeps you watching.

Humdrum facts like a publication's circulation figures can be made memorable with props and action. A salesman carries two piles of newspapers into a prospect's office. "This," he says, pointing to the big pile of his own publication, "is how many copies of my paper go into homes for one dollar you spend with us. And those"—pointing to a smaller stack of a competitor's newspapers—"are how many readers of the other paper you get for the same dollar."

John Theis, a CPA, dramatized an even duller subject—cost accounting. His prop was a 108-inch loaf of bread. It illustrated his breakdown of the cost elements of the baking business. He pulled the loaf apart in front of bakers. Inside each part of the loaf were figures explaining cost elements: 8 of the 108 inches, for example, represented waste from stale returns. If a CPA can dramatize facts, anybody can!

Take, for example, a salesman of industrial products. His product line was extensive. Like most long-line salesmen, he had a bulky catalog and a huge sample case—two reasons why purchasing agents try to fend off a long-line salesman. They're afraid he'll take an hour peddling his wares. But this man soothed them at the start—by catching their eye with a walnut shell.

"We handle two thousand items," he admitted, smiling, "but the reason you should deal with us is so simple that we put it in a nutshell." He dropped a walnut into the buyer's hand, saying, "Open it up."

Opening the shell, the buyer found a strip that read: "More items from one source—and from the most convenient warehouse." This was something purchasers wanted to hear about, since they must buy hundreds of items.

Gold-plated Furnaces

Here's how a new company sold conveyor furnaces for $35,000 and up. The company's founders, all furnace-design engineers, had developed a unique design that made the working parts of the furnace unusually durable. But how could they dramatize this difference?

They found a subtle way.

First, to make the sale, the company threw in a $45 gold-lettered nameplate. (Remember the tie-in technique?) Its salesman would ask a plant engineer, "Do you want gold or silver for your company nameplate on your furnace?"

While the engineer considered this startling question, the salesman pulled out gold letters and spelled the prospect's company name. "We always put the owner's name on our furnaces," he said. "Which letter style do you prefer, Old English or Gothic?" (Smart salesman ask which, not whether.)

Now, plant engineers are extremely proud of their equipment. This minor inducement made them see the furnace as almost a monument.

Without realizing it, by specifying the letter style on the nameplate, they decided to buy the furnace.

But the nameplate also played a long-term role. When the furnace was delivered, the gold letters spelled out: "THE ELKO FURNACE COMPANY'S MODEL 102, DELIVERED TO THE BENDIX CORPORATION ON MARCH 3, 1969."

Because of the durable working parts, Elko furnaces stayed on-line while others went down for repairs. Soon the facilities manager and plant engineer began observing that this furnace was several years old and hadn't needed any repair: "Every six months I have to change ABC furnaces' elements, manifold, and conveyor belt. But we've had Elko's unit four years now—see, it says on the plate it was delivered in March of '69—and would you believe that we haven't had to shut it down yet?" Since facilities managers and plant engineers talk to their peers at other companies, this still-young company soon had the best reliability image (Personality) in the industry. That reputation nets it 10 percent more in sales price over its competitors.

You Needn't Be Best

Sometimes *lack* of quality is an asset—if you make a point of it.

For example, a company turned out nothing but cassette transports, which are a component in computers. It sold only to computer manufacturers—a tightly limited market. Its components were simply built, to perform few functions. They were designed for users who needed only those few functions. The lack of versatility, reflected in the lower price, was their real selling asset.

The cassette maker, like most manufacturers, firmly believed that his product was the finest of its kind. But his advertising man was less emotional and more sales-minded. "Nobody cares how well we make our product," the adman insisted. "All they want to know is how well our product will work for them." Although pained, the company president finally okayed a campaign with the theme "Why pay for overcapability?" Computer manufacturers got the point. They'd been buying costly complicated units that could do more than they actually needed. So they switched.

Study Your Customers

As the American Institute of Banking keeps telling small business, "The easiest way to make money is to learn what people want and sell it to them. The fastest way to lose money is to offer something, regardless of what people want, and try to make them buy it.''

Nevertheless, a good many businessmen still try to promote unwanted products with look-damn-you advertising and high-pressure salesmen. But people are at least as intelligent as fish. A wise fisherman walks miles for the right bait. We seldom hear of a fisherman trying to train fish to bite at unattractive bait.

Which brings us to the first and most important of the five promotional P's: Product.

This means Product in the broadest sense of the term: whatever services or goods you plan to sell. It includes, for example, not only the food in a restaurant, not only the service by the waiters and busboys, but also the pleasant greeting at the door, the comfort of the seats, the atmosphere, perhaps the prestige of being seen there. (In this sense, Product and Personality sometimes overlap.)

Manufacturers, retailers, wholesalers, banks, insurance companies, Realtors, all kinds of service enterprises have a Product in this broad sense. For success, they need to match their Products to markets.

If a business is inefficient, if its goods or services are shoddy, or if customer-service people are rude or unskilled, then money budgeted for attracting customers can be better spent on improving these aspects— that is, on improving the image of the Product, as well as the product itself.

The market—the customers—should shape your Product. Ask what your customers want and need, and how you can satisfy them. Should you develop additional Products within your present line? Should you diversify with new Products quite different from what you now sell? Should you find new uses, new markets, for your present Product?

For example, if you've been selling replacement parts, you might try to expand by selling to original-equipment manufacturers. Or you might streamline your line, concentrating on the most profitable items. This might be a way to cut your operating costs sharply, and bring down that extremely important factor, Price.

Candy for the Firemen

Who would think of a candy maker's finding new customers among fire chiefs?

It was done by MacAndrews & Forbes, processors of licorice root. They saw that after they drew off the licorice extract and added soda ash to what remained, they had a liquid of remarkable foaming power. It billowed up, covered everything, and stuck to everything. They tried shooting it onto a fire. It cut off all oxygen and thus put out the fire. So the partners marketed a successful new product, Foamite Firefoam.

Robert Moore and Ernest Henderson were in the radio business. When the Great Depression of the 1930s ravaged their market, they salvaged $25,000 from the business and went looking for a new Product. They noticed that many hotels had fallen into the hands of insurance companies and mortgage lenders who knew little about running hotels. Moore and Henderson knew even less. But they decided to learn. They bought up debt-ridden hotels for next to nothing. Then they found ways to make their hotels attractive to customers. They began to decorate, air-condition, turn waste space to profitable uses, operate their own concessions in the hotels, cut costs by new methods, make it simple to get a room reservation. Then they advertised. Their hotels are now the Sheraton chain.

A small-city nursery wondered how to sell more flowers. The owner looked around. Upmost Avenue was declining from elegance into the in-between stage—no longer fully residential, not quite business. But it was a strategic artery and ought to look better. No one was allowed to park on Upmost, yet the avenue was very wide. The nurseryman's eyes lit up. "Let's rename this Avenue of the Roses," he suggested to the chamber of commerce. "I'll plant everbearing roses along both sides." He enlisted the garden club and the women's club. Soon his own Products were blooming not only on the avenue, but in the yards of property owners. Why not? All those roses enhanced prestige and boosted property values.

Merchants Who Tap the Subconscious

Anything that makes customers feel better may enhance your Product. A coal dealer wondered how to get more customers. He couldn't upgrade his coal. But he fired up the emotions of his customers by installing a huge gong inside the entrance of his yard, with a sign instructing customers to hit the gong to summon an attendant. We all secretly wish to hit something and make a loud noise. So this paid the coal dealer substantially.

Cashing in similarly, a doll maker thought up a figurine with which people could give vent to destructive urges at home. His silly-looking "Wackaroo" statue was of plaster, and sold for 60 cents. Some of the biggest department stores sold it, and the entrepreneur, John Melville, got widespread publicity.

An apartment-house owner had a good Product, but wanted to make it even more attractive. The windows had an interesting view. So he put $20 telescopes by the windows, and intrigued apartment prospects happily paid some $70 more a month than before.

Another apartment owner, pondering the same problem, added a sauna bath. A tract builder sold homes faster, for better prices, when he installed attractive curtains in the several windows of each of his empty houses.

(Techniques for making buildings more salable, at small expense, are numerous. You'll find chapters about them in my earlier Simon and Schuster books, *How You Can Become Financially Independent by Investing in Real Estate* and *How to Manage Real Estate Successfully—in Your Spare Time*.)

KEEP THESE BASIC POINTS IN MIND:

- *You must continuously cultivate customers and prospects—in order to replace lost ones, add new ones, and sell more.*
- *By being attractively different, you can promote business.*
- *Maybe you can sell more of your products with a tie-in or premium offer. Link products that complement each other. They enhance each other's image.*
- *Try to make your company name memorable through color, design, pictures. Give your products attractive names.*
- *Play up any differences that can give you an edge.*
- *In selling or advertising, use interesting objects and action to catch your prospects' attention.*
- *Look for customers' or prospects' needs you can satisfy, perhaps with new products or services.*

18
Small Improvements Can Mean Big Sales

An old adage among marketers says, "Color catches their eye, styling makes them buy, performance makes them re-buy." Veteran salesmen rank the strongest factors like this:

a) Industrial sales: (1) performance, (2) styling, (3) color.

b) Consumer sales: (1) styling, (2) color, (3) performance, (4) price.

These are grossly oversimplified, of course. But let's see how styling can sometimes capture customers without any other change in a Product.

The Overland Dry Goods Company of Overland, Missouri, was caught with broken color lines of towels. This is a familiar problem in the dry-goods business. The common "solution" is to mark these down and close them out. Instead, Overland grouped all its broken stocks by color and sent them out to be monogrammed in the same color scheme—green on green, gold on gold, and so on. Instead of the usual lettering it chose a variety of breezy inscriptions: His'n—Her'n . . . Mr.—Mrs. . . . Mine —Yours. Samples were draped on a display frame near the door. The towels sold out at full profit.

A jewelry store renamed some rings "divorce rings," to be worn by new singles desirous of showing their status, and attracted a whole new market with window displays and small ads. Another jeweler restyled a Product by using fishermen's flies and spinners—with the hooks filed off —as costume jewelry and advertising them as "Bait for the Boys."

Kid Customers for Machinists

Charles and Fred Doepke's machine shop in Rossmoyne, Ohio, prospered in wartime, but afterward the military stopped buying. The

Doepkes asked each other, "What shall we do for customers? We need new Products." To use their factory, they had to have something that could be stamped, pressed, and embossed in metal. Nothing was in sight.

One day Fred brought in his son's toy water truck for repair. It was wooden. The two men agreed, "Metal would be better." They had noticed that many toys were fragile. Why not make larger, stronger models, indestructible by the liveliest kids? Soon they sold models of everything from bulldozers to fire trucks, at $18 to $30, all made out of light metals. Their miniature concrete mixer actually made concrete. They'd found a hot new market, and devised Products to match it.

Had they chosen to expand their new business, they might have taken their marketing program a step further, as did John Tigrett, a toy manufacturer in Jackson, Tennessee. He'd learned that adults' ideas of what a child will enjoy can collect dust on dealers' shelves if the kids don't take to them. So to test his newly designed toys, he got local schools to let him put on a gadget show for kids. He mixed his new toys with those of other manufacturers and let the children have a delirious hour. Then he gave each child a dollar to buy whichever toy he wanted. This experiment, repeated yearly, keeps Mr. Tigrett attuned to his market.

When you think of restyling or innovating, try to test the market before you commit much capital. See how prospective dealers or users react. One entrepreneur could have saved himself much trouble and money by peddling his product to a few stores before getting in too deep. He had a fine silver cleaner, but people don't buy much silver cleaner. The market was too thin to justify stores' stocking it. Another company did better with a similar Product. The company sold it as a paint remover with silver cleaning as a sideline.

Be Color-conscious

Here are some examples that show why salesmen of consumer goods rate color next to styling in importance.

A candy manufacturer sold his sweets in blue boxes. Sales were poor. When he switched to red boxes, many people bought.

A manufacturer of hand shovels, perhaps the dullest of all tools, put a stripe of bright red paint on them. Sales climbed.

Frank E. Davis sells fish by mail out of Gloucester, Massachusetts. A black-and-white circular to fifty thousand families brought $9,388 worth of orders. The same circular next year to the same people, but with four colors on the cover (black and white inside), brought $12,482.

Until the 1940s, every bank looked like a cross between a mortuary and a powerhouse. Then banks awoke. They began to stylize and colorize their interiors (and often their exteriors). One of the first was the Valley National Bank, in Arizona. It created a magnificent lobby in warm mahogany tones with light pistachio walls and deep green leather seats. Within a decade it similarly restyled its other offices across the state. Bankers say this was one of the reasons the bank piled up a 25-fold increase in deposits in thirteen years.

Fred Rahr, a color engineer, enlarged the sales of Certain-Teed Products by redesigning its roofing shingles in new and brighter colors. He hired crews of college students and sent them out in multicolored autos. Cooperating with the local building-supply dealer, a crew would lie in wait outside an industrial plant. When workers streamed out, they found their paths lined with rows of resplendent shingles. This was tried first at Binghamton, New York, and brought 128 inquiries on the spot —from which 22 sales were made in a few days, at prices higher than before.

A color psychologist has made an experiment that enabled many retailers to attract more customers by making their places of business seem more spacious. He took a room of known dimensions and hung the walls with red draperies. Then he invited in various businessmen, workmen, and scientists—unimaginative, practical types. While chatting casually, he asked them to estimate the dimensions of the room.

After recording their guesses, he took out the red draperies and put in blue. He got other carefully chosen men to estimate the blue room's size.

Those who saw the room in red underestimated its true size by an average of 20 percent. Those who saw it in blue *overestimated* by almost 20 percent. So blue made the room seem one-fifth larger than it really was, while red had the opposite effect. This was because red is an advancing color, blue is retreating. (Thus a blue package seems smaller than a red one; no wonder the blue candy boxes sold weakly.)

One of many ways that business has used this discovery is in choosing colors for the company-supplied clothing worn by employees in banks, restaurants, department stores, and other service-oriented businesses. Because blue is unobtrusive, it is part of the ensembles favored by financial institutions, which don't want customers to feel intimidated. Conversely, waiters' garb often includes red, so that customers will feel the waiters are hustling toward them.

Even in industries where Performance and Price count for most, color helps cultivate customers. In Salt Lake City a printer gave his women employees colored smocks to wear (a different color every week) and painted each desk a different color—pink, yellow, blue, green, violet. The presses and paper cutters were in pastel hues too. It all attracted attention and made people remember his printing plant, which grows bigger yearly.

A Massachusetts shoe manufacturer stumbled onto the same idea while trying to help an old workman who couldn't keep up with production because of his eyes. The machinery was black; the leather was black. The manufacturer painted the machine light blue. Others in the factory liked the idea, and soon the plant was a rainbow. It became a showplace for factory tours—which hasn't hurt its sales.

It is a well-known fact that when Henry Ford started producing the old Model T on a production-line basis, it was suggested to him that he could sell more cars if he made them in a variety of colors. Thinking only of the production problems that could arise, he answered, "Give 'em any color they want—as long as it is black." The Ford Company very soon changed its marketing concept; today's cars come in all colors of the rainbow. The wildest colored and designed vans are the best sellers on the lot.

Wrong Place? Rise Above It

Now for the next of the promotional P's: Place. How can the location of your goods or services be used to improve sales?

The advantage of a strategic site is so obvious we needn't examine it. But suppose your business is in a bad location. What can you do? Promote!

Maybe you can glamorize the location with an imaginative name. A little restaurant deep in the Alabama woods attracted tourists by means of signs along roads advertising the "Swamp View" restaurant. Boca Raton, a rather out-of-the-way resort, advertised as "Florida's Secret Paradise."

The town of West Coulee is near Grand Coulee Dam, but a mountain hides it from the highway. This irked the townspeople, because tourists who drove to see the dam never turned off to visit West Coulee. So they set up roadside billboards advertising West Coulee as the "Hidden City," and soon had plenty of tourist business.

A young man in a corn belt university found another way to take advantage of an unpromising location. He organized a skiing tour for the students. You might not expect young people in the flatlands to go for this, but they did. During Christmas vacation he took several busloads to the mountains seven hundred miles away. He now makes a full-time business of such tours.

Basically, he was offering a desirable new Product in a Place that needed it. This is the principle followed by small truckers who buy up a load of fresh produce, bring it home six hundred miles, and sell it at a handsome profit.

Go Where the Market Is

This was also done by two frustrated automobile mechanics who were also cycle enthusiasts. They decided to quit their jobs and open a bicycle-accessories shop. Business was so-so—until they bought an old moving van, converted the interior into a bike-repair shop, and drove it to weekend bike meets. (This was in northern California—but bike meets are now held all over the United States on regularly scheduled dates.)

Next they bought a canvas tent, 50 feet by 18 feet. When they set up at a bike meet, they spread their tent and held a compact little bike-accessories show. Each participating manufacturer displayed his latest equipment. Not only did the manufacturers pay $250 to $400 for their display booths, but they also paid the two entrepreneurs commissions on everything they sold, and encouraged them to carry large inventories by giving them parts on consignment. After a couple of years, the mechanics' tiny business was netting them more than $150,000 a year. (If your business has salesmen on the road, would a demonstration van help?)

If you can't move your Place to where the customers are, then try hard to attract them to your Place, if business is slow.

You're lucky if you own a downtown corner drugstore. You may need little or no promotion. One of every twenty people who pass will probably step in to buy something. On the other hand, if you own something like an antique-furniture store on a side street, you'll starve if you count on walk-in business. You must advertise elsewhere to round up prospects from afar. In one way or another—perhaps in many ways—every side-street business must reach out for customers.

This is triply true of manufacturers. Along railroad tracks just beyond Syracuse, New York, stands a solitary factory. It makes rice- and coffee-grinding machines. Imagine such a company without a wide sweep in search of customers!

Come-hither for Your Business

"An interesting characteristic of most service businesses," says Professor William H. Brannen in *Successful Marketing for Your Small Business,* "is that a reputation for extra-high quality will attract customers in spite of a poor location."

However, this happens very slowly if not stimulated by advertising or publicity or other promotion. And since it happens only after the reputation is earned, a new business in a low-traffic site needs to be artful in attracting first-time customers.

To do this, its best bet is a curiosity-provoking Personality—the fourth promotional P, which we've seen in action here and there in this chapter, and will cover more intensively in the next chapter. First let's see how a manufacturer may solve his Place problems.

These problems may not be painful in this era of fast freight and instant long-distance dialing. But they still require the manufacturer to decide where, when, and by whom his products will be marketed. This takes alert research. Sometimes imagination helps too.

In marketing consumer goods, there's a saying that "Personal selling gets the merchandise on the shelves and advertising moves them off." It isn't always true that advertising moves them. But the saying does highlight the role of personal selling in almost any manufacturing business. That role is to sell to the trade—the wholesalers or retailers who must decide to put the merchandise on the shelves, or industrial purchasing agents.

Here are eight tactics to increase sales to the trade, retail or industrial:

1. Find out why some customers are buying less (or more) of your product than you'd expect. The answers can lead to new sales, and prevent the loss of customers.

2. Scan trade publications for news of contracts or purchases in your field—especially those which indicate new users for your product.

3. Don't overlook your own employees as sources of leads on new prospects. Your truck drivers, for example, often know about new stores or new owners. Some companies pay employees from $10 to $100 for valid tips on possible customers.

4. Keep building your mailing list. Send brochures and catalogs to all potential customers you can discover. When something interests them, they'll call you.

5. Try to sell whole lines, and special services, not individual items. Use every inquiry as a chance to tell the caller what else you can do for him.

6. Be alert to customers' special needs. If you become known for solving tough operating problems and meeting tough specifications, prospects will think of you when they need help.

7. Aim at the prospects that are the most demanding and hardest to see. They're the most promising targets, because your competitors probably don't even try to sell them.

8. Consider telephone selling. Now that the average cost of an in-person industrial sales call is $80, the cost advantages of telephone selling

loom larger. You may want to send for a publication, *How to Turn Telephone Inquiries into Sales,* available at no cost from Reuben H. Donnelley Corporation, 825 Third Avenue, New York 10022.

Wooing with IWATS

Saunders Archery Company makes and markets a broad line of archery equipment. Sometimes it sells through wholesalers, sometimes direct to retailers. But its only salesmen are its top executives. They call on key accounts and go to trade shows where they meet distributors. Until recently, Saunders' only other form of promotion was by mailing catalogs and announcements of new products.

Then Saunders investigated Wide Area Telecommunications Service (WATS). Service was available for either incoming or outgoing calls, or both. The company decided to use the inbound system (IWATS), by which customers using the IWATS line could call the company without a separate charge for each call. If middlemen wanted to call Saunders toll-free, they could do it without the bother of making a collect call. To make sure they knew this, Saunders sent them a special mailing, and urged them to phone regularly for new information.

It worked. Sporting-goods shows produced more sales than before, because new products that Saunders had suggested over the phone were in effect pre-sold to the trade. One product group showed a sales increase of 60 percent in two months. Yet IWATS cost Saunders, by its own calculation, only $14 for each $1,000 increase in sales.

Don't Block That Sale

Try to set up your business office in such a way that whoever takes telephone calls will make buying from you a pleasant experience.

When a customer or salesman calls in an order, don't put him through a cross-examination. Always accept the order first, and straighten out any problems after taking all the information he offers, in whatever way he wants to give it. After he has told you everything he can think of, ask questions in a cheery voice:

"How do you want us to make shipment—by freight, truck, or air? . . . I don't know if our rep told you, but you have your choice of shipping containers. Do you want a dozen to a box, 144 to a box, or would you like each individually boxed?"

290 How to Become Financially Successful by Owning Your Own Business

Even if a customer is mistaken about pricing, delivery, credit, or specifications, your clerk shouldn't refuse the order without top-management consent. Most field salesmen can straighten out such mix-ups personally with a customer, without jeopardizing the order he's already given.

When someone phones with an inquiry, he is getting ready to buy. Don't delay by mailing him literature, or answering his questions by mail; get the order *now*. However, don't try to sell him over the phone if it sounds like a sizable order and he isn't quite ready to give it. Go see him the same day yourself, or make an appointment for a salesman to see him. "I'll be over to talk to you about it" and "Our rep will come to see you immediately" are phrases that make sales.

Keep everything secondary to sale. When a customer needs something, he's pleased to find that you're giving him priority. Get your quotes out the day you're asked for them. If you can't do this because production and engineering must work out the costs, then send a letter to the prospect the same day, thanking him for the chance to bid, and saying you'll submit your quote no later than a specified date. And don't let that date slip.

Selling Big

If your company is angling for a first-time order from an important new prospect, your salesman may need higher-level help; probably his only contacts are with the prospect's purchasing department. Don't be afraid to approach top management, which will probably be involved in big-ticket buys.

Your best opening may be through a go-between who already has entrée. For example, a young TV production services company has one of its suppliers, a thirty-year company with many satisfied customers, introduce it to prospects. Even without an introduction, maybe your president can arrange an informal lunch with executives of the other company, just by phoning and suggesting it.

Another approach is for your president to write personal letters telling about your company, its products, and why the prospect should be interested. Mention other satisfied customers. Or if the record is bad, explain the improvements that will preclude past problems. Then you may decide to try to get your technical people acquainted with key technicians in the other company.

Finally, a top executive should then send another note to pave the way for your best salesman, telling the prospect who the salesman is, what his credentials are, and that he'll be calling for an appointment.

The Helpful Ghost

To help your salesmen negotiate with clients and prospects, several of your top people can have a scenario prearranged to play at the proper time in the prospect's office.

Your people must prepare themselves to play the role of a ghost executive in your office. Give the ghost a code name: Burlingame, perhaps. Give him a second-in-command title: general manager, operations vice president, or the like. This fictitious Mr. Burlingame, to be able to give an Oscar-winning performance, must appear to have wide authority, and must be able to delegate responsibility to any of your actual executives.

Here's how the performance is played. Suppose a prospect raises an objection that the salesman can't answer. Or suppose a customer demands something that the salesman hasn't authority to grant. Or suppose a salesman can't quote a price immediately on a possible big order. Or suppose a prospect is almost ready to give an order but can't quite make up his mind. In such situations, your salesman asks to use the phone for a collect call to your "executive vice president," Mr. Burlingame.

When your switchboard operator gets the call, she knows that it is a top-priority call. She goes instantly to her "Burlingame list" of various top executives who are qualified to handle it. She rings your president or chief engineer or whomever, telling him that he has a Burlingame call. So he knows that an important sale can possibly be made if he plays his role properly.

The operator must delay completing the call until the ghostly "vice president" gets back to his desk, pulls out the Burlingame notes (reminders of authorities, of responsibilities, and any technical guidelines), and signals to be put on the line.

After a brief introduction from the salesman, he proceeds to speak to the customer or prospect. Meanwhile, the salesman fills out his order form, so that when the conversation is complete, the order will be ready to sign.

A conversation might go like this: "Mr. Burlingame, I'm calling from Mr. John Jones's office. Mr. Jones is purchasing agent for the Superior Helipot Company, and he's concerned about delivery of our Model 2-T. Before he places the order, he must be sure we can meet his production needs. Since I don't know our delivery capabilities, I thought Mr. Jones should talk with you to help us work out his needs."

The pseudo vice president hears out Mr. Jones without interruption. He makes sure he understands Jones's doubts and requirements before he responds. Then, as one of the company's ace problem-solvers and negotiators, he should be able to work out a solution and to help close the sale, asking Jones to "please confirm our agreement" on the salesman's order blank.

Before ringing off, he must (a) impress on Jones that his name is Alvin Burlingame—so that the customer won't telephone plain Mr. Burlingame and get connected with a different executive; (b) make clear that he is delegating all responsibility and authority to Mr. Whoozis, a real executive—who rushes the customer a confirming letter.

The ghost-executive scenario plays prestige to the hilt. Your prospect's purchasing agent is impressed by talking to top management. He knows his order is getting high-level attention. If a problem arises, he can go direct to the top people and get satisfaction. He hasn't really been misled at all.

How to Keep Salesmen Enthusiastic

The biggest advantage of your ghost maneuver is that it takes heat off a salesman. He hands top management the ball, and is free of further responsibility. If all goes well, you all look good. If something goes wrong, the salesman is held blameless and can return to sell again.

Remember that recognition is a deep need and a real motivation in salesmen. Fill this need by having each of your top executives phone at least four different salesmen each month to thank them for their sales. This gets your salesmen onto a first-name footing with your executives, so that they feel free to phone when they need company help and feel they aren't getting it. Give salesmen your executives' home phone numbers, and instruct them to call collect whenever they need constructive help.

Sales promotion takes teamwork. If you have salesmen in the field, your team is built around them. So pass the credit to them for sales. Executives are prone to say, "I just landed a $100,000 order from Rockwell in Pittsburgh." However, you can be sure your man in Pittsburgh who made ten calls on Rockwell to soften it up will resent this.

Good salesmen want full responsibility for their accounts. They should always be in the loop between you and their customers. Some companies bypass them by sending quotes to a customer, with only a copy to the salesman. It's much better to mail any important quote to your salesman, so that he can deliver it and close the sale. Some smart companies type separate quotes at different prices and mail them all to the salesman. Then he can walk in, talk to the prospect, decide which of his bids will get the business, pull out the proper one, and land the order.

Salesmen like to sell. That's what you pay them for. Don't rob them of an opportunity. And don't ask them to be delivery boys, bad-debt collectors, repairmen, or record clerks. They hate paperwork and menial chores. They can't earn commissions when you take their time for other assignments.

Salesmen may want—and need—to know more than you're telling them: (1) Good news, such as high earnings or a big new order. Tell them before it's announced in the plant. They shouldn't have to learn about it secondhand. (2) Bad news, such as product problems, service breakdowns, recalls, company scandal, a disastrous quarter in sales or earnings. They can explain the company's side better if they're in the know. (3) Pending plans for new or changed products, facilities, services. These give them talking points with customers.

Send copies of your ads, and reprints of any publicity you wangle, to salesmen for distribution to customers—most of whom would never see them otherwise.

Words That Win Retailers

Advertising has been called "salesmanship in print." But studies show that an ad or a circular is only about half as effective as a personal conversation, even with a keenly interested prospect. And when it comes to "cold canvassing" of strangers, a salesman leaves the postman far behind. Let's see how some crack salesmen do it.

When Charles Luckman (later the president of Pepsodent, and then of Lever Brothers) was a young man, one of his first jobs was to draft a brochure for Palmolive soap. After a look at Luckman's draft, his boss said, "That won't sell soap."

"Let me learn by selling soap myself," the young man said. He went to Chicago's tough South Side. The first storekeeper he approached growled, "I don't need soap."

Luckman said, "I know you don't. That's why I'm here. If you needed soap you'd phone and order it. I came to find out *why* you don't need soap. Aren't your customers buying it?" (Good salesmen ask "why" a lot. They never say "Yes, but—")

The merchant said business was bad, nobody had money, nobody was buying, and so on. The talk turned (with some steering by Luckman) to ways of rearranging goods to catch customers' eyes.

Luckman peeled off his coat. "I'll help you. Let's put the cigarettes over there, where people will see them but can't get to them quite so easily. Candy bars too. Many people come in for candy or cigarettes, right? If we lead them past these other displays, something may catch their eyes and they'll buy it too."

Finally he got around to soap. "Everyone uses soap. They'll buy it here if they see it. So let's not hide it. We can stack it on this counter nose-high, so they smell that nice fragrance."

They built a soap pyramid. The owner thanked Luckman—and ordered more soap, since his whole supply was now stacked on display. "Better not order that much," Luckman advised. "We don't want you over-stocked."

He was building up welcome for the call-back. By similar helpfulness, he sold soap in seven of the first eight stores he visited. Soon he was a sales manager. He taught salesmen to concentrate on helping dealers—suggesting attractive displays, improvements in store layout, new products to carry. Good will was their goal. But orders rolled in.

Charles Austin Bates once wrote:

> Every businessman will talk about sales. Sales are his big problem. You won't find one in a hundred who is satisfied with his sales volume. If you can help him there, he will become your friend, and will think less about price.

A manufacturer thought up a slight improvement on an old and simple product, wooden clothespins. His were square instead of round. How to induce stores to stock them? His salesmen gave the stores three magic words for counter clerks: "They won't roll." Recognizing the convenience to housewives, the W. T. Grant chain stores sold 30 million clothespins with these words.

A sardine canner needed to show specialty stores how to sell his expensive brand of sardines. His tasted a little better, but the difference was too slight to be a selling point. The sentence that sold out the entire stock was "Rudd cans of sardines are turned upside down once a month in the warehouse prior to being shipped to our customers." This was followed by a quick explanation: reversing lets the oil seep through the sardines, making them look and taste better.

Salesmen Can Be Showmen

Salesmen often tackle prospects who don't want to see them. There are ways to change the minds of this type of prospect. Mandus Bridston, master salesman of appliances, once explained his way with busy buyers:

"I'll take out my watch and say, 'You've got seven minutes, haven't you?' He'll usually agree to that—but not a second more, he warns. Then I say, 'Put my watch here on the desk where you can see it, and please don't mind if I talk fast.'

"If he gets interested in my proposition, I ask his permission before I take more time. He grants it with a grin.

"If my prospect really is too busy to listen, I say, 'Suppose I come back at 2:40 tomorrow afternoon—or would 10:10 Friday morning suit you better?' Giving him a choice takes his mind off the impulse to say no. Also, asking for odd-hour appointments takes him by surprise."

Another clever operative puts on a show for the occasional rude dealer who never receives salesmen. He hires a silent assistant, some local young man who is willing to work ten minutes for a $5 bill. The assistant's job is merely to nod his head whenever the salesman looks at him.

They go into the store but make no effort to see the proprietor. Instead, the salesman pulls out a big card. He studies merchandise on the shelves, jotting notes and occasionally looking at his assistant, who nods as instructed. This worries the proprietor. He asks the men what he can do for them. The salesman says, "I see you're busy. Keep at it. I'll attend to your situation when you get through."

This convinces the owner they are officials of some kind. He soon finishes whatever he was doing, and hastens over to the salesman with uneasy cordiality. The salesman says, "Mr. Banghart, I've heard people talking around town. They say they won't do business with you because you don't treat them politely. I just wouldn't believe it, and I came in here to disprove those statements. I've already disproved them, because I saw how eager you were to greet me when I came in."

Startled but relieved, the prospect relaxes and listens to the salesman's proposition.

Suppose you're trying to sell not to retailers, but to business offices? Then the magic words are "It will save you money."

Salesmen for a copying machine are instructed to repeat this sentence no fewer than seven times in every conversation with a prospect. Harry Singer, a noted sales expert, found a way to dramatize this "money angle" and capture attention at the outset. He walked in with big bags of money. Before starting to talk, he opened several bags and let the jingle of falling coins transfix his prospect.

Another salesman makes thirty cold calls a day and can't haul heavy bags around. He nevertheless uses Singer's technique. He walks in with a $50 bill in hand. "Do you have all of these you want?" he asks.

Still another must get past receptionists who are instructed to fend off salesmen. He sends in a three-line message, written on a sheet borrowed from the receptionist. It usually gets the interview. It says:

> Will you give me three minutes of your time
> to prove that I can save you $500 a month
> without any investment on your part?

After a first-time sale, help your salesmen cultivate the customer for callback sales. Have someone phone or send a thank-you card while the order is in production. Let the customer know that his order is important and that the shipment is on its way and when it can be expected to arrive. It's sad how few companies send a real "thank you" for the business they've spent months or years trying to get.

After the order arrives, remind the customer what a good choice he made, and how much your company thinks of him. (Marketing research shows that customers are particularly happy when they're anticipating a purchase, and using it for the first time. Then they begin to wonder if they've made the wrong choice. You can ease them through this period of doubt.)

Persuasive Pricing

Now we come to the third promotional P, Price. Generally you set prices according to profit margins, competition, and what your customers can or will pay. Let's see how a little imagination in changing Price, or in talking about Price, can sometimes boost sales beyond what your money managers think likely.

Charles E. Finlay, a sales expert, designed extra sales appeal into apartment houses by the simple device of double pricing. He always had two identical apartments, say, directly across the hall from each other, but differing in price by as much as 10 percent. He always found one sort of prospect who would notice the difference, carefully compare the two apartments, and rush to rent the one at $395 before anyone else should notice the apparent error in pricing. On the other side, just as often, some customer who yearned for distinction was glad to pay $430 in order to have the highest-priced apartment in the building. One bought a bargain; the other bought prestige. The point is that a sale depends on the buyer's attitude, not the seller's.

"We're the Rolls-Royce of delicatessens," Marvin Saul tells his customers, and prints it across menu covers, matchbooks, and brochures. He pampers his customers with bizarre extras, including a limousine hot line near the cash register. He charges premium prices for ham baked in sherry and other delicacies. It works. His sales topped $2 million in 1980.

Well-heeled customers may pay extra when they consider that they're getting something special. This bigger markup can make it worthwhile to advertise a product to such customers. But be sure you advertise it correctly. One owner of a women's-wear shop considered that her merchandise was in the "moderate" price range. However, because her ads harped on Price and didn't mention quality, the public thought of her shop as a cut-rate place. When her ads started emphasizing quality and stylishness, she got a whole new group of customers, and found she could raise her Pricing. Indeed, they expected higher than she'd been charging.

On the other hand, the lure of an apparent bargain appeals to another —more numerous—group of customers. For them, you might try an auction. In order to move old merchandise and secondhand items taken on trade-ins, Charles Business Machines of Zanesville, Ohio, hired an auctioneer. He cleared out a big stock of discounted copiers, calculators, and used typewriters. The auction made money and generated good will. Bargain-hunting customers, asking when the next auction will be, are now good prospects for Charles's regular line.

"Bid" cards attached to slow-moving merchandise boosted sales for a Knoxville, Tennessee, retailer. The cards carried space for noting customers' bids, which were written in by store employees at the customer's request; the customer's name was written on the back, but only initials on the front. If a customer was overbid on any item, she could bid again. The promotion not only unloaded inventory at good prices, but attracted many customers who bought other items.

To celebrate the arrival of a new line of refrigerators, a shop in Reno ran newspaper ads offering a refrigerator to the person submitting the highest sealed bid. Merchandisers know that little cash is lost on such an offer, because the highest bid usually approximates the wholesale cost of the merchandise. And this plan gave the shop a fine list of prospects who were interested in the new model.

Help a Customer Unload

Here's a remarkable pricing concession that enables some industrial salesmen to get important new customers: they offer to buy unsold merchandise (made by their competitor) that's filling warehouse space their own product could occupy.

Sometimes they buy it outright and credit it against a specified minimum order from the customer. (You should do this only if you're reasonably sure that follow-up sales will justify the concession. This is a good bet if your product has a high price tag, or if it is part of a multiple-item line.) The next step is either to sell the dead merchandise at a closeout price or dump it and write it off as sales promotion. If the salesman does this, he is required to give up part of his commission in order to absorb the expense.

Other companies, instead of buying the customer's overstock, help him get rid of it by locating a closeout operator or distributor who'll take the stuff off his hands.

In either case, be tactful. The purchasing agent you deal with may be the one who bought that loser in the warehouse!

When You Cut Price, Tell Why

Decades ago, marketing expert Loren Deland taught that the *reason* for a price—particularly for a surprisingly low price—is as important as the price itself. Thousands of small merchants who never heard of Deland's dogma follow it unwittingly in their sales: "Lease Expired—Must Move." "Quitting Business." "Damaged by Fire."

Even a high-fashion merchant can fill his store to suffocation with low-priced merchandise if it can be explained in a believable manner. The most successful ad ever run by a certain elegant Fifth Avenue store was its final one—a few lines announcing "Receiver's Sale." Crowds were so big that mounted policemen had to be called.

Any merchant with suspiciously low prices has an extra job to do to convince shoppers that he isn't selling junk. From years of exploitation, people distrust unexplained generosity. He must either (a) show that he has no choice but to take a loss, or (b) explain how he himself benefits in the long run.

KEEP THESE BASIC POINTS IN MIND:

- *Use styling and color as sales-promotion devices. But test the market first, if possible.*
- *Make your location a selling point if you can. Maybe you should go where the customers are. If you can't do this, develop an image that will attract customers.*
- *Study your customers, and the trade news, for clues that can increase your sales.*
- *Maybe you should try selling by telephone. If you do, train your telephone people carefully.*
- *Give your salesmen maximum recognition and cooperation.*
- *Salesmen to retailers should concentrate on helping the retailers sell more merchandise.*
- *Salesmen to business should emphasize "It will save you money."*
- *Most buyers want bargain prices. Some wealthy consumers want prestige and luxury.*
- *When you cut price, tell why. Otherwise shoppers will be suspicious of your product.*

19
Recipe for a Reputation

Your business depends on what people think of it. If they think well of it, you may prosper even though you're in a hard-to-reach Place—and sometimes even though your Prices are higher than most.

Outsiders' opinion is formed primarily by whatever person-to-person experiences they have with your organization—through the mail, on the phone, face to face. They may judge your whole company by one experience with one person.

This can be fine for you, if you're the only person in your business and you have an engaging personality. It gives you a unique advantage over bigger businesses. If you expand, you should still stay out front as much as you can, because customers like to deal with "the owner" or "the boss." At the same time, try hard to be aware of your employees' attitudes toward the public, especially when you're not around. Each person is important in a small enterprise. Good personal selling is a way for many small firms to outdo competition.

And so (continuing what we started in Chapter 17) we come to your People, one of the five promotional P's.

Each employee who comes into contact with outsiders can help your enterprise immensely—or harm it. Your people give it a good or bad reputation. Reputation may be more important than reality, since customers tend to act as they perceive.

The Humble Optimist

What kind of impression should your People try to make? A "good" impression, obviously. But let's be more specific. Louis L. Allen, a noteworthy small-business man and venture capitalist who lectures yearly at the Harvard Business School, prescribes the characteristics he thinks any small business should try to manifest through its People:

> The image of the company is best put forward by demonstrating a *demeanor of cautious yet humble optimism, coupled with lots of hard work.* . . . The small-business man should be humble. He is small, he needs the business, he is asking for the order. Humility is an endearing quality and gives credibility to the other parts of the image. . . . As a small-business man, you can make someone believe he'll get extra service and attention simply because your organization is small. Your small size should be played up when calling on customers. Be humble about it, show cautious optimism and the willingness to work.

Whichever people in your organization are best at projecting this impression should do the selling and servicing of customers. They also should meet and mingle with the public and the trade as much as possible —attending conventions and trade shows, joining clubs, making speeches. They'll attract new business.

In addition, they should spend enough time with the other People in your organization so that their attitude will become contagious. Beyond that, your management should deliberately train employees in basic skills of public relations.

As prelude to the training, try a checkup. How do your company's outgoing letters look and sound? Is the language pleasant and clear? Is the typing perfect? Does the stationery give a good impression? If not, maybe you should call in a "better letter" expert. Such consultants are available.

A letter that seems simple and polite in its writer's mind may not seem so to the recipient. He may toss the letter away in disgust. And the writer won't ever know what happened. Surveys by several big companies have shown that many people didn't understand what the companies tried to say in their letters. Is this likely to be true in your company? Why not pre-test some of your important letters before mailing? Ask your wife and your freight clerk, perhaps, if they understand your letter well enough to sum up its meaning in their own words. (If they state it more clearly than the writer did, probably he should use their words instead of his own. Or if they say, "You're telling this guy, 'Drop dead!' " he should rethink his whole message. Why make an enemy needlessly?)

How Do We Look?

Outsiders judge by appearance. Often they have sharp eyes. If your receptionist greets visitors with a cigarette between her lips, they'll notice and remember. Many will also react unfavorably to conspicuous gum-chewing or hair-combing.

Inside the plant, your image in visitors' minds will be damaged by cluttered ashtrays, dust on filing cabinets, scraps on the floor. One immaculately clean print shop has a sign, "Five dollars for any piece of paper you find on the floor," and it pays immediately if a visitor does find one—which, of course, seldom happens. Its People take pride in their reputation for perfect housekeeping.

Employees' clothes and grooming give outsiders an impression of their personality and efficiency. In the drivers' room of the Horton Ice Cream Company in New York is a large mirror imprinted with the words, "This is how you look to the customer." Many other businesses might profitably use the same device.

Winning Ways

Dale Carnegie, the famous expert on techniques for winning friends, used to say that Stanford University was founded because of a mistake in the office of an Eastern university, which thereby lost $34 million. A shabby-looking couple came in and asked how much money it cost to run a university. The dignitary who received them considered their question stupid and impertinent. He replied brusquely. So instead of giving their millions to his university, as they'd planned, Mr. and Mrs. Leland Stanford went back to California to endow a university of their own.

"Every visitor is important to himself—and to us," warns a booklet given to employees of an aerospace company. "We must give friendly and fair treatment to all visitors—especially including salesmen and job-seekers. Even when our company can't do business with them, we want them to think well of us. Their opinions become part of our reputation."

With a little effort, you can probably train your employees to greet every visitor immediately—smiling and looking him in the eye. (Remember how annoyed you are when a haughty clerk in a hotel, or waiter in a restaurant, takes no notice of you for a while?) If delay is unavoidable, employees can explain why, and express regret.

When a visitor's request is outside the duties of the employees encountering him, they should automatically try to help him anyhow. They can pick up a phone and call someone in his behalf, or walk down the hall with him and introduce him to someone in a position to help. This takes longer, but it leaves the visitor with a warm feeling instead of the chill he gets from "Try calling So-and-So," or "You'll have to go to the Blank Department."

You and Your Telephones

One small-company president was lunching with an important customer when he discovered he'd left behind a chart he needed. He called from a phone booth to have someone bring it over. For some reason the switchboard operator didn't recognize his voice, and nonchalantly put him on hold for "what seemed like five minutes," he said later. When she got back to him, she didn't remember which extension he'd asked for.

Finally he was connected to his office, but his secretary was away from her desk, and a clerk picked up the phone after about twenty rings. Then, when the clerk tried to put the boss on hold, she disconnected him.

As you might expect, that afternoon the president had a few words to say to the whole office about how People should handle phones.

If customers say of your company, "They were very nice when I called," you're getting valuable free publicity. With a little training, your phone-answerers can make callers feel welcome with remarks like "Thank you *so* much for calling us, Mr. Orr."

Some companies impress on employees these ten tips for handling incoming calls:

1. Answer promptly—on the first ring if possible. This gives an impression of alertness and efficiency.
2. Identify yourself. Skip the hellos and yeses.
3. If the call is for someone absent, say "He's not at his desk," or "He's out just now." Then try to indicate when he'll return, and ask, "May I take a message, or can someone else help you?"
4. Nobody likes a blunt "Who's calling?" If you must screen calls (which isn't considered the best public relations), a better technique is to say "I'll see if he's here. May I tell him who's calling?"
5. If the call is for someone on another line, say "He's talking on another telephone. Would you care to wait, or may I have him call you?"
6. As you take a message, jot it down. Don't trust to memory, because an interruption may drive it out of your thoughts.
7. Take the caller's number. If he says, "He knows my number," you can pleasantly reply, "Let me leave it for him anyhow, just in case he doesn't have it handy." Also write down the time the call comes in; this can be important. Then put the message promptly on the right person's desk, in a prominent place where he won't overlook it.
8. Use the name of the caller when speaking to him, whether or not you know him personally.
9. Volunteer to transfer a call when advisable, but do it tactfully. Don't

say, "You'll have to talk to Blake." A better way is "I think Mr. Blake can help you with that. Shall I transfer you?" It's better yet, if possible, to offer "I'll be glad to get the information and call you back." (If a caller is shunted to several people before he finds one who can help him, it doesn't improve his opinion of the organization.)

10. If you must leave the line to get information or to answer another call, explain this to your caller so he won't think he's been cut off. It's friendly to ask "Will you wait, or shall I call you back?" If the caller waits, a "Thank you for waiting" is appreciated when you return to the line.

*Your Telephone Image—Good or Bad?**

The image that you project over the telephone may be a tool that you can effectively use to make a sale eventually. Or, it can be a handicap which will have a negative effect and create an unfavorable impression on the caller. It can prevent you from creating a favorable impression that will cause the individual at the other end of the line to react positively. Remember, the person to whom you are talking visualizes you and makes his judgment of you based on your attitude, voice, sincerity and manners.

At the same time, he judges the company you represent. Your company, as far as he is concerned, is you. All of the advertising and public relations efforts your company may have promoted over a period of years is riding on the manner in which you handle the prospect (buyer or seller) on the other end of the telephone line.

The Science of Saying No

Everyone in business is asked to do things he can't do—buy something, sell something, give something, join something, hire someone, divulge information. It's possible to refuse without irking the asker. Just take a little time and patience.

Before you refuse, make sure you understand the other person's viewpoint. Restate the request in your own words, to convince him that you understand. Make sure he agrees with your statement of it.

Explain fully why you can't do what he wants. (One successful executive says, "I give a quick yes, but I take a long time to say no. After I say no, I walk with the man to the door.") Try to be helpful. If his need is legitimate, look for some other way to meet it.

---

* Reprinted from the Lowry-Colman manual *Business Opportunities—Guide for the Professional*, published 1981 by Capital Printing, Reno, Nevada.

If he seems angry, don't interrupt, and don't argue. Nod earnestly. Perhaps you can remark that if you were in his place you'd probably feel as he does. (He'll feel better after he's blown off steam.) Then, gently, you might bring out facts he has overlooked. Usually you can phrase a few statements as questions, to steer him into reasoning out his mistake.

Remember that you want the good will of the visitor (and of his friends). Even if he is outrageously insulting, your job is to win him over without granting his demands. If you manage to do this, he'll probably be convinced forever that your company is a fine one.

Watch Your Language

Here are some words that lose friends:

Some that win friends:

What do you want?	May I help—
We're not interested.	I'll be glad to—
You're too late.	I see why—
I don't care.	Perhaps I can—
We're too busy for that.	Let me try—
Don't you understand?	I'd like to explain.
You can't—	I wish we could—
You must be mistaken.	Would you like to—
That makes no difference.	I'm certainly sorry.
It's no use trying—	Maybe you'd rather—
I don't know.	I'll find out for you.
I won't—	Shall I—
I don't see why you—	How about—
I guess so.	Thanks for being so patient.

A customer who wants to buy, only to be told, "We're all out," may not come back. Can you offer a good substitute? If not, try to tell him where to get what he wants, even if this means sending him to a competitor; he'll remember that you helped him. One store has another system: if a customer comes in for an item that's out of stock, he or she receives a "rain check" plus a 10-percent discount on it when it becomes available.

Whenever someone goes to the trouble of phoning or writing about buying something that you sell (or might sell), his name is worth money to you. Put him on a mailing list. Cultivate him.

The cheapest way to handle product inquiries is to answer all of them. It costs less than trying to figure out which are genuine leads. Of course not all inquiries need be answered the same way. An obvious prospect can get an immediate phone call. Less obvious ones might get a catalog or sales letter. Everyone should get something—a folder and a reply card, for example, or the answer to his specific questions.

If your office is too busy for this, there are services that will do it for you. Some will answer all queries, follow them up, keep track of results. Others provide trained interviewers who phone each prospect by WATS line and evaluate him as a prospect.

Who's Your Boss?

Most manufacturing (and even some service) businesses don't know who their boss really is. Ask them, and they say, "Why, Mr. Big, in the corner office." Wrong. The real boss is the customer—because that's who determines what goods or services should be offered, at what prices and in what styles.

Only rarely does a firm find out what customers really want and what they're willing to pay. Most companies are run by production and financial people who never talk to customers.

Try asking your sales and marketing people what the customer wants, how you should advertise it, where you should sell it. (Some astute companies require every executive to spend at least one month of the year behind counters, or calling on the trade.)

Of course, salespeople don't always understand customers either. Go out and listen to your spokesmen. Does their sales pitch match what the customer really wants *today?* Or does it play up selling points before the salesman finds out what the customer needs? Ask the customer why he's buying your product and how he uses it—or why he's *not* buying. Are you making the right promises for your product?

Match Promotions to People

Which brings us to a second major point about People.

Retail markets are People. What kind of People buy from you may be almost as important as what kind of People represent you.

If you can find a particular group of People who want something they're not getting elsewhere, maybe you can match your products or services —and your People—to them.

For example, a California bank recently opened for the purpose of serving a specific market: women. Naturally, it is owned and operated by women. Similarly, there are clothing stores for big and tall people; naturally, they use big, tall salespeople.

A furniture store picked out a new subdivision as a target market. It took photos of each of 500 homes there, keying each photo to its address. The owners of the homes were sent postcards on each of which was mounted a tiny photo of the house. They could get a free enlargement at the furniture store. Of the 500, 442 showed up for the enlargement, and most bought something. The whole promotion cost the store $325.

Frankenberger's, a men's-clothing store in West Virginia, aims a yearly promotion at high school boys. It gives each graduate a souvenir newspaper with his own name printed in the headline. Boys keep it all their lives. In Lincoln, Nebraska, a clothing store gives fashion previews for the college crowd, and has students vote on which clothes should be sold next season.

The Riviera Furniture Store sends you, a customer, a batch of discount tickets for you and your friends. The ones for friends are 10-percent coupons. Yours is a 15-percent coupon. Don't you feel good! You realize that Riviera considers you someone special.

The late Barney Dreyfuss, owner of the Pittsburgh Pirates baseball club, once spent $25,000 to build a temporary grandstand so that a few thousand fans could see three World Series games. He got back only $1,200. But he profited for years thereafter, because he had made a good investment in future customers.

On the same principle, a bit of promotion went over big in northern New Jersey when an ice cream parlor offered children free ice cream for A's on report cards. Here was a store doing what parents have been trying to do for generations.

Get People to Recommend You

Each of us is interested primarily in himself—but secondarily, and substantially, in other people. People find people more interesting than things. That's why the testimonial is a tried and proved (if not always honorable) promotion device. Its use gives the seller a chance to brag through another's voice, always a more engaging technique than self-praise. Americans have a healthy tendency to mutter, "Says you" when someone boasts about himself. A testimonial changes the comment to a second-level skepticism—"Says he, about you," which is a step in the right direction. And it substitutes a person for a thing as the object of interest—preferably a person whom the reader knows, or with whom he'd like to be identified.

Celebrities are okay in national advertising. But small business doesn't need them.

Instead, a Memphis motel owner bought several gross of drinking glasses salvaged from a warehouse fire. He mailed a postcard to households within a mile, asking them to recommend his motel to their out-of-town acquaintances if and when they came to visit. Anyone showing up for lodgings with the card in hand got a set of the drinking glasses, as did the person who sent the guest. This little promotion pulled in a surprising number of reservations. The supply of glasses ran out in four months.

Some retailers invite local high school and college students to write—and sign—ads for the stores' merchandise. This brings in more business than any ads the retailers themselves can devise.

The most productive ad ever run by a restaurant in Canton, Ohio, was a blowup of a scribbled postcard from a local patron traveling in Spain. The card was to the effect that "The food here is good, but no better than we get at your restaurant."

Pull Your Prospects into Your Act

Another way of aiming at People is by *involving* them, making them participants instead of idle bystanders. It doesn't always work, but it works often enough to make it worthwhile. A lunch counter attracts customers from miles around simply by letting them make their own sandwiches—at considerable profit to the owner, who spends much of his time washing the dishes.

McCurdy & Company sponsors clothes-designing contests for juniors in high schools, sets aside a special week and show window for displaying winning designs, and awards dresses as prizes. The same store runs essay contests about clothes, to get more schoolgirls involved.

You're partway to a sale whenever you get prospects *doing* something at your suggestion. Insurance salesmen hand a pen to a prospect and ask, "Will you write down these figures as I look them up?" Hardware stores sell more hammers by pointing the handles toward the customers' side of the counter, thus giving people an impulse to grasp one. The Cheney Hammer Company goes further: it has a counter display that capitalizes on this impulse. The display supplies a block of wood, a few nails, and a hammer. Customers are invited to grab the hammer and have a whacking good time.

A textile salesman carries a magnifying glass and invites prospects to peer at fabrics. Industrial salesmen bring along three-dimensional cardboard models of ships and tanks and even factories, so that prospects can take them apart and fit them together, selling themselves on the construction instead of trying to visualize it from blueprints or a sales talk. Even Girl Scouts, selling cookies door to door, get their prospects involved: they offer a cookie and say, "Here, won't you try one? Don't they taste good?" Sales experts say that "TRY can lead to BUY."

What They See Can Sell

If you even get people to stop and look at what you're offering, your chances of selling are much improved. That's what show windows are for. It's what point-of-purchase displays inside stores are for.

Have you watched to see how many passersby pause to look at your windows (or your dealers' windows) or stop to glance at various counters inside?

Once upon a time, salesclerks explained and sold. But the days of salespeople who care are almost over. Most stores are now self-service, whether or not they want to be. So a store becomes a battlefield, with every foot of space on counters and shelves fought for by manufacturers, wholesalers, and distributors. If you want to move goods, get them where People will look at them. One marketing study showed that of shoppers who made unplanned purchases, 80 percent bought an item because they saw it displayed.

A store chain on the Pacific Coast gave its buyers (who were charged with their own selling costs) a choice between window space and newspaper advertising. Out of 100 buyers, 88 chose window displays. Those experienced merchandisers knew that a good window will bring in from a quarter to a half of any ordinary store's sales.

Remember that three-fourths of the same People pass your window daily. You want them to form a favorable impression of your store. They take from three to six seconds to walk past. Normally, a window should attract a glance from about one man in ten, one woman in seven. So if your window doesn't get five of every hundred to turn around and glance, it isn't a display at all. And it should cause at least 2.5 percent of the glancers to stop. In other words, par for a window is stopping one of each 270 passersby. If you want to know how good your window is, take a count.

"I once criticized a merchant's display windows," wrote Kenneth M. Goode, an expert on sales promotion. "They were full of junk. He retorted that each buyer insisted on having an increased share of the show window. I pointed out his mistake. Strong advertising shouldn't be wasted on weak goods. Let the weak buyers bury their own mistakes. In store windows, as everywhere else, only the goods everybody wants will attract the right kind of attention, bring in prospects, and make customers. Don't waste window space. That's what you pay rent for."

A Philadelphia haberdasher suddenly awoke to his windows and hired a good window dresser. Within a year, sales jumped 170 percent.

However, bear in mind that most professional window men are artists first, merchants hardly at all. You may have to insist that your windows be vigorous sales displays. If you keep this in mind, you can probably design them yourself, without any artistic flair. Or ask manufacturers to provide some for you. Many will do this free.

Just by putting peppermint patties in the window, a drugstore sold five hundred pounds of them in two hours. An alarm-clock display sold $400 worth of clocks. A shoe store boosted sales by 30 percent when it tore out part of a blank wall and substituted a plate-glass window showing shoes. During football season, a liquor store pulled in extra customers each weekend by putting a "Game Special" package in the window; it was a quart of whiskey, a bottle of mixer, paper cups, and a container of ice cubes.

A retailer, stuck with several bushels of mixed buttons, knew they wouldn't sell as they were. But he put them into handy bags, displayed them in his window as "Assorted buttons for the mending basket," and quickly moved the whole lot.

Each of these windows displayed Price prominently. "The price ticket is the single thing that can surely break through the glass and start each looker thinking in terms of buying," Mr. Goode writes.

Your display should call attention to merchandise—not to the way it is presented. Keep the background simple: light materials against dark backdrops, and dark against light. Keep signs or placards to a minimum. Try to concentrate spotlights or high-intensity bulbs on a single central idea. People shouldn't say, "Oh, look how cleverly the stand has been covered with black so the jewelry seems to float in midair." You want them to say, "Isn't that watch magnificent! It looks like a bargain at the price. Let's go inside."

There are gimmicks that stop People, make them stare and then go in if what they see is something they want to buy. If nothing better occurs to you, put a mirror in your store window. Few People can resist the temptation of a glance. Many will linger for a second glance at the rest of your display.

Curiosity can be a strong gimmick. A store in Long Beach, California, frosted over one big window, leaving only a peephole in the center. A red circle was painted around this, and red arrows pointed to it. Big cards pasted to the glass warned, FOR MEN ONLY. Both men and women stopped to peer in—and saw a neat display of tools. A London dry-goods store marked its peephole, FOR THE CLEAN MINDED. Towels were selling. Lookers walked in and bought.

A big piece of wood, seemingly thrust through the plate glass, was used by W. E. Cooper in Alhambra, California, to make dozens of people walk across the street for a closer look. Jagged pieces of cellophane gave the impression of cracks in the glass. Half the wood was pasted inside the window, the other half outside. The Portis sporting-goods store in Chicago used the same trick, presenting an illusion of a football stuck halfway through the glass. Portis had cut the ball in half and attached part to each side of the glass.

Let Them Guess

Another successful show-window gimmick is a guessing contest. At Easter, some variety stores fill a huge jar with candies. A sign invites passersby to step inside and register their guess—for a prize—of the total in the jar.

Sporting-goods stores offer prizes to people who come in and register correct predictions of football, baseball, or basketball scores. An appliance dealer puts a refrigerator in a window and offers prizes for the best guesses of how much gas the refrigerator will use in thirty days. (This display is more than just a stopper; it also fixes prospects' attention on the refrigerator's low cost of operation.) Each summer a store on Long Island puts merchandise in a window along with a giant thermometer. Whoever guesses exactly what the temperature will be at noon on July 20 takes home all the items in the window. It draws thousands of guesses. Bookstores sold a mystery novel with a window full of clues and the question "How did these clues solve the murder of Sarah Giddings?"

Motion Is Promotion

We saw in the previous chapter that good salesmen put plenty of action into their sales pitches. Put action in your show window, and you'll attract People.

Dan Prosnit, a merchandising researcher, says the largest crowd he ever saw at a single exhibit in New York's Museum of Natural History was collected around a glass cage containing a small crawling sand snake. The museum was full of elaborate, costly still-life displays—but the little snake stole the show because it moved.

Another researcher, George Wellbaum, experimented with motion in display windows. He clocked the number of people who stopped at each window, including many windows that combined color and interesting design without movement. He found no other type of display with pulling power comparable to that of motion. Simply to pull the plug of any electrically powered moving display would cut the number of lookers by 60 to 80 percent.

An auto-supply store multiplied its sales of spark plugs tenfold by rigging a window mechanism that smashed an indestructible spark plug up and down against a rock. A bookstore attracted scores of browsers (and buyers) by putting a Linotype machine—operator and all—in the window. The manufacturer of Rat-tox, a rodent poison, gave dealers a window display including two live rats. Rat-tox sales were up 400 percent during the week of the display. A hobby store had an elaborate HO train layout, controlled by buttons outside the window. People stood in line to push buttons which activated trains—and many went in to buy.

One summer evening a dry-goods store took the merchandise out of one window and held a bathing-beauty show with five live models in the window. Two thousand people crushed against the window front. The show cost exactly $45—and sold more than a hundred swimsuits. The results were traceable because customers would come in and say, "I'd like to see that red-and-white suit the blond model wore."

You can use audiovisual equipment to give motion to your display. Slide projectors using circular trays can be set to rotate a showing of as many as eighty slides. The images are projected through a screen from the rear. Photographic-equipment stores sell the equipment; some rent it out.

Movies can be shown in your window too. Several manufacturers now offer players the size of a television set into which you insert a film cartridge and which continuously show the film. Sound can be transmitted through a speaker above the window or door—but be sure to keep the sound low enough so that it isn't obnoxious.

Even an impression of motion is better than no motion at all. Jumbled displays sell more than do neat, unbroken rows of merchandise. Knives sold faster when stuck three inches deep in a cake—which made them look as if they recently *had* been moving.

What Happens Inside the Store?

After People have been lured into the store, where do they go? If you own or manage the store, you ought to plan its layout to guide as many customers as possible past as much merchandise as possible, so that they'll see—and perhaps buy—many different items. If you manufacture or distribute something that's for sale in the store, you'll try to arrange for the maximum number of customers to see your merchandise. There are ways to accomplish each of these aims.

One strategy of store managers is to locate high-turnover or low-priced items which are natural traffic generators in less accessible areas of the store. So-called impulse items are almost always displayed at high-traffic locations such as ends of aisles and near checkout counters. This can be worth big money. A case in point is Tic-Tacs, a mint-flavored candy packaged in a small plastic container and usually placed in an attractive display case beside the cash register. At 25 cents for a half-ounce package, consumers are paying $8 per pound for this candy.

One drugstore owner thought up another traffic generator: a free phone in the rear of the store. It boosted traffic, which automatically boosted sales. Not only did people buy impulse items, but many of them called home to ask what items needed to be purchased at the drugstore.

If you manufacture some product that is tucked on inaccessible shelves, awaiting requests from a customer who is lucky enough to find a salesperson who'll reach for it, you can change your business history and your bank account by getting the stuff onto the selling floor. You need to make your merchandise visible and accessible to shoppers. The value of interior display is tremendous. In a food store where only 67 bottles of an undisplayed sauce were sold in three weeks, as soon as it was displayed sales jumped to 154. A well-known brand of soup jumped from 1,068 to 1,824 when displayed.

Selling a product to a store's buyer is hard. Placing a point-of-purchase display unit is easier. When you invade a new market and want to introduce your line, offer it in a display unit. The buyer will be more willing to take a chance on an item that you've packaged to sell itself.

In self-service and self-selection merchandising, stores want displays that create excitement on their own. Salespeople aren't there to do it. But a product can sell itself if it is displayed in a unit that shows it to advantage. This may be a floor display unit, or a display designed to stand on a counter.

Usually a display unit is shipped to a retailer as a reward for ordering a fairly large quantity. And it is usually designed in such a way that the order is shipped already packed in the display. That saves shipping costs, which can be important.

There are people who make a nice living designing and selling these displays, and you may want to get in touch with some of them. This is no task for an amateur.

How much should your display cost? As a rule-of-thumb, it shouldn't be more than 10 percent of the total net cost of the merchandise bought in the deal. Thus, a display for $100 worth of products shouldn't cost more than $10.

But before you invest in display units, you should study the kinds of stores you'll be selling in. There are a lot of places where you can't use a display, because of store policy.

In fact, most department stores permit no floor displays or counter displays except the ones they themselves design. This is because they've taken great pains to create a "personality" for their stores, and anything that mars this carefully calculated atmosphere is harmful, even if it increases sales for a particular item. (Incidentally, this is why some department stores and chains are branching out into discount operations under a different name. This enables them to share in the rack-and-display, self-service atmosphere of mass selling without disturbing their downtown Personality.)

Even if the store has no policy against displays, you may find that the store doesn't use them anyway. In small business, everyone is just too busy coping with the everyday turmoil of getting the work done, merchandise onto the shelves, and the bills paid to give time or thought to such "frills" as point-of-purchase displays. Even big manufacturers sometimes get fooled by this condition. Bristol-Myers once invested heavily in several thousand standing display units. They were handsome, and they sold the product briskly. Bristol-Myers shipped them out joyously to retailers, only to discover eventually that only about one out of ten displays was being used. The rest of the investment was gathering dust in storerooms, or had been consigned to trash bins. Bristol-Myers was memorably pained.

Your best insurance is to call some buyers at the stores you plan to be selling in, or at least at that type of store. Ask them for the lowdown on whether display units get used. They'll probably be glad to tell you, since it saves them trouble. The next step, once you're sure there's a chance of getting displays used, is to pick up pointers on the best kind of design for your particular business. Each market has its own special requirements, and if you violate them you're dead.

There are four ways to educate yourself about this. 1. Get in touch with the trade association. It can give invaluable information about the industry's design limits and specifications. 2. Talk to your salesmen in the field, or to sales reps you intend to engage. They know what sort of displays are around, which are working, and what your competition is doing. 3. Have lunch with a space salesman from a trade magazine. He's a gold mine of promotional information. 4. Hit the road yourself. Look at store displays, and ask opinions about the value of the types you see. Find out which kind sells, which kind the manager likes, and why. Analyze why some displays get better placement than others.

Personality for Your Business

As we saw a few pages ago, successful big stores like to create a Personality for themselves—an atmosphere, an image. Big advertisers use television and magazines for image-building attempts. But you're small. You need other ways of promoting sales through company Personality. The fewer personal contacts there are between your firm's People and your market's People, the more crucial your collective Personality —your reputation, your image—becomes.

If that's your problem, give a lot of thought to external appearances. Try to make your headquarters look distinctive. Roadside stands can take the form of a coffeepot, a shoe, or whatever. Even an inside office can have something distinctive; Leo Burnett always had a bowl of bright red apples for salesmen and other visitors in the reception room, and the apples became a well-known symbol of his firm.

How about your trucks? They should be rolling advertisements, distinctive and memorable. The delivery trucks of the Chock Full o' Nuts restaurants look like little cottages on wheels; the truck of the Standard Flashlight Company resembles a giant camera. Mange & Company in St. Louis uses a pony cart to deliver its children's-wear packages.

How about your company sign? Is it distinctive and memorable? Does it convey a "feel" of elegance, or sprightliness, or efficiency? Or is it just dull and stodgy?

How about your packaging and wrapping? It should look striking and attractive, always in the same colors. Your package should also be a billboard for its contents. But is it strong enough to withstand rough handling during delivery? Is it awkward to set up? Is it too easy, or too hard, to open?

Are you watching for chances to get publicity for yourself and your enterprise? Maybe service clubs and other organizations would like to book a talk by you, or one of your staff experts, on some interesting aspect of your business. Maybe there are anecdotes or oddities you can feed to a newspaper columnist or feature writer. Maybe your building has an interesting history. Take a bright newsman to lunch, and he may be able to suggest a dozen ways you can get publicity—especially if you hint at hiring him as a part-time consultant.

Aside from publicity, which any organization can wangle if it knows how, all these aforementioned techniques of image-building may be unavailable to certain businesses. Maybe you're in a field of industrial selling where the way your products are packaged and delivered can't possibly be distinctive. Maybe you're in shabby quarters far from heavy traffic. Maybe your products or services seem impossible to glamorize or even to make noticeably different. How then can you develop a striking Personality that will attract customers?

Ways to Brighten Up a Dull Business

This was the problem of the Los Angeles Brush Company. It manufactured a line of industrial brushes which weren't very different from competing brushes. It had a good mailing list of prospective users, but its few salesmen were spread thin, and couldn't call on a prospect more than a couple of times a year. How could it keep its market vividly aware of it?

It thought up a postcard campaign. Each month, every purchasing agent on its list received a card bearing a photograph and description of a brush such as no factory had imagined before.

One was a brush that could "be used as a cribbage board" when the bristles wore out. Another was a "street-sweeping brush" which could be fastened to the rear of any automobile. "Let's make every motorist a street sweeper," the card urged, and added that a special device would enable motorists to raise the brush when driving out of their tax area or when passing homes of people they disliked.

Another was an "improved shoe brush." As its photo showed, it was a brush fastened permanently to the shoe. "Ready to use anywhere," the description claimed. "In an elevator, instead of rubbing your shoes on the back of your trousers, just swing one foot across the other."

Guffawing recipients passed the cards around. L.A. Brush salesmen found themselves genially welcomed. Phone calls and fan mail surged in; one month's card brought 1,432 letters. The company's catalog, containing a year's collection of the postcard photos and descriptions (plus drawings of its actual brushes, almost as an afterthought) became a collectors' item—and the company became dominant in its industry. That's what humor can do.

A dealer in foreign automobiles, selling in an outlying suburb of Los Angeles, used humorous radio commercials with similar success. One spot announcement began "Come to the big fire sale at Nick Pastor Imported Cars. Later, come to the fire, date of which will be announced by the arson investigators and Nick Pastor's insurance adjuster." Another asked, "Doesn't it strike you as peculiar the way Nick Pastor's warehouse sale on imported cars just goes on and on? If the supply is limited, where are all the fresh cars coming from?" Every few days the radio audience heard fresh gibes at Pastor: "If you want something watertight, airtight and just plain tight, stop by 3451 East Firestone and read one of Nick Pastor's installment contracts. . . . Nick Pastor is running a contest, and it's easy to win, because the judges will accept bribes. As for prizes, everyone is out of luck. . . . Friends, if you have any goodness in your heart, if you feel sorry for poor Nick Pastor, from the bottom of my heart I ask you, won't you come out to his auto lot right now?"

Pastor had one lot, and was selling about 25 cars a month, when he began buying his peculiar radio spots. A year later he owned three auto lots and averaged 225 sales a month. Hundreds of customers told him they came because of what they heard about him on the radio.

An insurance agency gave itself Personality by sending out mail pieces offering to "cover any risk from cream to crumb." There were such insertions as a photo of the Venus de Milo with the caption "And when I asked him about full coverage, he handed me this silly blanket."

A statistical service advertised:

A CERTAIN RED-HEADED GIRL gets 10 dates to every 5 for a certain brunette. Who has the most appeal?

BUT WAIT. The boys buy sodas and movies for the redhead. The brunette gets orchids and seats on the aisle. NOW WHO?

A simple story. But it shows the importance of knowing *how much* as well as *how many*. My two-way analysis reveals both dimensions.

Search for Surveys

Of course, it takes a certain oddball turn of mind—which you probably don't possess—to write such ads. But if you want to develop a business Personality through memorable ads, you can ask for sample copy from a few small ad agencies or free-lance writers (of whom hundreds will answer a help-wanted ad) and engage one who seems to have the right touch. Or you can go to a public library and browse among the pages of the New York, Chicago, and San Francisco daily newspapers of thirty years ago. In those years after World War II, numerous small-space campaigns were using delightfully humorous selling copy, and you can pick up plenty of reusable ideas free. One of those memorable campaigns was run by Leon Lapides, a delicatessen owner. His brief ads carried headlines like MR. LAPIDES GETS AWAY WITH MURDER. . . . CAUGHT WITH YOUR PANTRY DOWN? . . . MR. LAPIDES IS A LADIES' MAN . . ."

Postcards, radio spots, and small ads are only a few of the media available for image-building campaigns. You can try handbills. You can put up small signs along the highway. (Signs like BE A THINKER—SEE THE STINKER lured motorists from all over the Northwest to a jovial Idaho retailer who called himself "The Stinker.") You can take a quarter-page ad in the Yellow Pages of phone books, or in trade journals. You can think up a slogan like one used by a maker of jellies and jams: "With a name like Smucker's, it's got to be good."

And your advertising can build an attractive image without necessarily being comical. Humor is best for taking dullness out of a humdrum product, and for making you stand out among deadly serious competitors. If your product is novel, or extremely useful, or a great bargain at its price, your promotion can build Personality (and boost sales) by simply telling the striking facts about it. Humorous ads make the prospect say, "This sounds like an interesting company. I'd like to get acquainted with them." But newsy ads make him say, "I think I'll try that product." The very best promotion aims at the prospect's self-interest.

Most advertising experts and most smart entrepreneurs prefer *quality* replies to quanity. Wouldn't you rather have 50 hot leads than 500 inquiries from warm bodies? Aim your promotion at People who are likely to buy your product, and spank your adman if he tries to change your direction for the sake of cleverness.

One company, offering computer services for profit-center accounting, realized that it needed only to establish its Personality vividly among company controllers. So it ran brief ads on financial pages:

> There is now a failproof and complete system for profit center controls. If you are a controller, visit booth 108 at the American Management Association convention for complete details.

Its booth at the convention was conservatively decorated with drapes, conference tables, and a sign that said "Controllers Only, Please." The booth next to it had free balloons, girls in swimsuits, audiovisual displays, fourteen salesmen to handle the crowds, and a carnival barker to attract everyone within earshot. The booth was for a company that handled fleet leasing.

At the end of three days the computer company's booth had logged only 385 visitors, of whom 320 were controllers. It had signed up 18 customers and gotten 73 prospects for follow-up. The sales manager of the leasing booth boasted that his extravaganza had pulled in 22,000 visitors. However, one of his salesmen confided that only a handful of visitors had leasing responsibilities, and not one had signed a lease. Which company did a better promotional job?

Whether your approach is quiet or gaudy, remember that your Personality must make a favorable impression on the *right* audience. You must catch that audience's attention within a few seconds. If you don't do this, you've lost a chance to convert someone into a customer. So your headline, or opening sentence, or picture if you use one, must whet interest enough to make your prospects invest a few additional seconds. In those seconds you can make your point or points. Give your audience instructions on how to get further details. Don't be afraid to ask people to respond by sending a request, if you're offering free information.

And don't be afraid to ask for their business. All business is gotten by asking for it. Personal salesmanship succeeds by asking one person after another. Advertising succeeds by asking many people all at once. The catch, of course, comes in the fact that few people will give you their business merely for the asking. You must prove that it will be advantageous to them—or you must convince them you're a likable organization —or both.

KEEP THESE BASIC POINTS IN MIND:

- *Each person in your organization should give an impression of cautious optimism, and of working hard. Outsiders often judge a small business by contacts with very few of its people.*
- *Check up on the appearance and the language of letters leaving your office.*
- *The appearance of your place of business, and the appearance of the people in it, are important. Emphasize neatness.*
- *Make sure that all visitors—including salesmen and job-seekers—are treated pleasantly.*
- *Make sure that all your people who answer telephones are taught the basic points of telephone courtesy.*
- *Learn how to say "no" without making people angry.*
- *Study the kinds of people who are your prospects. Try to find ways of making your business even more useful to them.*
- *Look for ways to obtain and use recommendations from customers.*
- *Whenever you get prospects doing something at your suggestion, you're partway to a sale. Even if they merely stop and look at your show window or counter display, more of them will buy.*
- *Look for something distinctive about your business, and build promotion campaigns around it.*

20
Bigger Money for
Bigger Ventures

If you're ambitious and your business venture is sound, a time will come when you'll need money for expansion—big money. To get ready for that time, you should learn an indispensable exercise called "making the presentation." That's what this chapter is all about—and Chapters 21 and 22 as well.

One way or another you'll probably make a lot of presentations as you strive for growth. Some presentations may be to manufacturers, urging them to manufacture your product or some of its components, or to go into partnership with you, or to send you carloads of stuff on the cuff. Other presentations may be to distributors or suppliers, for similar purposes. Maybe you'll try to sell your concept to big venture capitalists or other major investors. Most likely you'll make presentations to banks, since they're the most logical and accessible sources of capital. Second-round and third-round financing are usually much easier to obtain from banks than it is to secure start-up capital.

Expansion: A Capital Problem

Nursing your company through the difficult growth stages may take more artistry—and more time and energy—than finding the original seed money. Even the most successful entrepreneurs often recall horrendous experiences trying to keep their companies solvent while raising the big bankroll they need to continue.

Consider the case of two young fellows who went into the tent-making business. In 1970 they set up shop in Stearns, Kentucky. Three years later they were swamped with orders—far too many to fill all by themselves. They needed bigger machinery and dozens of workers, which the business couldn't afford. So they started hunting for capital. But southeast Kentucky lacks a lot of things, including good roads and big banks. Small-town bankers weren't familiar with financing manufacturing companies. When the tent company suggested loans collateralized by receivables, one country banker admitted, "I wouldn't know what to do with an account receivable if I had one."

From Lexington to Louisville and all the way up to Cleveland, the tentmakers kept hunting without finding the half-million dollars they knew they needed. But finally they heard of an organization in Belmont, Massachusetts, called Institute for New Enterprise Development, which specializes in counseling people who want to be in business for themselves. INED put them in touch with a small venture-capital firm they'd never heard of, although it was in London, Kentucky (a mile off the nearest highway), in their own part of the state. INED also advised the partners about how to most effectively package their proposal.

So after doing their homework, and with their well-documented proposal, they made their way to London and sold the Kentucky firm on their company, which they named Outdoor Venture Corporation to add glamour. They got a loan of $600,000. Five years later they had 120 employees and yearly sales of more than $8 million, and the venture-capital firm was reaping rich returns on its investment.

A story of many mistakes, but with a happy ending, is the story of the Trikilis brothers of Medina, Ohio. In 1967, with $500 to pay for supplies and rent, Ted and Mike started a small retail art-supply shop near Kent State University. They didn't know about shoplifting, and they didn't know how to keep track of inventory—so they thought they were prospering, because students swarmed in and the cash register kept ringing. Under their delusion of success, they decided to expand to a chain of art-supply stores, and persuaded friends to invest $13,000 to make this possible.

When the Trikilises finally realized that thefts by customers and employees were draining their profits, they switched to selling only posters designed by local artists. Their artistic tastes were sound, so their posters sold briskly. Soon they were able to buy out the printer who was producing their designs—but overlooked the fact that they were taking over the printer's debts as well as his plant, having signed the sales contract without asking any lawyer to read and approve it.

Even with this burden, their company kept growing. In 1970 they persuaded a Medina bank to lend them $120,000 to enable them to take over a 23,000-square-foot building. "That was our biggest mistake," they told a reporter later. "We overexpanded without enough working capital."

For three years they were on the brink of bankruptcy. The bank decided to call in its loan.

In this dire crisis the brothers persuaded an uncle, John Argile, to leave his job as a Chrysler executive and take over the firm's business management. Argile made a presentation to the bank that persuaded it to change its mind about the company, and it refinanced the loan. By 1974 the company was again making a modest profit, and the brothers offered to buy back the stock purchased six years earlier by their friends. "It was a matter of conscience," Ted Trikilis said. "We wanted to give them the chance to get their money out, and we gave them a 300-percent profit."

In 1976, by a magical stroke of luck, the brothers brought out the first Farrah Fawcett-Majors posters. These sold 7.5 million copies. The firm's sales for 1977 were $6 million, and in 1978 it expanded into 51,000 square feet of production space—mortgaged to the banker who had stuck with them in 1973.

The tentmakers and the poster publishers, and countless others like them, broke through the expansion barrier and became million-dollar enterprises because they somehow got money men enthusiastic. This is partly an art, partly a science. You can learn the scientific side of it, because there are clear principles to be followed. And with practice in following these rules, you'll develop artistry.

Get Some Doors Open Early

The first rule is to start thinking about your possible need for big money long before the need arises. The second rule is to start getting acquainted with possible sources, so that they'll know you and your business when the time comes to proposition them. Everybody knows the old saying "Banks will lend money if you prove you don't need it." Turn that around. The best time to talk to bankers is when you don't need to borrow.

Ignorance of these first two rules has been ruinous to many entrepreneurs. They didn't get to know any bankers in advance. They waited until they were hard-pressed, then rushed in, hat in hand, and said, "Business is great. How much can you lend me? And I need it today."

Go out of your way to get acquainted with several loan officers—and with some bank presidents if possible—while your business is still small. (Leave the venture capitalists alone until you can use a quarter-million-dollar loan or bigger and can work up a fully thought-out proposal. As we go through this chapter you'll see how to prepare such a presentation, as well as less elaborate ones for bank financing.)

List the twenty or so best bank prospects in your vicinity. If you aren't in a money center such as New York, Chicago, Boston, or the biggest cities of Texas or California, list the nearest big-city banks. If you don't expect to need more than $100,000, limit the prospects to local or regional banks. For the "big" deal, select a dozen major banks; nowadays even Bank of America and Citibank are competing to make million-dollar loans in the Midwest.

Get introductions from your accountant, your lawyer, or some friend who's prominent in business. In preliminary chats with each banker, see whether he seems to understand your business and what it hopes to become. If he seems cool and bored, try someone else. Shopping for a banker is almost like looking for a bride. A certain chemistry must exist between you.

One of the "right" bankers can give you good advice and help you make useful connections. He is in closer contact with business people all day long. His bank is a center for trade gossip. He has legitimate inside information that may help you.

Don't be intimidated by bankers. Most of them probably have smaller personal incomes than you do. They are selling money and services. Think about them as you would other suppliers. Find out their capabilities. Different banks have different policies, different specialties. Learn as much about the differences as you can.

Bankers tend to like bricks, machinery, inventories, and properties because, they say, these fixed assets are a protection to the company; new competitors can't spring into the field from nowhere. Also (though they seldom say so), physical properties can be attached by the bank if a loan goes sour. So when you find a banker you like, take him around your plant if it looks halfway impressive. Show him what the company is doing. Show preparations for the future. Introduce him to your key people.

Then take him to lunch. This is the time to feel him out about future transactions with the bank. You can remark casually, "Looks like we might need to do some borrowing next year."

If he answers, "Well, you know money is very tight," it means you haven't made a good impression. If he says, "Sounds like a good idea, but I'd have to see the papers on it," you've got a chance. In the less likely event that he says, "Anytime you want a loan just come in and see me," you know the door is open.

Much will depend on his first impression when he visits your place of business. He knows that poor housekeeping generally goes with poor management, so don't ever take a banker to visit a sloppy-looking office or shop. On the other hand, he'll be uneasy if he spots frills in your operation. Even though your sales manager may need to put up a front to attract customers, you'll look like a spendthrift to serious investors if you flaunt high-priced carpeting and drapes, original oil paintings, and expensive company cars.

If a banker asks you searching questions during this get-acquainted stage, be glad—even if you don't know the answers. It shows that he's getting interested. He won't fault you for saying "I don't know," or "I haven't thought of that," if you add "—but I'm certainly going to find out." Questions from a banker give you clues to the kind of information other bankers and capitalists will want. You can be ready with the answers later on, when you're ready to ask for money.

To repeat—don't be awed by bankers. Like CPA's, cleaning women, and lawyers, bankers work better if they sense that you aren't wedded to them, and that you may have alternatives waiting in the wings. They need you as much as you need them. They must make loans to earn their salaries. Few of them want the newer, riskier businesses—but when a small business seems to be making the grade, maybe growing toward bigness, bankers begin to jockey for the inside track with it. They sense a possible new arrival in the circle of successful companies to whom they want to lend. In fact, most financiers are always looking for that good investment or good loan.

You'll Need Photographs

Another thing you should do, months in advance of making a presentation, is gather material for it. Whether your presentation will be made to woo a sales rep, or sell a design to a manufacturer, or drum up financial backing, it should contain certain common elements. One of the effective ones is pictures.

Of course, these are frills. They won't convince a money man if the underlying numbers are wrong. But an entrepreneur can seldom get backing with numbers alone. Some companies used to be able to get bank loans merely by strolling into their banks and showing the loan officers their financial statements. But unless the financial statement looks overwhelmingly impressive, a more sophisticated strategy is needed today. The more complete and handsome your presentation, the more likely it will be to attract a lucrative lightning bolt.

Spend a few hundred dollars for a first-class professional photographer. Probably you'll need photos of your product anyway for catalog sheets, or for advertising, or for your package, so you'll probably spend this money even if you don't expand.

Cigar-smoking tycoons who never visit a plant can "see" your operation without leaving their paneled offices, if you provide good pictures of your facilities and products. Maybe you're not yet in production. Then take shots of prototype models. They're far better than drawings or blueprints. The models prove you've carried your homework one step further.

When you set up the photography session, arrange for each shot to be taken four ways: (a) in 4-by-5-inch color transparencies, for color slides in case you want to make a presentation to a group of people; (b) in 4-by-5 negative film, so you can make up color prints for your handsomely bound presentation book; (c) in 4-by-5 black-and-white, which can be enlarged for newspaper publicity or advertising; (d) in Polaroid for your own file reference.

Most successful presentations include a dozen—sometimes several dozen—8-by-10-inch glossy enlargements showing the management team working together, their products both in use and on display, the problems that their products solve, their facilities, their equipment, and anything else that makes the central idea more vivid. Pictures pay off because they can bring an abstract concept to life.

Does your product lend itself to demonstrations? Then plan to demonstrate as part of your presentation. But also photograph the demonstration if possible, so that your friend the banker can at least show the picture to his loan committee back at his headquarters.

Maybe you're thinking, "No, there's no way to demonstrate my product," but think about it some more. You might not think that a package of crackers would lend itself to demonstration, but listen to what the executives at Loose-Wiles Biscuit Company did with theirs.

They knew that their package resisted moisture and that the crackers inside stayed fresh. So the company put a package of crackers in a glass bowl of water. Later, in opening the package as part of the demonstration, it used a magnifying glass to prove that the crackers stayed "flakier" than competing products. All this was almost as impressive in photos as in the face-to-face demonstrations.

Loose-Wiles also found that its one-pound package of crackers contained 130 crackers. "Let's dramatize this," someone said. "Take 130 crackers and pile them one on top of another." It made a yard-high stack. The company showed a photo of the stack. Salesmen said, "All these crackers are for sale in one package. You don't believe it? Let's open a package and count them or stack them."

Pictures make people seem real. Maybe your presentation should contain a few photos of your major customers (with their consent, always) if you're a wholesaler or a manufacturer. Definitely it should contain a professional 8-by-10-inch color photo of you, as well as similar pictures of any other key management people in your organization.

They Want to Know About Your Team

What investors and lenders are looking for is a management team that blends financial, marketing, and technical skills with a reputation for integrity. William G. Brennan, a well-known expert at evaluating investment proposals for big clients, says his first—and sometimes only—step is an evaluation of the entrepreneur's reputation.

"Who does his accounting?" Brennan asks. "If it's a major firm, I can get references for him with one phone call to its local office. Also, I want to know what sort of associates he has. If he runs with anyone whose reputation is bad, that turns me off instantly. Then I look at his track record. Did he previously own some other company that went broke? Or is he a former high-paid executive of a big corporation setting out on his own? It makes a difference.

"I also want to know his net worth," Brennan continues, "so I can compare his company's financial strength with all the commitments and contingent liabilities it faces. If I see a shell corporation when I look, or can't determine net worth, I shy away."

Stanley Golders, president of a big venture-capital firm called First Capital Corporation of Chicago, says, "What we like to see is an owner who is a member of a team. That shows he's over the hurdle of thinking he knows it all."

From these experts' remarks you can see that it's important for your presentation to contain not only pictures of each major owner and top executive, but also résumés of their business background, and the personal financial statement of those who own any sizable part of the enterprise. These statements are essential. They should list all an owner's assets and liabilities outside the business—including real estate, interest in other businesses, savings accounts, automobiles and other personal property, bank loans, life insurance and its cash value.

Your presentation will make the best impression if it doesn't show too many people with a finger in the pie. Small companies trying to become big corporations tend to make a common mistake. They look at IBM or General Electric and see finance committees, advertising departments, purchasing departments, personnel departments, executive committees, and so on—and they say, "So that's how they do it! We need more executives, more departments, more activities," and a year later they're out of business.

If you're a small or middle-sized business looking to expand, you'd better study every proposal for a new expense or new activity closely, to see whether it's a necessity or an ornament. Otherwise you may be like the poor fellow who thought all he had to do to become a professional football player was consume big desserts at every meal. You'll be confusing fat with muscle.

So much for the showier "image-building" parts of your presentation. You'll weave them in as embroidery for the facts and figures that the money men will be most concerned with.

You Need a Business Plan

"We turn down many proposals because the entrepreneurs can't support their idea with a detailed business plan," says Robert MacDonald, a partner in the San Diego firm of Idanta, which buys part ownership of promising young enterprises. Golders of First Capital adds, "The business plan is a must. Financiers are experts at spotting flaws. This is where we can see if the guy really knows what he's talking about or just has cocktail-party chatter and big dreams."

The plan should give a summary of the business, outline its financing needs, show how the new capital will be used, and look ahead to financial goals. It shouldn't be longer than thirty pages. Many consultants feel that a smart entrepreneur might spend up to a year figuring out this plan.

"The key question to ask yourself before seeking money is 'Why should people want to invest with me?' " says David Ahlers, associate professor of management at the Cornell Business School. "Can you translate your ideas into their common denominator, which is money?"

The Small Business Administration has publications available on how to prepare a business plan. You can find numerous books in the public library providing the same information. Another excellent source of facts and advice is a CPA. Perhaps you should hire one to help you work up the presentation, especially if you're a little shaky on topics like inventory turnover or cost–sales ratios.

A good plan will include a pessimistic, an optimistic, and a realistic scenario for the business. "Start with what's most likely to happen," says Milton D. Stewart, who was appointed by President Carter in 1978 to serve as the entrepreneurs' advocate within the Federal Government. "Then ask yourself, 'How bad can it get? How good can it be?' If you go through that exercise for every item, you're less likely to shock yourself and your investors, and you're more likely to succeed."

A good financial man can look at your financial projections and tell more about you than you'd ever guess. He'll know a lot about your business judgment, your fiscal integrity, your management experience, and your ability to work with others. If your financial projections are poorly prepared, bankers can rip them apart in a few minutes.

How Sound Are Your Projections?

Financial projections (sometimes called pro forma sheets) are little more than your expected cash-in (sales forecasts) minus cash-out (the departmental budgets to meet those sales forecasts). If you have any money left over, you have profits. If you don't, you have losses.

"This is pretty simple," writes Richard White, a consultant who specializes in helping new businesses put together proposals for financing. "But would you believe that fewer than half the clients who come through our doors have attempted this projection? For example, if they're engineers, they frequently visualize optimum manufacturing conditions, make this the cornerstone of their business plan, and draw the foolish assumption that salesmen can sell everything they can produce—or even worse, that customers will buy their optimum production quantities without any sales efforts. These optimum figures become their sales forecasts.

"If the new companies are run by administrators," White continues, "their forecasts usually evolve from the profits that the founders want to make. So the desired profits become the cornerstone and the founders work back to the amount of sales needed to produce those profits. The third most common error is forecasts developed by sales-executive types. This type states either 'We can sell a jillion of 'em' or 'In X months we'll get 1 percent market penetration, in Y months 2 percent penetration, and in Z months 5 percent.' The forecasts, without supporting evidence, are worthless. And since the business plan is built on these forecasts, it too becomes worthless."

Get Set for These Hurdles

To avoid such mistakes, you should know about the hurdles you and your plan will face when you ask for financing.

The first hurdle comes when you describe your plan, and show your brochure of supporting facts and figures.

In that first session, financiers will judge the thoroughness of your planning. Few plans make it over this first hurdle—because either (1) they are complex, unreadable, and consequently unread; (2) they have obvious weaknesses, spotted quickly by readers or listeners; (3) their particular industry, product, or service doesn't interest the bank or venture-capital firm; or (4) the capital group doesn't have spare money to invest, or is so busy with other ventures that it doesn't have time to study the proposition.

The second hurdle, if you get past the first one, comes during the question period.

The questions will be few and perfunctory if the group has mentally rejected your plan already. But if your plan sounds interesting, the questions will come smoking in like tracer bullets. The financier and his researchers will be trying to get a feel for what kind of organization you have, how much you believe in what you're proposing, and how well you understand it. This hurdle may trip you the first few times. But with practice at answering questions, you'll improve.

The third hurdle will be the evaluation of your management team.

If the lender doesn't already know you well, expect to be investigated. He will want business references and will check them out. He will look into your credit record. He will want to know whether there are any past or present violations by the company, lawsuits, pending litigation. . . . If the loan you're asking is in the six-figure range, you'll probably be visited at home, your wife and children may be observed, your neighbors interviewed, your business acquaintances questioned. Capitalists won't risk big money on you until they're sure that you are honest, intelligent, energetic, and so on.

The fourth hurdle will be the evaluation of your financial planning.

Your plan probably got a fairly sharp financial analysis at the first hurdle. But bankers and venture capitalists realize that most owners of small businesses know little about leveraging, money controls, timing of cash injections, and forecasting. These are the areas in which money men excel. If your plan doesn't provide for the right reserves to be on tap at the times you may need them, you've blown it.

Now that you've seen the hurdles, maybe you have a better idea of how to write a plan that will clear them. That's what we'll consider in the next chapter.

KEEP THESE BASIC POINTS IN MIND:

- *While you're small, start preparing for a time when you may need big money for a major expansion. Otherwise you'll be caught short.*
- *Get acquainted with several bankers long before you need to borrow from them. Seek ones who'll take an interest in your business.*
- *As soon as your place of business looks shipshape and moderately impressive, bring some bankers out to see it. Beware of too costly furnishings or accessories.*

- *When bankers ask you questions, don't be afraid to say, "I don't know, but I'll find out."*
- *Begin gathering photos and testimonials that will add credibility to the presentations you'll eventually make.*
- *If you want to expand, build a well-balanced management team. One-man organizations can't borrow much money.*
- *Don't make your team bigger than you need. Spend only for necessities, not for ornaments.*
- *Begin roughing out a business plan to show to prospective lenders. You may need a year to prepare and refine it. Make sure your projections are based on solid facts, not on hopes or guesses.*

21

How to Write a Plan for Expansion

Beware of Slick Paper Jobs

Financiers are experts at spotting what they call "slick paper jobs" produced by professional writers of business plans. Every big city has proposal mills which crank out busines plans for clients too lazy or dumb to write their own. They charge fees ranging from $2,000 to $25,000, but all their plans sound noticeably similar. The financial ratios are always ideal, the graphs and milestones fall into recognizable patterns, the wording sounds familiar, and even the covers come from the same source. Loan officers and venture-capital researchers have learned to recognize these ghostwritten jobs. Naturally, they look unfavorably on these production-line proposals; or worse yet, toss them back unread.

Write your plan yourself. Or get the best writer in your company to do it, provided you're sure he's never worked in one of the proposal mills.

You need a presentation that sounds unique and vivid without being flashy. Keep it simple and easy to read. Make the body of the plan a concise, believable, and highly knowledgeable document, and back it up with appendixes that give the supporting data.

Some smart young companies put each appendix in its own booklet cover so that they can hold back design secrets or proprietary formulas until the lender needs them. And when one of these confidential sections is handed to the lender's consulting engineer or whomever, they make sure that it doesn't go through a copying machine; they sit with the researcher the entire time he studies it.

What to Put in Your Plan

A formal business plan—the kind submitted to prospective lenders or backers—usually consists of at least these parts:

1. A brief summary of your reasons for planning to expand. Describe the market to which you're selling, your present and planned products and services, their unusual features, how much money will be needed, and the anticipated return on this money. This first section must be well written enough to catch the reader's imagination and make him want to read further.

2. The table of contents. List each section, perhaps with a sentence summarizing it. Keep the table on one page if possible, but don't skimp. The table of contents is important because money men may want to turn immediately to some particular section as soon as they've read your introductory summary. The table of contents must help them find these details fast.

3. Your firm's history—again in brief, but told interestingly. Describe how and why you formed your company, any new technologies or concepts it is using, and how it has developed so far. Make the reader want to get aboard a winning venture. Never let him get the impression that you're just a me-too outfit imitating some bigger rival.

4. Your products or services. Describe them in nontechnical terms. Explain any special features that make customers want to buy from you instead of someone else. Show the price schedule. Mention and explain any patent applications, copyrights, or licenses. What did you apply for? When? What's the current status of your application?

5. Your production plans (or working methods, if you're a service or retailing firm). Describe how each product or service now progresses from inception to delivery, and how this will change as you expand. Mention your sources of supply. If you're an industrial enterprise, chart your manufacturing milestones and make sure your sales forecasts conform.

6. Your market and your sales history. This is a crucial section. We'll consider it in detail in a moment.

7. Your sales projection, based on the previous section. We'll also come back to this a little later.

8. Your cost-of-goods calculations. Just spell out neatly and concisely all the various costs involved in making and marketing your product. This part of the presentation will give people an idea of just how realistic and professional you really are in thinking about costs.

9. Your financial plans. Include summary tabulations of your projected (pro forma) balance sheets and income statements (profit-and-loss statements) for the next five years. In a financial appendix at the back of the book, show these projected statements done monthly for the first three years and quarterly for the fourth and fifth years. This much detail isn't necessary if you're merely seeking a five-figure loan from a bank, but it's essential if you'll be approaching bankers or venture capitalists for six-figure backing.

This section should also include a summary of the cash-flow charts, which should be set forth in detail in the financial appendix. Doing work costs money, selling makes money, but the crucial question is *when* does the money come in and *when* does it go out? There's seldom enough income to cover the outgo in the early years of a new enterprise. You're always finding yourself one cycle behind on the cash-flow chart, pinched for money to pay the outgo long before it can be replenished by the inflow. The same problem may arise, in fiercer form, when you expand. Make sure you're asking for a big enough loan to keep the cash flowing evenly.

10. Your money-leveraging plans. Explain how you'll use the investors' money to get maximum leverage. This section must be especially good, because bankers want to be sure you're aware of fiscal needs and opportunities. Obviously, unless finance is your own specialty, you'll be foolish to try to write sections 8, 9, and 10. These should be drafted by your treasurer or controller, if he's a real whiz at corporate finance. Otherwise you'll probably need a financial consultant to develop these sections.

11. Your proposal for distribution of ownership and control. Chart the structure of your enterprise (one-man ownership, partnership, limited partnership, stock corporation). Tell how you envision this structure changing in the next ten or twenty years. Bankers may not be concerned about this, but venture capitalists always are; they won't invest in anything, no matter how sound it is, unless they can foresee at least doubling or tripling their money when they sell their share. You might describe how you'll go public when the time is ripe, and ask the money man's advice on this question.

Also show an organization chart and define the job of each executive. Here is where the photos of these executives fit in. Refer the reader to a personnel appendix for complete résumés of and letters of reference about each person who helped start your enterprise and is still part of it.

12. Appendixes. If your operation is complex, and you're shooting for a quarter-million dollars or more, you may need separate appendixes, written and signed by the appropriate department heads, about (a) your designs, components, or special systems; (b) research and development; (c) production equipment used, manpower needed, and similar operational details such as shipping, purchasing, and the like, together with their budgets; (d) exactly how you developed the marketing and sales forecasts summarized in section 7; (e) finance, including full details on all departmental budgets, leverage strategies, and philosophy concerning whether surplus funds should be held as working capital, invested in fixed assets, or paid out as dividends; (f) personnel—venture capitalists like to see up-from-the-sidewalks stories, so it's a good idea to list every job each founder ever had back to the time he earned his first dollar; (g) management system, if you use management-by-objectives or management-by-exceptions or participative management or some other special approach; (h) list of assumptions about inflation, possible changes in laws that might affect your business, pending litigation, and other problem areas; (i) letters from distributors. Endorsements from people who want to sell your product to their customers will carry weight with financiers. Try to get ten or twenty distributors to write you letters saying that their markets are hungry for whatever it is you're producing. If these distributors list the larger customers in their territories, it will help. If they say they'll carry significant inventories, it will help even more.

Your Sales History Is Crucial

Section 6 of your presentation, describing your market and your sales, will be the hingepin of your whole presentation. You must show that your company has pulled in plenty of sales, or at least a big backlog of orders. Otherwise you're just an unproved start-up in the eyes of lenders.

This section can begin by analyzing your customers, your competitors, and your current sales. What are the typical sales patterns for products or services of the type you're selling? Define the market segment (or segments) you're shooting at. Define the geographics and demographics of your present market and your growth plans for expansion into additional markets—domestic or foreign. Try to find out, or at least estimate, what share of the market is going to you and each of your competitors. A marketing expert can help you do this.

Spell out your sales record in detail. How many units sold, how many outlets sold to, how many stock turns at retail, how long a period is covered by the sales history?

Then, using this sample as the base for your forecast, explain in section 7 what volume (in units and in dollars) of sales you foresee for each of your products when you begin your planned expansion.

Never say "if" you can borrow a specified amount you'll do thus-and-so. Always announce that you are going to take a certain course "when" the necessary capital is available. Assume you'll get it from one source or another. Explain that you plan to do such-and-such, with the unspoken implication that you'll do it through this money man or someone else. You are doing him the favor of offering him your business.

But he wants to see a good sales history. He wants to be sure that your product is selling well, even if only on a test basis in a limited market. He won't be much impressed by an announcement that some stores or wholesalers are stocking the product. That tells him only that you managed to make some sales to buyers for the stores or distributors. What he's really looking for is a good record of reorders. If your product is turning over four times a year at retail, or better, he's interested.

Obviously, the firmer the base for your sales projections, the more impressive they'll look. But one way or another, you must convince a potential backer that the company is likely to make a lot of money when it expands. There's no use giving a long explanation of the logic by which you arrived at your sales projection. Your own enthusiasm won't help much either. Give the person the background information (supported in the appendix with all the data you can muster) and let him decide for himself whether your forecast is sound. He'll do that anyway.

Also, you must show that you've planned well for what will happen as your sales increase. What new market segments are going to generate these sales? What sales and distribution network will be needed to hit the new market hard and fast? What strategies will you use—pricing, promotion, or whatever—to keep ahead of competitors? How much additional equipment and manpower and materials will you need?

Words and People Make a Difference

The wording of your plan is important. Much about a business can't be reflected in its financial data. A homely girl may have the same measurements as a beautiful one. The differences, if they can be described at all, come in details about the skin, the eyes, the hair, and so on. But observers may see the girls differently, and describe them differently. "Beauty is in the eye of the beholder," as a poet (female gender) once wrote.

So it is with financial statements. You must bring the measurements to life. That's why you need the details and the words that go beyond the numbers. "If I had to bet on a terrific idea with a lousy presentation versus a mediocre idea with a terrific presentation, I'd bet on the great presentation every time," writes Don Kracke, a specialist in developing ideas for marketing.

Always keep your reader in mind. Think about what he'd like, not what you'd like. G. A. Nichols, a noted expert on sales promotion, once sold stoves. When he went to a dealer he didn't ask him, "How would you like to buy a carload of stoves?'' He said, ''How would you like to *sell* a carload of stoves?''

Shun superlatives such as ''fantastic sales'' or ''huge profits.'' Transmit enthusiasm by selecting the significant details, and by choosing words that point up the meaning of these details.

As we've seen, you may want to call in an independent financial consultant during the months you're preparing a big-money proposal. Such an expert deals with bankers, accountants, attorneys, insurance brokers, business-opportunity brokers, and other professionals. He knows what the local financial groups look for. He may even know the preferences of individual loan officers. He can help you decide what form of financing is likely to be best for your company, and where you're likely to get the best terms. Then he'll help you think out the financial angles of your plan.

How to Package Your Plan

Having written your presentation and made the appendixes as complete as you possibly can, having figured out answers to all the questions the money men might ask and some they'll probably never think of—then you'll want to consider the physical format. The presentation must look visually attractive. It must even feel good to the touch.

Its binding and covers are important. You want a book that looks thoroughly professional from the first glance. When you hand it to a financier you're handing him something valuable, and the cover should convey this value. A 75-cent imitation-leather pocket folder is about right. It looks rich and feels rich, without being ostentatious. If your appendixes run to several pages each, you might well put each appendix in a separate one of these folders, so that the body of the plan doesn't look too bulky.

Naturally, the appearance of the inside pages is important too. You may want to hire a professional art director or an advanced advertising-art student to lay out the pages for you, including charts and graphs and pictures. A well-done heading for a page can help it immensely. Tell your artist the kind of audience he'll be aiming at, so that he'll go for elegance and dignity rather than look-damn-you layouts.

KEEP THESE BASIC POINTS IN MIND:

- *Don't commission a job by a proposal mill. You, or the best writer in your company, should do the writing.*
- *If you're not a financial expert, get one to work out every detail of the financial parts of your plan.*

- *Make sure your company has a good sales history, at least in a limited sample, before you present your plan to any prospective lenders.*
- *Package your plan attractively, with good binding and well-designed pages.*

22

How to Talk to a Capitalist

So now your presentation—your business plan for expansion—is typed, illustrated, duplicated, and bound. What do you do with it?

If you followed the suggestions in Chapters 20 and 21, you've been scouting among the banks for months past, and have picked out several that are prime prospects to finance you. By talking with their presidents or loan officers, or with financial consultants, you know they make the kind of loan you need.

At this point, if you follow the right strategy, you can open the door for what might otherwise be an unbankable loan request. You must execute it with care.

Now it's important to approach the right official of the bank. Banks have two separate tracks for management candidates. One track is for the corporate-officer candidates, the other for branch management. People on the first track draw good salaries, but those on the second may be paid less than engineers and salesmen. Banks give the title of "vice president" to almost everyone who comes into contact with wealthy customers, because the title helps them do business with such customers. But don't make the error of assuming that the average "vice president" has much authority or makes much money.

Early in your groundwork-laying process you got acquainted with branch loan officers. They're good to know. But remember that they're tightly limited in their authority. Now that you're ready to make your presentation, figure on making it to the highest-ranking officer you possibly can, preferably the president. At least the vice president in charge of the commercial-loan department, or the primary loan officer in the bank's main office.

Invite this bigwig to come for a day to visit your facilities, where you'll make the presentation. This is important, because only when the financier is on your turf can you make your full pitch without outside interruptions. Suggest that he bring along a few associates if he wishes.

The invitation is best handled by a third party, if possible—your CPA or attorney or financing consultant. If it's necessary to wait for a few days for an appointment with the right executive, wait. This shows you're not panicky, not a poor planner. Timing is a tool in business negotiations of all types; it's especially important when you're negotiating for financing. Make your presentation mostly in your office, if you're the company president. Have your right-hand man present, plus an aide whose only assignment is to take notes on questions asked by the visitors. Their questions may give you clues to problems that can be solved before you invite executives from the next bank on your list.

Prepare an agenda for the full day. Give it to the banker when he arrives. Also provide him with a clipboard so that he can clip additional notes to the board.

The first point on the agenda is your firm's history and prospects.

Hand him the introductory section of your corporate presentation, on one or two separate sheets which he can attach to his clipboard. (These are duplicates of the first few pages in the bound presentation, which should be handed to him later.)

Wait silently while he scans the section. Then go over it point by point, illustrating the firm's achievements with anecdotes. Convey your pride in the business and your involvement. Make clear that it's more than just a meal ticket for you. Don't hurry this part of the presentation, and don't let the banker hurry it. If he presses you on the size of your loan or your financial problem, ask him to hold off; tell him this will all be presented later. Point out that the agenda lists "financial data" as to be presented after lunch.

Section by Section

Next analyze your market and discuss your competition. At this point you may want to call in your marketing vice president and let him do the talking. Use the same technique as before: give the banker the written section of your presentation, let him read it, then go over the points one by one. It's a good idea to excuse yourself (assuming that you're the chief operating officer) while the marketing man makes his own presentation. This shows the banker that you have confidence in your next line of management. Of course, it is axiomatic that you are certain the person you select will be able to add strength to your proposal.

Other key executives may follow, again without your being present, but in your office. When it's the production expert's turn, he should conduct a tour of the premises—plus a short drive to nearby facilities if you have some. Sights and sounds have psychological impact. Big-money bond salesmen for power companies used to take prospects out to the waterfall sites and let them stand listening to the thunder of the water. Then they took them into the power plants and let them listen to the whirring of the turbines. In short, let the banker feel the energy that's driving your operations.

You should go along on this tour. Along the way, you may be confronted with a problem raised by a subordinate or a customer. Deal with it on the spot if you can. This will help give the banker a more convincing feeling for you and your business. But don't try to rig such a situation in advance. He'll sense it, and write you off as a phony.

Lunch: A Turning Point

It's best to serve luncheon right in your office. Order food that's simple but good. If your office isn't convenient, pick a nice but moderately priced restaurant. (The last thing you want is an image as a big spender.)

Serve liquor only if he asks for it. Check out the place in advance, to make sure it's quiet and well run, and tell the manager what you're planning. Don't have more than five or six people there—one of whom should still be taking notes on the questions the banker is asking.

Use the lunch to query the banker: Have you made loans to other firms like mine? What is your loan-approval procedure? How much can you yourself authorize? If the sum in question is above that amount, who are the people on the loan committee? Will you be the account manager of the loan? If not, who? What office will I work with? What reports will you want from us during the year?

If the banker asks financial questions, show him the agenda again, and point out, "We're coming to that soon." Fill his head with facts about what an asset you are, or can be, to the community. Tell him—in deep confidence, ostensibly—about your great plans for the future.

But also show some of your "soiled laundry." Find a way to tell him about your firm's shortcomings, before he spots them for himself. For instance, if a competitor caused trouble in the past, let the banker know it—and how you overcame it. A few dark spots will make a generally bright picture more believable.

At Last: The Loan Request

The final steps of the briefing should focus on your business plans, projections, estimates of market share, cash-flow forecasts, and the like. Your job here is to show that you know, and can convince the banker, how the bank will get its money back.

Now he'll need specific figures. He'll look at your rate of return—the ratio of your earnings to your capital. Earnings of 10 percent look good; occasionally he approves a loan where the return on invested capital is only 6 or 7 percent, especially if there are certain other circumstances to make the loan at this figure attractive.

He'll also mentally compute your ratio of quick assets to liabilities. A ratio of 1:1 may be acceptable. Closer to 2:1 is much better.

And he'll look at your growth rate. Some experts say that a business should be increasing its net worth by about 20 percent a year before its equity capital should be increased.

This is the time when he's entitled to ask tough questions. He knows about financial data. You shouldn't resent these questions, no matter how skeptical they seem. And you shouldn't bluff. Instead, learn from him. If he asks why your accounts receivable are high, you can say you didn't realize they were out of line. Or you may answer that the figure is normal for your business, and follow up by asking what information he has on new collection procedures. Or ask what your competition and other companies are doing, and how.

He'll be pleased by your eagerness to learn. And by now he'll have a feeling for you and your business, which will give him a deeper understanding of the data.

You can still be tentative about specifics of the loan proposal. Try to get him to say how much he thinks you need. If he won't mention any figure, try one or two for size, and watch his eyes. You might say, "Do you think we need as much as three hundred thousand?" (Or thirty thousand, if you're actually shooting for twenty-six thousand; the strategy outlined in Chapter 20 will work as well for five-figure financing as for several million.)

He'll probably cut down any figure you mention. This lets him play hero in the eyes of the bank. So if you specify an amount you actually need, you've goofed; you won't get that much. Ask for more than you hope to get; but on the other hand, you must at all times be realistic, especially now, when the chips are down.

If you've handled the interview well, he may say, "I think I might be able to convince our loan committee that you should have twenty-seven.'' You may counter by saying, ''You're probably right, but do you think they'd consider twenty-eight?'' Follow up with a point you've been saving, such as ''After all, our checking-account balance with your bank has been averaging almost six thousand.''

This average, called a compensating balance, may affect the amount you can borrow. On loans of certain types a bank may require you to keep a compensating balance in your account at all times during the term of the loan. If the bank's officers lend thirty thousand, they may expect you to keep somewhere between a fifth and a half of this amount on deposit in their bank. In other words, they can ask you to pay interest on a $30,000 loan while you're enjoying the use of only $15,000 or $24,000. By realizing this in advance, you will know better how much money you will need to ask for.

Computing your average balance is easy. Take your bank statement and add the daily balances together. Then divide by the number of days. Include your payroll account too.

In mentioning your average balance, which is another exhibit you might prepare for the presentation, pick whatever number of months makes you look best. If the average was $5,500 for the past five months but only $2,000 for the past year, show the five-month figure even though it's a shorter period.

What Terms?

You should know in advance just what terms and conditions you want. Do you want a term loan—that is, a loan of a set amount of money for a set amount of time, which comes due and payable with accrued interest on a fixed date? Since banks are the main source of short-term loans, they resist offering longer terms because these tie up their funds. They prefer quick turnover, which is safer and more profitable.

But long-term loans of three to five years are easier to get now because of the competition among banks. Such a loan may come through what is known as a line of credit, whereby the borrower applies and the bank agrees in advance that whenever the borrower needs any amount up to, say, $10,000, the bank will automatically advance it to him without delay. Some of this money may be needed for only a period of days or weeks, and you'll pay interest on it only for the number of days you actually keep it.

Maybe you'll want a loan commitment, which is a firm contractual agreement binding the bank to lend money in the future. It's used where money will be needed for longer periods, such as for construction of a new plant. There's usually a one-time commitment fee (maybe 0.5 percent of the maximum commitment), paid at the time the bank makes the commitment.

After you've said all you can and answered all questions as best you can, hand the banker your handsome brochure and explain that it's a duplicate of sections you showed him earlier, plus additional material. Give him extra copies for others who may need them.

He'll probably say that he'll take the matter up with the loan committee. This could be a dodge to avoid turning you down face to face. Or it could be the simple truth. Anyhow, don't make the blunder of asking, "Could I present our case to the committee?" This implies that you have no confidence in the banker, even as an errand boy. He certainly won't try to sell your loan to the committee if he thinks you want to bypass him.

Just act relaxed. This will impress him, since he knows only seasoned executives in well-managed companies can relax. But why shouldn't you relax? You know you can go on to other banks if the first one says no. The more often you make your presentation, the better it will become.

Sooner or later this banker, or some banker, will call to tell you your loan has been approved.

Beware Those Standard Terms

But you're not out of the woods yet.

While you're still aglow with satisfaction, the banker may try to slip a curve past you. "The note is all ready for you to sign," he'll say. "Shall I bring it to your office, or do you want to stop in here?"

If you sign on the dotted line before the glow is gone, you'll be sorry. He's hoping you'll buy his stiffest terms without balking. If you ask him what the terms are, he'll rattle them off, describing them as "currently standard terms."

Tell him you'll need to keep the note for a day or two before you sign, so that your attorney and financial advisers can go over it.

What is the interest? What kinds and amount of collateral will you have to supply? When must the money be repaid? These questions are almost more important to the banker than whether or not he makes the loan. They determine how much profit the bank will extract from you. He'll charge as much as he can get. It's up to you to negotiate.

Probably your presentation set forth the terms and conditions you wanted. And probably you'll find that the bank has tightened these up.

Now you need to come back with a counteroffer, a compromise between what you asked and what the bank put into the note.

If your company's credit is strong, try to get a lower interest rate, a lower compensating balance, a longer time to repay. Ask for elimination of service charges. Ask for free services such as preparation of payroll checks.

If the negotiations reach a deadlock, keep shopping around. After you've made your presentation to several banks, maybe you can get them bidding for your business. If you let your present banker know what the competition offers, he may match it to keep your company's business.

Venture-capital Firms Are Different

And don't be afraid to go outside the banking field, if you're seeking a quarter-million or more. Life-insurance companies have plenty of money available for long-term business loans. Most of their investment officers are willing to lend to privately owned companies, and a few will lend to companies with a worth of as little as $3 million.

Private investment firms usually won't touch anything under $250,000. They keep close track of a company they're backing, which may cost them $80,000 a year in salaries, office costs, and other expenses. Maybe they no longer look for the 50-percent annual return they expected in the 1960s, but they still hope for at least 20 percent a year as payoff for their risk and the time and money they spend nursing a young enterprise. Most new ventures simply can't afford such a high cost of money.

But if yours can, by all means aim your presentation at venture capitalists.

You needn't be as coy with them as you should be with a banker. You can—probably you must—announce at the outset how much capital you need. Venture-capital firms will insist on studying your presentation in their own office before deciding whether to come out for a visit. Expert researchers will pore through it.

And they'll want more detail than a bank would. They'll analyze your budget, department by department and line by line. They're primarily interested in whether your enterprise can grow into a leader in your industry within five to seven years. Meanwhile they won't expect dividends or an early repayment of the money they put in. But they'll expect to see the business growing fast, plowing back its profits into more growth.

They'll investigate you and your associates with brutal thoroughness. Don't be surprised if they talk to dozens of people who know you.

Even with their apparent interest in your company and the extensive efforts they seem to go through in turning your company inside-out in analysis, their rate of extending venture-capital loans is relatively small. Many venture capitalists may look at fifty to a hundred proposals before they make an actual commitment.

Whether from a venture-capital investor or a newly rich acquaintance or a bank, the money you need will be forthcoming if your enterprise is sound and you explain it well. Prepare your case thoroughly, and plan to present it to as many different prospects as need be. With time, you'll find the right door and pry it open.

KEEP THESE BASIC POINTS IN MIND:

- *Through an intermediary, get one of the top officers of a friendly bank to visit your facilities.*
- *Whoever extends the invitation should under no conditions tell the banker how much financing will be requested.*
- *Plan a meeting that will take most of a day, and draw up an agenda which you can hand to that banker when he arrives.*
- *Go through your presentation section by section, first handing the banker a section and giving him time to read it, then reviewing it orally with illustrative incidents and details.*
- *Let each of your key executives explain his own section personally, while you excuse yourself as a way of showing your confidence in these executives.*
- *Take the banker on a tour of any of your nearby facilities that will impress him.*
- *Serve a good but moderately priced lunch in your office or at some quiet place nearby.*
- *Put off all discussion of all financial matters, explaining that they're scheduled for later on the agenda. Keep them until the final sections.*
- *During the actual loan request, begin by showing how the bank will get its money back, and then try to get the banker to say how much he thinks you need. If he won't, name a considerably higher figure than you really expect.*
- *Know in advance what terms and conditions you want, and specify them after you and the banker have tentatively agreed on the amount of the loan.*
- *Then give the banker a bound copy of your presentation for further study, and wait to hear from him. If the delay lengthens, you can begin overtures to another bank.*
- *When a banker says, "The note is all ready for you to sign," take it*

away and study it. If the terms aren't what you asked, negotiate. Ask for other concessions to compensate for those he didn't include.
- *If you need a quarter-million or more, make an even more detailed presentation to venture-capital firms, but don't expect them to visit your facilities until they've studied your presentation.*

23
Rip-offs and Your Business

Stealing from business is an old sport, more widespread than bowling or hunting, say. Participants find it fun, practice it enthusiastically, and seldom encounter any unpleasant consequences. Business crime is far less risky than street crime, and much bigger statistically by every yardstick. In fact, surveys show that American businessmen lose a total of about $5 billion a year—far more than they pay in taxes—through rip-offs by employees, and about another $4 billion through rip-offs by outsiders. The losses are often hard to classify because insiders and outsiders may team up to do the ripping.

Let's scan the common kinds of crime against small business, and see how you can cope with them.

Phony Messengers, Inspectors and Their Ilk

Where do your employees go for lunch and coffee breaks? You should stroll there and join them occasionally—just on the off chance that you'll see some of them deep in conversation with a stranger.

If you notice the stranger more than once, better make careful inquiries. He may be a small-time hustler or buyer in search of bargains. Such operatives often get chummy with employees, then offer them one-fourth to one-third of the retail value of the company's products (or of its office furnishings, maybe) in cash. If employees know that small inventory losses have gone unnoticed in the past, they may be tempted.

And look out for any "messenger" who shows up at your back door. He may be the hustler. He'll say he's there to pick up "the order Mr. Jackson phoned in." Get identification. And if you don't know "Mr. Jackson," don't let your people fill the order until they've double-checked—or unless they get cash on the barrelhead.

Just phoning back to the number an unknown caller leaves isn't enough, for obvious reasons, unless the number is already known to your firm or can be verified in the directory. One way to check is by arranging for the caller to charge his order on a national credit card. When he gives his card number, you can verify his credit immediately by a call to the card-issuing company.

Deliverymen can be hustlers too, in cahoots with somebody in your stockroom. They can deliver less than you've ordered, then get their pal on your payroll to sign for the supposedly full quantity, and split the profit with him. This happens all the time in the restaurant business, for example. "You've always got to watch the 'back-door register' and not sign for any delivery unless it has been counted or weighed," according to Bernard Splaver, a veteran caterer, in a recent article in *Money* magazine. "As for your restaurant's own staff, treat 'em like brothers but watch 'em like thieves."

How Office Burglars Work

One Saturday afternoon a downtown business office telephoned a locksmith with an anguished message: "We can't get our safe open! The combination has been mislaid. Will you come down and open it?"

The locksmith was Charles Courtney, considered one of the best, and he doesn't go out on small jobs, especially on Saturday. "How big a safe is it?" he asked. "And can't it wait till Monday?"

"No! There are papers inside that we need right now. It's a big vault-type safe."

Courtney took a cab to the building. Most of its offices were closed and silent, he noticed as he rode up in the elevator. But the firm that had phoned him was wide open and buzzing with activity. Two girls were typing, and the office manager was toiling at a desk heaped with papers. He showed Courtney where the safe was, and hustled back to his desk.

Courtney went to work. After a few minutes he put down his tools with a discouraged sigh. "This is a tough one," he told the manager. "I'll have to go back for more tools."

"How long?" the manager asked briskly. Courtney said, "Oh, maybe an hour."

The manager said he'd wait. But when Courtney came back fifteen minutes later with police, the office was deserted.

"I had a hunch they were phony," he told police. "There was an odd atmosphere in that office. Maybe it was the way the girls typed. After all, it's interesting to watch a locksmith open a big safe, but these girls never gave me a glance. So when I went out, I asked the janitor if this office was usually open Saturdays. He said it never had been."

It was lucky for the business owners that Courtney, through occasional exposure to the wiles of clever criminals who wanted him to pick other people's locks, had become a suspicious man.

However, there are ways to rob an office without enlisting a locksmith. Melville E. Reeves, the "skyscraper burglar" of Chicago, who took more than $1 million before he was caught, told police, "If you roll up your sleeves and put a pencil behind your ear, you can rob any office without trouble."

This rule enriched him for twenty years. By day he visited offices—supposedly as a furniture-polish salesman, or as a fire inspector. By night he returned to whichever suites had looked most promising, and cleaned them out.

He had no trouble getting in. On the ground floor of the office building he signed a fictitious name to the after-hours registration sheet, then took the elevator to any floor he wished. There he entered offices either by (a) persuading cleaning people to open a door with their passkey, on the plea that he'd forgotten his own keys, or (b) scouting around until he found cleaners at work in one of the offices he had selected. He would stride in through the open door, sit down at a desk and busy himself with papers until the cleaners departed.

Once he got $30,000 in bonds from the office safe of a small company in Michigan City, Indiana. Another time he took $150,000 in government bonds. Finally he formed a partnership with John Worthington, a broker who specialized in stolen securities. Worthington eventually went to prison, but nothing could be proved against Reeves. He went free.

Not until years later, when Reeves grew careless in old age, was he nailed. As he left an office, somebody saw $38 worth of postage stamps drop from a package he'd sloppily wrapped. The witness mentioned it to a nearby guard, who stopped Reeves and found that the package also contained stolen currency. By then the police wanted him for bigger thefts. He was sent to prison, where he died.

Some of today's office thieves are smoother than Reeves.

The best of them never carry out anything incriminating. Instead they take with them manila envelopes, stamped and self-addressed. They steal only currency, checks, and negotiable securities, which fit into their envelopes. They drop these into the mail chute and walk out.

More sophisticated operators also steal blank checks (usually from the back of the book, where they aren't noticed) and a few cancelled checks (which they use to copy signatures onto the blanks).

But of course, crude rip-off types are thriving too. They steal portable office machines and equipment, even if it brings only a fraction of its value. One of them baffled the security men in the ultramodern office buildings of Century City, Los Angeles, night after night. The petty thievery seemed impossible, because night crews were in the buildings from 6:30 P.M. until 3 A.M., and were coached to keep their eyes open for skulking strangers. After 3 A.M. patrolmen were walking the halls, checking each office door to make sure it was locked. (In theory, cleaners and office workers lock doors when they leave. But in real life, some forget.)

Small items were disappearing from offices in all the buildings: clocks, pencil sharpeners, cigarette lighters, miniature TV sets, petty cash, postage stamps. The offices that were burgled were later found locked, when patrolmen made their rounds. This meant that someone had probably found the doors unlocked before the patrol got there, stepped in, and stolen whatever could be carried inconspicuously, locking the doors afterward. Nobody had passkeys; Building Security kept these for itself.

Almost surely, the thief had to be someone with legitimate business in the buildings at night; security guards would have noticed a stranger. Suspicion narrowed to a woman who delivered morning papers before dawn, dropping them in the hallways outside office doors. Security men shadowed her one night. She and her young son, who carried papers for her, were testing for unlocked doors as they went. The next night a guard was staked out behind an unlocked door, and caught the pair in the act of rifling the office.

How to Discourage Burglars

Maybe you think your office is burglarproof because your typewriters and other portable machines are bolted down, with numbers engraved on them for computerized identification, and because you keep cash and all equivalents of cash (including checkbooks and order blanks) locked in a safe—or tucked away in file folders inside a desk or filing cabinet. These precautions do give you a certain safety margin, but not enough.

When expert thieves are confronted by a safe or a dial padlock, the first thing they do is carefully turn the dial. Why? Because they know that employees responsible for a combination lock often make the lock easier to open the next morning by not completely turning the dial at the end of the day—which means that it will spring open when returned to the last number in the combination. Employees should be trained to spin the dial several times before leaving.

If burglars find a safe thoroughly locked, they search the room for a likely-looking set of numbers. They've learned that office workers seldom entrust a safe combination solely to memory. It's likely to be kept handy —in small, inconspicuous figures, of course—on a nearby wall, calendar, or memo pad. Or it's on a slip of paper in a desk drawer. Or somebody stashes it in a folder in the filing cabinet, feeling sure "No thief will look there.'' However, office thieves often make a point of going through desks and filing cabinets, on the chance of finding currency or bonds or other valuable papers—such as the combination to the safe.

So if you must keep the combination written down, don't write it anywhere in plain sight. And don't put it on a slip of paper that might catch a burglar's eye when he's glancing through the files and desks.

And if you must keep large amounts of cash or securities around the office, try to divide these up and keep them in separate safes with different combinations, rather than all in one place.

Another wise precaution is to set up a very obvious closed-circuit television camera near the safe. If you can't afford this, you can get a dummy camera with operating red light; it's inexpensive, and it scares off thieves.

If you're a retailer, or in some other business that collects wads of cash during the working day, you should know about one of the newer developments in safes. It's called a drop-depository safe. It has a slot atop its door, so all your employees can drop money in, but nobody can open it without the combination. Since there's no need to open the safe during the day, only one person need ever be entrusted with the combination. Such a safe costs about $65—and comes with decals that let any holdup men know that those present can't open the safe.

Maybe such precautions seem needless if you've never heard of an office burglary in your area. But just remember that the office burglaries which eventually led to the resignation of a U.S. President were planned by respectable government officials who had no trouble finding skilled burglars to do the jobs. The arts of office burglary are by no means little-known. In one city alone, Los Angeles, there are about 100 office burglaries every month, with the total loss averaging about $12,500 per month. And it's no longer uncommon for a company to find $10,000 worth of bolted-down equipment lifted by thieves who cut the bolts with hacksaws or torches.

Is Your Building Secure?

Small shops and offices in small buildings are especially vulnerable, of course, but a burglar alarm system can help, if it is really good. Many alarm systems are worse than worthless; they're an open invitation. A prowler sees their tape on windows and around the doors, and knows what to do. He uses a jumper wire to circumvent the alarm, or he simply enters and leaves through a roof vent.

Electronic-eye alarms aren't much better. A burglar can easily spot them, using optical equipment from a safe vantage place. Once he sees where they are, he just works around them.

If you want to learn about alarm systems, make friends with managers of big drugstores. Drugstores have to be security-minded, and they generally use the newest and best alarms. You'll probably find that they've installed ultrasonic or microwave "proximity alarms" or "intrusion detectors" triggered by noise or special kinds of vibration. Microphones are placed in key areas, to be turned on when the premises are empty. They can be programmed to register only certain noises—so that street sounds from outside won't trigger them, for example—and are highly sensitive to whatever kinds of noise they are designed to detect.

If your business includes a factory, warehouse, or some other self-contained building, of course you've thought about guard patrols, floodlights, fences, internal alarms, and other obvious security measures. But here's a new precaution you may not know about. You can literally paint out intruders. An "anticlimbing" paint can be applied to the top of your seven-foot fence. Fence climbers stain their hands and clothes with a sticky paint that shows up brightly and is easy to identify. Some varieties resist water and show up under ultraviolet light. These paints are easy to apply, and don't give your premises the grim look that comes with barbed wire or spikes atop your fence.

Safety in Skyscrapers

If your office is in a skyscraper office building, you may have to depend mainly on the building's own security system. Make sure it is tight and tough. Guards should insist that people entering or leaving after hours show valid proof that they belong there. The security director should teach janitors and cleaning people about office burglars' tricks, and should offer rewards for help in catching them. He should instruct watchmen to keep checking for unlocked doors, and to guard the passkeys like crown jewels.

Once burglars get inside the average office building, they are free to ransack it from top to bottom, especially at the end of a three-day weekend when there probably have been no tenants or cleaners in the building for a day or more. One Saturday night a pair of burglars invaded a building on 52nd Street in Manhattan. They went through fifty offices, using a janitor's passkey which they found in a closet. Then, after the robbery was discovered and reported Sunday morning, they returned that night and went through the other offices. Their haul totaled about $20,000. The building had only one man on duty. He slept in the basement, and his job was mainly to answer the bell if a tenant wanted admittance.

To combat top-to-bottom rip-offs, your building can easily install one-way door openers on all fire-exit doors, so that intruders are forced to go down to the ground level or up to the roof if they enter the fire staircase. What about the elevators? At the end of each working day, these should be set so that they can only return to the ground level and not open their doors at intermediate floors. Or they can be set so that they can be operated by only a night watchman or guard.

Another essential protection, of course, is insurance coverage. You may think you're insured against more kinds of crime than you really are. A safe-burglary policy, for example, won't pay off if a burglar finds the combination written down somewhere. For that, a money-and-securities policy is the answer. In Chapter 16 we saw other pitfalls to avoid in insuring against holdups, fraud, embezzlement, and the rest.

Don't Set Yourself Up for Robbers

During your working day, you need to beware of muggers, holdup men, and sneak thieves. Big office buildings are reporting more and more cases of business people being robbed in washrooms, elevators, corridors, and parking areas. A man with a gun may walk into almost any office and demand that the safe be emptied for him—or may phone an executive and wangle an appointment in his private office, then force him to write a personal check and/or business check, for whatever balance shows in his checkbooks. To get time to cash the checks, the robber may tie up the executive and gag him, or simply knock him unconscious. The smoothest holdup men work in pairs, with stolen credit cards to serve as identification when cashing checks. With a two-man team, they can then tell the victim, "Just relax. One of us will stay here with you while the other goes down to the bank and cashes your check." With a gun at your head, you would probably be willing to call downstairs.

Why not be prepared for holdups? Install a push button below your desk, and below the desks of others whose offices might be invaded by a gunman. These can connect with the desk of someone in the outer office, or with a security officer elsewhere in the building. By touching the button with a foot, anyone can summon help in a tight spot.

Unfortunately, it's easy for a robber to walk into almost any building during working hours. The constant coming and going of messengers, repairmen, deliverymen, customers, and clients enables criminals to enter and roam at will.

But you can make it hard for unwelcome visitors to penetrate your offices. Just put your receptionist in a small outer cubicle—maybe behind a counter or even a glass screen, for her own protection. Fix the door to the rest of the suite so that it won't open until the receptionist presses a hidden button unlocking it. By touching another hidden button, she should also be able to give the alarm if necessary. This type of layout has long been standard in high-security offices. Your firm can arrange it.

As for muggings and holdups in public areas of the building, that's the responsibility of the building owner. Most builders, owners, and renting agents act as if they were doing tenants a favor by establishing any strong security measures. Firemen visit buildings to make sure that fire regulations are obeyed, but who checks to see whether tenants are protected from crime? Probably you and other tenants ought to get together and talk sternly to the manager or owner. Point out that TV cameras in the corridors, elevators, and parking facilities are no longer a luxury; that remote-control alarms and other devices to summon help ought to be hooked up with a central guard station in the building; that a comprehensive security system can't be set up piecemeal by amateurs, but must be designed by an expert who knows how to leave no loopholes. If your requests don't get results, you can suggest that the owner or manager look up the whopping lawsuits against buildings found negligent in protecting their tenants.

But what if your office isn't in a big building? What if you have a storefront type of layout? What can you do to discourage the intruder bent on robbing you?

Above all, you can make sure that your place of business isn't an attractive target. Professional armed robbers look for a few key features that mark a business as ripe for rip-off. Here's what attracts them:

A cash-and-carry business that doesn't bank daily.

A business with a safe located where it's hidden from public view.

A business where plenty of cash is available to several employees.

If your business fits any of these descriptions, you're asking for a holdup or a nocturnal visit by safecrackers. Don't let cash or negotiable securities or other valuables pile up in your place of business, especially if your office is secluded. If you keep valuables in your safe, try to place the safe where it can be seen from the street or from a corridor—and keep the door to the corridor open. The more visible your safe, the better. Another precaution is to post several signs noting that your office uses a two-key system to protect all valuables.

If you can't arrange your offices to discourage criminals, you can at least train your employees to recognize prearranged signals for trouble. Stage frequent drills to keep them on their toes.

How to Stop Shoplifters

The American Management Association estimates that an average of 15 cents of every dollar paid over the counter at any store is stolen or embezzled, and that in some businesses this figure is as high as 30 cents.

The head of a supermarket chain says, "Replacing one stolen banana literally requires $20 in sales. That's an expensive banana." Too bad this fact isn't understood by more heads of small businesses.

If you operate on slim profit margins, a steady trickle of pilferage or shoplifting can bleed you to death. Maybe you don't realize this. Maybe the items stolen seem trivial in value, so you write them off to "inventory shrinkage" as an inevitable cost of doing business—and then wonder why the business doesn't show a profit. The AMA's study showed that one-fifth of all the businesses that go broke in a year are busted by losses from crime.

Shoplifters can be scared away, or caught. Some storekeepers are afraid to try to do either. Fear of lawsuits, and fear of disturbing customers with vigorous guard activity, keep merchants from developing an antishoplifting system. In fact, fear is the thieves' best friend.

Don't be afraid. Frighten the shoplifters instead. This can be done without bothering your customers.

Put mirrors behind counters and overhead, so that a would-be thief can never be sure he isn't observed from some odd angle. Also, thieves who know about two-way mirrors may fear that a guard is watching from behind a wall mirror. And you might consider installing dummy TV cameras.

Here's another low-cost system that scares thieves: a storewide loudspeaker system. Frequent announcements like "Officer Burke," please come to the Third Street entrance" can make it seem that your store has security officers all over the place.

But some professional "boosters," as the cops call them, won't be scared away by these devices, because they'll case the store carefully before going to work. These are the ones you must trap. Do it by training your salespeople to spot them on sight. Here's what to look for:

- shoppers who seem to know where they're going but don't wish to be helped, and don't buy anything
- shoppers whose elbows stay close to their sides, in position to hold something under their clothing
- shoppers wearing voluminous clothing or long coats or capes, or carrying big packages. The packages can have false bottoms that open to accommodate more merchandise.

Protecting Vulnerable Areas

Does your store have one of the new point-of-sale computerized cash-register systems? Find out if a security signaling button can be added to it. If not, look into the possibility of installing another button system, so that when a clerk or cashier observes a shoplifter, she can quickly and silently signal the manager or the security man, with an indication of the location of the alarm.

Expert shoplifters concentrate, if they can, on areas where merchandise is available in quantity and where there's little protection. You can direct your attention to those same areas. Can you put the more valuable items under glass, where shoppers can't pick them up? Can you station clerks near the open counters?

How about your stockroom? How about halls between departments? In sizable stores, these areas are the happy hunting grounds for thieves. Don't let merchandise be stored in the corridors, or in any other place where a stranger can stroll in. Discourage loitering near a stockroom.

Maybe you can't lock the stockroom because of fire regulations. Even so, you can install inexpensive signal devices that flash red lights in several places when a door leading to a vulnerable area is opened. Watch deliveries closely. All deliveries should be signed for and checked, or else marked "received unchecked."

Don't let everybody on your payroll walk into and out of the stockroom. Set up strict rules about who is authorized to enter it— and enforce the rules with a log sheet to be signed by everyone on entering and leaving.

If the law allows you to lock the stockroom during working hours, think about installing one of those electronic gadgets that use magnetic coded cards to unlock a door. They've been in use since the 1960s by Playboy Clubs, Elks Lodges and others, and recently hotels have begun using them on guest rooms. They're better than keys in several ways.

If you have a few employees whose main responsibility is your stockroom, sit down for a long talk with them. Make them see the need for security, and that you're concerned about it. Give them a feeling of "insider" status and a sense of responsibility.

What about visibility in the stockroom and other vulnerable areas? If it's poor, install windows (barred, of course) and keep the room well lighted. Thieves thrive in dim light.

They also prefer not to leave through the checkout stations. They look for a fire exit or loading dock, and slip away through this if they can. Here again, you can't lock fire doors, but you can put in the signals mentioned on the previous page. Train your guard or guards to respond to an alarm not at the door itself, but at the exit the door leads to. Then make a search back to the door. If the door leads to a parking zone, make that a checkpoint too.

Stolen goods can be smuggled out in trash containers. Some artful shoplifters pretend to be cleanup workers. So don't let trash accumulate or be picked up near any area where valuable merchandise is stored.

Cutting Employee Theft

Employees steal more than shoplifters do. Every survey and questionnaire shows this. Maybe your business is a type that can't be victimized by pilferage, but you're still vulnerable to dishonest employees. Every business is.

We saw at the start of this chapter that employees are sometimes cultivated by outside crooks who'll buy supplies stolen from your business. One way to counter this proposition is to make an announcement—probably by memo, circulated through all departments—about your awareness of such offers. Hint that your in-house surveillance may be followed up by a professional probe.

If supplies keep disappearing, you'd better have someone make checks of employee packages, briefcases, and handbags at irregular intervals. Don't tell either the manager or the employees when there'll be a spot check.

Also, provide lockers for employees to keep their personal belongings in. Don't let bulky coats, bags, or the like come into the working areas.

Watch the Managers, Too

Norman Jaspan, a leading expert on business theft and fraud, tells the story of an employee who was taught to steal by her boss. Jaspan says it's a fairly typical tale.

The employee, Mrs. X, was hired as a salesperson in a luggage store. The manager soon came to regard her as a treasure; she was careful and capable, and the customers liked her. After a couple of months, he had a chat with her because he wanted to make sure she was satisfied. "Oh, I like working here," she said—and hesitated. "But I feel a bit frustrated sometimes."

He pressed for an explanation. She said that her son would be going away to school, and she wished she could give him a gift—a Louis Vuitton suitcase, the best in the store. "But even with my employee discount, I just can't afford it." She never dreamed the manager could enable her to buy the suitcase. But the resourceful manager knew a way.

"Would you like this one here? It's a beautiful case." He did something she couldn't quite see. And suddenly the suitcase's metal nameplate was loose. "Look at that," he said. "Damaged merchandise. We'll have to let you have it for half price. Of course that nameplate can be fixed. I'll show you how."

Mrs. X got the idea.

Two weeks later she needed another gift—a present for her aunt. She picked up an overnight case, and used a pin to mar it. Soon she was at the adjustment counter. "A customer brought this back. There's a slight scratch here. You can hardly see it, but I guess she's just fussy." The overnight case was marked down. Mrs. X bought it for half price. And she was on her way.

Her manager had encouraged Mrs. X to be dishonest. He had just wanted to keep a fine employee. He didn't expect that she'd go on to bigger and worse things, but that was out of his control. Jaspan says that many managers, trying hard to keep workers happy, rob the owners in order to do so. Naturally, you trust your manager—but why not keep an eye on him?

Let employees buy at a generous discount. The bigger the discount, the less temptation to steal.

If stuff keeps disappearing from certain areas accessible only to employees, you can take a leaf from the Internal Revenue Service manual. Put out some "bait" in those areas—a few desirable and easily stolen articles, or perhaps some currency—after sprinkling phenolphthalein on the bait. When the culprit washes his hands, alkali in the soap turns the phenolphthalein on them red. This nearly colorless powder "can be obtained from any drugstore," the manual says.

If you use cash registers, they're an obvious temptation to your cashiers. Every cashier has occasional overages or shortages, but any suspiciously large discrepancy, or any run of small ones, should alert you. An overage in the register is as bad as a shortage—maybe worse, because it can mean that a clerk didn't ring a sale, or rang it too low, but hasn't had time to pocket the cash. That's why you or a trusted manager should be on hand when cash is balanced.

If there's chronic trouble about the cash, make spot checks during the day. On a random, surprise basis, balance cash registers before the day is over. If your cashiers never know when they'll be checked, they'll worry, and you may not have many more discrepancies.

All cash-register misrings should be documented by a detailed slip accompanying the register tape. All misring reports should be inspected by an employee assigned specifically to that duty.

How to Protect Your Loading Zone

Although many thieves operate at the retail counters and the cash registers, the big-scale rip-offs occur around platforms where merchandise is loaded and unloaded. Many a manager knows of disappearances of big

TV-stereo consoles, microwave ovens, expensive living-room rugs, and other merchandise that you wouldn't think could be carried off without attracting wide attention.

Such big thefts usually mean collusion between at least one outsider and one or more workers at the stockroom or loading platform. But occasionally they can be traced to a quick-witted truck driver or even a bystander who sees a chance to swipe some merchandise single-handed. Sometimes management isn't aware of thefts until long afterward. How about you?

Do you ever find unexplained shortages of goods—shrinkage of inventory in the stockroom or warehouse? Do you seem to be spending strangely high amounts to replenish your stock? If so, you're probably being systematically looted at the back door. Here are countermeasures you can consider.

Look around for empty closets or file cabinets, unused storage areas, or seldom-visited nooks in your warehouse or stockroom. Check these at irregular, unannounced intervals. Many systems for stealing hinge on hiding the loot in such places until it can be removed from the premises.

Other systems depend on simply tossing stuff out a window or over a fence to a confederate. Is this possible at your place? If so, surely you can find ways to make your windows and fences tossproof.

Do your incoming and outgoing deliveries use the same platform? Then there's bound to be confusion. Larceny-minded truckers like confusion. It enables them to divert a newly unloaded box onto their outbound truck, or unload less than their waybill calls for, or pull other dodges. So you'd better try to separate your incoming and outloading docks, and space them as far apart as you can.

You need a hard-nosed, hawk-eyed employee—maybe a security guard —on each platform, doing nothing but monitoring the movement of freight and vehicles, and watching for suspicious maneuvers. He should:

- never let a delivery be unloaded without a checker on hand
- prevent private vehicles, owned by employees or others, from getting close to cargo-handling areas
- question the presence of any person, car, or truck that doesn't seem to belong there; never let truck drivers or deliverymen walk around the premises unattended
- keep drivers and stockroom people apart as much as possible. Letting them roam or intermingle encourages them to work out sleight-of-hand for their own gain
- verify that a truck is really empty after it has supposedly unloaded
- be alert for extra containers on the dock or in the staging area
- find out why cargo is lying around unattended or lacking a waybill (especially high-value shipments, which should always be kept moving)

- verify (with the checker's help) that the right part of a load has been taken off, if the rest is to go elsewhere
- make sure that only your people, not drivers, move goods from truck to stockroom or the reverse
- verify the integrity of each container or trailer, inspecting latches and locks so that once a trailer is sealed it can't be entered secretly
- make sure that all incoming and outgoing cartons are sealed, or count their contents if they're unsealed.

Foiling Some Favorite Maneuvers

One of the common tricks of thieves at a loading dock is to pick up merchandise and walk away with it through the gap between the side of the truck and the building. If your losses in this area are serious and you can't discover why, you'd better take steps to rule out this possibility. Your handyman can make and install some thick bumpers of polyurethane foam, covered by fabric. He should mount them around the frame of the back door to your building. When a truck backs into your loading dock, the pads will compress, forming an airtight seal around the truck. Then if anyone steals something in the truck, he'll have to walk through your building with it.

Crooked truck drivers often use a helper who engages the checker in a chat (or an argument) while the driver returns to the truck some of the valuable goods he has just unloaded. Caution your checkers never to be distracted while goods are being moved.

Do you sometimes let a truck be loaded at the end of a working day, then parked until it starts its delivery route next morning? Thieves love this. It gives them all night to get into the truck and remove some of its contents. Such trucks should be parked with their rear doors flush against a solid wall, and their locks should be mounted on the kingpins. Or an empty truck should block the loaded truck.

Customers and salesmen can be sticky-fingered too. Don't allow them into the stockroom or warehouse unless one of your people is with them. It's always better to bring items to customers at the loading dock or over the counter.

Inventory thefts often depend on last-minute phone calls between inside and outside men. This is something else to watch if you can't find the cause of chronic losses. Delegate somebody to note outside calls to and from your dispatcher or your shipping office. If there are pay phones in your cargo-handling areas, remove them. Of course, you must provide a phone for outside truck drivers who need to inform their own dispatchers of their whereabouts. But this phone should be next to your dispatcher's window so he can hear the calls.

If you use guards, beware of personal friendships that may develop between a guard and other employees. You don't want a guard to be torn between loyalty to you and friendship with the gang around the shop. The way to prevent this is to rotate guards often, so that no one is assigned to a location (and a group of employees) long enough to develop real friendships.

Then too, a guard who has only one post and one target to watch—whether it be a parking lot or a shipping platform—is likely to be an unprofitable investment. A guard should have a variety of responsibilities. Changes will keep him more alert, more interested in the work.

Stopping Phantom Shipments

The most common theft isn't perpetrated by persons carrying things away.

It's done by means of phantom shipments—goods that are paid for but never actually delivered, or are received with a short count but are recorded as full count; and goods that are shipped out but never billed.

These can be big problems if you have the same person handling buying, receiving, and shipping. And if that person never takes any vacations or days off, it very likely means he's afraid to, because a substitute might stumble onto clues to his thievery. So you'd better take a hard look at that person's operations.

Often several employees are in on shipment frauds. Clerks record receipt of merchandise that goes into a buddy's hands rather than into inventory. Or they ship out stuff to an accomplice, with records rigged to hide the discrepancy.

Your best protection for materials shipped and received is good tight paperwork.

Your invoices, orders, and waybills should be numerically sequenced, with no more carbon copies than are absolutely needed. If there's an unused extra copy, insiders may realize that it can be used to authorize shipments. This trick enabled a $250-a-week clerk to steal a million dollars' worth of merchandise from one firm in less than a year.

If and when you introduce new forms, be sure to destroy all the old ones. Old forms are no longer under control, and can be used dishonestly by insiders.

Even if you haven't seen signs of fraud, it can go on under your nose. Anyhow, prevention is better than cure. You'll be wise to put somebody knowledgeable in charge of monitoring your company's shipping and receiving paperwork. This watchdog should be alert for:

- the same document number used for two shipments
- erasures or other alterations
- missing documents
- extra copies of documents
- figures on carbons that don't match those on originals
- records that indicate items or partial loads separated from shipments. This is a common first stage of inventory loss. The record should be followed up item by item.
- records of what happens to returned, cancelled, or delayed orders. These ought to be meticulously verified, because the goods are handled outside your normal operational channels, and thus are especially vulnerable to theft.
- continuous or sizable overages of inventory. At best these indicate sloppy record-keeping, which is tempting to insiders. At worst they're a way of hiding shortages for long periods.

Is your business partly computerized? Then you can probably put all loss notations on the computer, with a uniform code for cause, department, type of merchandise, and so on. A monthly computer run can show up patterns of loss, and can guide you in developing countermeasures.

Are Your Buyers Bribed?

The purchasing agent who takes bribes and kickbacks is an old, old story. If it happens in your company, it cripples you, because you're either buying more than you actually receive, or paying steep prices for what you get, or accepting shoddy goods.

Here are some signals that a buyer's palm may be greased:

- only one person decides what to purchase, with little or no advice from anyone else in the firm
- he or she takes no vacations
- his or her life-style is unusually luxurious
- the list of suppliers and vendors never changes. Most firms change at least one-fifth of their suppliers every year.
- the cost of supplies has risen faster than inflation in your industry
- large purchases are fragmented into small and confusing elements, such as add-ons, changes, or partial shipments, instead of being billed as one order
- the scales on your loading dock register more weight than is really put on them.

It's a good idea for you to chat with salesmen occasionally—especially those from high-quality companies who never get any orders from your buyer. If you pick up mutterings that they can't get appointments at your company, or can't understand why your buyer never orders from them, start digging.

If you suspect bribery, you can rotate the buying duties among several employees. It's also a good idea to make clear that purchasing isn't a blind-alley job. And take a look at your pay scales. Is there some way you can pay your purchasing agents better, maybe by setting up bonuses for performance?

Fraud in Your Office

The Research Institute of America says, "The big steal is usually committed by a 'completely trustworthy' employee, the one the boss would trust with his life. Insurance investigators find that behind the fantastic frauds and clever chicanery are open invitations to steal which top management does not perceive."

These trusted insiders are inherently just as honest as the next person. But their temptations and opportunities to steal are infinitely greater. And their subordinates almost always keep silent about their depredations—or connive with them—rather than blowing the whistle.

Consider the sales manager. Maybe he pays commissions to his salesmen as they bring in orders. And maybe some of the orders are faked, or given by deadbeats. So the company never collects—but maybe the manager splits those unearned commissions with his salesmen.

Or maybe the sales manager buys his company's repossessed merchandise at a fraction of its value, and resells it through channels of his own —to a landlord, say, who reciprocates by setting him up in a rent-free furnished apartment.

Consider the credit manager. Maybe he takes kickbacks from certain customers because he never presses them for payment. Have you looked at your delinquent accounts lately?

Maybe you have an export department. Maybe its manager sets up dummy sales agencies and companies, in collusion with people abroad, to siphon off big commissions. One export manager picked up an extra $50,000 or so every year, over a ten-year period, in this way. His company thought it was commissions to foreign sales reps when the money really went to him.

Consider your payroll department. What happens when, occasionally, a worker leaves without picking up his or her final paycheck? Can somebody in your department secretly endorse and cash such unclaimed checks?

Think about somebody on your order desk. Maybe his wife phones your store, orders merchandise, and has it sent COD to a wrong address. He knows the merchandise will come back to him for readdressing. But he doesn't try to track down this "customer's" real address. Instead he can just take home the parcel, because the department that made the "sale" will never know what happened afterward.

What happens when a customer brings something back to your company for exchange or refund? Can an employee take the stuff home, without the selling department ever realizing that the goods weren't sent back to the stockroom?

How about your manufacturing foreman? Is there any chance that he can grind out extra quantities of your goods without accounting for them? There's a black market for almost anything made, if a factory man will sell it under the table below cost. Maybe you think this is impossible in your company because, say, each of your products is stamped with a serial number. But what's to prevent someone in your factory rigging a machine to stamp out duplicate serial numbers?

One of your executives could be the hidden owner of some organization to which your company is funneling a good deal of money. He could be a silent partner of your architect, or of one of your suppliers, or of one of your landlords, or of one of your wholesalers.

There's probably no way you can uncover such frauds by yourself, unless you stumble onto them. But if your profits are dwindling for unknown reasons, or if your auditor tells you that certain figures look fishy, maybe you'd better call in one of the detective agencies that specialize in business fraud. They'll know how to investigate. Experience has taught them what to look for, and where to look.

Aside from all this, don't overlook the opportunities for minor but costly white-collar crime. Ask a trusted aide in your company to start a study of possible misuses of petty cash, checks, company credit cards. By asking tough questions about controls and access, you or your aide can make it clear that you're alert to potential abuses.

Defense Against Computer Frauds

Most small businesses don't use computers, but some do. More and more will be doing so each year. It's a fast way of handling payrolls, billing, inventory, and other detail work. Just keep in mind, if any part of your business is computerized, that any computer system can be ripped off. An abundance of controls or audits cannot outsmart a determined computer embezzler. That's the opinion of Dick H. Brandon, head of his own Manhattan consulting firm, which specializes in helping companies fight computer frauds.

Marsh & McLennan, the big insurance firm, which is trying to cut claims against the insurance policies it writes, takes the same view. It says that computer crime is the newest, the most sophisticated, and often the most difficult type of office fraud to combat.

For example, a 19-year-old computer programmer in California found a way to steal $4,100 from his company in a few days. He just programmed the computer to pay $100 cash each to 41 accounts he set up under false names. Then to make the company's total payout seem to balance, he instructed the computer to subtract $4,100 before showing the total.

"Computers are a particularly accessible and sophisticated tool for white-collar crime," Marsh & McLennan writes in a special report. "Used for all types of records and storage of accounting and payroll information, computers offer a method for white-collar criminals to embezzle large sums. . . . Businesses become most vulnerable to computer crime when they show lack of interest in the problem, or show ignorance about how to protect the system. Too often a company ignores safeguards until it suffers a big uninsured loss."

Manual systems of paperwork are slower, but they provide some security because the paper goes (or should go) through several different clerical and supervisory hands—so that a fraud has to pass scrutiny by a number of people. But with computerized systems, in which pounds of paperwork are crammed into recorded signals on a reel of magnetic tape, the number of people in the chain is sharply reduced. Fewer people are handling more data. Then too, manual systems require clerks to sign papers, whereas computers hide identity. "When I type a computer entry into the record from a keyboard terminal, it looks just the same as if you had typed it," one computer-security man told a business owner. "In a multiterminal system, there's no way of telling who is pushing the keys at the other end."

Dick Brandon says that the best defense against computer frauds is to maintain controls that are changed at odd times. People who run the computer should be aware that changes will be made at any time. Also, you can run audits at irregular intervals. Keep switching the people who do the audits, to make sure they're not part of a conspiracy.

Why They Bite the Hands That Feed Them

Contrary to the old maxim, love of money isn't necessarily the root of all evil. Some crime in business is rooted in other causes—resentment against higher-ups, for one example. Or, for another example, unwitting encouragement by higher-ups.

Take canny old Joe. He was assistant head of the records department. He turned down outside job offers because he figured he'd become head of the department when his boss retired or moved on. But just about the time his boss did leave, the company ran into financial troubles and had to retrench. One of its cost-cutting moves was to consolidate the records department with another department. Joe was made assistant to the head of the combined departments—a woman. Joe kept smiling, but smoldered. He began plundering the company in invisible ways he'd noticed were possible. Thus he got his revenge.

There is resentment, maybe, in the clerk who feels her extra efforts aren't appreciated. Or in the partner whose ideas for improving the business aren't accepted. Or in the department head whose bonuses dwindle; he just steals money that he considers is "rightfully" his.

Sometimes there's no resentment. There's just encouragement for dishonesty, given from above. Suppose the sales manager hires a young salesman who brings in some good accounts. The manager asks his bright subordinate to figure out a new marketing plan, which turns out to be great. The manager wonders how he can reward this achievement, how he can keep the youngster from being hired away by competitors. He can't give him a raise, because he did that last month. He can't give him extra time off, because the owner frowns on it. So he says, "Bob, you've gotta be tired after all you've been doing. And Sally hasn't seen much of you these past weeks while you worked on the marketing plan. Why don't the two of you just take off for a week? Go to Florida if you want. Do you both good."

The salesman wonders how this can be done. His expense account won't justify it, nor will his accumulated vacation time. The sales manager says, "Don't worry about it. I'll call it business. There must be some prospect, or a convention, or some damn thing, wherever you want to go. I'll cover for you, and I'll have the company pick up the tab for the whole thing. You've earned it."

This manager has given his subordinate a ready-made excuse for defrauding the company. Bob has "earned it." Next time Bob may decide to cheat without mentioning it to anyone.

"Rules were made to be broken" is a common saying in many a company. A superior bends the rules in order to bind good people to him, as he sees it. He isn't doing it to cheat the company, at least in the beginning. Almost imperceptibly, the process can slip into an unspoken conspiracy by which employees and others enrich themselves at company expense. Management encourages the process by apathy, or by handing down unworkable rules, or by breaking some rules itself.

Managers who pad expense accounts or use company property for their own benefit are creating a climate that encourages cheating. Do you, or some of the top people in your firm—

- avoid itemizing on the expense account, but require underlings to do so?
- take the family on business trips charged to the company?
- forget about billing a friend for something that was sent?
- use the company credit card to make personal purchases and buy gifts?
- put a relative in a good job, when better-qualified people are available in the company?
- get some work done for personal purposes by employees or suppliers?

KEEP THESE BASIC POINTS IN MIND:

- *Keep an eye on strangers who hang around your employees.*
- *Keep close watch on what goes in and out the delivery door.*
- *Check your premises to make sure they're burglarproof.*
- *You can prevent daylight holdups in your office by careful arrangement of the floor plan, and by training your employees.*
- *Shoplifters can nibble you to death. Take steps to discourage them, and train your floor people to spot them.*
- *Make your stockroom, warehouse, and delivery docks as invulnerable to pilferage as possible.*
- *Keep in mind the numerous ways that an employee can steal from the business or defraud it.*
- *If you use computer programs, keep switching the people in charge of them, and run unexpected audits.*
- *Don't let any of your top people set examples that could encourage subordinates in dishonesty.*

24.

How to Protect Your Business from Your Buddies

So your business has become a success. Congratulations. But also beware! Now is the time to be alert for unpleasant surprises from one or more of your close associates.

The more successful an enterprise, the more chance of trouble among partners or co-owners. The sort of people who go into business for themselves—in partnerships or in closely held corporations—are a different breed from the bland team players who seek safety within giant organizations. Entrepreneurs are in business to win. Often they're hard to get along with, because of their take-charge habits or prickly egos. They'll fight for whatever they consider their fair share of corporate assets. In fact, sometimes they'll fight for whatever they think they can grab. They may fight with velvet gloves—or with brass knuckles and steamrollers.

How Partners Turn Sour

Probably you and your associates teamed up smoothly during the hectic early years. Otherwise your business might not have come as far as it has. But a crew that works together in stormy seas can quarrel in a calm harbor. Just consider some kinds of change that can occur:

Maybe Joe taught Larry the insurance business. As equal shareholders they both worked hard and made good money. Now that renewal premiums are cascading in, Joe works even harder. He services the accounts. He calls on new prospects. He spends hours with accountants and lawyers. But Larry is contented. He sleeps late, goes to the races, dances the nights away at discotheques. He takes expensive vacations and charges them to the firm. So Joe wonders how to get rid of Larry. . . .

Paul, a hotshot promoter, raised the money that got Swellmart Stores started. But he's not smart at conserving money. He and his partners are in conflict over bad buys he makes, bad locations he picks. . . .

After building up a thriving machine shop, Buck dies. His widow, Mary, expects the same income as before, since he willed his shares of stock to her. But she contributes no skills. His nephews own some stock too, and they demand either well-paid jobs in the office or a big boost in dividends. Since the other owners balk at spreading the wealth, the nephews and Aunt Mary may decide to squeeze them out. Or maybe the others decide to get rid of Mary and the boys. . . .

The Expandrium Company was set up to exploit certain inventions by Oscar. The moneymen wound up in control; Oscar got minority stock interest in exchange for the patents he owned. He doesn't like the way Expandrium is run. So now he's selling his newest invention elsewhere. The board is furious. "You're working for Expandrium," they say. Battle lines are drawn. . . .

Angus, a hardheaded manager who kept the struggling Howzex factory in business when it could barely meet its small payroll, is no longer valued highly by the other owners now that Howzex is coining money. They think he's overpaid. He wonders how to protect himself from being forced out. He owns part of Howzex, but not a majority. . . .

Grover and Ted are senior and junior partners in a two-man importing firm. Years ago they signed a buy/sell agreement to cover the death, disability, or retirement of either partner. This agreement set a price on the stock, with a clause providing for readjustment of the price by mutual agreement at the end of each year. But years have passed with no price adjustment, maybe because both partners forgot. Now Grover wants to retire. The firm is doing very well, in his opinion, so he calls for readjustment of the price. He and Ted and their accountants consider all the usual approaches—book value, liquidation value, replacement cost, capitalized earnings, LIFO and FIFO methods of valuing inventory—and can't agree. Ted wants to buy Grover out at the price set years back, on the ground that they can't adjust the price by mutual consent. So Grover and his heirs decide to fight Ted, in court and out. . . .

Walt owns one-third of a printing company. His partners say he has become an alcoholic, and can't be trusted to call on customers anymore, but he won't admit it. He wants to continue taking a third of its profits. "Somebody's gotta go," all the owners say. . . .

Phil has set up kickback deals with several buddies outside the company. He lets them use company machinery for their own businesses. He leases an overpriced building from one, gives a maintenance contract to his incompetent cousin. When the board of directors challenges him, he swears to fight back. . . .

Imperious old Julius runs his lumberyard just as he did forty years ago; he is drawing a kingly salary while presiding over its decline. Connivers inside and outside the company are milking its profits without his knowledge. He's the majority shareholder. Other shareholders get together to try to salvage their investment. . . .

What's Fair?

Many inside conflicts aren't as clear-cut as most of the foregoing. Often there are no outright villains. Each combatant makes big contributions of brains and toil. Who can say what the fair shares should be? Probably you and your co-owners are all honorable people, all passionately sure they are right, all equally determined to get rid of "obnoxious" associates. Maybe a little diplomacy is all that's needed to work out a settlement. But if the personal incompatibilities cut deep, some kind of divorce may be the only answer. If so, look out! Business divorces can be just as messy as domestic ones.

When right and wrong are inextricably mixed up, the best tactician usually wins. So you ought to know at least the basic tactics for forcing out business associates—and for protecting yourself from being forced out.

Some tactics are legal, others not. In this chapter we'll give you a general guide to which is which. But remember that laws are intricate, with many exceptions. Be sure to get expert legal counsel when you're fighting for control.

You'll find more details on tactics in the book *Squeeze-Outs,* written by Bert Westlin, a New York attorney, and published by the Council for Business Research at 500 Fifth Avenue, New York. There are also good sections in *The Real Official Executive Survival Handbook,* by Herbert Lund, published by Dial Press, New York, and in *The Corporate Prince: A Handbook of Administrative Tactics,* by someone who calls himself Qass Aquarius, published by Van Nostrand Reinhold Company in New York.

The Tourniquet Treatment

One tactic for weakening an opponent within a corporation or partnership is to isolate him—cut him off from information, from power, from status, maybe even from income.

Using this treatment, his associates ignore him in making management decisions. They give him no work to do. Or they try to bury him in petty problem-solving work.

He can be sent out of town on various pretexts. In his absence his best clients or customers may be turned against him, his most loyal subordinates transferred elsewhere or fired. He may find his office moved to a remote location. There have been cases in which a partner or a top executive has been literally locked out, barred from access to his office or to files.

If the isolated officer is drawing a salary, it can be cut off, but this kind of amputation is dangerous. He may have an employment contract. Even if he doesn't, he may sue, claiming an implied or oral contract, or complaining of age discrimination or whatever. Then too, firing is an open declaration of war, and the victim and his friends may react more savagely than they would otherwise.

Maybe he owns a wad of stock, and gets his income from dividends rather than a salary. Then (unless he's the majority shareholder) the board of directors can suddenly vote to stop paying dividends. The law in most states doesn't give a minority shareholder much protection against this.

Still, the majority can conceivably get into trouble under Section 10 (b) of the Securities Exchange Act of 1934, which applies even to closely held corporations. If you're a victim of a squeeze by suspension of dividends, drop a word to the other side about SEC Rule 10 (b) 5. This may alarm their lawyer, and he may advise them to ease up, if he knows that the rule is a powerful weapon in the hands of minority shareholders pressured into selling their stock if there's been any concealment of material data (which there almost invariably has been). On the other hand, their lawyer may be completely ignorant of this SEC rule. If so, get a good attorney and start suit. Small companies often fall into Rule 10 (b) 5 traps because of their inexpert legal advice.

Assuming that the tourniquet hasn't cut off his income, how can a victim counter the tactic of isolating him?

Response: Hang in There

As long as his salary or dividends continue, he can't do much except stay where he is. They want him to quit his job and/or sell his stock. Probably they can't take over until he does.

He can circulate a lot, talk and write a lot, make sure everyone knows of the freeze-out being attempted. This may stir up sympathy for him, and make it harder for the enemy to shut him off from information and influence.

It's not illegal to isolate a company executive, or to limit his duties, or to withhold corporate data. But if anyone tries to undermine him by spreading rumors about him, he can probably sue for slander or libel. He may be able to collect without having to show actual damage. Therefore he'll be smart to use a tape recorder when he can, and to save any scrap of paper on which there's an innuendo against him.

He can also keep a diary of everything done against him—even the perfectly legal dirty tricks. Then if it later becomes clear that the opposition's moves were part of an illegal attempt to exclude him from something rightfully his, the diary can be evidence in court.

Partners Can Hit Back Harder

If he's in a general partnership rather than a corporation—ah, then! There's much more he can do. He's legally entitled to help run the firm, so he can get a court to intervene if he's excluded from any partnership matters. The Uniform Partnership Act (adopted by virtually all states) gives a partner a right to an accounting if he has been wrongfully excluded from possession of property or participation in the business.

Partners usually expect to share profits, rather than draw salaries. Furthermore, any general partner as such has a right to employment by the firm. So his normal remedy is a suit for an accounting if other partners try to lock him out. But he may need to tie this to a proceeding to break up the partnership and sell its assets. If the other partners are financially weaker than he is, they may not be able to outbid him for the assets—so the mere threat of liquidation may bring them to heel.

If he has less money than the other partners, by bidding boldly he may be able to bring the sale price up close to a fair value. At least it's a possible way to get most of his money out of the firm, and to rid himself of his partners.

If any partners go behind his back and negotiate deals for their personal benefit, or divert revenues into some other enterprise they control, they are probably breaking the law. This is circumventing the fiduciary duty they owe to every partner. He can compel them to account for any profits realized.

The law says a partner must be given full and truthful information about partnership business. This right is vital, because all partners are liable on business transactions.

Even Employees May Try a "Takeover"

Most of the stories you hear about squeeze plays are about partnerships or corporations. But it can happen even though you are the proprietor—the sole owner of your business. Many sole owners are fearful about teaching employees (George, Paula, Linette, James, or whomever) more and more about their business as it grows. But you must if you want to grow. You must delegate by assigning some of the responsibilities you've been handling and giving the corresponding authority for taking care of the assigned responsibility.

The danger of a takeover is real. Your key employees may begin to feel that they are indispensable and may present an ultimatum to you that you share ownership of your business with them. They may demand ownership of 51 percent or even more—and the active, controlling positions in your company—with you reporting to them!

If they don't succeed in taking over they may start a business in direct competition with yours. And that's O.K. if they don't take your files and your material with them. Don't worry about people of this nature. What they forget or don't know is:

- They don't realize that although you may have taught them everything they know about the business, you did not teach them everything *you* know.
- Carbon copies are never as good as the original.
- Competition can be good for your original business.

If you are confronted with a takeover attempt by one or more of your employees the best action is to wish them well and send them on their way—immediately!

Again, don't be overly concerned about the possibility of a takeover by employees. You must hire competent people in order to grow. Just do your best to hire persons who are capable, competent, loyal, innovative, creative, and self-motivated with the ability to Plan, Organize, Direct, and Control—and to motivate others. Keep your own goals in mind and devote your energies to the success of your own business.

Financial Strangulation

Now let's examine the more brutal tactic mentioned earlier—choking off a part owner's income from the business, or otherwise squeezing him financially. This may force him to sell out, unless he has other financial resources.

In any corporation, dividends can be stopped, or cut sharply. This is easy in the closely held corporation, if a majority of the directors want to do it. All that's needed is a majority vote at a board meeting where a quorum is present. Even if the company has ample surplus to cover a dividend payout, the directors can omit to declare the dividend. Or management can so arrange matters that there isn't any surplus for dividends. This can be done by extra-generous compensation to management, big expense accounts, misuse of assets, and/or tricky accounting.

If the owner under attack is wealthy, just the opposite technique may put pressure on him. Suppose he's in a 70-percent tax bracket. He doesn't want dividends, because he'll be able to keep only 30 cents on the dollar —or less, if he's also paying state income tax. A surge of dividends might make him sell part or all of his stock, possibly to help pay his taxes.

Suppose that instead of collecting dividends the part owner draws a salary from the company—as president or vice president or chief engineer, perhaps. He must need the money or he wouldn't be drawing salary. His salary can be stopped. A board of directors can fire an officer at will, with or without cause. Even if he's protected by an employment contract, the board majority may assert that he hasn't lived up to the contract; that they're removing him for "negligence" or "incompetence." His only recourse is to sue for breach of contract, paying legal fees from his own pocket. The corporation can use its treasury to fight the suit. Litigation can drag on for years. Unless the victim is remarkably determined and well heeled, he'll sell his piece of the business for whatever he can get.

Breaking the Squeeze

What can a victim of these pocketbook pinches do?

If he holds preferred stock, he may have a legal right to whatever dividends on it the company's earnings can cover. By suing, he stands a good chance of forcing the declaration of the dividends that he has coming.

But if he holds common stock, he's in worse trouble. He may have to convince a court that the board of directors was guilty of fraud or gross abuse of discretion in cutting dividends.

Still, this isn't impossible. Most courts will suspect bad faith if they see either (a) big pay or big bonuses to controlling shareholder-officers; (b) company loans to shareholder-directors; (c) hostility between those in control and those demanding the dividends; (d) evidence that those in control are in high tax brackets and therefore don't want dividends; (e) evidence that those in control want to drive down the company's stock in order to buy it cheaply. Even without these clues, a court will sometimes find in favor of minority shareholders in a closely held corporation, since there's little or no market for their shares.

Another strategy against the squeezers is to arouse the Internal Revenue Service's curiosity about the company. If a company hoards earnings unreasonably, this can be considered an attempt to avoid taxation of its shareholders, which would violate sections 531–37 of the Internal Revenue Code.

There's no penalty for accumulations up to $150,000. And the Code allows bigger accumulations without penalty if the reasonable needs of the company justify it. But if those in control can't justify it, there'll be a severe penalty tax. This is something to point out to the majority, if they try to throttle you financially.

Another way to hit back is through the federal securities laws. We've already mentioned SEC Rule 10 (b) 5, the antifraud rule. It's a violation of this rule to try to depress company stock by withholding or reducing dividends that can comfortably be paid. Of course, the company may plead a downturn in business and the need for belt-tightening as the reason for its parsimony. Then the plaintiff must prove that dividends were cut in order to force him out, rather than for some legitimate business purpose. The five elements mentioned on the previous page will also carry weight with the SEC.

What about the reverse tactic—pouring dividends on a shareholder in a high tax bracket? If this can be shown as a maneuver to make him sell his piece of a closely held corporation, Rule 10 (b) 5 might apply here too. As far as we know, no such cases have yet gone to court.

When an officer-shareholder is fired from his job, about the only way he can fight back is to make a nuisance of himself. He can try to harass management and the board with phone calls, personal visits, registered letters, court subpoenas, and whatever other moves he and his lawyers can devise to make life miserable.

For example, if he brings an action under the SEC's Rule 10 (b) 5, he gets the right to "discovery procedures," as lawyers call them. This means that the company officers can be compelled to give long depositions, and to compile written answers to long lists of questions called interrogatories. They can be forced to produce various company records. They won't like it.

If there's no way to get at board members directly, the victimized ex-officer may still cause time-consuming trouble for the company in other ways. With his inside knowledge, he may be able to stir up health inspectors, fire inspectors, building inspectors, OSHA agents, or the like, and get them concerned about company violations of some regulation or other. He can also talk to newsmen and perhaps start them prying into company affairs.

Probably his best bet is to dig deep for evidence of misbehavior by company personnel—bribes, kickbacks, overcharges, tax evasion, unfair competition, deceptive advertising, sweetheart deals, or anything else that will put them into hot water. A company that tries to force out an insider should expect the closest and most hostile scrutiny.

Steamroller Strategies

Now we come to more massive maneuvers—changes in the corporate structure to crush minority interests. All these require either a majority of shareholder votes or a majority on the board of directors.

One maneuver is to sell the company's assets cheaply to a newly formed corporation owned by the majority. The proceeds of the bargain sale are rationed out among shareholders, and that's all they get. Their company is liquidated and ceases to exist.

A variation is to sell only part of the assets—just its building and some of its inventory, say—and move the company to another part of the country. This doesn't necessarily freeze out the minority interests altogether, but it can sadly diminish their power and perhaps their income.

Almost every state has laws permitting a sale of all, or substantially all, corporate assets by a specified majority of shareholder votes. That majority may range from 80 percent down to a mere fraction over 50 percent (a simple majority) in Delaware. Many incorporators select Delaware because it gives them the greatest freedom to maneuver. A company can be incorporated there even though it conducts its business elsewhere.

How can a minority save their company from being sold out from under them?

Try for an Injunction

If they learn about it in advance, they may be able to delay the sale, and possibly block it, by getting a court injunction. To do this they must sometimes show fraud or bad faith—that is, establish that a big reason for the proposed sale is to get rid of them. But try anyway, even if you can't prove this. Some courts consider that controlling stockholders have a fiduciary responsibility (a position of trust) toward minority shareholders. In this view, the controlling owners may be required to prove that a sale is based on sound reasons and is inherently fair; the minority doesn't have to prove fraud and bad faith.

Even after a sale is completed, a judge sometimes grants an injunction, nullifying the sale and forcing the sellers to put everything back where it was. But he seldom takes such drastic action unless he's convinced that there was downright fraud.

Demand an Appraisal?

Another legal remedy—but not an extremely good one, as we'll see—is for the dissenters to get their shares appraised, and force the liquidating company to pay fair market value for them.

Appraisal probably won't take into account the future prospects and profits of the business, which the minority interests may prize more highly than the current value of their shares. In fact, appraised value is often less than the current true value. Then too, this procedure forces the shareholder to pay capital gains on his stock if he receives more than his tax basis for them.

The appraisal strategy may be out of reach altogether in some situations. Many laws giving the right of appraisal when assets are sold don't cover cash transactions. And a few of these laws apply unless there's a sale of virtually all the assets.

Nevertheless, the appraisal demand (or the threat of it) is worth considering. If you threaten it ahead of time, the mere possibility may hinder a sale, because it makes the majority realize they'll need enough cash to pay off all shareholders who invoke appraisal rights. Maybe the majority knows it can't lay hands on that much cash.

Beyond this, you're limited to the nuisance tactics mentioned in the prior section "Breaking the Squeeze."

Swallowed by a Dummy

Not only can part owners be unseated by a sale of assets, as we've just seen, but they can be smothered by a merger that swallows up their company.

A merger, of course, is the combination of two or more firms, with one surviving or with the assets of both pooled in a newly formed corporation. Under corporation law, mergers are easily made by those in control. All it takes in most states is a majority vote of the shareholders of both enterprises, although a two-thirds vote is required in some states. But a corporation can dispense with shareholder approval altogether if it owns a high percentage of the stock of a subsidiary it merges with. It can pay off the subsidiary's dissenting shareholders in cash and kiss them good-by.

This latter type of merger, known as a short-form merger, is sometimes used as a steamroller technique in fairly small enterprises that spread themselves among several corporate entities. For example, one business structure may include a corporation owning the firm's real estate, another corporation owning the equipment, a third managing the business, with maybe a fourth moving its freight, and a holding company pulling the strings of all the others. Each of the constituent corporations may be partly owned by minority shareholders—and each may disappear in a short-form merger.

More commonly, a power-play merger will fold the company inside a dummy corporation in which the majority shareholders, or their stooges, hold control. But this is legally questionable. In 1974 the Fifth Circuit Court of Appeals said:

> Where a corporation is unable, because of well-recognized contract law, to eliminate a minority stockholder by simply adopting a by-law or voting to purchase his stock, its majority stockholders cannot accomplish the same purpose by setting up a second corporation wholly owned by them whose sole purpose is to enable it to take advantage of the merger statutes which . . . result in the elimination of a dissenter.

So if you're threatened with extinction by absorption, ask your lawyer to look up this case (*Bergan v. Brock & Blevins Co., Inc.* CA-5, CCH Securities Law Reporter 94,414—2/27/74). He can probably use it to scare off the steamroller.

But there may be no time for this. Your opponents will probably try to confront you with an accomplished fact by springing the merger suddenly, with little or no warning. In that predicament, instead of trying to frighten them, you'll have to go to court, as Mr. Bergan did against Brock & Blevins. Try first for an injunction to nullify the sale. If this doesn't work, sue.

Here again, in addition to suing for damages or nullification, you can demand an appraisal of your share. To protect stockholders objecting to some basic change in company ownership, state laws generally give them the right to demand that the company pay them the appraised value of their shares.

A merger with an active corporation is much harder to stop than a merger with a dummy set up for the purpose. The mere fact that a minority will be ousted isn't enough to persuade a court to act. But if you can show that the majority misrepresented important facts, or withheld vital information, or betrayed their fiduciary duty to you, maybe your attorney can win.

Outvoted by New Stock

Let's say you're one-third owner of a dry-goods store. You've always understood that your block of stock gave you a veto on any proposals to change the nature of the business. Now the other owners want to expand by buying a drugstore. You're against it because none of you know much about drugstores.

"The corporate charter provides that agreement by three-fourths of all voting shares is needed to change the specified purpose of the corporation," you point out to the other owners. "I hold 3,333 of the 10,000 shares, and I say you have to give up the drugstore deal."

They smile grimly and go away. Soon you discover that they've caused the corporation to issue another 3,400 shares which they bought and divided between them. So now they hold a combined total of 10,066 shares—just over 75 percent of the 13,400 shares in existence. They outvote you, and put your company into the drugstore business.

What can you do? Not much, unless your lawyer made sure that the corporate charter was written to protect you. It should have given you "preemptive rights"—that is, the right to buy a proportionate number of the new shares to maintain your percentage of ownership in the company. Without this proviso in the charter, the majority can water the stock and weaken the power of any owner they're scheming to expel.

Even with preemptive rights, you'd better hope that your attorney made the charter airtight, because state laws about preemptive rights are sprinkled with loopholes. Even in closed corporations there can be legitimate reasons for issuing stock without letting all stockholders buy it on a pro rata basis. So some quirk of the law in your state may bar you from exercising the preemptive rights given you by the corporate charter, unless this quirk was taken into account when the charter was drawn up.

For example, your opponents might arrange for some of their own friends to perform services for the company, and to take pay in new stock instead of cash. So no actual sale of stock occurs. This is often done legitimately—while others do it too, legally but unethically, as part of their conspiracy against a minority owner.

Even if your opponents can't find any legal loophole, and are forced to recognize your preemptive rights, they may rig the stock offering so that it's hard for you to buy. Maybe they do it when you're away on a trip. They can sharply limit the time allowed for acceptance of the offer, so that the time expires before you get back. Or they can make the offering at a time when they know you're short of cash.

Courts seldom seem to worry about shareholders who lack cash to exercise their preemptive rights. They theorize that these people should be able to borrow money for the purchase, pledging the stock as collateral. Apparently they don't realize that few lenders will accept stock in a closely held corporation as security for a loan.

But if too short a time is allowed, courts are likely to rule in your favor. The law requires that a "reasonable" time be allowed for purchase—usually, in the case of a closed corporation, at least three weeks. Then too, if a court is convinced that the new shares are being issued to tilt the balance of power among warring factions, and are part of a plan to heave somebody out, your chances of judicial relief are much better.

Overpowering Amendments

Often the majority owners of a corporation can vote to amend the corporate charter and bylaws in ways that will weaken or eliminate dissenters.

They can vote to limit or deny preemptive rights; increase or decrease the number of shares; enlarge or reduce the number of directors; change the rights of different classes of stock; provide for redemption (company buy-out) of stock; call or devalue the preferred stock.

Sometimes they work out reasonable-sounding rules by which only their opponents' shares are called. For example, if their opponents aren't active in day-to-day operations, they might pass a corporate resolution calling for redemption of the shares of everyone who isn't a company employee. The resolution would probably stand up in court.

To ram through a resolution aimed at an unwanted co-owner, a faction that lacks majority control may call a directors' meeting on short notice or no notice at all; may schedule a meeting at a time and place that are inconvenient for the opposition; may spring the resolution without advance notice at a routine meeting where the opposition happens to be outnumbered; may recess a meeting and then reconvene it unexpectedly with the opposition absent; may try intimidation or trickery—such as fake messages or an "emergency"—to keep opponents away; may invoke some technicality of parliamentary law to overrule opponents at a meeting. Of course, such techniques depend on the active cooperation of the presiding officer. To protect your majority, it's a good idea to keep your own man in the chair at all times, if possible.

The No-quorum Defense

Another point to keep in mind, when you're guarding against dirty work in the boardroom, is the corporate rule about a quorum. Lack of a quorum can block action. Usually a majority of eligible voters is a quorum, but the certificate of incorporation may call for a higher percentage of voters in certain cases or all cases. If you know that a plot against you is afoot, and you can arrange for a majority to stay away from the meeting, you've stymied your opponents.

For example, if there's a nine-member board, with three members on your side and six against you, you might happen to know that two of your opponents won't be at the meeting for one reason or another. In that case, your three members can block action just by staying away; your four opponents at the meeting won't have a quorum. Just make very sure that your information is correct about the absence of two from the other side.

Similarly, if you walk into the meeting and see that your group's presence is needed to provide a quorum, maybe you can stall the steamroller by having your group walk out. However, in New York and some other states, the law is that once a quorum is present it can't be broken by withdrawal of any shareholders. If this law applies, and your antagonists aren't numerous enough to beat you, their strategy may be to try to provoke some of your group into walking out—or to recess the meeting and then call it to order again before your side returns.

Undermining a Partner

The various corporate power plays we've just been considering won't work in a partnership, because, as we've seen, partners have equal rights in management. They run the business directly, not indirectly through a board of directors or through stockholders. While a corporation's powers are hemmed in by state laws and its own corporate charter, the powers of partners are unlimited except as provided for in the partnership agreement. The Uniform Partnership Act gives each partner a right to an accounting of transactions and profits.

So when somebody is forced out of a partnership, it is usually done illegally. There are very few legal ways. One is for the majority partners to dissolve the partnership, force a sale of its assets, and outbid the minority for them. We'll examine this further in due course.

If a partnership owns a lease, the majority partners can't veto renewal of the lease and then make a deal with the landlord for a new lease excluding an unwanted partner. This is illegal, as the U.S. Supreme Court held in a famous case (*Meinhard v. Salmon*) in 1928. It's a violation of the partners' fiduciary duty toward one another.

Nor can some of the partners go behind the others' backs and negotiate a deal for their personal benefit, or divert business to some other firm owned solely by some of them. This too is a breach of fiduciary duty, and they may be compelled to account for any profits they make on the transactions.

More often than you might think, some partners falsify books in order to cheat another partner and perhaps lead him to sell out to them. Falsification is grounds for a partner to dissolve the firm and obtain an accounting; he can also sue for damages based on fraud and deceit. The law-enforcement agencies might also consider that criminal fraud—a penitentiary offense—is involved.

Seeking to stay on the right side of the law, partners who are secretly scheming against a copartner may say to him, "Let's incorporate. Look at the tax advantages." As we've seen, the corporate form offers many more ways for a majority (or sometimes a crafty minority) to overpower their opposition and seize the business for themselves. So be wary—especially if you have any inkling that partners might want you out.

Skimming Strategies

Whether in a partnership or a corporation, unscrupulous insiders may divert the firm's assets into their own pockets instead of trying to force out their associates. In the long run, they sometimes calculate, the result will be the same: the business will be (or seem) so pinched that the opposition will sell out at sacrifice prices. This is how the Mafia works when it muscles into control of a legitimate business.

In its crude forms, diverting the assets simply means tapping the till or emptying the shelves. Employees' tricks for doing so, and management's best means of control, were covered in an earlier chapter. But when the grabs are made by a part owner, they're harder to control. A co-owner or partner may have to use different remedies, as we'll see in a moment.

More devious forms of skimming are likely to involve sweetheart deals with outside accomplices: leasing, buying, selling, or lending on terms that enrich the outsider. Sweetheart deals are made in seclusion. How can the other owners know, and prove, that a new supplier is controlled by their own partner or his henchmen? How can they prove that fees for outside services are exorbitant?

Even if a deal is made openly, it can be deceptive. Property sold to the company by some stranger may not be worth what the company-retained appraiser says it is. Executives' expense accounts can be padded almost invisibly.

Reversing the Cash Flow

An expert skimmer may conceal his plunderings by removing certain records, or falsifying them. Conversely, if he's even more adroit, he can make a healthy business look sick without falsifying anything. He can pay debts before they're due, and slow down collection of receivables, so that the company's bank account is depleted even though its underlying balance sheet is solid. His motive is to drive the firm into bankruptcy—wiping out the other owners—then buy it up at a few cents on the dollar.

Other ways of impoverishing a business while enriching oneself, without actual fraud, are to assign accounts receivable to banks (or to factors) for discounted cash; or to borrow heavily, putting up company property as collateral.

What can a victim do about skimming? (Maybe "skimming" is the wrong word. In the extreme forms we've just described, it's more like draining.)

Don't Threaten

Never try to whip plunderers into line by overtly threatening to sue or to file criminal charges. Such threats can boomerang. They can be interpreted as a form of extortion, which would open you to possible criminal prosecution.

Either go to the district attorney and lodge a complaint, if you've collected strong evidence, or else ignore criminal aspects of the case. (Remember, too, that prosecution and conviction of company officers may damage the company's reputation. What will customers and creditors think? What will happen to the value of your share of the business?)

If you do go to the authorities, or if your enemies think you're going although you haven't said so, they may make restitution or offer you some settlement in order to escape prosecution. But make sure you have strong evidence when you make your first call, or the authorities are likely to brush you off.

Appeal to the Board

A better bet (unless you're in a partnership) is the board of directors. The board can remove an officer or director, and certainly should do so if you point to grossly unethical transactions. The problem, again, is gathering evidence that will impress the board. Your proof needn't be strong enough for prosecution, but it should shock insiders. To get what you need, maybe you can hire an investigator with a good background in business and accounting.

If you do collect some fairly damning facts and figures, take them to the directors, even though you know the board is stacked against you. If a board ratifies an improper act by an executive, its members may become personally liable. Remind them of this.

Most sweetheart deals violate conflict-of-interest rules under which firms are incorporated. For example, Section 42 of the Model Business Corporation Act, adopted in numerous states, forbids corporate loans to officers or directors, or loans secured by company assets. And under Section 43, directors who knowingly assent to such loans are liable to the corporation for the amount of the loan until repaid.

Incidentally, this applies to you too as a dissident on the board. If you're in a board meeting when an improper action is taken, and neglect to have your dissent noted in the minutes, you may have lost the right to challenge. Even if a transaction doesn't require board approval, if the board receives notice of it (buried in some executive's written report, perhaps), just your silence, in some situations, may give consent. Check with your lawyer.

Also ask your lawyer to check the company's charter or certificate of incorporation, and its bylaws. These may contain provisions that can give a minority on the board some weapons in forcing an end to the skimming.

Minority shareholders can start legal action on behalf of their company to recover assets that have been improperly dealt away, or to hold certain directors personally liable. If they can trace the movement of company assets into another business, a court may declare what is called a constructive trust, giving the company some of the profits of the other business—or sometimes even transferring part ownership of it.

No Proof? Call the IRS

Suppose you haven't enough solid proof to cause a ripple at a board meeting. You have nothing but suspicions. Then try to get the Internal Revenue Service interested. It can investigate without any proof. The burden of proof in a tax audit is on the company, to show the IRS that any questionable transactions were legitimate.

Section 1239 of the Internal Revenue Code can transform a capital gain into ordinary income (and thus taxable at a higher rate) if the gain was made by a loan, sale, or transfer of property between an individual and a firm he controlled.

The IRS takes a keen interest in many transactions between a closed corporation and its officers or directors. It often rules that more taxes are due. For example, if it finds that a company paid too-high rent for property owned by a shareholder, it can deny the company a deduction for whatever part of the rent it considers excessive. Contrariwise, if the company rents property to an officer-shareholder at a bargain rate, the IRS can rule that the bargain is taxable to him as a dividend. The same is true of any kickbacks he received; and if he didn't show them on his personal income-tax return, he's in obvious danger of prosecution for tax evasion.

IRS field agents are expert at sniffing out tax fraud. Even when they find no fraud, if they hit the company and/or skimmer with big additional tax bills, they'll discourage future sweetheart deals. And the IRS findings may give you ammunition for a civil suit to recover company assets.

A Drastic Cure: Dissolve the Company

There's one final card you can play against skimmers, in either a partnership or a corporation. You can threaten to force the dissolution of the firm. Then its assets would be put up for public sale. If you and your allies can buy them, you can put the business back together without the skimmers.

Under the law in most states, a corporation can be dissolved by a board of directors' resolution that is confirmed by vote of, say, two-thirds of the shareholders. Of course, this doesn't help if your side is the minority. But some statutes, as in New York, provide that a company can be dissolved by only one shareholder under certain conditions. Thus you can be a continuing threat to those in control, even if you're a minority of one.

So ask your attorney about petitioning a court to dissolve the firm. In some states the court will act if it is shown that assets are smaller than liabilities, or merely that dissolution will be beneficial to the shareholders. One of the ways to do this is to specify in the petition that there is internal dissension, with two or more factions of shareholders so deadlocked that dissolution would benefit the shareholders. If a court believes this, the company can be dissolved even though the business is showing a profit

If you can show that officers or directors defrauded or abused minority shareholders, or otherwise flagrantly mismanaged the company, you may well be able to get a court to appoint a receiver to wind up the company's affairs and dissolve it. In such a situation, those opposing dissolution have no right to get their shares appraised and be paid appraised value. So by threatening dissolution, you may be able to scare the other side into buying you out, or selling out if you prefer.

But the cure may be worse than the ailment. Don't go through with dissolution until you've explored all possibilities for less destructive solutions. Breaking up a business is almost always costly for both sides. But keep it in mind as a way that a minority can actually force out a majority, taking over the business themselves if their financial backing is strong enough.

In partnerships there's worse danger of skimming, because it's easier for one partner to snatch money or property of the partnership and put it to his own use, or to make sweetheart deals. But all this is illegal. The Uniform Partnership Act says:

> Every partner must account to the partnership for any benefit, and hold as trustee for it any profits derived by him without the consent of the other partners.

A partner's normal remedy for skimming, or any other diversion of profits, is to sue for an accounting and petition for a liquidation of the partnership. If the skimmer doesn't want the partnership dissolved, he may render the accounting and pay you back at least part of what he's grabbed.

Look Before You Join

Let's hope that you've read this chapter before going into business with anyone else—certainly before giving up majority control. By now you must see more clearly the reasons for making sure (as we advised in an earlier chapter) that nobody else can outvote you in your own business. When you form a corporation with others, get the best attorney you can find and have him help draft the articles of incorporation with an eye to protecting you against any possible conspiracy against you by the other owners. (You may want to ask him to read this chapter.)

If other people offer you a chance to buy into a partnership or a closely held corporation, take a long hard look at what you're getting into, and have your attorney look—not only at the soundness of the enterprise as an investment, but also at the legal protection for minority shareholders. What could happen if an executive-shareholder dies, or if the firm is torn by dissension? If someone turns out to be mismanaging the business, are there legal ways to dislodge him?

Why are you being invited to join with the present owners of the firm? Do they need your money? Your contacts, your talent, your patents or technical know-how? Maybe they need you so badly that you can negotiate adjustments that will give you protection without imposing minority rule on the majority.

Here are some legal points on which you should try to protect yourself:

You should have an unbreakable right to buy a proportionate fraction of any new shares issued. Without this, a group of insiders can rob you by watering the stock.

Make sure you'll be on the board of directors, or will be represented on it. Ask for cumulative voting for directors, and staggered terms of office, so that only one-third of the board, say, can be voted in during any one year.

Consider putting top limits on the total compensation for officer-shareholders, so that they can't vote themselves a big share of your money in salaries and bonuses.

Look closely at the dividend rules. Try to stipulate that a certain percentage of earnings must be paid out as dividends. And spell out your right of access to corporate records, so that you and your auditor can always find out where the money goes. Require audited reports and financial statements at specified intervals, probably at least quarterly. Name an auditor independent of the majority.

Ask for restrictions on the transfer of shares, to prevent a majority from selling out to undesirable buyers. Nonselling shareholders should have the option to purchase, if shares are put up for sale.

Ask for a requirement that all important decisions, whether by the board or by the shareholders, must be by more than a bare majority. Check the state laws applying to this. What voting percentage do they require for which actions? Can a corporation change the percentage by charter, bylaw, or other provisions?

If state laws won't allow high vote requirements, try for a corporate provision for a high quorum.

If you're considering joining a Subchapter S corporation, be sure to read Chapter 10, which covers such corporations, before you commit yourself.

KEEP THESE BASIC POINTS IN MIND:

• *It's always possible that good friends sharing control of a business may fall out. Be prepared.*
• *One tactic used against an insider is to isolate him. His best response is to do everything possible to maintain his contacts and flow of information. He should also keep a detailed record of everything done to try to pressure him into leaving.*
• *No partner can legally be excluded from any part of the firm's business affairs.*
• *Insiders sometimes cut off another insider's flow of income from the*

business. His response may be to appeal to the courts, or the Securities and Exchange Commission, or the Internal Revenue Service. He can also undertake a campaign of harassment against the company and its directors.

- *Owners of the majority interest in a closely held corporation may try to sell its assets to some other firm they control. This can sometimes be blocked by a court injunction. Otherwise the dissenters may be able to take legal action to get their shares appraised, and force the liquidating corporation to pay fair market value for them.*
- *Another squeeze-out play by insiders is to merge the company into some other company controlled by them. The same countermoves are available as when a company's assets are sold.*
- *Majority owners sometimes water the stock to diminish the voting power of minority shareholders. To prevent this, the minority should make sure in advance that preemptive rights are available to them.*
- *A group on a board of directors may try to amend the corporate charter to weaken or eliminate their opponents. One possible defense against this is to prevent the group from obtaining a quorum at the meeting.*
- *Squeeze-out moves are more difficult in a partnership than in a corporation. So a partner should be wary of a proposal to incorporate.*
- *There are many ways of diverting a firm's assets by collusion between an insider and an outsider. These tactics are virtually always illegal. Victims should do their best to gather evidence, then complain to the board or to law-enforcement authorities. A civil suit is also a possibility.*
- *When dissidents can't find proof that assets have been diverted, they may be able to get the IRS to investigate on mere suspicion.*
- *Forcing the dissolution of a corporation is a last-ditch remedy that dissidents can attempt.*
- *When you pool business interests with partners or co-owners, first investigate thoroughly, with your attorney's help, to make sure that the partnership agreement or the articles of incorporation will give you recourse against mismanagement or attempts to force you out.*

Epilogue

This book has been written to help you avoid every conceivable problem you might encounter in buying and operating your own small business. With careful planning, following the guidelines and cautions set forth, you can see how very possible it is for you to realize the Great American Dream of achieving success on your own terms, as your own boss, with your own business.

Happily, it is a dream that more and more men and women are fulfilling. Now that you have read this book, you know what steps you need to take to make such success a reality. There will be times when things will go wrong, and when you will feel terribly discouraged. But obstacles can be overcome, if you have the determination and the know-how. No matter what type of business interests you—real estate, a dress shop, TV repair, or whatever—what you have read in these pages will help you take stock of your talents, knowledge, experience and drive, and choose the business in which you can best attain personal satisfaction and high financial rewards. Opportunities are everywhere. Take yourself in hand and get going. You can succeed as a small-business owner!

Index

Courses by Albert J. Lowry, Ph.D.

Lowry Real Estate Investment Seminar
Lowry Creative Real Estate Financing Seminar
Lowry Business Opportunities—Cash Flow and Profits Seminar

Manual by Albert J. Lowry, Ph.D.

Lowry/Colman ''Business Opportunities—Cash Flow and Profits''

Newsletters

Lowry Real Estate Insider Letter
Lowry Small Business Insider Letter
For a schedule of seminars to be given in your area and for further information on the newsletter and manuals write to Dr. Albert J. Lowry, Director, Education Advancement Institute, 50 Washington Street, Reno, Nevada 89503 or call (toll free) 800-648-5955.

About the Author

Raised in an orphanage, Albert Lowry went to work at sixteen as a day laborer in a Canadian steel mill, and later became a butcher. He moved to the United States and began to study business and real estate in his spare time. Without a fixed income, credit or savings, he began his own business. By leveraging his investments, he acquired other businesses, purchased large properties, and became a multimillionaire.

Once Albert Lowry had attained some of his business goals he decided to pursue his formal education, and has Master's degrees in both Real Estate and Business Administration, and a Doctorate in Business Administration.

Dr. Lowry's expertise as a financial and investment counselor has gained him national multimedia recognition. He is a member of the Institute of certified Business Counselors and is founder and director of Education Advancement Institute, one of the largest seminar operations centers in the country.